An American Epic

Famine in Forty-Five Nations

The Battle on the Front Line

1914–1923

VOLUME III

THE HOOVER INSTITUTION ON WAR, REVOLUTION, AND PEACE

HERBERT HOOVER

An American Epic

Famine in Forty-Five Nations

The Battle on the Front Line

1914–1923

VOLUME III

**THE HOOVER INSTITUTION ON
WAR, REVOLUTION, AND PEACE**

HENRY REGNERY COMPANY

CHICAGO: 1961

This book
is dedicated to the tens of thousands of
men and women who served
that their fellow men should not perish

IN ACKNOWLEDGMENT

This volume includes an immense number of facts and many quotations which were gathered from the examination of hundreds of thousands of documents. I wrote the original text of the volume and have revised it twice in order that it should be accurate and complete. I have received valuable assistance from many friends and my staff.

Among these are former colleagues associated with me in our work in Europe—Perrin C. Galpin, Sidney A. Mitchell, Lewis L. Strauss, John L. Simpson, W. Hallam Tuck, and Hugo Meier.

Neil MacNeil, H. V. Kaltenborn, Diana Hirsh, and Herbert H. Hyde commented on the text for me.

Those of my staff who assisted by research, checking of figures and quotations, and in the mechanical preparation, include Bernice Miller, Arthur Kemp, Loretta Camp, Thomas Thalken, Ellen Brumback, Mary Elizabeth Dempsey, Joan Dydo, Aileen Edwards, and Kay Stalcup. They have given devoted service.

CONTENTS

PART TWO

AFTER THE PEACE

SECTION X

Organization Behind the Front

SECTION XI

Finland, the Baltic States, Poland, and the Danzig Free State

SECTION XII

Germany, Czechoslovakia, Albania, Austria, Hungary, and Yugoslavia

SECTION XIII

Rumania, Greece, Armenia, China, and Ireland

SECTION XIV

Expressions of Appreciation from the European Nations

SECTION XV

The Relief of Communist Russia from 1921 to 1923

THE BATTLE ON THE FRONT LINE

This memoir—An American Epic—is concerned with the American relief which provided the margins of food, medical aid, clothing, and assistance in reconstruction that saved the lives of more than 1,400,000,000 human beings overseas during the two world wars.

Volume I gave an introduction to the whole series of four volumes and an account of the relief to ten million people in Belgium and Northern France during four and one-half years of German occupation and its aftermath.

Volume II told of American relief to the 170,000,000 people in the Allied and Neutral nations from the American entry into the war in April, 1917, until the Armistice in November, 1918. This volume also described the "organization behind the front" in forty-five nations to meet the food shortages, acute famine, and reconstruction problems created by the First World War.

This, Volume III, describes the "front line" of relief—nation by nation—to more than 1,281,150,000 people from the American entry into the war in April, 1917, to the final victory over famine and pestilence in September, 1923.[1]

When the restrictions on information from over the world were relaxed by the Armistice, we were able better to appraise the degree

---

[1] Volume IV will relate these American activities during the Second World War, when more than 800,000,000 people were involved in shortages of food or acute famine.

of famine in various countries and the populations involved. More than 400,000,000 people required overseas imports of food from the United States and financial aid or gifts to obtain it.[2] In order to give the reader a clearer picture of world food needs, I introduce here the results of a survey made about two months after the Armistice.

THOSE NATIONS IN NEED OF FOOD BUT
NOT IN ACUTE FAMINE

Country	Population
Britain	43,000,000
France	39,600,000
Italy	36,500,000
Belgium	8,000,000
Portugal	6,000,000
Greece	5,000,000
Cape Colony *	6,000,000
Transvaal *	4,000,000
Holland	6,600,000
Denmark	2,900,000
Norway	2,600,000
Sweden	5,800,000
Switzerland	3,900,000
Spain	21,000,000
India *	300,000,000
Azerbaijan	4,000,000
Georgia	3,000,000
Lebanon	700,000
Mesopotamia (Iraq)	2,850,000
Saudia Arabia	5,000,000
Egypt	20,000,000
Abyssinia	10,000,000
	536,450,000

* These nations provided their own imports.

[2] The population figures for many countries were approximations of the new map of the world—there could be no census.

NATIONS WHOLLY OR IN PART
IN ACUTE FAMINE

Country	Population
Finland	4,000,000
Estonia	1,100,000
Latvia	1,600,000
Lithuania	2,000,000
Poland	28,000,000
Bohemia	8,000,000
Slovakia	7,000,000
Serbia	8,000,000
Montenegro	2,000,000
Slovenia	3,000,000
Rumania	16,000,000
Albania	1,000,000
Dalmatia	1,500,000
Armenia	2,000,000
Syria	2,200,000
Palestine	800,000
Persia (Iran)	10,000,000
Communist Russia	140,000,000
"White" Siberia	10,000,000
Germany	68,000,000
Austria	6,500,000
Hungary	8,000,000
Bulgaria	6,000,000
Turkey	8,000,000
China	400,000,000
	744,700,000

A narrative of the measures required to prevent starvation in these forty-five nations presents many complexities. Our research shows that there were more than 200 governmental agencies and over 211 American charitable agencies engaged in this battle to save human lives. Now, nearly forty-three years after the Armistice, although most of the governmental records have been preserved, some of them are incomplete, and information from many of the charitable organizations is but fragmentary. A further difficulty arises from the fact that the accounts of even the major charitable agencies are kept under headings of several countries and their aid to these countries can only be estimated. However, after extensive research into the records of both governmental and private agencies, we have been able to boil down the unknowns to a few minor residues.

❖   ❖   ❖

The financial burden of relief from the United States' entry into the war in April, 1917, to the signing of the Peace in June, 1919, exceeded $7,000,000,000. Except for cash purchases from overseas (mostly from former enemy countries or Neutrals), United States Government agencies had financed more than 80 per cent of the overseas supplies. The other 20 per cent came from American charitable agencies and the Allied governments.

❖   ❖   ❖

Aid from the Allies on a large scale could not be expected. They themselves were dependent upon the American people for the margin of supplies upon which they could survive. Moreover, their resources were greatly depleted by the four years of war. So far as the records are available, I record their contributions to other stricken nations.

❖   ❖   ❖

While the American charitable agencies' expenditures on relief were small compared to those of the United States Government, they still played a great part in protecting religious minorities from persecution and a very large part in providing medical services. Their total expenditures during the nine years of war and its aftermath exceeded a billion dollars.

❖   ❖   ❖

Some kind of common denominator is necessary to express the dimensions of the gifts from the host of American relief activities. The American governmental agencies accurately documented the quantities of food and clothing which saved the lives of these hundreds of millions. After more than forty years, the records of American charitable agencies seldom give quantities, although their accounts often record dollars raised and dollars spent. However, in order to give some idea of relative service, I use their statements of dollar expenditures, even though quantities and dollars do not express the compassion and sacrifice which lie in their saving of life and suffering.

*   *   *

In describing the relief undertaken in many countries, it has been necessary to give an account of their economic and political situations. Many of the descriptions are a contribution of hitherto unknown history of these nations. And the struggles of these nations for independence and liberty are an inspiration to all free men.

*   *   *

After the Armistice, our official American governmental relief agencies maintained representatives, or missions, in thirty-two countries. The relief of another thirteen stricken nations was carried on under the leadership of the American charitable agencies.

*   *   *

With our American staff of more than four thousand able men and our telegraph system connecting thirty-two countries, our organization was frequently called upon by President Wilson and the Supreme Council (the "Big Four") for information—and at times for political action. Our men were in constant touch with Prime Ministers and cabinet members throughout Europe. The records of these matters and our staff members' appraisals of the abilities and character of these men comprise many lights hitherto unknown to history.

*   *   *

It is necessary for me to explain some of the terms used in this volume. I frequently refer to "the Allies." By that term I mean Britain, France, and Italy, for they alone participated in decisions relating to matters of finance and supplies. I do not include Belgium, Portugal, and Greece because their major policies and actions were determined by the three former countries. I do not include the United States in the term "Allies," thus following President Wilson's insistence that we were not an "Ally" but an "Associated Power." Where the United States joined with the Allies, I say so.

*   *   *

Throughout the text, I frequently refer to the "Lodge amendment." When Congress appropriated $100,000,000 to aid the new nations that were ineligible for loans from the United States Treasury and to provide for systematic rehabilitation of the children who were ailing greatly from the effects of famine, Senator Henry Cabot Lodge, despite the protests of President Wilson, myself, and many members of Congress and the public, secured an amendment to the act. This amendment prevented the use of the appropriation in former enemy countries, except among the small minorities of Christians and Jews in Turkey. I need not relate the constant grief of our staff, who, thwarted in their organization of systematic rehabilitation, were compelled to witness the plight of the children in these countries and the malign inheritance the world was to receive. Instead of repeating the text of this amendment each time it is needed, I merely refer to it as the "Lodge amendment."

❖ ❖ ❖

During the war, the modern terms "Communist" or "Communism" were less frequently used than "Bolshevik" or "Bolshevism." In Germany, the Communists were labeled "Spartacists" and likewise had special names in some other countries. Where I can do so, I either use the term "Communist," or, in documentation, I bracket the word "Communist" in place of the other terms.

❖ ❖ ❖

As explained in Volume II, the United States Treasury lent the countries which had participated in the war against the Central Powers vast sums of money with which to purchase supplies from the United States. These so-called loans were funded at low rates of interest, with installments on principal over sixty years, and were, in fact, a great reduction of the debts. For a few years, the debtors paid the stipulated amounts of principal and interest of the funding agreements, but by 1933, except for Finland, all of the debtors had ceased payments. In no case, except Finland, did their temporary payments of principal in total exceed 5 per cent.

The interest on the United States bonds which were issued to enable these loans to be made amounted, over the years, to probably twenty times any payments made to the United States by the debtors. Now, in 1961, this burden on American taxpayers still continues as a part of our national debt.

It should be said here that in time, the American people realized that the impoverishment of the borrowers by war and the economic impossibility of transferring such huge sums into either gold or goods made repayment of these sums impossible. In this volume, I refer to these loans as gifts, which they were. I analyze and summarize them—nation by nation—in the Appendix.

* * *

The huge surplus of food on our farms, in our warehouses, and in the reserves of our Army and Navy at the time of the Armistice was no climatic accident. Despite the drafting of four million men into the armed services and other millions into war industries, we were able to export three times the volume of farm products that had been our prewar average. This huge surplus was produced by the older men, women, and the children, most of whom had not worked in the fields before. Theirs was no eight-hour day or five-day week. They worked from dawn to dark, and often seven days a week.

A substantial part of this surplus was made possible by the saving of waste by the food processors. But the major part of these savings was a result of the self-denial in every public eating place and, above all, in the homes of the American people.

* * *

Most of the administrative positions during the American participation in the war and its aftermath were conducted by volunteers who left their professions and businesses without remuneration in order that they might serve. Their total number probably exceeded fifty thousand. In the activities under my direction alone there were, including the food administrators, at least fifteen thousand. The leaders in the American charitable agencies were likewise mostly volunteers dedicated to the relief of suffering humanity.

During the period between the Armistice and the Peace, there were some four thousand men on my staff. During the Armistice period, several hundred volunteers remained at their posts in the

Food Administration, and a large number of our staff were officers and men from the Army and Navy who, with encouragement from General Pershing and Admiral Benson, volunteered for our service.

❋   ❋   ❋

Through the charitable organizations, American physicians gave treatment to millions of the sick in foreign countries. American surgeons performed hundreds of thousands of operations on the injured and wounded. They received little or, usually, no compensation. American nurses won back life to hundreds of thousands; and they gave consolation to the bereaved. American organizations protected the persecuted. American women established employment and aid for the wives of fighting men. And in the train of relief was the building of new homes, restoration from war damage, the rebuilding of churches and schools, and the establishment of new hospitals and orphanages. And not the least of these services was the restoration to health of tens of millions of war-damaged children.

❋   ❋   ❋

The religious denominations of the United States participated in the aid to our armed forces during the war and to countries over the world during the famine. Through these services, religious faith was revived and courage was given to those in despair.

❋   ❋   ❋

In the course of this volume, I will indicate the gratitude of the oppressed masses who were blessed with American ministrations. And I will relate the co-operation of great statesmen who paved the way for these services.

❋   ❋   ❋

I believe I will be pardoned if, out of pride in my country, I recall the extra hours of labor on the farms, the self-sacrifice in the homes, the administrative abilities and volunteer services without remuneration which made possible the lessening of suffering, the saving of hundreds of millions of lives, and the restoration of health and happiness to tens of millions of famine children.

❋   ❋   ❋

From a relief point of view, the recital of the front line of relief and reconstruction during the First World War was dominated by the momentous event of the signing of Peace on June 28, 1919, when the whole world scene shifted. The major burden of overseas relief and reconstruction prior to the Peace was borne by the United States Government, with a supplement from the Allies and charitable relief agencies. After the Peace, the burden, with minor exceptions, fell upon the American charitable agencies until the job was mostly completed by September, 1923.

Thus the narrative of the front line in many ways falls into two parts: part one, before the Peace, and part two, after the Peace. But even this cannot be a universal rule since in some nations and in some groups the work of relief before the Peace was so far advanced that it adds to clarity to state the whole record of relief in one place. With these complexities in mind, I have divided this volume into parts and sections as described below.

PART ONE

BEFORE THE PEACE

Section I discusses the Allies—Great Britain, France, and Italy— and Belgium, Portugal, and Greece. Since the major relief measures ended, for the most part, at the Peace, I have completed the narrative of these nations in this section, with the exception of Greece, which I deal with in Section XIII.

In Section II, I describe the relief, prior to the Peace, of Finland, the Baltic States (Estonia, Latvia, and Lithuania), and Poland.

Section III is devoted to relief in the Neutral nations of Europe— Norway, Sweden, Denmark, Holland, Switzerland, and Spain. Relief measures were unnecessary in these countries after the Peace.

Section IV records our relief work in Germany before the Peace.

Section V tells the story of relief, prior to the Peace, to Czechoslovakia, Austria, Hungary, Bulgaria, Yugoslavia, and Rumania.

In Section VI, I discuss the relief of Russia (before the Peace), Siberia, and the areas behind the "White" Russian armies.

Section VII recites the relief and protection of the Christian and Jewish minorities in the Moslem states of Mesopotamia (Iraq), Palestine (Israel), Syria, Turkey, Persia (Iran), Egypt, Saudi Arabia,

Tunisia, Algeria, Morocco, and Azerbaijan. The relief of these states was not seriously affected by the Peace, and I have therefore recorded in this section their relief for the entire period of relief activities.

The relief of Armenia (prior to the Peace), Georgia, and Abyssinia is related in Section VIII. Since the relief of Georgia and Abyssinia was little affected by the signing of Peace, I have completed their narrative within this section.

I have relegated Section IX, the last section of Part One, to a discussion of the approach of peace and the winding up of American participation in inter-Allied economic activities. Also recorded here are details of continued American economic co-operation after the Peace and some expressions of appreciation from the countries involved in our relief work.

PART TWO

AFTER THE PEACE

Section X, the first section of Part Two, begins with a description of the world scene at the Peace and an appraisal of the European food situation. I also recorded the creation of the American Relief Administration, finance of the relief, the building of our organization and the extracurricular activities of the American Relief Administration. The European coal chaos is also recorded. The last chapter of this section describes the repatriation of prisoners of war.

Section XI discusses relief work in Finland, the Baltic States, Poland, and Danzig after the Peace.

In Section XII, I relate the relief of Germany after the Peace. Our work there was fraught with difficulties because of the rising tide of Communism. I also relate the relief of Czechoslovakia and Albania, Austria, Hungary, and Yugoslavia.

The post-Peace relief of Rumania, Greece, Armenia, China, and Ireland makes up Section XIII.

Section XIV records the expressions of gratitude to the people of America from the people in Central and Southern Europe.

In Section XV, I record aid to Russia from 1921 to 1923. Except for this brief period, the world knew or could learn little about conditions in Russia after the Bolshevik Revolution.

Section XVI, the final section of this volume, is devoted to the winding up of relief activities in the needy or war-torn nations of the world. I also record some of the tributes paid the American people by these countries. And included here are statistics relating to relief and reconstruction.

PART ONE
BEFORE THE PEACE

SECTION I
THE ALLIES

CHAPTER 1

GREAT BRITAIN

From the United States' entry into the war in April, 1917, until the Armistice, Great Britain received 7,988,400 tons of farm products from the United States, aside from raw and manufactured textiles. During the Armistice period of nine months, the British obtained from us, through the United States Food Administration, 3,013,500 tons of supplies and from the United States Army Liquidation Commission we secured an additional 15,000 tons for them. Thus the total amount of farm products sent to Great Britain from the United States' entry into the war until the Peace was more than 11,300,000 tons.[1]

For clothing purposes, the United States furnished the British raw cotton, wool, and cotton and woolen manufactured products amounting to $798,962,675 during the period from April, 1917, to the signing of the Peace. These figures do not include the medical or reconstruction supplies, since American records do not permit a detailed breakdown of items.

United States loans to Great Britain (enabling the British to purchase American supplies) totaled $4,715,310,000—as agreed upon with the United States World War Foreign Debt Commission. How much of this could be attributed to farm products and textiles is impossible to determine, since the loans were not connected with the export of goods in the Treasury books. In any event, as explained in the

[1] This amount included West Indian sugar purchased by the United States.

1

Introduction to this volume, the whole of the British debt to the United States, like the debts owed the United States by many other countries, became a gift from the American people.

Although we have no record of the full amount, the British contributed substantially to the aid of other nations during the war and its aftermath. One instance was their subsidy to the Belgian Relief Commission of $109,045,328, plus charitable gifts from the Commonwealth to the Commission of $16,641,034. This volume will show many other contributions by the British to the famine-stricken nations. As in the case of the United States, such contributions of supplies and services were made by "loans." We do not have a record of repayments—if there were any.

AID TO GREAT BRITAIN FROM AMERICAN CHARITABLE AGENCIES

The American Red Cross supplied the major portion of aid to Great Britain by American charitable institutions. Its expenditures in the United Kingdom from the outbreak of the war until the Peace in June, 1919, were $12,473,702. Additional expenditures after the Peace brought the total to $13,428,104. A large part of this was used for the care of American armed forces personnel in transit. However, more than $5,000,000 was donated to British relief organizations, particularly the British Red Cross. In addition, $23,800 was used for the care of shell-shocked children, and a workshop was maintained to give employment to more than two thousand women who were in financial difficulty because of the war.

One of the American charitable activities in Great Britain bore the formidable title "American Overseas Charities and Patriotic League of Britain." The only record of this group's activities we have been able to find is a contribution of $13,489 to the British Red Cross for hospital beds.

A second American effort which aided the British was put forth by American women residents in England during the war. Mrs. Hoover was one of the organizers and managers of this work, the major accomplishment of which was the establishing and equipping of a hospital for wounded men at Paignton. The hospital was in operation for nearly the entire war period.

Another activity in which Mrs. Hoover participated was the creation and management of a committee which bore the title of "American Women's Committee for Economic Relief." This group established a knitting factory for the employment of women in need and distributed the factory's products to the armed forces. It also made direct contributions to needy women. Nearly all of the expenditures for these operations came from Americans then resident in Great Britain.

The Young Men's Christian Association was mostly concerned with American armed forces personnel in transit. Its expenditures in this service were $1,580,324. In addition, it established a service to enemy prisoners of war in Great Britain upon which it expended $211,351.

Compared to the relief of the American Red Cross, other activities were of minor order, but they were daily proof of devotion to the British cause.

CHAPTER 2

FRANCE

Some review of the military operations in France during the four war years is desirable in order that the reader may understand the relief problems involved. When the Germans attacked France in August, 1914, it was the second time within the recollection of men that German hobnailed boots had trampled French soil. After their armies were stopped on the Marne in September, 1914, the Germans retreated to trench lines which stretched about four hundred miles from the Belgian Canal locks at Nieuport to the Swiss border. The German armies occupied the French provinces north of these lines, where 2,500,000 French people were kept alive by the Commission for Relief in Belgium.

The Allied and German armies were locked in attack and counterattack along these trench lines for more than three and one-half years. When in March, 1918, the Germans defeated and made peace with Communist Russia, they brought their eastern armies to an area some sixty miles from the Western Front and smashed through the French and British lines to Amiens. Here they were stopped by the British, French, and American armies. On September 12, 1918, the American armies at St. Mihiel began the great counterattack by all the Allied armies. They drove the German armies into retreat and final surrender at the Armistice on November 11, 1918.

Prior to the Armistice, because of the strict censorship and restrictions on travel which were necessary to prevent leakage of in-

4

formation to the enemy, the free world had little comprehension of the suffering of France during almost four years of continuous war. When the curtain was raised at the Armistice, there came into view destroyed cities, homes, and farms. A belt of once fertile land on both sides of the trench lines was so torn that it required years for restoration. Factories remained as charred walls. Railways, canals, and coal mines in the whole fighting area were to require a decade for recovery.

The human picture was even more tragic. Tens of thousands of French soldiers who had been held as prisoners of war by the Germans streamed along the roads, determined to reach home again. From German work camps, hundreds of thousands of gaunt Frenchmen in tattered clothes, many almost shoeless, were making their way along the same crowded roads. And to these were added thousands of refugee men, women, and children who had fled to Holland and Belgium with the original German attack, while many mothers and children had remained in hovels built from their former homes, determined to stay at the old address in order that their men could find them.

This ghastly horde of refugees, plodding along the broken roads, was without food or shelter. I was an eyewitness to these tragedies. Later, I relate how our relief organization undertook to organize and support this heartbreaking parade.

Added to these tragedies, there were throughout France the widows, the orphans, and the *mutilés* of those who had sacrificed their lives and limbs in defense of their country.

THE WORK OF RELIEF

During the war, France received American aid from several quarters. The official United States Government relief agencies bore the major burden of French overseas supplies from the American entry into the war in April, 1917, to the Peace in June, 1919. The Belgian Relief Commission directed the relief of the German-occupied northern provinces from March, 1915, to June, 1919. Certain American charitable agencies gave service from the outbreak of the war until after the Peace.

The exposure of the suffering of France at the Armistice deeply stirred the sympathy of the American people. At once there sprang into being a host of new voluntary charitable agencies. Although the story of these efforts can be told in a few words, it is an epic of American compassion in itself. Statistics carry no emotion. But the background of the statistics I give below was the self-denial and the long hours of labor of the American people in the provision of these supplies.

After our entry into the war and prior to the Armistice, the American people had sent to France 6,790,280 tons of farm products, exclusive of textile raw materials and their manufactured products. During the Armistice, the official American relief agencies, under my direction, provided 3,618,560 tons of food and subsidiary supplies, which came from the Food Administration, United States Army surplus, and the Belgian Relief Commission.[1] Thus the total amount of supplies sent to France during the war and the Armistice was 10,408,840 tons. In addition, France was furnished cotton and wool and their manufactured products with a total value of $224,560,002. These totals do not include medical supplies, but they do include sugar from American purchases in the West Indies.

American aid in providing farm supplies, textiles, raw materials, and munitions appears in the French debt to the United States, which was agreed upon with France at $4,230,777,000 and funded by the United States World War Foreign Debt Commission. However, as stated in the Introduction to this volume, this debt to the United States became a gift. But the American people, remembering the sacrifices of France to free men and to civilization and the economic impossibility of such repayments, have no regrets over the outcome.

---

[1] A final sale by the United States Army of all remaining property and equipment in France for $400,000,000 (on credit) contained some food and clothing, but the amount is not recorded.

CHARITABLE ORGANIZATIONS IN AID OF FRANCE

In Volume I of this memoir, I have related the service to France of the Commission for Relief in Belgium, and in Volume II, I have related the organization and aids to France of the American Red Cross, the Salvation Army, the Jewish Joint Distribution Committee, and the American Friends Service Committee.

THE COMMISSION FOR RELIEF IN BELGIUM

In narrating the relief of France, I may recall that for four and one-half years the C.R.B. managed the relief of 2,500,000 French people in the northern provinces occupied by the German Army.

The Commission was mainly supported by government subsidies. Of these, the United States provided $386,632,260, Great Britain $109,045,328, and France $204,862,854. Added to this was a total of $52,290,795 from the charity of the world, profits from the sale of food to other countries, and other receipts, making a total of nearly $1,000,000,000. Of this, the supplies to Northern France during the war and its aftermath were 1,091,879 tons at a cost of $220,283,551.

Our American staff in Northern France had to be recalled when the United States entered the war. We substituted a Dutch staff, and the Commission continued to deliver supplies throughout this period. Most of our American staff had joined the American Army, and our former director in the North of France, Hallam Tuck, had joined the British Army. All of these men had distinguished themselves during the war. At the Armistice, with General Pershing's help, we recruited our old hands for the Armistice relief of Northern France, and Mr. Tuck came back to take charge.

The French Government urgently requested us to provide care for the steady stream of French men, women, and children pouring down the roads to their old villages, farms, and cities in Northern France or en route to places farther south. Their total exceeded a

million persons. To assist our staff, I secured from Admiral W. S.
Benson, who was in command of the American Navy, the delegation
of Admiral Thomas Craven and about 150 naval officers and sailors,
together with a vast amount of building materials. Almost overnight
these men erected barracks along the roads and fitted them with
beds and kitchens. General Pershing lent us a number of worn trucks
with drivers who managed their repairs.

The expenditures of the Army and Navy (a gift) amounted to
$3,660,000; our organization furnished free food to the migrants. We
had created in Northern France during the war years a system of
canteens for subnormal children, expectant mothers, and infirm
adults. The system was managed by devoted French women, and
when our staff returned to the scene at the Armistice, they were still
devotedly providing for over 500,000 persons. We maintained the
service until the Commission disbanded at the Peace.

From Commission profits accruing through trade with other nations and some remittances of charity, we allotted, at the Armistice,
$5,000,000 to create a permanent service to French children.

THE AMERICAN RED CROSS

This the greatest of all American charitable agencies centered its
major activity in France, where it was most needed. Prior to our
entry into the war, the Red Cross had given considerable service to
the French, which I have related in Volume II.[2] At the entry of the
United States into the war, a special committee was set up by the
Red Cross for its war work. This committee was originally directed
by Henry P. Davison, who was succeeded in March, 1919, by Dr.
Livingston Farrand. Its organization in France was first directed by
Major Grayson M.-P. Murphy, who in September, 1917, was succeeded by James H. Perkins and later by Harvey D. Gibson.

It is impossible to include in this text an adequate description of
the gigantic tasks performed by the Red Cross in France. The reader

[2] Herbert Hoover, *An American Epic* (Chicago, Henry Regnery Company, 1959—),
Vol. II, Chap. 21.

can learn this only from the annual reports of the organization. But I may recite briefly that its work included service to our armed forces in France and to the French Army through the provision of medical staffs and supplies. It also created a host of "huts" for the rest and recreation of the fighting men.

The Red Cross set up 25 children's hospitals and convalescent homes, and 99 mobile dispensaries and clinics—which, altogether, treated more than 200,000 patients. It set up canteens which served food to more than 32,000 school children. It gave aid in cash allowances to 37,652 needy families of French soldiers. It established a factory to make artificial limbs for *mutilés*. It gave food, clothing, medical aid, and repatriation to 1,726,534 refugees.

Although expenditures are not an adequate expression of the saving of life by its American physicians and surgeons, the care and encouragement of its nurses, or the feeding of the hungry, they do indicate the dimensions of this organization's service. The Red Cross expended in France, from the inception of its work in 1914 to the end of its activities abroad in 1922, a total of $124,946,996. This represented savings of the American people given to trusted hands.

THE AMERICAN FRIENDS SERVICE COMMITTEE

In Volume II,[3] I have given an account of this committee, its organization, and its service in France prior to the Armistice. From the Armistice in November, 1918, to April, 1920, when their French mission closed, the primary concern of the Friends was the rehabilitation of the Verdun area—a 200-square-mile district containing about 40 villages and some of the war's worst wreckage. This task, undertaken at the request of the French Government, was solely in Quaker hands. It covered every phase of rehabilitation—medical, agricultural, and economic—or, as the Friends themselves put it, "the reconstruction of the social fabric." An estimated 7,775 families and 32,118 individuals were restored to self-support.

At the height of the operation, the personnel of the Friends'

[3] *Ibid.*, Chap. 25.

French mission totaled 547, of whom 363 were Americans, directed successively by Charles J. Rhoads and Wilmer J. Young. The American Friends Service Committee's expenditures for France from July, 1917, to the close of the mission in April, 1920, totaled $917,529.

THE SALVATION ARMY

I have described the work of the Salvation Army in France prior to the Armistice in Volume II.[4] Evangeline Booth directed its work from Washington, and Lieutenant Colonel William S. Barker was in charge in France. Aside from its great services to the American men in uniform, it gave certain aids to civilians.

THE JEWISH JOINT DISTRIBUTION COMMITTEE

I have given a narrative of this organization and its work in Volume II.[5] Under the direction of Felix M. Warburg, it gave support to Jewish refugees in France at an expenditure of $27,714.

THE NEW CHARITABLE ORGANIZATIONS
FOR FRENCH RELIEF

As I have stated, when the suffering of France came into the full view of the American people at the Armistice, there followed a great outburst of sympathy, one expression of which was a multitude of new voluntary charitable agencies determined to help. Our research into the records which have survived after more than forty years disclosed that in many cases parts of them had been lost, while in other instances they were discernible only by references in the press or in reports of other organizations. The following list of organizations and expenditures represents what we have been able to discover so far.

[4] *Ibid.*, Chap. 24.
[5] *Ibid.*, Chap. 23.

American Artists Committee of One Hundred, WILLIAM A. COFFIN, Chairman .... $ 8,701

American Committee for Devastated France, MYRON T. HERRICK, President 1,262,915

American Committee for "La Renaissance des Cités," A. F. BEMIS, Chairman 10,574

American Committee for Training in Suitable Trades the Maimed Soldiers in France, MRS. EDMUND L. BAYLIES, President 34,112

American Committee of the Argonne Association, EDGAR V. FROTHINGHAM, President 129,307

American Memorial Hospital Committee of the American Fund for French Wounded, MRS. BENJAMIN G. LATHROP, Managing Director 728,193

American Ouvroir Funds, MRS. HENRY P. LOOMIS, President 740,953

American Students Committee of the École des Beaux Arts, HENRY R. SEDGWICK, Chairman 16,347

Children's Tin Box Fund, MRS. E. C. LARNED, President 35,361

Committee of Hope, HOWARD TOWNSEND, President 6,919

Duryea War Relief, MRS. NINA LARREY DURYEA, President 64,585

Fatherless Children of France, SEYMOUR L. CROWELL, President 13,835,229

Food for France Fund, MISS CARITA SPENCER, President 8,611

Franco-American Committee for the Protection of Children of the Frontier, FREDERIC R. COUDERT, Chairman 555,413

French Heroes' La Fayette Memorial Fund, MRS. WILLIAM ASTOR CHANLER, President 1,758,819

French Restoration Fund, JAMES M. HALSTED, President 135,274

French Tubercular Children's Fund, WALTER E. MAYNARD, President 291,315

French Tuberculous Soldiers' Relief Committee, DUCHESSE DE RICHELIEU, President 57,413

International Kindergarten Unit, FANNIEBELLE CURTIS, Director 168,107

Les Maisons Claires, MRS. EMILE VILLEMIN, Chairman 6,693

Secours Franco-American, MRS. JOHN A. LOGAN, Chairman .. 25,083

Secours National, New York Committee, MRS. WHITNEY WARREN, Treasurer 606,120

For the following organizations which worked in France we have no information concerning officers but do have amounts expended, in part or in whole:

Le Paquet du Soldat	$ 6,236
S. R. Fuller Lecture Fund	33,000
Winifred Holt's American Committee for Helping Blind	69,759

For the following relief organizations which worked in more than one country, including France, we have some information concerning officers and sums expended, in part or in whole:

American Allies Cooperative Committee, MRS. MARY HATCH WILLARD, Chairman	$ 25,079
American Women's Hospitals, DR. MARY M. CRAWFORD, Chairman	266,556
Carnegie Endowment for International Peace, ELIHU ROOT, President of Board of Trustees	300,000
Permanent Blind Relief War Fund, GEORGE A. KESSLER, Chairman	96,837
St. Vincent de Paul Society, GEORGE J. GILLESPIE, President ..	52,904
Smith College War Service Board, MISS MARY B. LEWIS, Chairman	61,422
The New York Sun Tobacco Fund	442,000
Women's Overseas Hospital, MRS. CHARLES L. TIFFANY, Chairman	8,057

For the following organizations giving relief in France we have the names of officers but no information concerning expenditures:

American Committee of the Villages Libérés, MISS BELLE SKINNER, President
American Friends of Musicians in France, WALTER DAMROSCH, President
Committee for Men Blinded in Battle, JOHN H. FINLEY, President
Edith Wharton War Charities, WALTER E. MAYNARD, President
Free Milk for France, MRS. WARREN McCONIHE, Chairman
Le Paquet de l'Orphelin, MISS BYRD W. HAMBLEN, President
Ligue Fraternelle des Enfants de France, MISS ANNE PARKER MINER, President
National Allied Relief Committee, JOHN MOFFAT, President

Scottish Women's Hospitals, Miss Kathleen Burke, American Representative

Society to Help Devastated Churches of France, Morgan J. O'Brien, President

The Needlework Guild of America, Department of War Relief, Mrs. John Wood Stuart, Chairman

For the following organizations giving relief in France we have no information concerning either officers or funds expended:

American French Service Committee
American Fund for Charité Maternal
American Society for the Relief of French War Orphans
Appui aux Artistes
Committee on American Hostels for Belgian Refugees in Paris
French Actors' Fund
French Tuberculosis War Victims' Fund
Le Bien-Etre du Blessé
Le Sou de Mutilé
Mon Soldat
Our Boys in France Tobacco Fund
Save the Children for the France of Tomorrow
Secours de Guerre
Secours d'Urgence
Société Secours Blessés Militaires
Union des Arts
Union Nationale des Églises Reformées Evangeliques de France
Villiers Fund

THE AMERICAN RELIGIOUS DENOMINATIONS

Prior to the Armistice, the leading American religious denominations had devoted themselves strictly to religion and morale-building in the American armed forces and among their co-religionists in France. With the lifting of the curtain on the condition of the French people, several of them undertook the additional service of physical relief to civilians in some form.

After the Armistice, the American Methodist Episcopal Church undertook the relief and reconstruction of thirty-two villages. Food and clothing supplies were sold at low prices, and the receipts were used for medical aid and the support of "social centers." The supplies were purchased from the American Army and other sources at a value of $65,000. The Church worked with babies and the young and established one orphanage for girls and another for boys.

The Northern Baptist Convention undertook relief work in France and Belgium. Its efforts were largely centered around the destroyed city of Lens. A three-year budget of $166,000 per annum was provided. With it, this group erected some temporary housing, aided women and orphans, provided textbooks for schools, and bought farm implements for peasants. These war activities continued until the spring of 1923.

The National Lutheran Council spent a total of $114,731 for its work in France.

The National Catholic Welfare Council (which included the Knights of Columbus and its work with the American armed forces) provided civilian aid by establishing two lunch canteens for girls and women working in factories and two playgrounds for children in Paris. It opened six welfare centers in congested factory sections and in devastated areas, where social, recreational, and educational programs were carried on; set up vacation homes for working girls in two country locations; and maintained "Maisons de famille" in four French cities. Destroyed churches were reconstructed. The total expenditures in France, as far as we can analyze the records, were $1,644,182.

The Mennonite Emergency Relief Committee expended some funds in France directly, but its major service was in support, by staff and funds, of the American Friends Service Committee. Its total expenditures were $290,856.

The Presbyterian Church in the United States (South) erected the French Reformed Church at Compiègne, France, as a memorial to our soldiers at a cost of $25,000.

The Protestant Episcopal Church's unofficial publication, *The Living Church*, sponsored a "War Relief Fund" for many years.

Besides receiving contributions for relief, it secured sponsors for more than one thousand fatherless children of Belgium and, especially, France.

In June, 1919, the Reformed Church in America gave $25,000 to the Interchurch Committee for Christian Relief in France and Belgium for the restoration of Protestant churches.

The Church of Jesus Christ of Latter-day Saints (Mormons) provided food, medical aid, clothing, and reconstruction aids, but records of their expenditures are unobtainable.

During the war, the world-wide organization of the Young Men's Christian Association devoted itself primarily to religion and morale-building among the armed forces and to the care or guardianship of war prisoners of every nation at war. For the French Army, it established Les Foyers du Soldat, rest places with recreational activities and an advisory staff. It opened and operated 1,534 foyers, upon which $7,600,000 was expended.

The Y.M.C.A. gave attention to the welfare of about 400,000 prisoners of war (mostly German and Austrian) held by the French. However, the French Government placed most of these prisoners as farm laborers; they received board, lodging, and experience in farming.

The Y.M.C.A. was also concerned with the welfare of more than 150,000 Chinese laborers brought into France by the Allied armies. Unable to speak either English or French, they rapidly sank into sullen despair. However, the Y.M.C.A. remedied the situation by teaching the Chinese to speak English or French and by providing the usual "huts." Expenditures in France by the Y.M.C.A. from April, 1917, to March, 1921, totaled $9,089,913.

The Young Women's Christian Association also established "foyers" for the military forces and for French factory workers, especially those living in barracks, who had little opportunity for rest and recreation. They provided lessons in sewing and English or simply provided good cheer. From 1917 to 1920, the Y.W.C.A. provided thirty-one foyers and eleven recreation camps. Its expenditures in France were $633,603.

THE TOTALS

A rough estimate of the gifts by American charitable agencies comes to more than $165,000,000. To this should be added the gift of the whole French war debt, or a total of $4,395,777,000. But I have stated repeatedly that sums of money are poor expressions of the American contribution to France, which helped bring victory to the cause of independence of nations, of free men, of the preservation of civilized governments, and, above all, the relief of suffering, restoration of courage among the disheartened, and the saving of human lives.

CHAPTER 3

ITALY, BELGIUM, AND PORTUGAL

ITALY

Italy joined in the war against Austria-Hungary on May 23, 1915, and declared war on Germany on August 28, 1916. Except for farms and water power, Italy was a country without great natural resources. Before the war she was dependent upon imports for much of her food, medicine, clothing, practically all her coal, and many raw materials. She had built up a large manufacturing industry and supported herself with the export of her products. After Italy's entry into the war, because of her slender resources, she was not able to finance her necessary imports. The British and French extended her loans with which to pay for supplies. After the United States entered the war in April, 1917, our Government extended loans to Italy with which to purchase American supplies.

From the United States' entry into the war and prior to the Armistice, American Government agencies furnished 5,215,000 tons of farm supplies (not including textiles). During the Armistice, the United States Food Administration furnished 3,256,400 tons, making a total of 8,471,400 tons. From April, 1917, to the Peace in July, 1919, the United States furnished raw cotton, wool, and their manufactured products valued at $140,516,700. During the war and the Armistice period, the United States also extended a total of $2,150,150,000 in loans to Italy for all purposes, including the pur-

17

chase of her food, raw materials, and military supplies. And, as explained in the Introduction to this volume, this became a gift from the American people.

AID TO ITALY FROM AMERICAN CHARITABLE AGENCIES

The American Red Cross was the leading American charitable agency giving aid to Italy. Its total outlay from July, 1917, through 1920 amounted to $22,885,678.

The Red Cross commission initially sent to Italy in the summer of 1917 returned home in October, reporting a relatively small need for relief. Within a few weeks, however, came the Italian military disaster of the Austro-Hungarian breakthrough at Caporetto. This ignited a mass flight of soldiers and some 500,000 civilians southward from the Venetian plains. The Red Cross once again sent its workers to Italy.

In its refugee relief up to March, 1919, the Red Cross distributed 891,000 garments, 148,000 pairs of shoes, a million yards of cloth, and 971,000 bedding and household articles. It organized and operated three hospitals, three dispensaries, 50 kitchens, 88 workrooms, and five refugee colonies. At Pisa, the Red Cross furnished two thousand residents with food, housing, medical attention, schooling for their children, and employment in factories especially constructed for the production of war materials.

In January, 1918, the Red Cross undertook a longer-range program of child welfare, aid to needy families of soldiers, rehabilitation of refugees in co-operation with private and official Italian agencies—ultimately expanding its activities to 141 cities and thousands of villages from the Alps to Sicily. Within the next year, an estimated 155,000 children were cared for through orphanages, special kitchens, day nurseries, schools, playgrounds, health centers, and summer colonies partially financed by Red Cross funds and in some cases operated by its personnel. Cash was distributed to 326,000 families of needy soldiers, and a number of their dependents were employed, along with refugee women, at Red Cross workrooms for the repair and manufacture of clothing.

The Red Cross and its work had a profound effect in restoring Italian morale.

OTHER AMERICAN CHARITABLE AIDS TO ITALY

The Young Men's Christian Association established its first "hut" in Italy in July, 1916, to aid civilian and war prisoners from Austria, Hungary, Poland, and Turkey. It distributed books, games, and tools for wood carving. From January, 1918, the Y.M.C.A. increased its efforts in Italy, working with the Allied armies. It set up huts, athletic programs, entertainment, and emergency stations, serving hot drinks, bread, and cigarettes to soldiers. We have been unable to learn the initial expenditures of the Y.M.C.A. in Italy, but available statistics from April, 1917, through March, 1921, reveal an expenditure of $3,840,988.

Early in 1919, the Young Women's Christian Association sent a small staff to Rome to assist the Italian women's organization, *Christiana Delle Giovani*, in setting up hostels for working girls and refugees. From 1919 through 1922, the Y.W.C.A. expended $228,202 in Italy.

There were a number of less extensive American charitable aids to Italy. The records preserved are incomplete, but, as far as our research shows, they were:

American Free Milk and Relief for Italy, Inc., MRS. JOHN ADAMS DRAKE, President
   Supplies in kind: $165,972
American Poets' Ambulances in Italy, ROBERT U. JOHNSON, Chairman
   Funds: $176,807
Italian War Relief Fund of America, ROBERT U. JOHNSON, President
   Funds: $130,116
Jewish Joint Distribution Committee, FELIX WARBURG, Chairman
   Care of Jewish refugees
   Funds: $30,054

Methodist Episcopal Church, Bishop JOSEPH F. BERRY, President, National
   War Council
   Relief efforts were concentrated in the devastated northern areas from
   Trento to Trieste; food, clothing, and shoes were distributed to widows
   and orphans; $25,000 was given to the Italian Government for agri-
   cultural implements.
National Catholic War Council
   Established *Case Sant' Elena* in Turin as a residence for young women;
   also gave aid to war orphans in homes and at a trade school in Rome.
National Fund for War Orphans in Italy, MRS. BENJAMIN MILLER, Presi-
   dent
   Funds: $100,000
   Maintained and educated war orphans.

The Christian Science War Relief Fund, the National Lutheran
Council, and the Presbyterians also spent minor amounts of money
in Italy.

Our research developed the following references to relief for
which no information except the names of the organizations can be
found:

   American Committee in Aid of Italian Soldiers Crippled in the War
   New England Italian War Relief Fund
   War Orphans of Italy Fund.

BELGIUM

I have given a detailed account of the relief of German-occupied
Belgium in Volume I of this series. To make this narrative of the
"front line" complete, I give a brief account of these operations.

When the curtain over German-occupied Belgium was lifted by
the retreat of the German armies and the Armistice, there came into
view the first food administration in history. It had sustained Belgium's 8,000,000 people for four intensely difficult years. During its
operations, the organization had inaugurated a system of canteens
where subnormal children, expectant mothers, and the aged were
given special food in addition to the necessarily drastic rations. The
experience and skills developed with this system later enabled us to
spread this service over Europe to more than 15,000,000 children.

Prior to the Armistice, the Commission for Relief in Belgium had imported into Belgium 3,036,317 tons of food, clothing, and medical and other supplies. During the Armistice, the Commission delivered 858,624 tons of supplies, making a total of 3,894,941 tons. To this quantity might be added 277,000 tons of supplies in ships torpedoed by the Germans, wrecked at sea, or marooned in foreign ports. These supplies came from the United States, except for comparatively minor quantities in cargoes purchased en route and some supplies from the Neutral nations.

I have recited the American, British, and French governmental subsidies to the Commission's support in the chapter on the relief of France. Funds from charity, the sale of requisitioned food, and other sources gave it total financial resources of more than $1,000,000,000. The organization had been conducted by more than 50,000 American and Belgian volunteers.

With the Armistice, the Belgian Government requested the Commission for Relief in Belgium to continue—which it did for five months after the Armistice.

During the years of its operations, the Commission had made a profit from trading in food, mostly with other nations, and had in hand some unspent charitable gifts totaling more than $38,000,000. At the request of Prime Minister Leon Delacroix, I determined the disposal of this fund. It was used to reconstruct and endow the universities and technical schools; to create scientific research institutions; to provide for education of destitute students; and to establish a system of exchanges of students and professors between America and Belgium.

As was the case in all countries, American aid to Belgium was in the form of so-called "loans." The total Belgian debt to the United States for food, medical supplies, raw materials, and munitions was settled in 1923, by agreement, at $483,426,000. For reasons stated in the Introduction to this series, the whole of this sum proved to be a gift from the American people to Belgium.

Other American charitable organizations gave great service to the 600,000 Belgian refugees who had escaped during the German invasion. The American Red Cross undertook the major role in organizing this relief. More than half the refugees drifted into France, where the Red Cross aided their support through contributions to local Belgian organizations. It subsidized schools for the children and supplies of medicine and clothing for adult refugees.

In its work, the Red Cross established or aided nine hospitals with American physicians, surgeons, and nurses. It supplied food, clothing, and housing. In this latter field, it built a sawmill to provide housing—and even the making of wooden shoes. Sewing machines were furnished to Belgian women in organized workshops, and they were paid for their work.

The Red Cross expended a total of $4,481,433.

OTHER CHARITABLE ACTIVITIES

The Rockefeller Foundation expended $1,498,471 for the relief of Belgium and the Belgian people through the Commission for Relief in Belgium, the American Red Cross, the War Relief Commission, and aid to Belgian professors in England.

The Jewish Joint Distribution Committee expended $2,500 in support of Jewish refugees.

The National Catholic Welfare Council provided a home for working girls in Brussels and community centers in three Belgian cities.

In the fall of 1919, the Young Women's Christian Association sent an American mission to Belgium. It co-operated with Belgian organizations in establishing foyers for girls, and expended $126,927.

The Methodist Episcopal Church, South established an orphanage in Brussels and a relief station in Ypres.

Also making minor contributions were the Northern Baptists and the Presbyterian Church.

After the Armistice, a fund was organized by Nicholas Murray Butler, President of Columbia University, for the rebuilding of the destroyed library at the University of Louvain. Work was started, and about $150,000 was raised (the Carnegie Endowment for International Peace contributed more than $100,000 of this). However, at this point the fund died and the Commission for Relief in Belgium, from its profits (noted above), completed the building at a total cost to the Commission of about $425,000.

Our research revealed no records beyond the mere names of the following Belgian relief efforts:

American Committee Collecting for the Charities of the Queen of the
    Belgians
Belgian Refugees Knitting Yarn Fund
Belgian Soldiers' Tobacco Fund
Children of Flanders
Committee for Relief of Belgian Refugees
Dollar Christmas Fund for Homeless Belgians.

PORTUGAL

From the beginning of World War I in 1914, Portugal declared her loyalty to the British. In February, 1916, the Portuguese requisitioned German ships in their ports. Germany then formally declared war on Portugal on March 9, 1916, and was followed by Austria on March 15.

The Portuguese organized an expeditionary force which arrived in France on February 3, 1917, and took over a small part of the front. By July, 1917, there were more than 40,000 Portuguese troops on the Western Front.

Portugal was self-supporting and needed no aid from the American official relief agencies.

The American Red Cross indicates a small expenditure to Portugal of $6,000 before the Armistice, but no further aid.

The American Young Men's Christian Association helped the Portuguese soldiers at the front with their language problems. It provided canteens and dormitories to care for the Portuguese officers in Paris.

GREECE

Greece was an Ally, but since her narrative involves problems occurring after the Peace, I deal with it in Part Two of this volume.

FINLAND, THE BALTIC STATES, AND POLAND

CHAPTER 4

FINLAND

The Finns were a tribe which had migrated from somewhere in Asia in the dim past. Their closest racial ties were with the Hungarians.

For three hundred years Finland had enjoyed independence and representative government. Then she was invaded by the Russians and for the next hundred years was subjected to their domination— with no self-government. She declared her independence in December, 1917, after the Bolshevik Revolution in Russia. A civil war then ensued, with Finland's domestic Communists aided and abetted by Moscow. With Germany's help, the Communists were defeated, and the Finns were then compelled to elect the Kaiser's brother-in-law as their king. After the Armistice, on December 12, 1918, they threw off the German yoke and established self-government under the leadership of General Baron Carl Gustav Mannerheim. The German king sank without a trace in history. The native Communists were still active, and the measures taken under Mannerheim to remove them were positive enough, but not so inhuman as those applied by the Communists against the non-Communists in Russia. The Finnish Communists were permitted to emigrate to the United States. Many came and were for years a national pest.

The population of Finland at the time of the First World War approximated 4,000,000 people, about half of whom were engaged in agriculture. The northern portions of the country were a bleak annex

27

of the Arctic. Of some 82,000,000 acres, only about 4,100,000 could be cultivated.

The Finns' major industry dealt with forest products from their Arctic holdings. Under Czarist domination, Finland had received a large part of her food supply from Russia in exchange for these forest products. During the year of German occupation prior to the Armistice, Finland was blockaded by the Allies, barring both her imports and her exports. This, together with the Communist disturbances and a bad crop, doomed Finnish towns and cities to complete starvation within sixty days after the Armistice.

Soon after I arrived in London on November 22, 1918, a Finnish deputation called upon me to relate their plight. They were led by Rudolf Holsti, who later became Minister of Foreign Affairs. Theirs was a heartbreaking story of invaders, destroyed crops, plundered and burned granaries, prohibited imports and exports, people eating bread made from a mixture which contained the bark of trees, and a terrible death toll among the weak and the young. Their earnestness was so overwhelming that without further investigation I replied at once that I would direct to their ports some of our food cargoes which we had already loaded in the United States before I left for Europe. They had made arrangements to get a loan of 10,000 tons of emergency supplies from Denmark, provided that we would guarantee to replace these amounts later. The Finns had arranged to pay for these supplies sometime in the future. We at once gave our guarantee.

The deputation informed me that the Finns had a small cargo fleet sufficient to handle their exports and imports. However, their ships were under Russian registry and the Russian flag. The Allied blockade authorities would not allow them to go to sea or to change their registry. The Finns added that their government, or their banks, had about $5,000,000 on deposit in London and about $8,000,000 in the United States. Since they were still under blockade restrictions, they could not use these funds. Also, the United States Government owed Finland about $5,000,000 for goods seized as alien enemy property while the Finns were under German occupation.

I suggested to my visitors that in view of the impending arrival of the 10,000 tons from Denmark and of our ships soon to be en route, they could instruct their people to release all reserves of food for immediate consumption. They wanted to know if I was certain that the new supplies would arrive from the United States. I assured them again that the ships were loaded and would be directed to them at once.

It is seldom that men of the North show emotion. Some few minutes after they had left, they returned. They wanted to know how much the operation would cost. I explained that I did not know what the cost would be but that supplies would be furnished without profit and that I was confident we could arrange to advance the food against the various foreign assets they had mentioned. (We later arranged for the Grain Corporation to do so.) They said: "We will pay. Our people will work and pay." I replied that they could take their time to pay and added that I hoped the American Congress would furnish me resources to provide extra food for their children without cost.

The desperate situation in Finland is best described in quotations from two of the many letters I received while we were progressing with our task. The local committee at Nurmes wrote:

The three scourges, war, hunger and disease, have ravaged in Finland. They have sown suffering and tears into many homes. But in addition to all this, the continued shortage of foodstuffs brought sufferings especially into the homes of the poor families. . . . The mother had to add bark, peat and straw when making bread. As a result of such nourishment the members of the poor families have changed into emaciated, pitiable looking human beings. Often the small ones tell their mothers, "Please, mother, give us real bread," and just as often the mothers had to reply with heavy hearts, "At present there is none, my little child, but wait, perhaps sometime we shall get it."

And then arrived the gift of the American people for the children of Finland. When the poor mothers heard this their hearts brightened and their hopes revived. Now our small ones at least shall receive of God's real food.

And then when the father or mother brought home the gift of the noble American people there was a holiday. The eyes of the children shone for joy and thankfulness toward their good benefactors. They were prepared into a meal which with glad hearts and thankful minds was eaten. Benedictions were asked for the great and noble American people living beyond the sea. . . .

The committee of Pielisjarvi Parish wrote:

We wish to express our thanks for the assistance which we have received as a gift from America. We were in great want. The weaker ones amongst us already looked the hunger death in the eyes and then the help arrived, arrived from far beyond the sea, from an entirely foreign part of the world and from which we had no idea of expecting it. The noble people of America hastened to our help in the hour of our greatest need. It conveyed us luckily past the threatening danger, through its great gifts to us.

We cannot make any return gift, but we wish to send our regards and most sincere thanks for your great help.

We sent Mr. Magnus Swenson of our staff to make a preliminary examination of Finland and the Baltic States. When President Wilson recommended the appropriation of $100,000,000 for relief and the Congressional committees asked for more information concerning needs, Mr. Swenson's report on the situation carried conviction.

STAFF ARRANGEMENTS

Mr. Swenson continued to represent us in Finland and the Baltic States until we could make more ample arrangements. On March 19, 1919, we sent a full mission to Finland to succeed him. The mission comprised:

MAJOR FERRY K. HEATH, *Chief of Mission*
CAPTAIN JOHN C. MILLER, *Chief Assistant*
LIEUTENANT MORRIS G. BISHOP, *Secretary to Mission*
LIEUTENANT IVAR W. WAHREN, *Chief of Children's Relief,* aided by
LIEUTENANT ANGUS I. WARD, *Financial Officer*

OUR "BALTIC BASE"

We established our headquarters for all of the Baltic region at Rotterdam, later moving it to Copenhagen. We discharged most of our larger cross-Atlantic cargoes at these ports, where we built up stocks and distributed the supplies with small American Shipping Board "Lake" steamers in order to save our larger ships for the trans-oceanic voyages.

FOOD SUPPLY AND FINANCE

In addition to our plan for Danish supplies, I arranged for the Grain Corporation (a division of the Food Administration) to undertake shipments to Finland on the pledge of her balances abroad. Under my authority from the President to use Army surpluses for relief, we secured for the Finns substantial amounts of food on credit. When Congress made the $100,000,000 appropriation available to us at the end of February, 1919, we were out of financial trouble as far as Finland was concerned.

THE BLOCKADE

The blockade under the Allied declaration of December 31, 1918, applied to food as well as imports of raw materials and exports of products. It immobilized Finnish ships and prevented the Finns from using their funds abroad. Under the assurance from Admiral Benson that American-flag ships carrying food supplies to starving people would not meet interference, we carried on our delivery of food, clothing, and medical supplies.

Both Vance McCormick (Chairman of the Superior Blockade Council) and I repeatedly urged the Allied blockade committees to allow the Finns to register their ships under the Swedish flag. However, the first tenet of bureaucracy is to prevent the establishment of a precedent, and this would have been a crack in the whole block-ade system.

Finally, on June 4, seven months after the Armistice, McCormick secured the following from the Superior Blockade Council:

> . . . the Council *determined* that for the present foodstuffs could be shipped to Finland without the prior issuance of a permit. . . .

We were glad to know this because we had been doing it without permission from anybody except Admiral Benson.

CHILDREN'S REHABILITATION

There could be no doubt about the needs of Finnish children, for the population was on the edge of mass starvation when we began shipments. With regard to the needs of children, I may add to the letters from local committees which I quoted earlier some comments from three of our staff reports:

> . . . It is imperative that early shipments arrive, if some of the localities most desperately in need of this help shall receive them before the roads become impassable. . . .
> [At a] . . . children's home for orphans and poor children . . . [the] matron informed me that due to insufficient bedclothes, it was necessary on cold nights to put the children to bed wearing all their clothes. . . .
> . . . We visited . . . [in central eastern Finland] a home for children which at present, owing to lack of clothing, only accommodated thirty children although originally intended to accommodate fifty. . . .

During the war years previous to the Armistice, the Finns had fully organized the care of children. We had only to furnish them supplies. We shipped them 2,272 tons of special food at a cost of $560,275. At the time of the Peace, there were 1,600 kitchens in operation feeding 43,000 children. And many more children had already been rehabilitated.

HELP FROM OTHER QUARTERS

The British furnished Finland 3,467 tons of food valued at $920,250.

As I have mentioned previously, from Denmark the Finns obtained 10,000 tons of food, which we replaced.

Mr. Swenson secured from the Norwegians 4,442 tons of coffee and fish products valued at $1,177,130.

The American Red Cross contributed 282 tons of clothing valued at $56,400.

The Methodist Episcopal Church War Relief Committee sent some clothing to Finland, the amount of which we do not know.

Total supplies sent to Finland from the Armistice to the Peace included (in tons):

	Food	Clothing	Total	$ Value
American Relief Administration:				
Children's relief	2,272		2,272	$ 560,275
General relief	167,561		167,561	24,308,914
(Including freight)				
American Red Cross ...		282	282	56,400
United Kingdom	3,467		3,467	920,250
Denmark	10,000		10,000	1,141,700
Norway	4,442		4,442	1,177,130
	187,742	282	188,024	$28,164,669

For these supplies the Finns paid the United Kingdom, Denmark, and Norway in cash or in goods.

The United States received $16,004,404 in cash and received Finnish obligations to pay $9,190,000.

THE INDEPENDENCE OF FINLAND

The real solution for Finland's troubles was the recognition of her independence by the Supreme Council (the Big Four). I repeatedly urged this upon the lesser authority—the Council of Ten. The French Foreign Office was the stumbling block, for it believed that the Communist Government of Russia would collapse and that questions of Finland's destiny ought to be kept open for settlement with the expected new Russian Government, all of which was nonsense.

Finally, I appealed to President Wilson to raise this question with the Big Four and let me do the talking. My letter was:

26 April 1919

MY DEAR MR. PRESIDENT:

I am wondering if there is not some method by which the recognition of the full independence of Finland could be expedited. They have now had a general election, they have created a responsible ministry: this ministry is of liberal character. There are many reasons why this matter should be undertaken, and at once.

1. The United States has always had a great sentiment for the suffering of the Finnish people, and their struggle over a century to gain independence.

2. By lack of recognition, they are absolutely isolated from . . . the rest of the world. They are unable to market their products. . . . They have ships without flags; have no right to sail the seas. They are totally unable to establish credits, although they have a great deal of resource, as no bank can loan money to a country of unrecognized government. They are isolated by censorship. Their citizens are not allowed to move as their passports do not run. . . .

I then described the relief operation, the Finnish financial situation, the burden upon us, and continued:

If ever there was a case for helping a people who are making a sturdy fight to get on a basis of liberal democracy, and are asking no charity of the world whatever, this is the case. I am convinced from our reports that unless Finland is recognized within a very short time . . . the present government cannot survive the difficulties with which it is faced. . . .

Nor do I see why any half measures need to be taken in this matter. They have gone through every cycle that the world could demand in political evolution, to the point of an independent people, and I feel that they would long since have been recognized had it not been for the terrible cloud of other questions that surrounds the world. . . .

HERBERT HOOVER

The President suggested that I discuss the matter with Premier Clemenceau. As always with me, the Premier was most considerate. He agreed to my proposals and at once instructed the French Minister of Foreign Affairs accordingly. Secretary of State Lansing sent my letter to the Council of Ten, and the President added to the urging on May 3 with the following note for Secretary Lansing's use:

MY DEAR LANSING:

I am pretty clear in my view that the case of Finland stands by itself. It never was in any true sense an integral part of Russia. It has been a most uneasy and unwilling partner and I think that action in regard to the recognition of the Finnish Government would not commit us or embarrass us with regard to the recognition of any other part of the former Russian Empire that might be separately set up. I am very keen for the recognition of Finland, as you know.

WOODROW WILSON

As a result, I did not appear before the Big Four with my prepared oration.

The Council of Ten met the same day and agreed to recognition. But it was also agreed that the decision should be kept secret until it could be announced simultaneously by the Council members. A few hours after the decision was made, Rudolf Holsti, the Finnish representative in Paris, came to see me; he was full of emotion and gratitude. He informed me that he had seen my letter, that both the French and the British had communicated to him confidentially what had been done, and that both had said they hoped Finland would appreciate their efforts.

As soon as the decision was made public, Colonel James Logan of my staff telegraphed Major Ferry Heath that recognition had been granted, adding:

. . . The recognition of Finland has been brought about entirely by Mr. Hoover by his urgent and repeated representations to the various governments. . . .

Heath's reply makes illuminating reading:

. . . You doubtless know that the news of England's recognition arrived three days prior to the news that we had also recognized Finland. Naturally, this resulted in a feeling of obligation towards England which was only partially dispelled by the tardy arrival of the news from the United States.

EPILOGUE

The government of Finland had repeatedly invited me to visit that country in order that the Finns might express their appreciation. I did so early in 1938. Their reception was tremendous, with events staged over five days. I found a prosperous nation of happy people with but one fear—Communist Russia.

And Finland was the only country in the world which continued payments upon her debt to the United States.

An innocent Polish victim of World War I.

A Russian lad from Ufa with food from the A.R.A.

Finnish children eating A.R.A. rations.

Polish children with receptacles for food.

CHAPTER 5

THE BALTIC STATES— ESTONIA, LATVIA, AND LITHUANIA

We set up a central administration of the official United States relief agencies in the Baltic States—Estonia, Latvia, and Lithuania. As problems developed, we secured forty-seven officers and men from the Army and Navy. Because the names of our leaders appear frequently in this text, I give them here:

MAGNUS SWENSON, *Chief of Mission to the Baltic States*
COLONEL JOHN C. GROOME, *Successor, Chief of Mission to the Baltic States*
MAJOR GEORGE F. FELKER, *Assistant*
CAPTAIN EVAN H. FOREMAN, *Assistant*
LIEUTENANT JOHN THORS, *Assistant*
CAPTAIN JOHN C. MILLER, *Chief of Mission to Estonia*
MAJOR WALTER DuB. BROOKINGS, *Chief of Mission to Latvia*
LIEUTENANT GEORGE P. HARRINGTON, *Assistant*
CAPTAIN JOHN B. HOLLISTER, *Chief of Mission to Lithuania*
MAJOR W. A. BURBANK, *Successor, Chief of Mission to Lithuania*
CAPTAIN JAMES T. SCOTT, *Assistant*

The people of these three little states had a common pattern in their migration from Asia to the rich lands on the Baltic in the dim past: (1) constant oppression from the more powerful nations for more than a thousand years; (2) a determination to hold their own racial mores and culture of all these years; and (3) their break for freedom at the Armistice. They had been dominated by either Russians, Poles, Germans, or, in the Middle Ages, the Teutonic Knights —colloquially called the "Baltic Barons." The latter left in each of these peoples a strain of race out of which grew a class known as the Balts.

Centuries prior to the First World War, the Baltic States had been provinces of the Russian Empire. Under the more liberal policies of the later Czars, the people of these states emerged from serfdom to become peasants and industrial workers, but oppressions continued under Balt and Russian industrialists and landlords. During all of these centuries, they had never been allowed a semblance of self-government, but they had maintained an extraordinary intellectual independence. They had withstood Russianization, and they had clung to a determination that freedom would come to them some day.

Russia was interested in these states because of the possibility of developing the Baltic ports as outlets from the hinterland to the Baltic and because she wanted to establish herself as the ruling landlord and industrialist.

We of the American Government relief agencies were the major contact of these states with the outside world. We were eyewitnesses on the ground, and members of our staff were often participants in their struggles for freedom. We repeatedly presented their difficulties to the Supreme Council in Paris and at times secured some aid for them. We alone knew their story.

Rather than repeat the major conditions and problems of each state in separate chapters, we shall, for clarity, consider them collectively in their common patterns.

THE GEOGRAPHIC SETTING AND POPULATION OF THE BALTIC STATES

Estonia, the northernmost state, with its port of Tallinn, was the smallest of the three. It had an area of 18,358 square miles (about half the size of Indiana) and a population of about 1,100,000, half of which were farmers.

Latvia was made up of the former Russian provinces of Kurland and part of Livonia. It comprised an area of 25,402 square miles (about that of West Virginia) with a population of about 1,600,000, of which over 500,000 were concentrated in Riga, the great Russian commercial outlet to the Baltic. About 500,000 were farmers.

Lithuania, with its port on the Baltic at Memel, comprised an area of about 28,000 square miles (about half the size of Illinois) and had a population of about 2,000,000 of which more than 1,600,000 were farmers.

These people had little mineral resources, but they possessed two great economic assets: fertile soils and devotion to hard work.

THE COMING OF THE WAR—AND FREEDOM

In 1915 the Germans had driven the Russians from the Baltic States and annexed them to the German Empire, but with the Bolshevik Revolution in Russia in 1917 and the defeat of Germany by the Allied and American forces in 1918, the opportunity for independence and freedom came at last.

The Estonians declared their independence at the time of the Communist Revolution in November, 1917, but it was snuffed out by German invasion. They again declared their independence thirteen days before the Armistice—October 28, 1918. They created a provisional government and adopted a provisional constitution providing for the basic freedoms and the British form of parliamentary government. They formally elected a parliament on April 13, 1919.

Latvia produced the greatest leader of the Baltic States' drive for independence—Karl Ulmanis. Probably more than any other man's, his devotion to freedom was responsible for the independence movement in all three states; he was one of the unique figures to emerge from the war. As a refugee from Latvia he arrived in Nebraska in 1907. By working his way through college, he graduated from the University of Nebraska in February, 1909, and engaged in farming and in teaching until 1914, when he returned to Latvia to minister to his mother and was caught in the draft of the Russian Army. Returning to Latvia seven days after the Armistice, he, in council with leading Letts, declared the independence of Latvia. A provisional parliamentary government was set up, with Ulmanis as its president. But his frail government was at once opposed by the Balts. Because of their refusal of support, he was unable to overcome the Communist seizure of Riga on January 2, 1919, and fled to South Latvia, where he held out until the Communists were driven back.

The Lithuanians proclaimed their independence shortly after the Communist Revolution in Russia, but the new nation was eclipsed by the German invasion. After the German defeat, they followed the lead of the other Baltic States, declared their independence, and in January, 1919, called a national assembly which set up a provisional parliamentary form of government.

The individualism of the three states was such that they could not, and would not, unite into one nation, although their racial affinities, aspirations, economic problems, future defense, and independence all pointed to that necessity. Each of the parliaments— and all were inexperienced in government—was divided among twelve to sixteen political parties of religious, racial, industrial, and ideological groups. But the political parties agreed on certain things: they would maintain their independence, they would be free men, and they would divide the landholdings of the Balt and Russian overlords.

These states were fighting for freedom on many fronts, and their struggle did not end with the creation of free governments. The Germans, during their short period of occupation of the three peoples, had plundered them of their cattle, their farm machinery, their food, and their household goods.

The Germans had created an army of occupation consisting of Germans and Balts under the command of General von der Goltz. At the Armistice, the Allies, fearing widespread chaos in these new and inexperienced governments, stipulated that von der Goltz's army, subject to Allied direction, should remain to preserve order. His army lived on requisitions from the people, and in the recruitment of it, every German and Balt soldier had been promised a landed estate.

The Russian Communists not only created conspiracies to overthrow these governments but also invaded them with armies; the

Balt element tried to seize control of the new governments; von der Goltz's army was a constant threat of aid to the Balts; the Allies maintained the blockade, which prevented the restoration of their industry. Rank starvation, epidemics, and poverty were everywhere.

Never in history had there been an emancipation of nations to freedom under such appalling difficulties or with such courage and sacrifice as in these three little Baltic States. Theirs was a heroic and tragic epic of man striving to be free. And this struggle should be part of the story of freedom for mankind.

CHAPTER 6

THE COMMUNIST INVASIONS

On November 22, 1918, the Soviet Army invaded Estonia, not only in an effort to spread Communism, but also to regain the major Russian outlets to the Baltic Sea which had been cut off when the Baltic States secured their independence.

The Estonians, with a makeshift army composed mainly of peasants, assisted by Finnish, Swedish, White Russian, and Latvian volunteers, defeated and drove the Communists out by the first of February, 1919. Our staff reported that George Washington's army at Valley Forge was better clothed, better fed, and better armed. There can be no doubt about the Estonians' heroism. One division alone sustained 50 per cent casualties in a single action. But they held their country.

The newly independent Latvian Government, born at the Armistice, scarcely had time to breathe before it was invaded by Soviet armies. They drove through Latvia and occupied Riga, the great Baltic port, on January 4, 1919.

The Communists invaded Lithuania in November, 1918. The Lithuanians repelled the invasion with an army of 25,000 ragged and ill-equipped men.

I determined that if we were to give relief to these people we had to have military protection. I requested Admiral Benson to place American destroyers at the various ports to give moral support to the people and to protect our staff, which he did.

The grip of the Communist armies on Riga was the cancer threatening all the states. We could obtain little or only partial information as to what was taking place in Riga until early in May. At once, I presented the situation to the President for the information of the Supreme War Council in a memorandum dated May 7. It read:

The situation at Riga appears to have developed into a most distressing form. From advices received from different quarters, it appears that the Bolshevik Government being unable to provide foodstuffs was mobbed by the populace and withdrew entirely from the city, which was given over to complete anarchy resulting in the wholesale massacre and murder of the so-called bourgeois population. It appears that a large number of women and children were transported to an island in the bay . . . [and have been] slowly starving under the guardianship of a lot of female harpies.

We are endeavoring to arrange for a shipload of food [for Riga], but the question arises at once as to any form of guardianship by which the food could be discharged and distributed. It seems almost impossible to contemplate sending any merchant ship in without naval escort and to secure anything like a reasonable distribution without some kind of military protection. . . .

My information, as given above, was incorrect in the detail that the Communist Army had withdrawn from the city. It was still on the job and doing its worst. Because only the Big Four could take adequate action, two days later I addressed to President Wilson a personal letter which I hoped he would lay before them. In this letter, I was again mistaken that the Communists had withdrawn from the city:

9 May 1919

MY DEAR MR. PRESIDENT:

I feel that the time has come when it is necessary to take some more definite action with regard to the situation in the three Baltic States of Esthonia, Latvia and Lithuania. I enclose herewith a sketch map showing approximately the ethnological boundaries and at the same time the present military status.

The food conditions in these states are simply terrible. From a shipping, finance, and food point of view, we could overcome this if some kind of order can be established. We are gradually extending our distribution along the coastal fringe of the non- [Communist] . . . area, but even in such areas the hinterland is in a state of chaos due to [Communist] . . . invasions, with the resultant arson and slaughter. About one-half of the coast area is held by the [Communists] . . . or is in such a state of anarchy as to make it impossible to send ships in. At Riga, for instance, the Red Army withdrew some days ago, leaving the town in the hands of a starving mob, among whose actions was to drive some twenty thousand bourgeoise women and children into an island in the bay, and the results are beyond all description.

From a relief point of view, the situation is hopeless except to a few coastal towns, unless we can have some sort of order and protection. The Germans, of course, occupy Lithuania, and some instruction must be given them to cease interfering with the development of the government there—for something must be established to succeed the German occupation.

The population in none of these states is [Communist]. . . . In many places they are putting up a good fight to try and establish their independence from the Moscow tyranny. They insist if they were given military supplies they require no other help to establish their boundaries and to maintain order, and our [representatives] . . . concur in this opinion.

The problem seems to me as follows:

(a) To place enough naval strength (not large) in each of the ports to protect the relief of all the coastal towns;

(b) To furnish military supplies to the established governments so as to enable them to maintain order in the interior and to defend their borders;

Sheerly as a matter of preserving human life, it does appear to me worth while to give them this support. All this requires collective action by the Allies, and a definition of policies.

The situation is one that is so appealing from every human point of view, that I am wondering whether or not it would be possible for yourself and the Premiers to set aside a short period, when the British and American naval authorities, who are familiar with this situation, could appear, together with myself on the food side, in the hope that some definite political relief policy could be arrived at.

HERBERT HOOVER

The President promptly had my letter referred to the Council of Ten. I met with them the same day, and they came to the following conclusions:

"That a committee consisting of an American, British, French and Italian economic, naval, and military representative should be appointed to report on the best means of keeping and maintaining order in the Baltic States and of revictualling the population. . . ."

This new committee, of which I was a member, met on May 13 and decided to submit to the Council of Ten the following recommendations:

1. In accordance with Article XII of the Armistice the Germans will be required to withdraw from Latvia and Lithuania as soon as they can be replaced by local organized forces but must remain where they are until orders are issued. The organization of local forces should be carried out with the least possible delay.

2. A competent Military Mission under British Command to be organized under a Lieutenant or Major-General with Headquarters at Libau or Reval, for the purpose of advising the Governments of Esthonia, Latvia and Lithuania on questions of organization, equipment and training of all local forces and such volunteer forces as may be raised from external sources. . . .

3. Volunteer forces mentioned in (2) to be raised by voluntary recruitment in the Scandinavian States, including Finland.

4. A credit of £10,000,000 to be placed at the disposal of the Baltic States by the Allied and Associated Governments and to be applied as required under the arrangements of the political and military missions.

5. Food supplies, equipment, clothing, arms, munitions, et cetera, to be supplied by the Allied and Associated Powers, the cost being defrayed from the credit referred to in (4).

6. It will be the duty of the political and economic missions to see what collateral securities can be obtained from the three Baltic States, to cover the credit referred to in (4) wholly or in part.

The President replied to my letter of the ninth as follows:

PARIS, 21 May, 1919

MY DEAR HOOVER:

I read with deep interest and concern your letter of the ninth of May

about the situation in the Baltic Provinces, and yesterday had an opportunity to read it to the other members of the "Council of Four." Mr. Lloyd
George suggested that I request you to have a conference with Admiral
Hope, or anyone else who represents the British Admiralty here, in order
to ascertain whether it was feasible from a naval point of view to carry out
the programme you suggest. If the programme were adopted, it would,
I suppose, necessarily be the British Navy that executed it, and we would
very much appreciate a memorandum from you as to the result of your
conference with the British Admiralty.

WOODROW WILSON

I immediately described the situation to Admiral Hope and urged
that a strong Allied military mission with naval support be sent at
once. But with the usual slow motion in selecting officers and equipment, it did not arrive until June 26—over five weeks later. If the
people of Riga were to be saved, we could not wait all these weeks.

Admiral Benson could not occupy Riga by means of an offshore
destroyer or stop the butchering and starvation. We therefore determined on action on our own responsibility. Under the Armistice
terms, it was the duty of General von der Goltz to preserve order in
the Baltic States. We surmised that he would like to do something
at Riga, especially as the Communists there were executing Balts
daily. Colonel Logan, our Paris liaison officer with the various military forces, got in touch with von der Goltz, and the General agreed
to occupy Riga at once with the help of such remnants of the Latvian Army as he could find.

On May 17, Baron Taube of von der Goltz's staff notified our office
in Libau that they were attacking the Communists at Riga and asked
that we send food quickly. Von der Goltz's army, with the aid of the
Latvians, took the city on May 22, or more than a month before the
Allied military forces, under General Gough, arrived. With Baron
Taube's notice of the attack, our staff at Libau loaded a train of
forty cars with supplies and sent it to Riga under Lieutenant Harrington, two sergeants, and a half-dozen doughboys. The train
reached a point ten miles from the city; beyond that the tracks had
been torn up. Lieutenant Harrington, being the kind of American

he was, set his doughboys to recruiting labor and repairing tracks. His train arrived on May 29, one week after leaving Libau.

Fighting between von der Goltz and the Communists was still raging in the suburbs. Many were dead in the streets, either from starvation or as a result of the fighting. From one of Harrington's sergeants there came to me this story of what happened when Harrington arrived in the city:

... Harrington did not quite know how to get hold of the situation. He inquired if there was an American Consulate. There was. He sent the sergeant, who found a small American flag nailed to the door and a type-written notice in Lettish and vigorous English warning all comers to stay away—signed "The Acting Consul of the United States of America." The sergeant had some difficulty in rousing anybody, but finally a girl peeked through a crack and, seeing his uniform, threw the door open— and broke into tears. She was the Consulate stenographer, an American of Lettish birth, who had stood by the ship when the Consul had been re-called in advance of the German [army] ... a year before. She pulled herself together quickly when told that they had a trainload of food at the edge of the city and that they wanted to find somebody in authority to organize its distribution. She knew whom to contact and managed it as if she had been the very mother of Riga itself. She was very thin and hungry, and the sergeant assumed the duty of caring for her needs. With her aid, Lieutenant Harrington set up a committee of citizens to distribute his food.

When I told President Wilson about our American lieutenant and his entry into Riga, he remarked: "We need a lot of Harringtons and his sergeants at home."

We had ordered one of our cargo ships, the *Lake Mary*, into Riga, and Admiral Benson sent a destroyer along to protect it. The ship arrived amid much rejoicing. Colonel Groome, head of our Baltic mission, sent Major George F. Felker to take charge in Riga with the aid of Lieutenant Colonel A. J. Carlson, Captain Evan H. Fore-man, and an adequate staff. They arrived on June 7.

The history of Communist actions in Riga and Northern Latvia from January to May, 1919, has never been told adequately in English. The Latvian Soviet Republic had been set up with the aid of Lettish and Finnish Communists. The prisons were opened, and the dregs of Riga—once a city of 500,000 people—were turned loose on the populace. Together with the Communists, this mob looted every store and every house. The banks and public institutions were plundered. Literally hundreds of innocent people were executed daily without trial in a sadistic orgy of blood of which the world has known few equals. Clergymen, doctors, teachers, and young girls were taken to prison and mowed down by machine guns. On some days, as many as one thousand were executed. The deaths from starvation, disease, and executions were so great that coffins could not be provided, and bodies were dumped into trenches by the hundreds.

The condition of the people in Riga and Northern Latvia may be roughly indicated by the reports of two members of our staff. One report written by Captain Evan H. Foreman contains the following:

Freed from [Communism] . . . after four months of "Red Terror," the city of Riga, hungry and helpless, without national or city government, turned yesterday to the American Relief Administration as the only barrier against famine. The story of what this once prosperous old Russian port has undergone during the years of the war and the months of the more horrible [Communism] . . . is incredible to one who is not here on the ground to see what the "red" handiwork has wrought. Although the [Communist] . . . Army has now been cleared from the environs of the city, the red . . . [gang] has left Riga only a shell of a city. The people, feeble and foodless, counting themselves fortunate to have survived, stalk the silent streets in a ghastly sort of a way, and hundreds of emaciated children besiege the food kitchens for scraps. Corpses are being cleared from the prison yards, which were strewn with the bodies of intelligent, well-dressed citizens, including seven pastors and many women, all murdered by the [Communists]. . . .

Another report from Lieutenant Colonel A. J. Carlson serves to bring home even more the incredible suffering of these people:

. . . Scores of children and old people lined up on the quay all day long before the American food ship "Lake Mary" . . . in mute appeal for food. They fought for garbage from the ship's kitchens. With old tin cans tied to a stick they picked up the garbage that was thrown overboard, even to raw potato peelings, a piece of gristle or a crust of bread. Children and old women begged for the privilege of sweeping the quay where American flour was being unloaded and put in the warehouse. With their bare hands, or with a rag, they would sweep the stones for the little flour that dusted through the sacks, then pick out the larger particles of dust or dirt and put the remaining meagre gleanings into their pockets, in a handkerchief, or even directly into their mouths. After viewing these distressing scenes, I could not help thinking of my home city (Chicago), where enough good food to support more than half the population of Riga is thrown out as garbage every day. . . .

Since it is difficult to believe these barbarities from mere assertion of them, I introduce here a condensation of a letter written by a woman who went through the terror:

DEAR SISTER,

. . . It is a miracle I am still alive! . . . Erich . . . is no more. . . . In our apartment they have taken everything. . . . They were perfect devils. . . . Eight days after the perquisition in our house, I was arrested one night & taken to the Police Station. I remained there two days without food except ⅛ of a pound of bread . . . a little hot water; Besides myself there were 9 people in the same room. The next day they did not give us any bread. . . . At 4 o'clock we were led away to prison in the "Citadelle." . . . At midnight we at last arrived in a small dark cell after we had been searched & nearly everything had been taken from us. . . . The first night behind locked doors on a hard uneven bench, bugs everywhere, was dreadful. . . . Twice a day we were let out for 5 minutes to wash & clean the cell. . . . And then we were famished. At night, we woke up with hunger. In the morning we were given a jug of water for tea & ⅛ of bread! At mid-day, some watery soup in which floated a few grains of porridge or a few turnips. . . . At 5 o'clock once more the same soup & that was all. . . . The most fearful thing was the nights. *Generally at midnight the unfortunate ones who were to be shot would be fetched out.* One heard them being abused in the most brutal way, then immediately after, the shots under our window which delivered them! . . . As there was only one bench in our cell & there were 3 of us, I had to sleep for some time on the stone floor . . . which was intensely cold. . . . Next to me lay the daughter of Pastor Kleman, who for 4 weeks was ill with spotted typhus & had 40° of fever. . . .

Opposite our cells were the poor prisoners brought from Mitau . . . among them the sisters of Vally Lieven . . . very sweet old ladies. It was hard to see these old, starving ladies . . . abused by the women-warders & not to be able to help them! I spent over 7 weeks in prison. It was constantly said that we should be transported or shot. I was never brought before any tribunal nor do I know why I was arrested. . . . How we longed for deliverance, but always in vain! And then it came so suddenly! We heard much firing, saw many aeroplanes flying. . . . At the last moment they still dragged off 3 men to be shot. We heard them lamenting & imploring . . . then we heard the shots. *"Now,"* we thought, *"it is our turn!"* . . . Already the doors were being unlocked & we were free! . . . Then we saw the first of our Officers who told us to remain quietly in the cells as there was still firing going on in the streets—perhaps we might go home in the evening. . . . Four warders who had been perfect demons were at once arrested & shot before the prison . . . . the hand-grenades already lay on a table to be thrown into the cells. Unhappily, in the Central Prison they arrived just too late. *Ten ladies were shot there,* among them poor Marion Klot, aged 21. . . . Were also shot Elsie de Hahnfeldt . . . & her sister-in-law, Baroness Wöhrman, née Brakel, Baron K. Oelsen & his wife. (Their son belonged to the rescue-party & found his parents' bodies still warm.) Were also shot 8 Pastors & many others. Thirty unfortunate people have been dragged off, nobody knows where, among them Clara Vegesack. . . . In the streets there were many murdered people whose boots had been stolen. When I went home in the evening I had to pass many corpses. . . . But the poor victims in the other prisons! "Mouse" Klot knew she would not be deported but killed—she told her fellow-prisoners so. *They drove all these victims into the yard & mowed them down with machine-guns!* "Mouse" looked so peaceful. A bullet had passed through her heart & lungs. But others were terribly mutilated. . . .

Our men at Riga quickly got the food distributed, but we were soon to experience another kind of trouble. A Balt colonel, placed in charge of the city by von der Goltz, set up a military court, made up mostly of Balts, to find and try the persons guilty of executions under the Red regime. There were men on the court whose wives, sons, and daughters had been victims of the Communists. At once a "White Terror" replaced the "Red Terror," with a new round of executions. Our staff not only protested but asked me to protest. I had no particular authority in the matter but sent a telegram to Colonel Groome for him to transmit:

. . . The Germans alone are responsible for this white terror which succeeded the red terror. . . . As soon as you get to Reval see the various military commanders, communicate to them my views and secure from them a definite assurance that the Riga incidents will not be repeated. Tell them plainly that you are directed by me to see that these unlawful and inhumane acts do not occur. . . . The American people will not lend their support for an instant to any movement which would countenance such actions. . . .

HOOVER

The Balt court then reduced its executions mostly to proven criminals.

OTHER WARS

The organization of relief in these states was indeed a hectic operation because there were other wars besides the one started by the Communists.

In Latvia, Ulmanis, fleeing from the Communist seizure of Riga, stirred a revolt in South Latvia and again pulled his government together on March 1, 1919, with headquarters in Libau. We sent into that port a cargo which arrived early in April, and within a week our organization had kitchens operating and was feeding some 20,000 of the most distressed people. But on April 16, a mixed German-Balt-White Russian army under Baron von Stryck seized Libau in an attempt to take all three Baltic States. Ulmanis took refuge on a boat in the harbor, and our men suspended food distribution for a few days to see what would happen. On April 20, one of Admiral Benson's destroyers appeared. General von der Goltz issued a proclamation announcing that he had nothing to do with the overthrow of the Latvian Government, whereupon our men resumed distribution.

Still another war developed. This was a revolt of the Balts against the Latvian Government. Colonel Groome, with Lieutenant Harrington, brought about an armistice and combined the various elements in a temporary coalition under Ulmanis.

The only bit of humor from the Baltic was provided by Lieutenant John Thors, who had charge of child relief in Estonia. He reported that upon the arrival of our ship the *Lake Dancey,* the captain asked for a field for his crew to determine whether the sailors or the firemen had the better baseball team. Thors had a field marked out and decided that he would charge the Estonians admission to this strange performance. He borrowed a band from the town and saw to it that full publicity appeared in the press. The sailors and firemen donated cigarettes to be sold for 1.50 marks a pack—say 25 cents—a reduction of about 80 per cent of the current price. The band, cigarettes, and baseball game proved a huge success. After the performance, Lieutenant Thors counted up 3,200 marks for the Children's Relief.

THE ALLIED BLOCKADE

Added to the other stupendous difficulties of the Baltic States in their fight for freedom was the Allied blockade. Under Admiral Benson's interpretation of what constituted a righteous blockade, we were sending food, medicine, and clothing into areas which were free of the Communist invaders. For areas which were not free, a rigid blockade was imposed by the Allies on the import of raw materials and exports. This not only created much unemployment but prevented the Balts from contributing to their own support and imposed on the United States a greater burden for their relief. But the story of the continued blockade is more than a matter of economics; it is a story of human tragedies and death—and stupid bureaucracy.

When Vance McCormick arrived in Paris early in February, 1919, and created the Superior Blockade Council, he took up the battle of removing the blockade in the Baltic States. He got nowhere. He again raised the question in the Superior Blockade Council in meetings on March 12, 15, 19, 24, and 29 and on April 7. He secured some relaxations. But the Council of Ten then rescinded all previous relaxations because of a Balt attempt to seize South Latvia. A protest from our American staff reads as follows:

The blockade should be lifted at once, not only in reference to food, but touching all articles of commerce. At present Riga is dead industrially and commercially and in consequence thousands of men and women are out of employment. This adds to the starvation and misery, to the unrest and the chances for political disturbance and violence.

Except for a few cracks, the blockade of the Baltic States was not removed until the signing of the Peace.

Obviously, the real solution to these problems was a recognition by the Supreme Council in Paris of the independence of these states. But the French stopped it on the theory that the Communist Government of Russia would fall under the impact of the "White" armies and that the new government of Russia should have the privilege of determining the fate of these states. All of this was utterly foolish because the people of the Baltics had already demonstrated their willingness to die rather than lose their independence.

CHAPTER 7

FOOD FOR THE BALTIC STATES

There is little necessity after these chapters on the history and tribulations of the Baltic States to elaborate on their need for relief. Extracts from our staff reports will show what was happening in these states. In January, 1919, we sent Magnus Swenson to report on the situation. He said:

It is dreadful. In the midst of their fighting the Communists, the women and children were dying from starvation. Disease was rampant. In some towns child mortality hit a rate of 35 per cent per annum.

Captain John C. Miller, in an extensive report on the situation in Estonia, stated:

. . . the Russian . . . army, in retreating, took with it much of the available foodstuffs, rolling stock and farming implements. The German army of occupation followed, requisitioning everything that was left. . . . Then came the Russian Bolsheviks, laying waste and devastating all that they laid their hands upon, and committing the most horrible atrocities. The Bolsheviks . . . advanced to within a short distance of Reval. . . .

A few Estonian patriots . . . with the aid of a British naval detachment, succeeded in repulsing the Bolshevik attack. . . . After three weeks, the enemy was entirely driven from the country . . . [but left it] in a dreadful condition. . . .

There are only two public soup kitchens in all of Esthonia, both in Reval, where about 2,000 meals are served daily. The meal consists of vegetable soup and meat, and costs two marks. Soup alone is served for 50 pennies.

I have already described the situation in Latvia, Riga in particular.

The situation in Lithuania was not as serious as that in the other states. Being an almost wholly farm population, the people managed to hide some food from the invaders. But their needs were revealed later.

THE CHILDREN'S NEEDS

The needs of the children were particularly acute. The invaders not only plundered the food in general but they also drove off the cattle so that there was little milk available. A few paragraphs from reports of our staff in Estonia are quoted here:

Even after this preliminary inspection it was apparent that child relief must begin in Esthonia as soon as general relief . . . the people were bordering on starvation. . . . Every house in the city [of Reval] was visited, and conditions were found which were really deplorable. Children were without clothing, and had to be kept indoors because they had no warm things to protect them against the cold winter weather. Most of the schoolboys of fourteen years and older were at the front with the army. The cupboards were empty of even the bare necessities of life. The people were living almost entirely on a diet of bread made from potato flour, oat flour and sawdust. . . .

The natural consequence of the confinement of the children was a great prevalence of tuberculosis and rickets. Their bodies were shrunken, their eyes bulging and glassy, they had an appearance of marked stupidity, and were yellow-skinned and distinctly unhealthy looking. . . .

Before the distribution of the clothing by the administration . . . American Relief Administration flour sacks were in great demand. Many an Esthonian youngster went to school in blouses and trousers decorated with the trademark of an American flour miller. . . .

For the entire city [of Pskoff on the border of Russia and Estonia] there were only sixty cows, which furnished some milk for the hospital and the ten asylums for orphan and refugee children. . . . The condition of the children was exceptionally pitiful. Many were begging and several came to the armored train on which the Lieutenant was living to beg for potato peelings.

. . . children in school in the city [Tartu] numbered some 7,000 out of which 50 percent are ill due to underfeeding. 2,000 have not sufficient money to purchase clothing so can not attend school regularly but stay at home. The food supply for the children is practically nothing. . . .

In the country the conditions are particularly bad as around the Peipus Sea there live from 12,000 to 15,000 children whose diet consists chiefly of fish and potatoes, with no milk or other foods.

The men have practically every one been mobilized for the Army, leaving no one but the women and old men to look after the interests of the children, and as a result the children suffer.

The procuring of milk is almost impossible due to the fact that as the different armies passed through the country they drove all the cattle off with them.

The difficulties of the selection of the needy children to whom clothing was to be issued, were immense. . . . only those children most in need would be furnished with the new shoes and overcoats.

Our reports from Lithuania contain the following sentences:

. . . [There were among the] children . . . marked signs and symptoms of anemia, malaise, and quite evident mal-nutrition. . . .

. . . Death rate among children estimated to be twenty per cent of total deaths caused by lack of food, such as milk, which is not obtainable. . . .

FINANCING THE RELIEF

The Baltic States were ruled ineligible for loans from the United States Treasury since Russia had previously made peace with Germany. In consequence, we were unable to finance the relief until the $100,000,000 Congressional appropriation was available. However, we supplied food to them from Army surplus stocks, and we lent them food temporarily from our Rotterdam stocks.

REHABILITATION OF SUBNORMAL AND DISEASED CHILDREN

Prior to the passage of the $100,000,000 relief appropriation by the Congress, our staff was unable to establish the systematic rehabilitation of the children through our canteen system or to aid expectant mothers and the aged. But our staff set up its relief organization and was ready for the enactment of this appropriation at the end of February, 1919. We spread the system rapidly in those parts of the Baltic States free from Communist control.

In Estonia and Latvia, there was no difficulty in organizing capable and intelligent women into the necessary nation-wide and local committees which provided eating places, furniture, and services to the children.[1]

Although our reports showed that the children of Lithuania were suffering terribly, we found it impossible to set up our usual committees of women to organize the canteens because there was little leadership among them.

The supplies of special food from the American Relief Administration for children in the Baltic States included cereals, peas, beans, meat, fats, condensed milk, cocoa, sugar, and clothing:

	Amount	$ Value
Estonia	1,445 tons	$ 376,621
Latvia	1,763 "	493,575
Lithuania	1,001 "	279,721
	4,209	$1,149,917

CLOTHING FOR CHILDREN AND ADULTS

Our major source of clothing was the United States Army's surplus stocks. From them we got new uniforms, new repair cloth, and

[1] Captain Thomas J. Orbison, in charge of the work in Latvia, wrote a most touching and interesting book on the subject entitled *Children, Inc.* (Boston, The Stratford Company, 1933).

used clothing. We secured 8,658 tons from this source, the British contributed 400 tons of used clothing, and American charitable agencies sent fourteen tons—a total of 9,072 tons. Workrooms were set up by the women for sewing appropriate garments. The number of garments they obtained from this tonnage of clothing and cloth was estimated by one of our staff to be at least 6,000,000.

AMERICAN CHARITABLE AGENCIES

We received assistance from two of the great American charitable agencies, the American Red Cross and the Jewish Joint Distribution Committee.

THE AMERICAN RED CROSS

We include but two small items of Red Cross expenditures. In Estonia, under the American Relief Administration the Red Cross expended $89,800 for 312 tons of medical supplies, and in Lithuania, $221,560 was expended. Large expenditures were made after the Peace, and I will include these later in this memoir.

THE JEWISH JOINT DISTRIBUTION COMMITTEE

The J.D.C.'s accounts likewise cannot be broken down. The records show expenditures of $11,543,198 in Poland, Lithuania, and Kurland (South Latvia) from 1914 to December 31, 1919. I have estimated its expenditures, which were handled by European sub-committees, to be $578,000 in Latvia and $2,608,000 in Lithuania.

The relief operations can best be illustrated statistically by the tons of supplies and services furnished to the Baltic States as a whole.

OTHER CHARITABLE AGENCIES

The Christian Science War Relief Committee sent knitted goods amounting to nearly ten tons. The Methodist Episcopal Church sent some food and clothing of similar amount.

TOTAL SUPPLIES TO LITHUANIA *
FROM THE ARMISTICE TO THE PEACE

	Food	Clothing & Misc.	Total	Dollar Value
American Relief Administration:				
Children's relief	1,001		1,001	$ 279,721
General relief .... (including freight)	3,357		3,357	871,066
Army surplus	4,700	3,620	8,320	4,414,861
American Red Cross	(quantities unknown)			221,560
Jewish Joint Distribution Committee †	(quantities unknown)			2,608,000
United Kingdom .... (freight)				57,120
	9,058	3,620	12,678	$8,452,328

* In tons.
† Total also includes some contributions prior to the Armistice.

TOTAL SUPPLIES TO ESTONIA *
FROM THE ARMISTICE TO THE PEACE

	Food	Clothing & Misc.	Total	Dollar Value
American Relief Administration:				
Children's relief	1,445		1,445	$ 376,621
General relief .... (including freight)	9,977	14	9,991	2,103,743
Army surplus	26,000	4,120	30,120	12,262,819
American Red Cross		312	312	89,800
United Kingdom .... (supplies and freight)	8,224	400	8,624	2,342,360
Denmark	462		462	35,208
	46,108	4,846	50,954	$17,210,551

* In tons.

TOTAL SUPPLIES TO LATVIA *

FROM THE ARMISTICE TO THE PEACE

	Food	Clothing & Misc.	Total	Dollar Value
American Relief Administration:				
Children's relief	1,763		1,763	$ 493,575
General relief .... (including freight)	13,304		13,304	2,610,578
Army surplus	5,378	918	6,296	2,556,953
Jewish Joint Distribution Committee †	(quantities unknown)			578,000
United Kingdom .... (freight)				80,920
	20,445	918	21,363	$6,320,026

* In tons.

† Total also includes some contributions prior to the Armistice.

Total supplies to the three Baltic States during the Armistice period amounted to a value of $31,982,905.

DEBT SETTLEMENTS

Except for Children's Relief, the food to the three states was paid for by loans from the $100,000,000 Congressional appropriation. The United States World War Foreign Debt Commission and the Baltic States agreed on the amounts of their total loans plus accumulated interest and funded them over a long term. The totals were:

Estonia	$14,143,000
Latvia	5,893,000
Lithuania	6,216,000

For reasons stated in the Introduction, these were all gifts from the American people.

THE PEACE IN THE BALTICS

When the Peace was signed at Versailles, the citizens of all these states came to the offices of our organization with their children in parades of thousands, bearing flowers and with bands playing "Yankee Doodle" (their idea of our national anthem); they also brought tears and prayers of thanksgiving.

CHAPTER 8

POLAND

For an understanding of the relief of Poland, there is need for some historical background of the Polish people.

More than a thousand years ago, the Poles settled on plains which became the periodic battleground of three great military empires— Germany, Austria, and Russia. In their wars, the Poles had been overrun time and again; their territory had been partitioned repeatedly. But just as often, they had renewed their struggle for freedom. And their indomitable spirit had led them out of oppression time and again.

The Poles are the world's greatest proof that oppression cannot kill the spirit of a race. There is more to nations than their soil, their cities, their wealth, or their governments. There is a soul in a people. That soul is forged in the instincts of the race, its traditions, its heroic struggles, its strong men and women and its genius in art, music, literature, and industry. It is steeled in sufferings.

Poland's last partition before the First World War was a division among the German, Russian, and Austrian empires, and for almost 150 years, the Poles were an exploited and impoverished people. Most of their rich agricultural lands had been divided among great Russian, Austrian, German, and Polish landlords, who wrested every bit of produce from the peasants and who exploited the industrial workers. Under their foreign oppressors, the people had been allowed no real role in government; but despite their oppressors, they had developed great leaders in art, literature, and music. Millions of them had migrated to foreign countries, the largest group coming to the United States. Then came the war between Germany and Austria on one side and Russia on the other, when Poland was the battleground of repeated invasions, retreats, pillage, and destruction.

Early in the war, the great musician Ignace Paderewski had organized "The Freedom for Poland Committee," supported by overseas Poles. The unification and independence of Poland were a part of President Wilson's basis of peace, which was agreed upon by the Allies. At the Peace Conference, Paderewski was recognized by the Allies as the representative of Poland. He was ably assisted in negotiations by his long-time associate, Roman Dmowski.

I had known Paderewski for many years. As a boy in college, with partners, I had conducted a sort of lecture bureau to relieve our financial deficits. We had scheduled Paderewski for an appearance. I met him in these negotiations, but the appearance did not come off for some reason. In 1915 I had met him again when he requested that the Belgian Relief Commission organize relief for Poland. I had sent Dr. Vernon Kellogg of our staff to investigate the possibilities, but the military situation made it impossible. When I returned to Washington as Food Administrator, Paderewski came frequently to discuss with me the work of his Committee, and he was often my house guest.

The Poles in the three partitioned areas had been drafted into the Russian, Austrian, and German armies. Immediately after the Armistice, these demobilized officers and men erected provisional governments in the three areas. They were finally brought into cohesion under the leadership of General Joseph Pilsudski, who quickly organized a substantial army but with little equipment. The General was a revolutionary soldier, wholly without experience in civil government. He was a dictatorial person with a strange mélange of social and economic ideas. He was jealous of Paderewski's recognition by the Allies and was not co-operative with him. It was in this setting that we undertook the imperative relief of Poland.

The need was enormous. About 28,000,000 people dwelled within the boundaries of the new state. During the preceding four years, the Poles had endured four separate invasions, with the repeated havoc of battle and plunder by advancing and retreating armies. Many had died of starvation. The homes of millions had been destroyed, and many were living in hovels built of the rubble. Their farm implements were depleted; their crops had been only partly planted and even then only partly harvested. Industry was suspended from a lack of raw materials. Their workers were unemployed, and millions were destitute. The country was being flooded with printing-press rubles, marks, and kronen by Russia, Germany, and Austria in purchase of any Polish supplies they could obtain. The railroads were barely functioning. The cities were almost without food. Typhus and other contagious diseases raged over whole provinces. But despite rats and lice, famine and pestilence, the people were determined to build a nation.

THE RELIEF

It was in these surroundings that the official United States relief agencies under my direction began the relief of Poland. I appointed Dr. Vernon Kellogg head of our initial mission to Poland. Dr. Kellogg had served as one of the leaders of the Commission for Relief in Belgium. He had been the Food Administration representative in Europe during the period we participated in the war. His work there was to analyze constantly the needs of the Allied nations for food, clothing, and medical supplies, and he possessed great political and economic insight. His mission included Colonel William R. Grove and Captain Chauncey McCormick, both experienced administrators.

The mission arrived in Warsaw on January 4, 1919. On January 6, Dr. Kellogg sent me the following preliminary report on needs:

. . . Poland normally produces sufficient food to maintain itself but Germans carried away 60 per cent of last harvest, and through unguarded borders due to lack of Polish military organization more has passed. German agents are constantly busy in getting food out of Poland. In certain cities the misery is terrible; in Vilna and Lemberg people are actually dying of starvation. Especially are the children suffering. The account of the situation in Lemberg as given by [the] Mayor . . . who ran great personal risk to reach Warsaw, their train being under fire and several passengers killed. . . . Vilna is reported to be as bad.

Later, in a report on the military situation, Dr. Kellogg stated:

The critical region of Poland is the East front. Lemberg is beseiged by Ukrainians: Vilna has just been taken by the . . . [Communists]: Brest seems about to be taken. The Poles are desperately short of ammunition, uniforms, boots. . . . What is needed imperatively and at once, if they are to succeed in holding back the . . . [Communist] hordes of Russia, is Allied supply of these things plus, if not a small force of Allied troops, at least some Allied officers to give training and moral support to the Polish volunteers. Or, if Gen. Haller's Polish army in France could come— or even part of it, the difficulty would probably be solved. Also they need [in order] to fight . . . [Communist conspiracies] food, clothing, shoes and raw materials to put the thousands of idle workmen at work. . . .

Paderewski returned to Poland to find that General Pilsudski had set up a ministry composed mostly of doctrinaire Socialists and Army officers wholly unfriendly to him. On January 6, Dr. Kellogg made the following report on the political situation:

. . . The Government here is purely Socialist—except perhaps for a couple of Ministers who assume the curious position of being heads of their departments, but not members of the governmental cabinet. Paderewski's arrival . . . has set things boiling and the night after we got here a little opera-bouffe coup d'Etat was pulled off—with a little firing of rifles and machine guns, one man killed, six Ministers arrested—but Pilsudski left in charge as chief of the State. Yesterday came the reverse and the Ministers were freed—and several of the heads of the opposition arrested—then last night a little more fighting—and everybody seems to be free again today. In the meantime Paderewski had a long conference with Pilsudski—making various demands all refused by . . . [the General]. So Paderewski makes a hurried trip to Crakow the coup d'Etat comes off, and Pilsudski sends his Chief of Staff to Crakow to bring Paderewski back and offering certain concessions, varying according to different reports,—the most extreme report and apparently the most credible one being that Paderewski is to be allowed to form a new Government. So Paderewski is expected back tomorrow morning. However something may happen again tonight. In the meantime the people here take it all very quietly so far—and barring the shooting at night and a few machine guns in the streets—there is no sign of civil war. . . .

On January 9, Dr. Kellogg sent me a long message describing the frictions and negotiations between Paderewski and Pilsudski. The fundamental differences was that Paderewski was determined to set up representative government in Poland, while Pilsudski was endeavoring to set up a government where he and his appointed ministry would hold the seat of power. Kellogg stated that

Colonel Wade, the head of the British Military Mission has been definite in his statements that the Allies will do nothing for Poland in the way of Army or military supplies or money as long as the present socialist group is in power—or there is no stable Government. . . .

Pilsudski did not give way, and Dr. Kellogg's conclusion was that the one hope of unity in Poland was for Paderewski, who was beloved by all Poles, to be Prime Minister, with a strong Cabinet in full control of the civil government. Dr. Kellogg asked that Pilsudski be informed by the Supreme War Council that unless Paderewski were given this position, Allied and American co-operation and aid would be futile.

I laid the matter before President Wilson, and a messenger was sent to deliver to Pilsudski a statement from the Supreme Council that they had recognized Paderewski alone in Polish affairs and that unless he was made Prime Minister, there could be no aid in the present chaos. Pilsudski gave way.

Paderewski, now Prime Minister, at once called for the election of a national assembly. The elections were held on January 26, and the newly elected members gave Paderewski an overwhelming vote of confidence on February 10. At the same time, they confirmed Pilsudski as "Chief of State," which did not add to clarification.

The new government setup was a sort of hybrid of the American and British systems whereby the "Chief of State" controlled the Army and the Prime Minister and his Cabinet were responsible to a parliament for civil affairs. President Wilson arranged that the independence of Poland be immediately "recognized" by the Allies. It was, however, the beginning of a most troubled life for the world's greatest musician.

Paderewski was in constant motion between Warsaw and the Peace Conference at Paris. Adding to the Prime Minister's persuasiveness was his colleague, Dmowski, a shrewd, hard-headed negotiator. Together they succeeded in enlarging the boundaries of Poland beyond the powers of the nation to assimilate the minorities taken in. They secured entirely too many fringe groups of Germans, Ruthenians, and Lithuanians for Poland's good. And the too-wide Polish Corridor to Danzig was to add to their subsequent grief.

THE POLISH PARLIAMENT

When Paderewski assembled his parliament, it was divided into seventeen different groups representing every political theory on earth except Communism, and the confusion was compounded by the old three-way division of the Poles, from which there survived great factionalism. As a political leader, Paderewski had one superb quality. He was fired by a patriotism which made him one of the greatest orators of his time. His voice, his burning devotion, shamed and reconciled even the bitter and selfish factions of Poland through the dreadful winter of 1919. He was resolute on representative government, despite the lack of popular preparedness for liberal institutions. He knew well that the canker of Poland was the terrible subjection and poverty of the peasants under the system of great landholdings which had been installed under the German, Russian, and Austrian regimes. He proposed land reform by purchase of these estates from the owners and their sale to the peasants on long time payments.

At once he incurred the disfavor of the landlord class. He was already hated by Pilsudski's military clique, and defeats piled upon him in his parliament. It was doubtful that he could survive these attacks. (He resigned a few months after the Peace.) All these cross-currents added to the difficulties of organizing rations of food and clothing, agricultural expansion, and reconstruction of the railways and factories.

Paderewski was not particularly strong as an administrator. At his request, we sent a whole staff of expert advisers for his governmental departments of finance, railways, coal, and food.

REARRANGEMENT OF OUR STAFF

Since we needed Dr. Kellogg in Paris, in mid-January we appointed his principal assistant, Colonel William R. Grove, to be chief of our mission. We strengthened his staff with the addition, on February 9, of Captains Franklin R. Baackes and Frank Nowak, Lieutenants James H. Becker and Maurice Pate, and Private Roscoe C. Butler.

FINANCE OF POLISH RELIEF

We were confronted at once with the difficulty of financing the relief. Poland was not eligible for loans from the United States Treasury, since she had not been in the war on the Allied side.

On January 18, 1919, we began shipments of food from Switzerland. We guaranteed the Swiss that we would pay if the Poles could not. I had in hand some part of the $5,000,000 allotted to me the previous December from President Wilson's emergency fund.

We received great financial help at this time from the combined action of the Jewish Joint Distribution Committee and the Polish National Relief Committee. They paid us cash for one of the cargoes which was en route to another destination. This ship—the *Westward Ho*—carried 6,486 tons of food, for which we received $2,000,000.

When our cargoes from the War Department and the Food Administration (which I had arranged for before I left Washington) began to arrive, they were supposed to be paid for at delivery. We solved this problem by simply delaying demand for payment.

In these critical days, there were increased deaths from lack of

Refugees at home in a dugout in Dixmude, Belgium.

Amerikanische
Kinder-Hilfs-Aktion

An A.R.A. health clinic in Vienna, Austria.

Belgian women making clothing in a C.R.B. workroom.

Unemployed Belgians working at a job created by the C.R.B.

food, but Americans saved Poland from mass starvation. The President had placed the United States Army surplus supplies at my disposal, and we gave them "on credit," to be paid for sometime in the future. When the $100,000,000 Congressional appropriation became available at the end of February, 1919, we were able to clean up all of our liabilities and deliver increasing supplies.

Our total American Government supplies to Poland during the Armistice came to more than 380,000 tons valued at over $116,-000,000. At the Peace Conference, Count Jan Horodyski of the Polish mission remarked to me:

This is the first time in history that any government has made a promise to Poland and kept it.

Our deliveries to Poland increased to a rate of 70,000 tons per month. It was entirely insufficient, but the shortage of shipping [1] and the total demoralization of the railways in Poland prevented us from doing more.

THE CHILDREN'S RELIEF

There was one bright spot in all this murk of trouble. Out of the $100,000,000 Congressional appropriation, we were able to set up, as an American charity, our canteen system, which was based on our long experience in Belgium and Northern France. From our canteens a full meal was given daily to debilitated and diseased children, expectant mothers, and the aged.

When approval of the appropriation began to appear likely, we started shipping from the United States the special food required, and Maurice Pate, with long experience in this work in Belgium, went into action. He created a whole system of committees of superb, devoted Polish women on a national, provincial, and school-district basis. This system went into full swing almost overnight.

The need was imperative. Lieutenant Pate estimated that there were 2,000,000 subnormal children. Our Paris office challenged his estimates. In his reply he said:

[1] See *An American Epic,* Vol. II, Chap. 42.

. . . In the village homes . . . visited . . . the children were generally in bad condition and undernourished. If we had the means of reaching them, 40% of these children up to 15 years of age, or over 10% of the total population, requires assistance.

In the Eastern District . . . recently retaken from the Bolshevists the population as a whole is under famine conditions. It would be safe to say that 80% of the children are not receiving anywhere near sufficient nourishment, or 25% of the total population.

. . . I feel that 10% of the total population is a very conservative estimate . . .

Lieutenant Harwood Stacy, one of Pate's assistants, in a report on the institutions and hospitals for the children, had this to say about one place he visited:

The majority of the employees were barefooted. Some of the nurses were barefooted. Only the Sisters of Charity wore shoes. There were two hundred babes under two years of age. The supply of rubber nipples was totally exhausted and none could be had for the past ten months. They had no effective substitute. There was great need for condensed milk. Milk was as precious as gold, as the Germans had killed or carried away all of the cattle. There was no substitute for milk. . . .

Some of the infants looked terribly emaciated. . . . There were practically no pillow cases on the beds. The sheets, such as they were, were a mosaic of patches—done with minute care. . . . The hospital was totally without heat, though it was a very cold, wet day, and I was wearing a sweater and overcoat. They could not heat the operating room during an operation, for lack of coal.

Practically every child from 2 to 10 years of age was barefooted and those of school age were unable to go during the winter months . . . on account of lack of clothes and shoes. The fact of being barefooted in winter . . . led to unnecessary chilling and much croup and influenza.

There was an extreme shortage of all kinds of medicines.

. . . the Director's final words were, "We are doing the best we can. . . . If there exist in the world supplies that are not being actually used, share them with us, so we may supply the needs of these little ones who cannot comprehend why they are not fed." . . .

After examination of another institution, he said:

After climbing three rickety stairs I was admitted to this Children's Home. . . . No picture in Bleak House could equal it. . . . bare and cold and foreboding. They housed 63 children under ten years of age and 73 others came for meals. They stated that they could feed more, if they had the food. . . .

Before the Peace, we shipped 16,618 tons of special food and clothing, of which there were 858 tons of breadstuffs, 2,898 tons of beans and peas, 2,077 tons of rice, 765 tons of meats and fats, 6,294 tons of condensed milk, 2,433 tons of cocoa and sugar, 827 tons of clothing, and 466 tons of miscellaneous supplies, at a cost of $4,743,147—a gift from the American people.

Before the signing of the Peace, we were feeding more than 500,000 subnormal children daily, and we could have provided more supplies but for the shortage of shipping [2] and the almost total collapse of Polish railways.[3] Our great expansion of the canteen system after the Peace is recorded in a later section of this volume.

CLOTHING

The clothing need in Poland was as acute as the food and medical needs. Colonel Grove of our mission reported:

Investigations . . . and reports . . . from various parts of the country show that the clothing situation is fully as serious as the lack of food . . .

A considerable proportion of the population, especially children in the mining and industrial region, are unable to get out of their houses because they have no shoes and insufficient clothing. The shortage of shoes is preventing miners and workers from going to their work and gaining a living for their families. The lack of underwear, shirts, and stockings is the cause of bad sanitary conditions which are giving a great deal of trouble in skin and eye diseases. . . .

Colonel Grove stated that the price of clothing had increased 1,000 per cent over prewar:

. . . The very small amount of clothing here if either purchased or requisitioned by the government would be insignificant in relieving the situation for the poor. . . .

[2] *Ibid.*
[3] *Ibid.*, Chap. 43.

The big thing is to get immediate action as the situation is rapidly growing worse and should be relieved before summer. . . .

The demand for soap here is very pressing and I think an import of 1 lb. per person, or 2,000 tons, would mean a great improvement in sanitary conditions. Particularly throughout the mining district there is a great deal of contagious disease, trachoma, and skin maladies. Investigation has shown that the poorer people as a rule use no soap, the market price . . . being beyond their means.

I have stated that we had shipped 827 tons of clothing for children. We arranged for shipment of a total of 2,775,000 garments and 50,000 yards of cloth valued at $4,420,375 from American Army surplus. We also shipped more than 3,000 tons of used clothing from our stocks accumulated for the Belgian Relief, which were no longer needed, and from other sources. In addition to these supplies, we shipped 5,000 tons of raw cotton for making clothing in the Polish mills.

TROUBLE WITH TRANSPORTATION

Just as we started to send food to the Poles, we found ourselves in trouble with the Germans over the use of the railways out of Danzig. On January 6, Dr. Kellogg advised me:

. . . While the Poles seem to be in possession of Dantzig itself, and British and American War Ships are in the harbor, the country behind Dantzig up to Polish frontier is in hands of Germans and no movements of supplies or personnel between Poland and Dantzig can be made without definite arrangement of Armistice Commission. . . .

The Germans refused to allow passage of supplies through their territory until the blockade on their food was removed, as provided in the Armistice agreement. But their authorities were friendly to our organization because of our fight to remove the food blockade. Our staff arranged with local German officials to issue temporary shipping permits to Poland. This problem was finally resolved at the Brussels Conference on March 14, and thereafter we were able to ship regularly.

THE BLOCKADE OF POLAND

Amid all our other problems, we also had to fuss continually with the Allies over the blockade on Poland. We shipped our food, medicine, and clothing in American-flag ships under the assurances of Admiral Benson. This, however, did not cover import of raw materials or export of manufactures so necessary to support Poland's economy or to enable her to carry part of the financial load of relief. I will not describe these negotiations to relax the blockade or its long documentation, other than to state that Mr. McCormick began urging this relaxation through the Superior Blockade Council on February 24. Curiously, the Council granted permission to ship a "small amount of foodstuffs into Poland." This action was more amusing than of intrinsic importance. We had been shipping all the food we could get for the previous seven weeks. On March 12, McCormick again urged that the blockade be taken down on raw materials and export of goods. It was refused. On March 18, after the Brussels agreement with the Germans which removed the food blockade, our organization presented the situation again by a letter from Colonel Logan to McCormick:

MY DEAR MR. MCCORMICK:

On March 12th I sent you a letter relative to . . . the importation of raw materials through the port of Dantzig. This letter also pointed out the beneficial moral effect that would result in Poland by a formal relaxation of the existing blockade of that country by the associated governments. . . .

. . . It is also difficult for us to understand why any restrictions should be placed upon the importation of raw material into Poland. . . .

In view of the fact that America is the only country which is today actually supplying foodstuffs to Poland it follows that it . . . [is] penalized under existing circumstances. We are presenting the foregoing views to you . . . should you consider it advisable to use your good offices in securing the desired action from the Allied Blockade authorities.

JAMES A. LOGAN, JR.

On March 20, the Blockade Council recommended to the Supreme Economic Council that all blockade restrictions on Poland be taken down as of April 1. The Supreme Economic Council approved this four days later and recommended it to the Big Four. It was referred to the Council of Ten, which approved it on March 28, subject to some minor controls, and it was confirmed by the Big Four on April 7. The long delay of five months after the Armistice brought great suffering through unemployment in Poland and created a larger cost for relief because of the inability of the Poles to operate their factories and export their goods.

ANOTHER TROUBLE

On April 10, 1919, a news dispatch reported that fifty Jews had been lined up against a wall and executed by command of a major in the Polish Army. A great outcry rose in the American press. We sent one of our staff to investigate and found that the number killed was greatly exaggerated but that things were bad. The story began to threaten American public support of our relief work. On June 2, I wrote to the President, saying that I had suggested to Paderewski that he request the President to send an official American mission to Poland to investigate the matter.

On June 3, I received the following note from the President:

MY DEAR HOOVER:

I have received the request of Mr. Paderewski to which you refer in your letter of the second, and I am going to try to act upon it, for I have the deepest interest, as you have, in assisting Poland in every way and, amongst other things, in this troublesome question of the treatment of the Jewish people.

WOODROW WILSON

The President appointed a three-man mission: Henry Morgenthau, Sr., as Chairman, Chief of the Army Engineers General Edgar Jadwin, and Congressman Homer Johnson. These gentlemen performed a fine service by sifting out truth from exaggeration and creating a generally more wholesome atmosphere in the relations of the Poles and the Jews.

OTHER AIDS TO POLAND PRIOR TO THE PEACE

As will be shown later in our statistical tables, more than 96 per cent of the burden of finance and supplies to Poland was provided by the official relief agencies of the United States Government. The remaining 4 per cent of finance was provided by British and American charitable organizations.

THE BRITISH

The British gave substantial aid. Our records show that they furnished 21,462 tons of supplies valued at $6,304,620. They also furnished transportation for our Army surplus stocks, whose value amounted to $1,389,920.

THE AMERICAN CHARITABLE ORGANIZATIONS

While our official governmental agencies carried the burden of food and collateral supplies, the American charitable agencies performed a vital part in saving life in Poland by providing medical and other aids.

THE AMERICAN RED CROSS

In August, 1917, the General Relief Committee in Poland, with headquarters at Vevey, Switzerland, notified the Red Cross of the serious conditions in Poland, particularly among the children. A Red Cross investigation confirmed these reports. Finally, in late 1917, with the consent of the State Department and the Food Administration, the Red Cross donated $200,000 to Poland on condition that the funds would be used solely for relief. Through the American Legation at Berne, arrangements were made to use the money specifically for food and clothing for destitute children under ten years of age. The Archbishop of Warsaw headed a committee especially appointed to administer this relief.

After the Armistice, the Red Cross sent a unit into Poland to co-operate with the American Relief Administration. It furnished clothing and medical service, assisted in the establishment of a national health bureau, and set up dispensaries for treating the sick and suffering.

The method of Red Cross accounting does not permit an accurate statement of its expenditures in Poland as separate from surrounding states. From our organization records and such deductions as one can make from Red Cross accounts, we estimate its expenditures prior to the Peace at $813,800.

THE JEWISH JOINT DISTRIBUTION COMMITTEE

The Jewish Joint Distribution Committee was a major lifeline to the Jews in Poland. Prior to the Armistice, its channel for aid to Poland was the Jüdisches Hilfskomite für Polen und Litauen, a group formed in Berlin soon after the German advance into Russian territory. At one point in the pre-Armistice period (February, 1916), fully 700,000 Jews in Poland and Lithuania were entirely dependent upon the J.D.C. for their continued existence.

A large part of the J.D.C. activities prior to the Armistice was directed toward protection of the Jews from their terrible persecutions. With the Armistice, the Western powers stopped these persecutions, and the J.D.C. was able to turn its activities to the restoration of Jewish life.

In February, 1919, the J.D.C. appointed Dr. Boris D. Bogen director of its operations in Poland; he co-operated with Colonel William R. Grove, head of our mission in Poland. The J.D.C. undertook the restoration of homes, the creation of workshops, aids to small business, and placing of Jews on the land.

It is impossible, from the method of accounting, to separate the J.D.C.'s outlays in Poland from those of neighboring Kurland and

Lithuania. From the beginning of the J.D.C.'s work in November, 1914, to the Peace, its expenditures for these three areas are given as $11,543,198. From an analysis of the J.D.C.'s annual statements and by taking into account the number of Jews in Poland, Kurland, and Lithuania, it is possible to make a reasonable estimate of expenditures in Poland from the Armistice until the Peace. I have included in our summary of American aids during this period the sum of $8,357,000.

OTHER ORGANIZATIONS (PRIOR TO THE PEACE)

The Christian Science War Relief Committee distributed knitted garments and other clothing.

The Methodist Episcopal Church sent clothing and some condensed milk.

The Polish League of Women contributed $1,640 to the American Relief Administration Children's Fund, and the Russo-Carpathian Commission contributed $200 to this fund.

The Polish Victim's Relief Fund provided relief for war sufferers in Poland and for Polish refugees in France, England, and Switzerland.

The Rockefeller Foundation, in 1916–1917, gave $86,781 to the War Relief Commission for purchases of clothing for inhabitants of Poland.

The Young Men's Christian Association provided forty huts and eight rolling canteens for the Polish Legion, now returned to Poland, and for other Polish Army units.

The American Government supplies (except Children's Relief) were in the form of "loans" to the Polish Government. The total debt of Poland to the United States was settled by the United States World War Foreign Debt Commission as at $182,324,000, which included supplies and other items in addition to those furnished by our organization. For reasons given in the Introduction to this volume, the whole "loan" was a gift.

The British supplies were also in the form of loans, and they probably met the same fate.

TOTAL SUPPLIES TO POLAND *

FROM THE ARMISTICE TO THE PEACE

	Food	Medicine, Clothing, & Misc.	Total	$ Value
American Relief Administration:				
Children's relief	15,326	1,292	16,618	$ 4,743,147
General relief .... (including freight)	254,427	5,775	260,202	52,215,784
U.S. Liquidation Commission	44,360	62,766	107,126	59,365,112
Jewish Joint Distribution Committee	7,802	1,904	9,706	3,412,497 †
American Red Cross		4,043	4,043	813,800
Jewish Joint Distribution Committee .... (additional money spent which did not go through A.R.A.) ‡	(quantities unknown)			5,944,503
Polish League of Women ...		4	4	1,640
Russo-Carpathian Commission		1	1	200
United Kingdom .... (including freight)	12,210	9,252	21,462	7,694,540
	334,125	85,037	419,162	$134,191,223

* In tons.
† The Polish National Committee should be credited for $1,000,000 of this; they paid the J.D.C. for part of the *Westward Ho*'s cargo.
‡ Total also includes some contributions prior to the Armistice.

THE NEUTRAL NATIONS OF EUROPE

CHAPTER 9

THE NEUTRALS

The Neutral nations were continuously blockaded until the Peace and were thus held to rations less than their needs. We Americans made a great effort to obtain relaxation of the blockade for them, but we failed. The Neutral nations were generous in gifts to their neighbors, and they co-operated fully with our organizations in arranging distribution of the few special surplus foods which they produced. Sweden and Norway provided a surplus of fish products, Denmark and Holland of dairy products.

The Neutrals paid for and transported the supplies which they were allowed under the blockade "rations." We have no statistics of their total food imports. Their purchases from the United States from October 15, 1918 (approximately the Armistice), until September, 1919 (two months after the Peace), were as follows:

Country	Food (Tons)	$ Value	Animal Feed (Tons)	$ Value	Total Tons	Total $ Value
Norway	216,240	51,777,144	17,706	1,198,242	233,946	52,975,386
Sweden	138,829	51,879,433	62,059	3,816,102	200,888	55,695,535
Denmark ...	236,870	57,772,629	124,553	8,525,502	361,423	66,298,131
Holland	653,298	126,400,269	54,409	3,981,734	707,707	130,382,003
Switzerland .	348,777	43,726,025	549	31,988	349,326	43,758,013
Spain	45,539	8,717,198	—	———	45,539	8,717,198
Total	1,639,553	$340,272,698	259,276	$17,553,568	1,898,829	$357,826,266

AIDS FROM AMERICAN CHARITABLE AGENCIES
DURING THE ARMISTICE

The Neutrals were not in need of charity for their own people, but the American charitable organizations had given extensive aid to them for the support of refugees from other nations. The contributions were:

HOLLAND

Jewish Joint Distribution Committee—for refugees	$ 92,116
American Red Cross	15,600

SWITZERLAND

Jewish Joint Distribution Committee—for refugees	$ 37,281
Near East Relief Committee	13,000
American Red Cross	2,222,937

The American Red Cross not only gave aid to refugees in Switzerland, but from that base it assisted Allied prisoners in Germany and elsewhere, upon whom $859,129 of the above amount was spent.

DENMARK

Jewish Joint Distribution Committee—for refugees and co-religionists	$ 1,740

SPAIN

Jewish Joint Distribution Committee	$18,000

GERMANY

CHAPTER 10

THE RELIEF OF GERMANY
PRIOR TO THE PEACE

In Volume II of this memoir, I have described the desperate food, economic, and political situation in Germany at the Armistice.[1] I have also given in that volume an account of the American efforts to remove the blockade, since it was a violation of promises of food in the Armistice agreement under which Germany surrendered to the Allies.[2] And I have given an account of the vigorous American protests and the settlements at the Brussels Conference of March 14, 1919, when the food blockade was relaxed.[3]

The delay of food supplies for four months following the Armistice promise was not only immoral and inhumane, it sowed dragon's teeth for another war. It made it doubtful that Germany could be saved from Communism. Before the Brussels Conference the Communists had at different times seized the municipal governments of Hamburg, Munich, Stettin, and at one time the governments of the states of Bavaria, Saxony, and the Ruhr. And at the very moment of the Brussels agreement, machine guns were chattering in the streets of Berlin and Hamburg.

The Brussels agreement was the beginning of an enormous political and administrative problem for our official American relief organizations. We were pledged to find, buy, and ship more than

---

[1] *An American Epic,* Vol. II, Chap. 34.
[2] *Ibid.,* Chap. 35.
[3] *Ibid.,* Chap. 36.

1,800,000 tons of food to Germany, which duty fell upon our already overworked New York and London staffs.

We appointed Edwin Sherman chief of our mission and gave him adequate staff. We established offices in both Rotterdam and Berlin, with Dr. Vernon Kellogg as the liaison officer for both Sherman's mission and our Paris office. We did not wait for the gold agreed upon for payment of supplies to arrive at my credit in the bank vaults in Brussels, Antwerp, and Rotterdam. We had huge stocks of food awaiting the opening of the blockade at Antwerp, Rotterdam, and Copenhagen. We instantly opened our doors to German barges and railway cars, and we diverted cargoes en route to German ports, hoping our supplies would arrive in time to save the new German Republic under President Ebert.

When the gold arrived, it came in carloads of boxes and bags. We had no way of knowing whether the boxes and bags actually contained gold coin or iron washers. We had some sample boxes and bags opened and found that a considerable part was American gold coins. Also included were some of the French gold coins paid on the indemnity of the Franco-Prussian War of 1871.

We arranged with the New York Federal Reserve Bank to take possession of the gold and advance us at once 92 per cent of the estimated value, the balance to be paid as it was melted at the American mints.

On March 23, the 2,700,000 tons of German and Austrian merchant shipping which had taken refuge during the war started coming out to Allied ports. In two days, 23 ships arrived, but, as was described in Volume II,[4] they were distributed among the Allies, and we had a constant battle to get even a few of them for relief uses.

The assurance given the Germans in the Brussels agreement of 300,000 tons of cereals and 70,000 tons of fats or condensed milk monthly added a huge strain on world-short food supplies. We had made a reservation in that agreement that this assured monthly supply was subject to availability from world supplies. But with the raging starvation and the political situation in Germany, we drew on

[4] Chap. 42.

every source to the utmost, although it added to the already short supply of other nations. Among other sources, I diverted the entire food reserve held by the Belgian Relief Commission, which was estimated at a value of $45,000,000.

Our hundreds of thousands of tons stored in the ports poured like manna over all Germany. The German press expressed astonishment that the Americans had acted so quickly without waiting for the gold and interpreted it as a mark of confidence in the Ebert Government.

Since we were barred by the Lodge amendment to the Congressional appropriation from using any of that $100,000,000 in former enemy countries, we were therefore unable to set up our usual canteen system for the rehabilitation of children. However, we hoped that our monthly supply of 70,000 tons of fats and condensed milk would enable the Germans to give their youngsters rehabilitating nourishment. Aside from all decent men's sympathy for starving children, we also hoped from these supplies to prevent a generation of hoodlums with stunted minds and warped bodies from haunting the world.

SOME BAD ADVICE

On April 21, Mr. Wilson handed me a memorandum from some important British official advocating that the way out of Germany's internal dangers was to reorganize the German Government to include Spartacist (Communist) elements in it. I replied as follows:

21 April, 1919.

DEAR MR. PRESIDENT:

I enclose you, herewith, memorandum on the note which you handed me today with regard to the situation in Germany. I have put it in the form of a memorandum in case you wish to hand it to . . . your colleagues for their edification.

HERBERT HOOVER

In this memorandum I pointed out the foolishness of any such proposal in relation to free men and continued:

. . . You and all of us have proposed, fought and plead for the last
. . . [four] months that the blockade on Germany should be taken off,
that these people should be allowed to return to production [and export
of certain commodities] . . . that there should be awakened in them
some resolution for continued National Life [under free institutions]. The
situation in Germany today is to a large degree one of complete aban-
donment of hope. The people have simply lain down under the threat of
Bolshevism in front and the demands of the Allies behind. The people
are . . . in a state of moral collapse and there is no resurrection from
this except through the restoration of the normal processes of economic
life and hope. We have for the last month held that it is now too late
to save the situation. We do think, however, that it is worth one more
great effort to bring the Allied countries to realize that all the bars on
exports and imports should be [relaxed] . . . that the Germans should
be given an assurance that a certain amount of ships and working capital
will be left in their hands with which to re-start the National machine.

We feel also from an American point of view that the refusal of the
Allies to accept these primary considerations during the last three months
leaves them with the total responsibility for . . . [what] is now impending.

. . . We do not believe the blockade was ever an effective instrument
to force peace; it is effective, however, to force . . . [Communism].

To this the President replied the following day:

MY DEAR HOOVER:
Thank you warmly for your letter of yesterday enclosing your memorandum on the situation in Germany apropos of the British memorandum
which I handed you. It will be very serviceable to me indeed.

                                              WOODROW WILSON

AN INCIDENT OF BAD FOOD

There was one item in the provision of food for Germany which
temporarily gave me a much troubled mind. The Allies, including
the United States, through the British, had purchased during the
war large quantities of salted fish from the Norwegians to prevent
its going to the enemy. Beyond this, Britain had a quantity of bacon

stored as a reserve against submarine attack. It had been reconditioned often and was now inedible. The Allied governments arranged with the Germans to sell them these commodities for part of the gold. When this came to my attention, I instructed Dr. Kellogg in Berlin to inform the German Food Ministry that our organization had nothing to do with this transaction and that we wanted no implication that we had taken any part in purveying rotten food— even to a former enemy. Their astonishing reply was:

The Allies will no doubt take our gold reserve for reparations, and if we can get some material for fertilizers and soap in exchange, we would be glad to have it.

Thus the transaction seemed to be all right with everyone. The British and French got about $45,000,000 in gold (which they deserved as war damages), and the Germans were satisfied to get anything back. We had cleared our skirts of the charge of selling bad food.

ANOTHER PHASE OF THE BLOCKADE

Although we were able to supply Germany with food, the blockade prevented the import of raw materials and the export of goods, which would have contributed to her support and required less demand on the gold. More gold would have remained for reparations. We fully recognized the rightness of preventing Germany from restoring her world trade in advance of the Allies, but there were certain goods, such as chemicals, which were not competitive. However, we were unable to secure any relaxation of this sort.

THE FOOD SUPPLY OF GERMANY IS MIXED
WITH POLITICAL POLICIES

At the Peace Conference, that fierce old tiger Premier Clemenceau demanded every device for dismembering Germany in order to keep a reunited Germany from attacking France again. He had ample justification for dismemberment from past French sufferings at the hands of German aggressors, but our organization could not go along with proposals to base this dismemberment on distribution of food.

On March 27, I was called to a meeting of the Foreign Ministers, held at the French Foreign Office, where French proposals to provision Bavaria separately were being considered. Some extracts from the minutes are as follows:

. . . *M. Pichon* explained the political importance of allowing Bavaria to get supplies from other directions than the north. At present all the supplies for Bavaria were sent by the Berlin organization, and this tended to increase the political influence of Prussia. The best way to obviate this was to enable Bavaria to receive supplies from the south. . . .

M. Seydoux thought that the revictualling of Bavaria from the south could be carried on outside of the decisions taken at Brussels. There it had been decided that the revictualling of Germany should be compensated for by exports. France needed coal and glass, which Bavaria could export, and he suggested that food might be supplied in exchange. . . . His proposal was to supply Bavaria by rail from Strassburg. In the same manner the goods which Bavaria could supply would be brought back through Strassburg. . . .

Mr. Lansing said that the real question involved was one of policy. Did we want to separate Bavaria from Germany?

Mr. Hoover said that the Allied and Associated Powers had entered into a series of contracts with the . . . [Ebert] Government, under which the latter had undertaken the fair distribution of supplies throughout the whole of Germany, including Bavaria. There was a financial problem involved. The people with whom the Allied and Associated Powers were dealing drew on the resources of the whole of Germany for payments. To make a separate financial arrangement would involve separate means of payment being found for Bavaria. If these goods came to France from Bavaria, it was doubtful if France had [food] supplies to furnish in return. To replace them . . . food supplies would have to be imported from elsewhere, and dollars or credits would have to be found. One difficulty was that there was a serious shortage of foodstuffs available for Europe. . . .

Mr. Hoover . . . said that in any event the supplies would have to receive access to Bavaria by the Rhine. Otherwise, they would have to be brought from Bordeaux right across France, whereas, by using the Rhine, an immediate and easy transport was available. . . .

. . . He estimated the value of the food supplies that Germany must import in the next three months at 300 million dollars. The amount she could export did not exceed 40 million dollars in value. . . .

Mr. Hoover said that the arrangement with the Germans comprised two methods. (1) An arrangement with the Central Government at Berlin, (2) a relaxation of the Blockade which would enable German merchants to buy in neutral countries on the understanding that what they bought would be deducted from the total ration for Germany. There was nothing to prevent Bavarian merchants purchasing from the Swiss and we had undertaken to make good to Switzerland what [food] they sold, but without increase to the total ration. . . .

Mr. Lansing said that if our object was to get rid of Bolshevism the best way was to . . . [support] the Berlin Government which was certainly not Bolshevist. He doubted the expediency of interfering with the internal affairs of any country. . . .

Mr. Balfour proposed to send the matter to the Supreme Economic Council.

Mr. Hoover said that if the question was sent to the Supreme Economic Council the first thing they would do was to ask "What was the policy?" . . .

(After some further discussion the following question was referred to the Supreme Economic Council:—
Whether, having regard to the terms of the Brussels agreement, it is economically possible to send food independently to Bavaria, apart altogether from the political expediency of doing so.)

When the subject came before the Supreme Economic Council, the American and British members gently buried it.

President Wilson requested that I give him a note on my opinion of the whole business, which I did:

April 3, 1919

Dear Mr. President:

With respect to feeding Bavaria through Switzerland, this is totally infeasible in any volume worth considering, both from a transportation, food and financial point of view.

For your confidential information, the whole of this question has been repeatedly agitated . . . by the French Minister at Berne, who is constantly endeavoring to create a Separatist spirit in Bavaria and who wishes to send a few carloads . . . into Bavaria under the French flag.

The pressure from this quarter became so great in this particular about ten days ago that it was raised before the Council of Four Ministers of Foreign Affairs. . . .

Foodstuffs are moving into the ports of Germany as rapidly as we can secure transportation and the large industrial centers in the North are in far more acute distress than Bavaria. While we are insistent that some portion of shipments should be made to Bavaria, I myself consider it fundamental that we should get some American food at the earliest possible moment into the larger centers of the North and East.

As quickly as the first German . . . ship left the German harbors, and before any of the financial arrangements were completed, I diverted several cargoes intended for other quarters into German harbors. . . . I may add, however, that the situation in Germany is extremely dangerous and that I am not at all sure that our food supplies have not arrived sixty days too late. In any event, it is a neck and neck race as to whether food will maintain stability as against the other forces that have grown out of hunger in the meantime.

HERBERT HOOVER

Premier Clemenceau pursued the matter no further, and we did not set up Bavaria as an independent state based on food supply. However, he and Marshal Foch found another case for dismemberment based on food. Marshal Foch proposed that we set up a separate distribution for the Rhineland. We refused for the same reasons that we did in the case of Bavaria. The French and German industrialists in the Rhineland started a movement for a "Rhenish Republic." When they asked for an assurance of a separate food supply, we again had to decline for the same old reasons. This affair ended when President Ebert put the German conspirators in jail. Nevertheless, Premier Clemenceau secured the separation of the Rhineland in the Versailles Treaty.

THE BLOCKADE QUESTION FLARES UP AGAIN

Marshal Foch had insisted at all times that the reimposition of the blockade (and thus starvation, mostly of women, children, and the old people in the impoverished districts) was the way to make the Germans sign the Treaty on the dotted line. To him, this was much simpler than marching a few divisions of Allied troops into a disarmed country.

On May 5, 1919, the French delegates on the Supreme Economic Council submitted plans for reimposing the blockade if the Germans showed any hesitation in accepting Allied terms.

The Big Four asked a representative of the Economic Council to discuss reimposing the blockade with them on May 8. McCormick's diary entry for May 9 sheds light on what happened:

Went to special committee of the Supreme Blockade Council at the Commerce Department to discuss plans for blockade in the event of Germany refusing to sign Treaty. We came to agreement. I notified Council, while approving the plan, that I hoped the Allies would not use it as it would make more chaos. In my opinion, the only solution of the question would be military occupation. . . .

On May 7, the Treaty was given to the Germans, and they were allowed two weeks to comment on it. The Big Four now requested from the Supreme Economic Council a detailed plan for reimposing the blockade. The Council proposed to transmit a plan which had been prepared by the French. While I could not prevent the Council staff from presenting a plan in response to a request from the Big Four, I objected to the whole idea because it meant the starvation of women and children. I stated that a peace treaty signed under such pressure would not survive the revulsion of world public opinion. It was then proposed that the Council make public its plan. Both McCormick and I objected on the ground that we never had approved it. By way of obstruction, I raised a secondary question concerning what would happen to food then en route. According to the minutes, I explained that large advance commitments had been made by the American relief agencies for the purchase and transport of food for Germany from both the United States and the Argentine and that a sudden reimposition of the blockade might leave us with great losses. A further extract from the minutes shows:

The British Delegates remarked upon the gravity of the situation and expressed the opinion that proper steps should be taken to the end that all losses should be borne by the various governments as an expense incident to the conduct of the war.

It was agreed:—

(a) That all shipments by the Relief Administration landed at, or en route for, European ports and intended for the revictualling of Germany which may be kept from going into Germany by the re-establishment of the blockade, shall be taken off the hands of the American Relief Administration by purchase by the Allied Governments. . . .

By this time we had learned the meaning of the last two words. It may as well have read "by loans from the United States."

The Big Four, on May 13, made this nebulous statement with respect to the blockade:

. . . Arrangements have been made to remove the blockade against Germany immediately and completely as soon as the German representatives have signed the Treaty of Peace.

In the meantime the following temporary relaxations have already been made for the duration of the armistice. . . .

The statement went on to describe a list of minor relaxations of the blockade. They were of little importance.

I did not like any aspect of reimposing the blockade, and I addressed this letter of protest to Mr. Wilson:

PARIS, 14 May 1919

DEAR MR. PRESIDENT:

. . . my strong view that we should not be led into joining with the Allies in a food blockade against Germany as a method of forcing peace. The margins on which the German people must live from now until next harvest are so small that any cessation of the stream of food, even for a short time, will bring the most wholesale loss of life. It might be that the imposition of a blockade would be effectual in securing the German signature to the peace. *I seriously doubt whether when the world has recovered its moral equilibrium that it would consider a peace obtained upon such a device as the starving of women and children as being binding upon the German people.* If the Germans did resist, it is my impression that it would throw Germany into complete chaos and military occupation would need to follow in order to save Europe. . . .[5]

HERBERT HOOVER

[5] Italics added.

McCormick's diary contains this entry for the same day:

Was called to the President's house at 11:00 to submit to Big Four our plan for blockade in the event of Germany refusing to sign. . . . When we started meeting I handed the President a letter I had just written him strongly recommending the use of military occupation instead of blockade in the event of Germany not signing and told him of Lord Robert's opinion that for financial and other reasons he thought military occupation impossible. I told the President this could not be and that the alternative was starvation and revolution in Germany. Everything would be lost to the Allies while occupation would save something out of the wreck. President made this statement to the Big Four and urged occupation. . . .

McCormick's diary for the next day contains this entry:

At 2:00 went to President's house with Hoover, Davis and Baruch to discuss with the President the blockade policy as to food if Germany refused to sign. Hoover urging food should go to Germany in any event. . . . President told him of our conversation with Big Four yesterday and that he advocated military occupation rather than starvation methods. President discussed freely his difficulties with his colleagues in Council—called them mad men, particularly Clemenceau, whom he now understands better since he has read some of his earlier writing in which he advocated the "survival of the fittest." He says he has a great pity for them. They have such fear of the Germans and such great self pity. He spoke feelingly of his struggles with Clemenceau and Lloyd George to hold them down to justice and reason and could not vouch for his being able to convince them that military occupation was better than the starvation method because the military occupation would cost more in money. . . .

On June 13, the Big Four gave their final verdict on reimposing the blockade in a communication to the Supreme Economic Council:

The Council of the Principal Allied and Associated Powers have considered the Note of the Superior Blockade Council, dated June 11th 1919. . . .

They have decided that the Blockade Council should make every preparation for the re-imposition of the Blockade but that its actual enforcement should not be undertaken, even in the event of the refusal by the Germans to sign the Treaty of Peace, without a decision from the

Council of the Principal Allied and Associated Powers. No actual threat should be made public that the Blockade is to be re-imposed but, short of this, steps should be taken to give the public impression that preparations are in hand. If practicable, these steps should include the despatch of destroyers to show themselves in the Baltic.

(Initld) W. W.

G. C.

D. L. G.

S. S.

N. M.

McCormick's diary of June 14 contains this item:

After cleaning up routine in office, I attended the final meeting of the Blockade Council on preparations for re-imposing blockade in event the governments decide it wise to do so. The machinery is all set and we are ready to shoot. I hope it may not be necessary. I am convinced that military occupation is the real thing and blockade unnecessary.

Lunched with advisers in my room—General Bliss, Admiral Knapp, Hoover, Baruch, Davis, B. Palmer present. Hot discussion on treaty and blockade. Hoover and Bliss think it too hard; Baruch and I think it just and workable. Hoover says if blockade imposed he will resign. . . .

On June 16, the Allies replied to the German criticisms in vigorous terms, offering few concessions. The German delegation to Paris returned to Germany the same day and resigned.

Also on June 16, a British naval official jumped the gun on the executionary phase of the plan to reimpose the blockade. He seized fourteen of our food ships in German ports. I had to appeal to the President to get the ships released. The red tape involved required a week for this to be done.

McCormick's diary of June 24 contains this entry:

I caught the President at the Crillon . . . and asked him to bring up the [blockade] question at the next meeting of the "Chiefs." He said he thought it bad policy to do so, as Clemenceau was in such a rage at the action of the Germans in sinking the fleet [at Scapa Flow] and lowering the flags that he was having great difficulty in preventing him from making war again on the Germans, and that this was the wrong time to submit the question of removing the [proposed] blockade. . . .

PEACE IS SIGNED BUT DOES NOT REIGN

President Ebert sent two representatives to Versailles, and on June 28, they signed the Treaty on the dotted line. A detailed account of these negotiations, President Wilson's endeavors to revise the Treaty, and my protests that it would breed further wars are given in detail with documentation in my book *The Ordeal of Woodrow Wilson*.

FOOD SUPPLIES TO GERMANY

In the meantime, we had furnished to Germany as much food as the scant world resources would permit. Our supplies, under the Brussels agreement of March 14, 1919, could not be fully completed at the Peace, and, in any event, the Brussels Agreement contemplated supplies until the German harvest of August was available.

During this period, however, the Federal Reserve Bank had advanced us 92 per cent of the estimated value of the German gold, the remainder to be paid when the gold was melted, which required some months after the Peace. Since this final settlement of the gold and other services during the Armistice period was affected after the Peace, I discuss it in Part Two of this volume.

FOOD SUPPLIES SENT TO GERMANY UNDER TERMS OF THE
BRUSSELS AGREEMENT OF MARCH 14, 1919

	Total Tons	$ Value
American Relief Administration * ...	846,608	$190,475,228
United Kingdom	299,144	75,653,861
France	69,404	16,262,889
American Friends Service Committee	60	29,687
	1,215,216	$282,421,665

* Included in the supplies furnished by the American Relief Administration are the following purchased in:

	Total Tons	$ Value
Argentina	155,000	$16,774,000
Holland	44,648	9,784,989
Switzerland	28,886	5,825,812

CZECHOSLOVAKIA, AUSTRIA, HUNGARY, BULGARIA, YUGOSLAVIA, AND RUMANIA

INTRODUCTION

There were certain impediments to the relief of Czechoslovakia, Austria, Hungary, Bulgaria, Yugoslavia, and Rumania. Possibly the worst was the truncation of the old railway systems which radiated from Vienna. With the Armistice, communications between these states were cut at the will of any one of them. In addition, each state was seizing railway stock and refusing to cooperate in railway connections across its borders.

On February 28, 1919, I proposed to President Wilson that the only solution was to give our organization certain control of these railways. On March 7, the Supreme Council established a priority of supply trains to be operated by us under my direction, and we established a method of control by which all trains would go to their destinations over the frontiers. The effect was instantaneous, and we were able to increase our rail shipments out of Trieste to all destinations from 700 tons a day to over 4,000 tons.

WATERWAYS

Likewise, the separation of these states had divided the waterway transport system into segments where politics and the seizure of barges reigned.

COAL SUPPLIES

Coal supplies practically fell into the hands of one of these countries—Czechoslovakia. It was not until a mandate was given my organization by the Supreme Council on August 5, 1919, for managing these operations that we could provide heat for homes and hospitals and also keep the wheels of commerce going around in this area of the earth.[1]

THE BLOCKADE

Another impediment to the relief of these nations was the demon blockade, which, under Allied orders of December 31, 1918, was made absolute on all commodities. Under Admiral Benson's bold statement that American-flag ships would not be stopped on missions to save dying people, we simply ignored the blockade. And curiously enough, while still maintaining the threat for political purposes, the Allies also ignored it—except in the relief of Germany.

The blockade was supposed to prohibit the exchange of raw materials and manufactured goods between these states. This was also ignored by both our organization and the Allies.

However, the blockade was strictly enforced on overseas imports of raw material and exports of manufactured goods. The efforts of the President, Vance McCormick, and my organization were of no avail, although we proposed that goods competitive with Allied trade should not be permitted.

POLITICS AND HATE

A violent impediment arose from the Pact of London, in which the Italians had been promised certain annexations in return for their joining the Allies in the war. Italy was to have a segment of Austria, the port of Trieste, Adriatic islands, part of Dalmatia, and other privileges. At Paris she demanded the port of Fiume and its hinterland, although this had been reserved for Yugoslavia in the Pact of London. Italy's general policy was to obstruct everything,

---

[1] For details on railways, waterways, and coal, see *An American Epic,* Vol. II. Chaps. 43, 44, and 45.

including the railway operations which were vital to the relief of Czechoslovakia, Austria, Hungary, and Yugoslavia. Italy used her strategic railway and port facilities as pressure to secure the promises of the London Pact. And she had absolutely no love for her former enemies, which included Czechoslovakia, Austria, and Hungary, and parts of Yugoslavia. In fact, hate was an ever present force between all these states and Italy, and our relief organization was the victim.

Early in February, 1919, these contentions, plus hatred, flared up into what became known as the Lubiana Incident. The Italians claimed that the Yugoslavs had insulted their flag and as a reprisal embargoed Yugoslav food and other supplies from passage through the Adriatic ports and over their connecting railways—which action incidentally stopped our railway connections with Austria, Hungary, and Czechoslovakia.

On February 28, I received, through the American Embassy in Paris, this note from the American Minister to Serbia:

Major Ryan, representative of Food Administration here reports that he is informed by his agent Trieste that on account interference local Italian authorities he is unable to forward any flour from Trieste to Slovenia and that . . . [their] supply . . . is exhausted and famine conditions imminent. Ryan has telegraphed to Hoover requesting immediate action with Italian representative Paris.

It was not until late in March, 1919, that these obstructions to our work were at least partly solved. Many of the weak and aged perished in the meantime.

CHAPTER 11

CZECHOSLOVAKIA

Two world figures emerged into leadership of the Czechs—Dr. Thomas G. Masaryk and Professor Eduard Beneš. For many years Dr. Masaryk had spearheaded Czech (Bohemian) demands in the old Austrian Parliament for wider liberties. At the outbreak of the war he came to the Allied side and created an effective liberation committee composed of Czechs abroad. Before the war ended, he had become so influential that he was able to induce the Czech divisions in the Austrian armies to desert to the Russians, thus contributing to the defeat of the Central Empires. But with the Communist Revolution, followed by the peace with Germany in March, 1918, this army was left stranded. There is no greater odyssey in history than that of this army, which, by superb courage, held together and fought its way five thousand miles across Russia and Siberia to Vladivostok on the Pacific and then joined the Allied armies on the Western Front.

Dr. Masaryk was a noble figure—scholarly, wide visioned, tolerant, yet with an iron resolve. He had an honest, philosophical mind, and was a deep student of the art of government. I knew Dr. Masaryk when he was leading his liberation forces during the war. At that time, Eduard Beneš was a sort of man Friday to Masaryk. Beneš was an academic man and a Socialist. He was a great master of diplomatic formula and rather intolerant. But since he had lived under the Austrian heel all his life, struggling to bring freedom and relief to his people mostly by conspiracy, he had some rights to tolerance.

The Austrian and Sudeten Germans had dominated Bohemia for most of the previous three hundred years. They had, with the utmost brutality, tried to crush Czech racial aspirations. Only by sheer intellectual fortitude had this intelligent and plucky people been able to preserve their language, their culture, and their moral independence.

As an indication of the hates which poisoned the air in Central Europe after the Armistice, I may relate an incident between Czechoslovakia and Austria. In December, 1918, our organization was advised that the Czechs were refusing to send coal to Vienna. The municipal services of light and heat, which would include hospitals and the already distressed civilians, were faced with this additional disaster. I took the matter up with President Masaryk in Paris, and he gave orders that coal should be sent. But his letter of December 14 to me indicates the prevailing situation. He said:

Right after our conversation I sent orders home to send to Vienna all coal available. . . .

The situation in Vienna seems grave; but I am not quite sure of the good will of the Vienna Government and of some of the political leaders. Our government has positive evidence of the fact that Vienna is sending arms to the German population in Bohemia through Bavaria and to the German population in Silesia through Prussia; and . . . the coal-mining districts of Silesia and Moravia have been occupied by German bands, and, I am sorry to say, by the Poles. By reason of this fact it is not only Vienna, but also our cities, especially our capital, Prague, which suffer of serious coal-shortage. Another factor in the situation is the very great shortage of rolling stock, locomotives and freight cars, many thousands of which were taken by the Italians in the last Austrian *debacle*. . . .

At any rate you must take into account the evident endeavor of the Austrian Germans (I mean the known Pan-German leaders) to discredit us. . . .

At the Armistice, the abilities of Masaryk had brought about a quick revolution and an effective organization of the new nation of

Czechoslovakia, with constitutional government in parliamentary form. He brought home his experienced army.

The setup of the new state was a perplexing problem at the Peace Conference. The French, partly to create a better military frontier for their Czech ally against Germany and partly to dismember the Germans, insisted upon including the Sudeten Germans in the new nation. Masaryk came to see me in Paris to express his doubt about this proposal. He asked me to suggest to Mr. Wilson that the President oppose inclusion of the Sudetenland in Czechoslovakia. He explained that to ask for this himself would place him in a difficult position with the French. Mr. Wilson soon found that the French were adamant on this point as a part of France's wish to dismember Germany.

The Czechs otherwise were busy at the Peace Conference expanding the boundaries of the new republic in other directions. It finally embraced Bohemia, the Sudeten Germans, Moravia, Slovakia, and parts of Ruthenia and Silesia, approximately 14,000,000 people. During the Armistice, the Hungarians attacked Czechoslovakia, but in the end, the victorious Czechs secured some more Hungarian territory. Also, they were in competition with the Poles for the Duchy of Teschen.

The original setup of Czechoslovakia, as agreed to by both Masaryk and Beneš in writing to the Peace Conference, was that its government was to be a cantonal state, like Switzerland, thus preserving a certain autonomy for each of the four races, and possibly also for some Moravian and Hungarian areas. The separate races were represented in the new parliament and quickly coagulated into opposition to Czech domination. The Czechs, having the majority, gradually increased their iron grip.[1]

[1] The great tragedy of Czechoslovakia was Masaryk's death in 1937. He had the tolerance and vision required to overcome a hate centuries deep and to weld together and lead the Sudeten Germans, the Slovaks, and Slovenes to accept the new republic and co-operate with the Czechs. After Masaryk died, Beneš, who succeeded him, did not evince such qualities. Even the names of the streets and roads in the Sudeten areas, which had been there hundreds of years, were changed to Czech names. When Hitler began his integration of all Germans, the Sudeten Germans were ripe for revolt. Then came Munich and, later, Hitler's hideous invasion of the truncated state and with it the disintegration of the Czechoslovak state—for a while.

Since, under the old Austrian Empire, all finance, transportation, communication, and commerce had centered in Vienna, the difficulties confronting the new Czech republic were enormous because a whole new economic order had to be built and centered in Prague.

RELIEF OF CZECHOSLOVAKIA

Our American relief operations got off to a bad start. Early in December, 1918, we had telegraphed Beneš, then acting Prime Minister, for some estimate of his country's food needs. On December 18, he replied to me and to the American Red Cross as follows:

. . . Thanks to the productive wealth of our soil, thanks to the spirit of economy which has been shown by the population, there is no need to consider this important question. The local resources will meet the needs.

We therefore did nothing for the moment. As a matter of fact, Beneš was a stranger to his own country. Despite his optimism, reports soon began to show that the Czech potato crop had been a failure and that during the war the Czechs' cattle had been reduced 40 per cent and their swine 85 per cent. With a shortage of fats and dairy products, Czech children were in a deplorable state.

A few quotations from our staff further indicate the Beneš illusion:

. . . In addition to the food problem, which is foremost, lack of clothing, insufficient heating, and especially the almost total lack of soap, contribute largely to the increased death rate. Housing is also very insufficient, due partially to the return of Czecho-Slovaks who had been driven abroad by various causes. . . .

Apart from actual starvation, the lack of certain foods has produced bad effects on the general health in various ways, affecting notably the teeth. Dentists have never had so much to do as at present. The particular shortcoming throughout the war had been in fats, which are required for the manufacture of explosives and other army uses. The food ration which was progressively increased for a time immediately after the inauguration of the republic, has since been decreased. This subsequent decrease, in addition to the fact that the ration is at times only a paper ration. . . .

A report on the Kladno district reads:

. . . A large percentage of the population are iron and steel workers and coal miners, while in the four smaller towns mentioned the population is almost totally iron workers and coal miners. . . .

It is the opinion of the local committee at Kladno, who have been doing relief work during the war, that help is needed. . . .

I give reports on the condition of the children in a later section of this chapter. In any event, frantic appeals came to us from Czechoslovakia, including a personal appeal to me from Dr. Masaryk.

STAFF ARRANGEMENTS

In February, 1919, we replaced our single representative in Prague with a full staff as follows:

LINCOLN HUTCHINSON, *Chief of Mission in Czechoslovakia*

LIEUTENANT R. S. BYFIELD, *Assistant* (who was in charge of the office during the absence of Mr. Hutchinson)

LIEUTENANT C. H. GRIESA, *Remittances, Supplies & Office Management*

MAJOR G. E. BURKE, *Barge Movements on Elbe*

R. C. PURCELL, *Accountant and Disbursing Officer*

CAPTAIN J. T. SHAW, *Chief of Children's Relief Bureau*

CAPTAIN A. C. RINGLAND, *Assistant Chief of Children's Relief*

We sent in additional American army officers to reinforce this staff.

TRANSPORT PROBLEMS

In February, 1919, we started supplies by rail from Trieste, but the demoralization of the Eastern European railways was such that it was only a trickle. I have already given a full account of our railway troubles and the non-co-operation of the Italians, who controlled one segment of the railroads to Czechoslovakia.[2] After the removal of the food blockade on Germany on March 14, we began shipments over the River Elbe from Hamburg to Prague. Our shipments steadily increased until we were delivering over 70,000 tons a month.

[2] See *An American Epic*, Vol. II, Chap. 43.

BARTER OF SUPPLIES BETWEEN CZECHOSLOVAKIA AND THE NEIGHBORING COUNTRIES

Our mission was the catalyst of a series of exchanges of supplies between Czechoslovakia, Poland, Austria, Hungary, Yugoslavia, and Italy. The Allied governments participated in these exchanges, despite their bureaucratic rulings pertaining to the blockade.

Czechoslovakia had a surplus of sugar, some metals, and, ultimately, coal. Such exchanges were reported by our mission to have the following value:

	Tons	Value
With France	16,531	$ 7,535,780
" Italy	75,861	16,653,920
" Poland	50,000	1,000,000
" Yugoslavia	550	587,050
" Austria	520	281,600
	143,462	$26,058,350

FINANCE OF SUPPLIES

Czechoslovakia was accepted by the United States Treasury as a belligerent on the Allied side and thus became entitled to loans from the United States. With the enactment of the Congressional appropriation of $100,000,000 at the end of February, 1919, we were able to handle the entire situation.

REHABILITATION OF CHILDREN

That a great number of children in Czechoslovakia were in desperate need can be indicated by a few sentences from our reports:

Infant mortality in Prague, according to Professor Svehla of the Foundlings Hospital, is now ten times greater than before the war. This statement is presumably based upon cases under his own observation. . . .

. . . Deprived of essential food values for four or five years, there has been a considerable development of tuberculosis, scrofula and Rachitis, while many children in the impoverished sections are far below normal in stature and health. . . .

. . . very urgent need exists for the relief of children, particularly among the congested and mining sections. A mild form of disease is breaking out among the children due to the lack of nutrition, lack of soup, and the lack of clothing.

. . . The appearance of the children in these places leaves no doubt as to the greet need of the A.R.A. child relief work in this country, and I am credibly informed that the condition in Prague is not the worst in Czecho-Slovakia; in other words, the food conditions along the German border is even worse than in Prague. A notable thing is the stunted growth of many of the children, showing that the undernourishment has continued for the greater part of the War.

. . . In the Republic, excluding Slovakia (where there are no reliable statistics at present) there are 497,000 boys and 488,000 girls under 6 years; 599,000 boys, 582,000 girls from 6 to 10; 332,000 boys, 330,000 girls from 11 to 13. . . .

With magnificent support from the Czech Government and the devoted Czech women, our staff rapidly spread our canteen system over the country. The estimated number of children cared for rose to as high as 428,000 daily. The special food supplied totaled 6,506 tons.

CLOTHING

Our major source of clothing was the United States Army surplus placed at our disposal by the President. Some of it was new, some worn. The total, including miscellaneous supplies, was 5,850 tons. The American Red Cross delivered to our headquarters in New York some 875 tons of adult clothing, and 325 tons of clothes for children were provided from the Congressional appropriation—in all a total of 7,050 tons from the United States. The British contributed 1,120 tons, making a total supply to Czechoslovakia of 8,170 tons.

Some of the American charitable organizations valued such clothing at $1.00 per pound, or $2,000 per ton. However, we indulged in no such estimates.

AIDS FROM OTHER QUARTERS

The United Kingdom furnished 7,132 tons of supplies valued at $1,599,836.

Norway furnished, as charity, supplies to the value of $6,060.

The French furnished $5,138 worth of free supplies.

I have stated above the barter transactions with other nations, which yielded 143,462 tons, of a value of $26,058,350.

The American Red Cross, convinced that the medical facilities in Czechoslovakia were ample, did not establish a service there before the Peace but gave aids through our organization.

The Jewish Joint Distribution Committee found little need for its co-religionists and made only minor contributions for refugees. Its figures are not separable from aid to other states.

SOME GOOD BUT WASTED ADVICE

My colleagues and I concluded that the newborn states in Eastern Europe should begin to plan for the inevitable when, at the signing of the Peace, all our Congressional authorizations and appropriations, along with the blockade, would end. Our reason was that the attitude of the American people was changing. The war had been a great burden and these European states were not likely to get much aid from governments after the Peace was signed. I therefore addressed the following letter to Dr. Beneš:

Paris, 11 March 1919

Dear Doctor Beneš:

It appears to me that the time has arrived when the Czecho-Slovak National government can well consider a second step towards the rehabilitation of economic life. The first step is obviously to secure the relief of the population in the vital foodstuffs, which is in progress. . . . It is impossible, however, to conceive that relief of this character can be carried on indefinitely, not only from the press of world finance but also from the transcendent necessity to return the population to productive labor. . . .

. . . My project is as follows:

1. That the Czecho-Slovak Government should organize an official commission, (or perhaps a corporation) comprised of leading commercial men of Czecho-Slovak nationality.

2. That this commission should establish its head office in Czecho-Slovakia, with branch offices at Trieste, (as soon as possible at Hamburg), in Paris, in London, in the United States and elsewhere, as occasion may develop.

3. That the Czecho-Slovak Government should open a credit in local currency to this commission and should, if possible, secure at least small initial credits in England, France and the United States as a basis of working capital for this commission.

4. That the commission should charter its own shipping for the movement of food supplies inward from overseas and for the movement of manufactured products outward from Czecho-Slovakia.

5. The commission, [should take over] . . . the advances being provided by the United States Government . . . purchase food supplies in the United States, transport . . . these food supplies into Czecho-Slovakia . . . [should] sell these . . . supplies to the population; with the funds thus secured . . . [the Commission] will be in position to purchase in Czecho-Slovakia various commodities for export. These commodities then sold in the markets of France, England and the United States and elsewhere will replenish the funds of the commission. Ultimately with the growth of export productivity, the commission should become self-supporting. . . .

During the period while the commission is establishing itself, the American Relief Administration will continue to function as at present, handing over its operations to the commission as rapidly as the development of the commission permits their absorption. There will thus be no interruption of the progress from economic illness to convalescence.

I earnestly commend the above project to . . . [your] Government for early consideration. I am fully aware of the perplexities of the tasks which confront . . . [you] at the present moment, but I believe that . . . [such organization will] expedite the rehabilitation of the economic life in Czecho-Slovakia. . . .

HERBERT HOOVER

Beneš merely acknowledged the letter. The Czechs would have avoided many troubles if they had taken this advice. All other states to whom I addressed this letter also acknowledged it.

TOTAL SUPPLIES TO CZECHOSLOVAKIA
FROM THE ARMISTICE TO THE PEACE *

	Food	Clothing & Misc.	Total	$ Value
American Relief Administration: †				
Children's relief	6,506	325	6,831	$ 2,261,230
General relief	311,361		311,361	56,699,512
Army surplus	34,500	5,850	40,350	19,098,874
American Red Cross		875	875	175,040
United Kingdom †	6,012	1,120	7,132	1,599,836
Aids from other quarters . . .				11,198
The barters yielded	143,462		143,462	26,058,350
	501,841	8,170	510,011	$105,904,040

* In tons.

† The American supplies, except for the children's relief and $33,000 paid in cash, were in the form of loans. The British supplies were also in this form. As was explained in the Introduction to this volume, the American supplies became a gift from the American taxpayer.

CHAPTER 12

AUSTRIA

Austria, at any odds, was the worst relief and reconstruction problem with which we had to deal. Austria was not a nation; she was a wreck. During the war, with her partners—Hungary and Germany —she had taken part in the invasions of Serbia, Rumania, Italy, and Russia and had certainly incurred a lasting hate from each of them.

Austria-Hungary's ancient provinces of Bohemia, Slovakia, Galicia, Croatia, Serbia, Montenegro, Herzegovina, and Transylvania, the Tyrol, and her Adriatic ports had been amputated at the Peace Conference. After these operations, Austria was left with a population of about 6,500,000 people, more than 2,500,000 of whom were living in the city of Vienna. That city had been the cultural, industrial, financial, railway, and trading center for 50,000,000 subject people and of many more in the Danube Basin. The dismemberment had left Austrian industries and export trade paralyzed. Because of the small agricultural area left to her, Austria was, except for imports, foodless for nine months of the year.

To the United States, Austria was an enemy country, and the Lodge amendment prevented charity, even for her debilitated and diseased children, from the $100,000,000 Congressional appropriation.

The day after I arrived in Europe, prayers for help from Vienna began to pour in upon us with vivid and pathetic details. We at once sent Dr. Alonzo Taylor to report. He said that even if all the harvest remaining in the hands of the comparatively few Austrian farmers were requisitioned as of January 1, it would not feed Vienna for three weeks—and there were eight months to go before the next harvest. He reported that the death rate had risen from 14 to 38 per 1,000 and that infant and child mortality was even worse. He estimated that, at the lowest ration in Europe, Austria would need 60,000 tons of breadstuffs and 5,000 tons of fats or dairy products monthly—a program that would cost about $20,000,000 monthly—until the Peace was signed, with no solution for her future supplies after that time.

Such was the scene when our mission arrived in Vienna. I appointed Captain T. T. C. Gregory, an able lawyer, head of the mission, with Lieutenant Gilchrist B. Stockton, Captain Clare M. Torrey, Captain F. Dorsey Stephens, John L. Simpson, and Dr. Raymond Geist as members of Captain Gregory's staff.

Elsewhere I have described the steps taken for immediate relief— which were mainly an allocation to us of $5,000,000 by President Wilson from his unrestricted funds.[1] Captain Gregory found in the Vienna banks some negotiable securities, from which, at his urging, the Austrian Government realized $4,642,723 and handed it over to us. This and the $5,000,000 Presidential fund started a stream of food into Austria from our cargoes in Trieste in late December, 1918; but these funds were only a drop in the bucket for Austria's needs.

On December 19, 1918, we invited the British, French, and Italian representatives to join us in meeting with an Austrian delegation at Berne, Switzerland, to consider financial measures for Austrian supplies. The meeting began on December 24, with Dr. Taylor, Captain Gregory, and Hugh Gibson representing us. At the end of the third day, Dr. Taylor reported to me the conferees' estimates of possible assets with which Austria could pay for food. They catalogued these as (1) the Austrian claim on part of the gold reserve of the old Austrian National Bank, the total of which was about $50,000,000 and which the Hungarians had taken away and would not give up; (2) the possible sale of art treasures; (3) possible loans from Neutral countries; and (4) the possible sale of Austria's refugee cargo ships.

[1] *An American Epic*, Vol. II, Chap. 37.

The essential paragraphs of Dr. Taylor's report on the conference were:

1. That the British refuse to allow the Austrians to sell an Austrian boat or exchange a boat for wheat, on the grounds that it is the British policy of indemnity to claim ton for ton in repair of sinkings by submarines. 2. It is obviously and openly the policy of the Italian Government to prevent the use of Austrian gold, securities or valuables on any account for the purchase of wheat, on the grounds that this will minimize Austria's power to pay indemnity to Italy. I cannot refrain from the observation that the Austrian delegates understand this position of the Italians, and the tendency of both parties is, therefore, to force the Americans into a corner to loan to Austria-Hungary in order that she may be fed on the humanitarian side . . . [while] on the indemnity side Italy's interests are maintained intact. I have taken the liberty of explaining to the Italians the exact meaning of their position and have tried to induce them to see that one cannot take one's cake and eat it at the same time.

. . . The Austrians request specifically that they be given permission to open negotiations with Spain and in the United Kingdom, France and in the United States for the purpose of obtaining dollars, which they profess to be able to obtain up to a certain figure, though they stated frankly at the last conference that only a loan could carry them over until the new harvest.

Hungary has grain. . . . [She] is at present offering . . . [it] to Switzerland in exchange for textiles. Hungary could probably be forced to send grain to Vienna. Hungary's statement is that they have supplied Austria with 37,000 tons of flour in the last three months [which was completely false]. I have talked with Madame Schwimmer [2] and she does not deny Hungary's power to give a certain amount of cereals, indeed a large amount, but states that, as long as Hungary is being encroached upon from four directions, she cannot be expected to strip herself of foodstuffs. . . .

TAYLOR

THE BLOCKADE

This series has already dealt with the problems of the Allied blockade. Simply to show that we Americans were not idle in this

[2] Madame Rosika Schwimmer, the Hungarian Minister to Switzerland.

matter, I may relate that either Vance McCormick or I protested and demanded relaxations for Austria during at least twelve meetings of the various Allied councils.

On March 29, 1919, Mr. McCormick's diary showed the first signs of daylight. He stated:

Meeting. . . . 10:30 Blockade Council. Fixed dates of announcement for relaxation of blockade Poland, Esthonia and Austria. Hard fight on suspending black list. All against me but will bring it up at Supreme Economic Council. I will not take the responsibility of economic chaos in world due to artificial restrictions. . . .

Finally, on April 2, nearly five months after the Armistice, good sense prevailed; Austria was allowed to import raw materials and to export goods.

GENERAL RELIEF

One great aid to the general relief of Austria was the exchange of commodities and services between Austria and her neighboring states. Austria collected freight charges over her railways; she had machinery to sell from her idle factories; she had surplus railway rolling stock; her factories, although hobbled by the blockade, produced substantial amounts of goods; and she had a great stock of munitions and military equipment which her neighbors needed for their defense or their wars of aggression. Our missions did not hesitate to use any of these assets which would produce necessary supplies.

Our missions in Austria and Czechoslovakia initiated exchanges between these states—mostly coal and sugar from Czechoslovakia and munitions, arms, and railway rolling stock valued at $9,914,858 [3] from Austria. Our missions also initiated barters between Italy and Austria valued at $18,856,872, and Italy contributed $2,021,250 for freight. The barters between Yugoslavia and Austria amounted to $2,464,561; between Hungary and Austria, $805,063; between Poland and Austria, $204,896; and between the Netherlands and Aus-

[3] These dollar values are based on a conversion of the local currency into dollars at local rates of exchange.

tria, $112,400. Sundry other exchanges were arranged, these amounting to $23,308.

Switzerland, on her own initiative, carried out barters of food for Austrian goods amounting to $1,529,537.

Britain furnished $1,916,640 worth of supplies and $4,760,000 for overseas transport for future payment. France, likewise, furnished $4,500,000 worth of transport.

Norway made a gift in the amount of $4,980.

FINANCE

As I have stated, we started Austrian relief with two funds of $5,000,000 and $4,642,723. I have already described the arrangement we set up by which the United States would lend to Britain, France, and Italy $30,000,000 each, which amounts these countries would then lend Austria to be administered by our organization.[4] We used less than $50,000,000 of the $90,000,000, and the Allies never repaid the loans to the United States.

However, that this arrangement was not without conditions is indicated by the following minutes of the Supreme War Council at a meeting on March 5, 1919:

. . . That as security for such credits the Austrian Government should formally agree to place at the disposal of a Commission or Commissioners representative of the three leading powers a suitable lien on (a) the salt mines in Austria, (b) the properties of the City of Vienna, and (c) such other assets as may be agreed upon, in Austria, immediate steps being taken in the case of the salt mines to clear these mines of all prior claims. . . .

. . . That the repayment of such credits be a first charge on the future resources of Austria, ranking in front of any payment for reparation. . . .

Despite these precautions, Austria was not able to repay loans to anybody.

[4] *An American Epic*, Vol. II, Chap. 37.

REHABILITATION OF AUSTRIAN CHILDREN

Because of the appalling situation among the Austrian children, we started our canteen system of rehabilitation early in January, 1919, with President Wilson's fund and the securities discovered by Captain Gregory. When the funds through Allied loans became available, we expanded the program with great rapidity, serving a total of more than 400,000 children.

The highly skilled physicians of Vienna greatly aided the relief organization. They developed a series of simple tests based on weight, height, and symptoms to determine the degree of under-nourishment. We adopted these tests in all of our European child-feeding operations.

Colonel A. J. Carlson, chief of our children's-rehabilitation division in Paris, reported after an inspection trip in Austria in early July:

. . . In every place the food was most excellently prepared and the premises a model of neatness, cleanliness, and order. The meals served average about six hundred fifty (650) calories per day. Our own officers, as well as the Austrian officials, report a marked improvement already in the children as a result of the feeding. At the present time fully eighty (80) per cent of the children fed are distinctly under-nourished, and an unusually high percentage of the children are stunted in growth. The degree of stunted growth varies from one to three years, so that children at the age of eight have the height and appearance of children of five. This fact shows that the under-nourishment of these children has virtually extended for the whole period of the War. . . .

RELIEF OF INTELLECTUALS

During the Armistice period, our organization started a relief program for intellectuals with a contribution from the Commonwealth Fund of $200,000. In the section of this memoir dealing with relief after the signing of Peace, I give a full description of this undertaking.[5]

[5] See Chap. 43.

AIDS OF AMERICAN CHARITABLE AGENCIES

The substantial support of the American Red Cross began after the Peace, and is therefore recorded in the second section of this volume.

Prior to the Armistice, the Jewish Joint Distribution Committee was concerned with the protection and relief of its co-religionists. With the triumph of the Allies, all major persecutions of the Jews were ended instantly. The Committee turned its program in Austria toward restoring normal conditions in agriculture and industry and also toward the repatriation of refugees. It did not confine its efforts to Jews, but contributed largely to the other organizations which were giving food, medical aid, and clothing.

The J.D.C.'s expenditures prior to the Peace cannot be broken down for Austria alone. Under the title "Austria-Hungary," it shows expenditures of $2,881,591 from November, 1914, to the end of December, 1919. From our staff information and for statistical purposes, we have estimated the Committee's expenditures for Austria (prior to the Peace) to be $1,500,000.

TROUBLES WITH THE COMMUNISTS

As I pore over the thousands of telegrams, letters, and reports in our Austrian files, I find the words "hate," "Communist," and "Bolshevism" always looming in the background of discussion. The relief was indeed a race against both death and Communism.

Bela Kun had headed a Communist seizure of Hungary on March 22, 1919. Immediately thereafter, he extended his services to Austria, as a conspirator, and expended some of the Hungarian National Bank gold, which he had seized. The Austrian authorities notified us that May 1 had been fixed by the Communists as zero hour for the overthrow of the Austrian Government. We authorized them to post city walls with a proclamation saying:

Any disturbance of public order will render food shipments impossible and bring Vienna face to face with absolute famine.

HERBERT HOOVER

May 1 came and went quietly.

TOTAL SUPPLIES TO AUSTRIA
FROM THE ARMISTICE TO THE PEACE *

	Food	Clothing & Misc.	Total	$ Value
American Relief Administration:				
Children's relief	8,282		8,282	$ 3,167,365
General relief	354,164		354,164	51,293,470
(Including Joint Allied Loans and freight from A.R.A.)				
Jewish Joint Distribution Committee †	(quantities unknown)			1,500,000
Norway (gift)				4,980
United Kingdom	11,500	6,500	18,000	1,916,640
Transportation expenses provided by:				
United Kingdom				4,760,000
France				4,500,000
Italy				2,021,250
Barters initiated by American missions ‡	161,685	26,946	188,631	33,911,495
	535,631	33,446	569,077	$103,075,200

* In tons.
† Total also includes some contributions prior to the Armistice.
‡ Here is a breakdown of the barters initiated by American missions (in tons):

	Food	Clothing & Misc.	Total	$ Value
Czechoslovakia	39,873	23,025	62,898	$ 9,914,858
Denmark	19		19	10,108
Germany	330		330	13,200
Hungary	8,878		8,878	805,063
Italy	64,061		64,061	18,856,872
The Netherlands	2,810		2,810	112,400
Poland	105	3,921	4,026	204,896
Switzerland	11,723		11,723	1,529,537
Yugoslavia	33,886		33,886	2,464,561
	161,685	26,946	188,631	$33,911,495

Except for the realization of Austrian securities, amounting to $4,642,723, the whole of American expenditures was a gift to Austria, as is explained in the Introduction to this chapter. The relief of Austria had to be continued after the Peace, the burden of which was carried mainly by the charitable organizations, and will be recorded in a later chapter.

CHAPTER 13

HUNGARY

Defeat in modern war means more than surrender of a sword. Defeated Hungary, after her surrender in November, 1918, presented a sort of unending, formless procession of tragedies with occasional comic relief. Across our American efforts in relief and reconstruction marched revolution, Socialism, Communism, terror, wanton executions, murder, suicide, falling ministries, the revival of imperialism, invading armies, medieval looting—all against a constant backdrop of threatening starvation.

Added to these woes was the Allies' natural dislike for Hungary—for her part in starting the war and her conduct during those four years. Besides this unfriendly atmosphere, there were the hates of the peoples that Hungary, together with Austria, had oppressed for centuries. The Poles, Czechoslovaks, Rumanians, and all the southern Slavs which made up Yugoslavia had little reason for sympathy with her plight, and, in fact, hate and revenge were the current bases of their statecraft.

Hungary had five revolutions during the Armistice period while we were trying to feed her capital city. At the Armistice, the Hapsburgs had been dethroned and a republic proclaimed. A parliamentary government was established under the presidency of Count Michael Károlyi. He was not a strong man. He had been a liberal thinker on paper but not a man of action. His appeals to the Allies for consideration of Hungary's new conversion from imperialism received little sympathy.

In February, 1919, the Peace Conference announced preliminary boundaries for Hungary, giving Czechoslovakia, Yugoslavia, and Rumania chunks of undoubtedly Hungarian population, which seriously denuded her industrial and agricultural resources. Károlyi appealed to us for food for Budapest, whose children were in great distress.

We had no finances for food, since Hungary was an enemy state and therefore not eligible for loans from the United States Treasury. Nor, because of the Lodge amendment, could we use any of the $100,000,000 Congressional appropriation—even for children. However, as I have mentioned, the Hungarians had taken possession of the old Austrian National Bank gold reserves of about $50,000,000. Károlyi arranged to pay in gold the amount necessary for us to set up our canteen system for children and to provide supplies for hospitals. We were also in the midst of completing a purchase of wheat for Hungary from a corner of Yugoslavia—the Banat—which, because of transportation problems, could not reach that country.

We had just started from Trieste to Budapest twenty-five carloads of food for the children. Apparently, at this time Károlyi got the notion that should the country go Communist, it would frighten the Peace Conference into reconsidering his claims. Whether or not this was the case, the Communists had no difficulty in taking over his government.

Bela Kun, as a Hungarian prisoner of war in Russia, had been indoctrinated in Moscow. Financed by confiscated Czarist gold, he had been sent back to his native land to conspire against the government. On March 22, 1919, he seized power from Károlyi without friction and installed the usual Soviet forms and practices. He inaugurated a Red terror, with a typically sadistic liquidation of some 2,000 people without semblance of trial, and decreed the seizure of all private property.

The Big Four had imposed a tight blockade on Hungary after the Communist Revolution and the French officials in charge refused to permit our food train from Trieste to pass through, although our mission had arranged with Bela Kun that the distribution would be conducted under our organization. I appealed to President Wilson for help. On April 3, he arranged with Premier Clemenceau that an order be issued to allow our food train to pass. We continued for a while, but under great difficulties, for Bela Kun was arresting, and in some cases executing, the Hungarian leaders of our distribution committees. On April 15, I transmitted to the President the following telegram from Captain Gregory, who managed our Hungarian activities from Vienna:

Trains of food recently held up by the French arrived yesterday Budapest. Created most favorable feeling for Americans as demonstrating their integrity in carrying out their engagements, more particularly among the anti-Bolshevik labor element in Budapest.

We had other problems with Bela Kun. Certain railway connections from the Adriatic to Czechoslovakia and Poland passed through his realm, and he was soon at war with the Czechs. If these states were not to starve, we had to secure some railway co-operation from him. Captain Gregory proposed an agreement with Kun by which he would permit us to operate our trains over the Hungarian lines and we would sell him some food. That would require action by the Big Four in relaxation of the blockade. On April 15, I wrote Mr. Wilson:

DEAR MR. PRESIDENT:

I regret the necessity to trouble you to secure the approval of the three premiers to a short statement that I desire to make to the Hungarian Government . . . vital to the relief of Central Europe.

After explaining our dilemmas, I continued:

. . . I propose to complete the negotiations with the Hungarian [Communist] Government as to transportation and supply of food with the preliminary announcement on the following lines:

The proposed economic arrangement with the . . . [Relief] Administration as to railway transportation and food supplies for Hungary is provisional and purely humanitarian and has no relationship to the settlement of any political questions.

. . . the Associated Governments will for the present . . . advance food supplies for such services and funds as may be acceptable to the . . . [Relief] Administration. . . .

The matter is of urgent character and it is impossible for anyone to agree to the political issue involved except yourself and the three premiers. Any amount of discussion between the members of the bodies in which I sit cannot possibly result in other than a reference to yourself in the end. . . .

The President answered my letter the same day in his own handwriting as follows:

MY DEAR HOOVER:

The Four this morning approved the enclosed plan and I beg that you will proceed with it.

W. W.

Day by day, at the President's request, I transmitted to him accounts from Captain Gregory of Bela Kun's progress.

Kun was a busy man. He mobilized a considerable army under the command of a General Boehm and officers of the old regime. His army occupied an area of Czechoslovakia, and he threatened to do the same in Rumania. He bought some arms from Italian army officers with the National Bank's gold and in his spare time used some of this gold to subsidize Communist conspiracies in Austria.

In their retreat after the Armistice, the Hungarian and German armies had plundered Rumania unmercifully, helping themselves to food, household goods, farm machinery, and nearly all of her railway rolling stock.

On May 2, Rumania advanced her armies over the Hungarian border, demanding return of this loot, but they were stopped by order of the Allies. We continued to supply food to Hungary, under our agreement, until July 1, at which time the harvest would be sufficient for Hungarian needs.

AMERICAN CHARITABLE AGENCIES

We have been unable to learn the details of aid to Hungary by the American Red Cross, but its accounts reveal an expenditure of $22,917 for Austria-Hungary from 1914 to 1918.

The Jewish Joint Distribution Committee was a major contributor in the relief of Austria-Hungary from early 1915 until February, 1917, when the United States broke off relations with the Central Powers. Up to that time, the J.D.C. provided great aid to the refugees clogging the large cities, particularly Budapest and Vienna. It provided medical allowances, clothing, money for food, and emergency barracks for shelter; potatoes and other foodstuffs and wood for fuel were distributed; people's kitchens and tearooms were set up; special shelters housed orphans; rabbis, teachers, students and schools were given direct financial help. After the Armistice, the J.D.C. resumed its activities. From 1915 to the Peace, its accounts cannot be broken down, but they reveal an expenditure of $2,881,591 for the relief of Austria-Hungary, including Galicia. For statistical purposes, I have estimated the expenditure of the J.D.C. for Hungary prior to the Peace as $1,381,591.

TOTAL SUPPLIES TO HUNGARY
FROM THE ARMISTICE TO THE PEACE *

	Food	Clothing & Misc.	Total	$ Value
American Relief Administration:				
Supplies sold for Hungarian gold	319		319	$245,520
American Red Cross †	(quantities unknown)			22,917
Jewish Joint Distribution Committee †	(quantities unknown)			1,381,591
	319		319	$1,650,028

* In tons.
† Total includes some contributions prior to the Armistice.

Shortly after the Peace, a full invasion came from Rumania with further drama and miseries. I record these events in the part of this memoir which deals with the period following the signing of the Peace.[1]

[1] See Chap. 44.

CHAPTER 14

BULGARIA

Bulgaria organized a republic three days after her surrender in 1918. Because of the war and a bad harvest, decreased production had left this normally surplus-food–producing country in difficulties. Early in January, 1919, through the American Minister at Sofia, the Bulgarians presented an urgent appeal to us for food, and our staff in Constantinople confirmed that the townspeople were suffering greatly.

Bulgaria, as a former enemy, was not eligible for relief under the Lodge amendment or from U.S. Treasury loans. However, she had a gold reserve of about $30,000,000, some negotiable securities in her banks, and a considerable surplus of tobacco and other non-food commodities, which she could export. Therefore, in response to American Chargé d'Affaires Charles S. Wilson's urging that we aid the feeble republic, we cabled him that we would place 10,000 tons of food at the Bulgarians' disposal, saying:

> . . . Bulgaria should deposit with you at once a sum in gold or American exchange amounting to two million two hundred thousand dollars, to cover this shipment. It is our view that we should make wheat flour in this quantity available in Constantinople and that the Bulgarian Government should arrange transportation from that point. . . .
>
> HERBERT HOOVER

However, the French authorities objected to Bulgaria's parting with her gold, demanding that it be used for reparations. I urged

French Minister of Commerce Clémentel to relax their opposition. He replied:

PARIS, 15 January 1919

DEAR MR. HOOVER,

Thank you for your letter of January 14. . . .

As for . . . Sofia, as our Treasuries have not yet agreed . . . I [will] transmit this [letter] . . . to Mr. Klotz and will let you know his advice as soon as I hear from him.

I deem it advisable to point out to you that, according to my information, the United States is said to have bought enormous quantities of Bulgarian tobacco, which could perhaps be used in exchange for contemplated supplies, thus avoiding diminishing the . . . [gold] of Bulgaria, which are the common guarantee of the Allies. . . .

CLÉMENTEL

For a minister of commerce, this seemed somewhat lacking in information about commerce. The United States, being the greatest tobacco-producing country in the world, would hardly be purchasing much of it from Bulgaria.

Our difficulty in Bulgaria is further indicated in a letter I wrote to Norman Davis, our Treasury representative in Paris:

PARIS, 26 February 1919

MY DEAR DAVIS:

. . . The Bulgarians are starving. The French military authorities are demanding that they have food; the French civil authorities prevent the Bulgarians from using the gold and negotiable securities which they own. . . . I can see no reason why Bulgaria should not be allowed to trade her securities.

HERBERT HOOVER

I had to appeal to the Big Four over the heads of the French. The Big Four finally agreed that we could take gold in payment, but we were so delayed that it was not until March 28 that Howard Heinz, chief of our mission at Constantinople, was able to arrange to begin delivery of 22,862 tons of flour worth $4,856,647. He had the Bulgarian gold placed upon an American destroyer at Constantinople. In due time, the destroyer was ordered home, and we arranged that it should take the gold along. The gold realized $5,210,357. We returned the balance to the Bulgarian Government.

Some months later, I was astonished to learn that the Food Administration, and/or I, was being sued for a percentage of the Bulgarian gold in the name of the captain and crew of the destroyer which had transported it to the United States. They were proceeding under a law, some one hundred years old, which provided that "valuables" could be transported in American war vessels if a toll were payable to its human complement. Robert Taft defended us and won judgment in the lower courts and finally in the Supreme Court on the ground that the law did not apply to Government "valuables." In any event, the food had long been delivered and was sufficient to get the Bulgarians through to the next harvest without further loss of life.

Certain American charities had taken an interest in Bulgaria. The Jewish Joint Distribution Committee expended a total of $26,000 in Bulgaria and Occupied Serbia from 1914 to December 1918 in protection and relief of its co-religionists. The American Red Cross expended $6,000 prior to the United States' entry into the war. Its accounts carry an item of $5,250,995 appropriated for the Balkan States during the Armistice period, part of which may have been expended in Bulgaria. Bulgaria also shared, with nine other countries, an expenditure of $402,369 from January 1 to June 30, 1917.

SUPPLIES TO BULGARIA

FROM THE ARMISTICE TO THE PEACE *

	Food	Clothing & Misc.	Total	$ Value
American Relief Administration:				
General relief	22,862		22,862	$4,856,647

* In tons.

CHAPTER 15

YUGOSLAVIA

The conquests of the armies of Serbia, the revolutions of the Slav states from the old Austrian empire, and the decisions of the Peace Conference unified the southern Slavs for the first time in hundreds of years. From Serbia, with 33,891 square miles of territory and 4,500,000 people, and from twelve states comprising 64,493 square miles and over 8,200,000 people, the new kingdom of Yugoslavia sprang up. Some of the population figures given below are estimates, but the table illustrates the composition of the new state:

	Area in Sq. Miles	Population
Serbia	33,891	4,500,000
Montenegro	5,603	400,000
Annexed from the old Austrian empire:		
Bosnia and Herzegovina	19,768	2,000,000
Slavic Carinthia	900	85,000
Slavic Styria	3,000	450,000
Carniola	3,845	524,000
Dalmatia	4,956	655,000
Croatia and Slavonia	16,421	2,680,000
Banat, Batchka and Baranya	10,000	1,500,000
Total	98,384	12,794,000

None of these states except Serbia had experienced either battle or devastation by enemy armies. When the armies of Germany, Hungary, and Austria retreated from the Russian front, these southern Slavs were regarded as part of the Austrian empire and were not looted. They not only had sufficient food supplies, but in the Banat there was a substantial surplus.

Serbia had been ravished by invading and retreating armies time and again. Her people were starving, destitute, and afflicted by typhus. The death of her men in battles of defense had left her with a horde of widows and orphans.

RELIEF OF YUGOSLAVIA

On December 15, 1918, I enlisted Colonel William G. Atwood of the Army Engineers to head our mission to Yugoslavia, and we sent along one of our best old Belgian hands, John L. Simpson, as his assistant in charge of the children's relief. Subsequently, we needed Colonel Atwood in Paris; we then assigned Major W. B. Ryan temporarily to Belgrade and by March, 1919, placed Simpson in charge. The staff included:

MR. JOHN A. CHUMBLEY, *Assistant* (January–July, 1919)
LIEUTENANT COLONEL ANTON J. CARLSON, *Director, Children's Relief* (January–March, 1919)
  He was succeeded by:
    MAJOR FRANK C. GEPHART (April–June, 1919)
    LIEUTENANT AUSTIN A. HOWE (June–July, 1919)
    MAJOR DAVID KLEIN (July–August, 1919)
    CAPTAIN MOWATT M. MITCHELL
MAJOR ALVA E. McKENNET, *Railroad Transportation*
CAPTAIN OSCAR L. CARSON, *Communications* (May–July, 1919)
    CAPTAIN HUBERT S. TURNER, *Successor*
    LIEUTENANT L. W. CAPSER, *Successor*
MAJOR F. E. LAWRENCE, *Port Operations*
    LIEUTENANT ORVILLE C. BELL, JR., *Assistant*
LIEUTENANT CHARLES B. McDANIELS, *Monetary Remittances to Individuals*
LIEUTENANT CHARLES E. FOX, *First Financial Officer*
    LIEUTENANT DORR K. TAYLOR, *Successor*

I have recorded the operation of the railways in Southeastern Europe under Colonel W. B. Causey and the assignment to us of a place for our operations in the ports of Trieste, Fiume, and Cattaro.[1] Colonel J. W. McIntosh was in charge of our port operations.

FINANCE

Serbia, as a nation which had been at war against the Central Powers, was eligible for loans from the United States Treasury to pay for our supplies. I have mentioned President Wilson's directive to the Secretary of the Treasury on December 16, 1918, to advance us $35,000,000.[2] We used only $13,191,246 for overseas supplies from the United States. To avoid transportation costs, we drew heavily on supplies from United States Army surplus, and our relief missions were able to obtain a considerable amount of supplies through barter with Yugoslavia's neighbors.

With the enactment of the $100,000,000 appropriation by Congress at the end of February, 1919, we undertook more systematic rehabilitation of subnormal children—a gift to the people of Yugoslavia.

The major burden of relief of Yugoslavia fell upon the United States and Great Britain. The American official agencies furnished 86,927 tons of supplies valued at $33,736,578. The British official agencies furnished 33,655 tons of supplies, which included 19,567 tons of food and 14,088 tons of clothing, valued at $9,261,532. They gave additional aid in transportation; this amounted to $373,660.

SUPPLIES BY BARTER

The Banat surplus was isolated from Serbia by the fragmentation of the old Austrian railway system. The traditional recipients of the Banat's surplus were neighboring Hungary, Austria, and Czecho-

[1] *An American Epic,* Vol. II, Chap. 43.
[2] *Ibid.,* Chap. 31.

slovakia. Our missions worked out a plan by which the Banat supplies were divided among three other countries in exchange for their commodities. It took much patient negotiation, since hate was the dominant emotion in these neighborhoods—and it was quite vocal. The trades included coal and sugar to Yugoslavia from Czechoslovakia in exchange for food from the Banat, the sale of Banat food to Hungary for gold, and its exchange to Austria for manufactured goods and railway rolling stock.

As a consideration for the Yugoslav Government's consent to this setup by our organization, we agreed to supply Serbia and Montenegro with overseas provisions through Adriatic ports.

Another of the results of truncation of the old railway system was the isolation of the districts around Nish along the Bulgarian frontier. On February 22, 1919, Mr. Heinz telegraphed me from Constantinople:

. . . there is an acute shortage of all food stuffs especially of flour, the Bulgarians having carried off almost all of the wheat with the result that there is great destitution and misery among the inhabitants of this district. . . . Milk for the children seems to be as necessary in this district as flour and it would appear also that some seed grain will be required this spring. Meat is more plentiful than any other food because of lack of fodder which is causing the killing off of . . . cattle. Clothing is another of the great needs . . . it being stated that newborn babes are wrapped in paper for want of the necessary clothing. Other supplies needed are soap and medicines. Illness is said to be prevalent, due to the famine conditions in which the people have been living and typhus is spreading. . . . Apparently the greatest difficulty in reaching the suffering regions of Serbia will be the matter of transportation the railroads having been almost entirely destroyed by the Bulgarians in their retreat while the highways are so bad and the distances so great that automobiles and motor trucks cannot be operated efficiently. . . .

We arranged to supply this area from Salonika under the supervision of our Constantinople office. The British also contributed generously to this area from their military stocks in Greece.

CARE OF DEBILITATED CHILDREN

In the Balkan Wars a few years previously and in World War I, it was estimated that Serbia alone had lost half her male population and that in the new state there were more than 500,000 fatherless children.

Our chief of mission, John Simpson, from his Belgian experience, began to organize our canteen and orphan support as soon as the $100,000,000 appropriation from Congress became evident. He labored under many difficulties for lack of capable native organization and local personnel. However, he soon was serving from canteens some 300,000 children, expectant mothers, and the aged and was supplying a host of children in orphanages with food and clothing.

We shipped overseas 3,445 tons of special food and clothing and purchased considerable local supplies. The expenditures, which were a gift from the American people, were—prior to the Peace—$1,035,407.

CLOTHING

During Colonel Atwood's term as chief of our mission, he wrote to me:

1. The need for clothing in the whole of Serbia is really more urgent than that of food. As I remember requests had been made by the Serbian Government for clothing. . . . Nothing has been heard by the Serbian Government regarding clothing from any source.

2. There is some typhus in Belgrade and there are no clothes available to permit disinfection and the issue of new clothing. Most of the old . . . [clothes] will not stand disinfection. A part of these supplies would be issued as charity by the government and a part sold in the same manner as the food.

3. The Red Cross have a very small supply of summer clothing which is necessarily for charity use, while some very urgent cases of need are people who can and are perfectly willing to pay. . . .

We solved the major clothing problem by securing 15,550 tons from American Army surplus. This, together with the distribution of 667 tons given by the American Red Cross and 166 tons from the United States Treasury loan, totaled 16,383 tons of clothing and miscellaneous supplies. The British contribution was 14,088 tons, making a grand total of 30,471 tons of clothing and miscellaneous supplies. Many American charitable agencies also contributed clothing but we have no record of the amounts.

A TOUCH OF HUMOR

Amid all the tragedies and our difficulties, there was little to laugh about. But a spark of humor did fly from the Italian-Yugoslav frictions.

A fight broke out between Montenegrin troops and purported Italian-subsidized mercenaries. Some months after this "war," a first lieutenant on our Montenegrin staff asked for special leave to come to our Paris office on an urgent personal matter. When he arrived, Lewis Strauss, my invaluable secretary, came to me and urged that I listen to the lieutenant with a straight face. The officer, an upstanding, earnest American, told me that he and two sergeants with two trucks of food, had come under fire on the mountain road from Cattaro to the capital of Montenegro. He had stopped, investigated, and made contact with the general of the army at hand and through his interpreter expressed wonder and indignation that the general did not know that an armistice was on and the war over. He found that the general liked neither his war nor his own military situation. Our American offered to negotiate an armistice. It was promptly accepted.

With his interpreter and a guide, our peacemaker made his way around the mountain trails to the headquarters of the opposing army. He found the same attitude in the commanding general there and a welcome acceptance of his offer to negotiate an armistice. All of that part was easy, but neither side would surrender to the other or admit defeat. Being of a direct mind, the lieutenant decided to draw up in writing a surrender of each general and his army to the

United States of America, but when he came to put it down on paper he grew fearful that he was taking responsibilities on behalf of his government that were far beyond his powers and that he might involve the United States in some dire political consequences. He finally solved the problem by making out the surrender to me as United States Food Administrator. In military tradition he demanded a formal surrender of the generals' swords and, remembering General Grant, allowed the men to keep their horses and small arms—everything except machine guns and artillery.

Our staff at Cattaro was short of labor needed to unload a ship in the harbor, so it occurred to the lieutenant to offer a wage in flour and bacon if one of the armies would help unload it. This was promptly accepted, and he marched them down the mountain to the harbor under the command of one of his sergeants. Then the other army, hearing of this, also wanted a job. So our staff put one army on the night shift and one on the day shift, and they got along all right. There were about 300 soldiers on each side.

When the lieutenant thought all of this over, he became greatly worried for fear that he had used my name wrongly. He fretted for weeks and resolved to come to Paris to explain it all and take whatever was coming to him. He was plainly anxious. Without even a smile, I asked him what had become of the two swords. He said that he had brought them along with the idea that if he were sent home he would want them as souvenirs. I told him that if he gave me one and kept the other for himself, I would take all the responsibilities for his actions off his shoulders. He was relieved. Lewis got him a week's leave from the Army, and I wrote him a note to say that he was of the stuff that had made America great.

The lieutenant and his superior officer at Cattaro, Major Gallagher, both told me of the large amount of lire in the pockets of the mercenaries who had been on the Italian side.

RED CROSS RELIEF EFFORTS

The American Red Cross had established a medical relief program in Serbia in 1914 to serve her countrymen wounded at the time of the Austrian invasion and occupation. Its services during this time included the establishment of three hospitals, an organized attack on typhus and cholera epidemics, and the importation of agricultural implements, seed, and food for Belgrade.

At the Armistice, the Red Cross continued its widespread medical service in Yugoslavia. The services included the creation and support of hospitals, clinics, and medical aid generally through teams of physicians, nurses, and sanitary engineers, all of whom played major roles in stamping out contagious diseases.

The following expenditures were made by the Red Cross in Yugoslavia up to the Peace:

Montenegro	$ 1,095
Serbia and Montenegro (1915)	117
Serbia	1,616,349
	$1,617,561
Clothing (distributed by A.R.A.) ..	224,800
	$1,842,361

In addition to these funds, Red Cross records indicate an appropriation of $5,250,995 for aid to the Balkan States during the Armistice period, but it is impossible to determine what part of this amount was designated for Yugoslavia.

RELIEF FROM OTHER ORGANIZATIONS

Before the Peace, the Jewish Joint Distribution Committee undertook rehabilitation of agriculture, the creation of work enterprises, and training in new occupations, not only to Jewish sufferers and refugees, but to those of other religious faiths. It is not possible from its accounts to segregate what was spent on Yugoslavia.

The Christian Science War Relief Committee gave a small amount of money and knitted garments to the Serbian Relief Committee.

In January, 1919, the Methodist Episcopal Church shipped one ton of sugar and 28,000 cans of evaporated milk to Yugoslavia.

The Rockefeller Foundation donated $163,894 to the American Red Cross for relief in Serbia in 1915 and 1916.

We are unable to obtain an exact figure for the expenditures of all of the American charitable organizations working in Yugoslavia during the period prior to the Peace, but their contributions were considerable. For our purposes, I have estimated them to be $2,500,000. (This includes the additional Red Cross expenditures which were distributed directly by it.)

TOTAL SUPPLIES TO YUGOSLAVIA
FROM THE ARMISTICE TO THE PEACE *

	Food	Clothing & Misc.	Total	$ Value
American Relief Administration:				
Children's relief	3,376	69	3,445	$ 1,035,407
General relief	54,911	166	55,077	13,191,246
Army surplus	16,300	15,550	31,850	20,464,191
American Red Cross		667	667	224,800
Other American charitable organizations †	(quantities unknown)			2,500,000
United Kingdom .... (supplies and freight)	19,567	14,088	33,655	9,635,192
	94,154	30,540	124,694	$47,050,836

* In tons.
† Total includes some contributions prior to the Armistice.

The expenditures of the official United States agencies, other than the children's relief and the gifts of American charities, were made in the form of loans to the Yugoslav Government. As explained in the Introduction to this volume, the whole sum was a gift to the people of Yugoslavia. Our records do not show what the British obtained in repayment of loans—probably little or nothing.

The relief of Yugoslavia prior to the Peace may be summed up as costing the American taxpayers and their subscriptions to American charities about $38,000,000. But the lives saved, the suffering relieved, the children restored to mental and physical health, a nation given stability and courage—these things cannot be measured in dollars. It is a part of a great epic in American history.

CHAPTER 16

RUMANIA

Rumania entered the war on the Allied side in August, 1916. As the price for coming into it, she was to receive slices of territory from neighboring Hungary and Bulgaria. The military strategy developed in the summer of 1916 was for Rumania and Russia to attack the Central Powers from the East simultaneously, with a great Allied assault from the West. But the Germans, Hungarians, and Bulgarians promptly defeated Rumania's armies and occupied most of her territory, taking Bucharest within sixty days. The great Allied attacks from the West were repulsed with huge losses. Rumania surrendered to Germany and Austria in March, 1918.

The German, Hungarian, and Bulgarian armies unmercifully plundered the country, not only during their invasion and occupation, but especially in their retreat at the Armistice. Their loot included all the food they could find, 80 per cent of Rumania's animals, most of the agricultural implements, and even much household furniture. Never in all history had there been such gigantic theft of railway rolling stock. The plunderers left only sixty-two workable locomotives and a few thousand cars to serve sixteen million people.

At the surrender of the Central Powers, the Rumanian monarchy was restored, with a weak king and a strong, British-born queen. With French aid, Rumania at once began to rebuild an army, and with this and Allied decisions at the Peace Conference, she doubled her former territory. She annexed Transylvania from Hungary, Bessarabia from Russia, and part of the Banat from Yugoslavia. Thus Rumania expanded from an area of 53,000 square miles before the war to about 100,000, and from a population of 7,500,000 to over 16,000,000.

On December 18, 1918, about a month after the Armistice, the American, British, and French Ministers at Bucharest cabled their governments, urging immediate food, clothing, and medical supplies. They added warnings of mushrooming Communist conspiracies. On December 23, they again cabled, even more urgently. On December 27, I received the following cable from the American Minister in Bucharest:

. . . I beg to again plead for Roumania where, unless immediate help is received, hunger will most certainly press within 30 days. . . .

Thirty days was a long time in our relief life and ample time in which to turn around. At once we ordered two of our cargoes already in the Mediterranean to proceed to Constanta on the Black Sea, and the British added two cargoes then en route to the United Kingdom through the Suez Canal. All these cargoes—carrying about 27,000 tons of supplies—arrived in time to relieve the starvation threat.

On January 10, 1919, we directed Captain Joseph C. Green, who was one of our able former C.R.B. hands, to be chief of our mission, with an adequate staff to take charge of our operations in Rumania. They reached Bucharest early in February. Shortly thereafter we established our mission at Constantinople under Howard Heinz to expedite supplies to the Black Sea and the Eastern Mediterranean. Just a few scraps from the dispatches of these men are poignant enough:

. . . the most starved looking lot of people I have seen in Europe. The women and children for the most part are without shoes and stockings, everyone had patched ragged clothing. . . . All of them complained that their children had died for lack of food. . . . I visited many homes or hovels. . . . I found no food. . . . Cattle, pigs, even dogs are about half their normal weight. . . . Eggs $1.80 per dozen, butter $3.00 per pound, ham $2.20 per pound.

In the areas occupied by the Germans and Hungarians the country was

pillaged, all manner of commodities extorted from the inhabitants. . . .
It is difficult to describe the minuteness of the German despoliation.
Every town house and farm was visited. . . . [They] removed table
linen, silver, kitchen utensils, furniture, blankets, clocks, metal articles,
wagons, work animals, livestock. They gave not even a receipt or a requisition . . . packed and sent to Germany. . . . An examination showed in
one area alone the horses reduced from 745,000 to 149,000. Cattle from
3,445,000 to 1,125,000. Sheep from 5,550,000 to 445,000.

In accord with our agreements to co-operate fully with the Allies,
I requested the British, French, and Italian governments, on January
7, to appoint their representatives on an inter-Allied mission to
Rumania to co-ordinate the support from the Allied governments.
On February 10, Captain Green commented on the Allied repre-
sentatives:

. . . Have had conference with American, British, Italian Ministers,
French Charge d'Affaires. . . . French Military authorities causing some
trouble claiming right to preside over all ravitaillement but [Rumanian]
Minister Economic Reconstruction angrily refuses recognize them . . .
[other] diplomats in agreement [with him]. . . .

On the same day, Captain Green also telegraphed us:

. . . Daily conference with Constantinescu Minister Economic Reconstruction. The strongest man in cabinet running things in premier's absence. . . . Present administration insufficient. Suggest you supply Prime
Minister now in Paris with information . . . to show him magnitude of
work involved in feeding a whole country. No conception of it here. . . .

On February 16, Captain Green elaborated on his troubles:

. . . Request information re organization inter-allied Food Council and
our relation to it. . . . American, British, and Italian Ministers and
French Charge d'Affaires form food council in name only. These ministers
strongly desire to leave practical work in hands of myself and colleagues
believing their body sufficiently preserves international aspect and that
actual international administration will lead to inefficiency. British Minister has sent strong despatch in this sense to foreign office but he is handi-
capped by direct orders sent by British Ministry shipping to British com-

mercial firm here instructing them to take charge of British cargoes. That firm's unloading charges exactly double ours. . . .

French military authorities acting on instructions dated December from French Minister Blockade organizing so called inter-allied ravitaillement committee for Rumania. . . . This committee claims to represent inter-allied food council of London and claims control over distribution all foodstuffs imported. Rumanian Minister Economic Reconstruction refuses to recognize it or deal directly with it. Great indignation here because head of French Economic bureau is member of committee. That bureau purely commercial affair wasting tonnage importing French wines, perfumes, soaps, sardines, etc., transporting same to interior . . . and selling at exorbitant prices. Rumanian Government threatens confiscation. . . . Despatch from French Government states that I will be member his committee under his presidency. I cannot do this because of impossible relations existing between him and Rumanians. My relations with Rumanian Government entirely satisfactory. . . .

CAPTAIN GREEN

On February 19, we informed Captain Green that we could not and would not handle the Rumanian situation alone and that the Rumanians would have to look to other nations for a large part of their support:

. . . we do not wish to take upon the U.S. either psychologically or actually the whole problem of provisioning Roumania. . . . In view of our obligations to other countries and the limitation of our shipping and financial abilities we cannot undertake to find more than one-half of the Roumanian food program, that is, not more than 25,000 tons of cereals per month, and that it must be made perfectly clear to the Roumanian public that this is a contribution from the U.S. to their food necessities and is not an undertaking of the U.S. to find the whole food required by Roumania and that they must look to the British and French for equal quantities with the U.S.

In addition to this the Roumanians must bestir themselves to trade oil and lubricants and other supplies to the [adjoining] Jugo-Slav areas for the surplus of cereals that exist . . . [in the Banat] and can be transported up and down the Danube.

. . . We are able to expend only about $5,000,000 a month on Roumanian food supply. Roumania should insist on obtaining credits in

England and in France and upon these Governments furnishing them shipping and food in return for these credits. The Roumanians must make up their minds to help themselves and cannot expect to lay down on us. . . .

HOOVER

On March 6, Captain Green was even more explicit concerning the nature of the current Rumanian Government:

The present Ministry is formed of politicians. . . . Alexandre Constantinescu . . . was already Minister of Commerce, Industry, Labor and Economic Reconstruction, when I arrived here, and last week he took over the portefolio of public works, which gives him control of the railroads and of navigation. . . . in the absence of the Prime Minister . . . he is to all intents and purposes the Government. He is one of the ablest and certainly the most detested man in the country. . . .

I doubt whether any man could do efficiently all the work which Monsieur Constantinescu has undertaken, but this is especially impossible in this country. . . . Public service here has never been regarded as anything but a matter of private interest. Pecuniary corruption is so widespread as to be considered as a matter of course. It is generally believed here that everyone connected with the distribution of foodstuffs is making something for his own benefit and that of his family and political friends. This may be true but I am convinced that the Minister is honestly endeavoring to avoid anything of this kind as far as possible in the distribution of our [American] imports.

Later on, Captain Green sent this added comment to our Paris office:

This is a curious government. The Minister of Commerce, Industry, Labor, Economic Reconstruction and Public Works has fallen ill again, and all government work is at a standstill. This is almost literally true. The Minister keeps everything in his own hands and personally decides upon such matters as the import and export and shipment of every kilo of merchandise in this country. This is paternalism with a vengeance, and paternalism of such an inefficient character that it would become intolerable in any but a semi oriental country like this. The import of vegetable seeds from Bulgaria, the export of petroleum, the organization of the children's relief committees and a half a dozen other important matters in which we are interested will have to wait until the Minister's recovery. . . .

Our whole relationship with the Rumanian Government in our relief measures became confused. On April 24, I addressed Prime Minister Jon Bratianu, who headed the Rumanian Peace Delegation in Paris, as follows:

SIR:

. . . The American Relief Administration in the month of January undertook the shipment of foodstuffs to Roumania for the relief of the civil population of Roumania on the urgent representations of the Roumanian Government that the people both of the city and country districts were practically without . . . food supplies and were threatened with starvation. . . . the American Relief Administration during the months of February and March delivered in Roumania 40,786 tons of wheat flour costing . . . more than $8,500,000. Deliveries during the month of April from American sources will amount to approximately 15,000 tons of wheat flour, 3,000 tons of pork products and 1,000 tons of milk, costing about $6,000,000.

Since it appeared that the Roumanian Government had no resources available for payment, the United States Treasury at my request, has extended three credits of Five Million Dollars each to the Roumanian Government without making conditions with regard to the disposal of the proceeds which the Roumanian Government has been able to collect from the sale of these supplies.

I have further urged on the French and British Governments the necessity of extending credits to the Roumanian Government for additional food supplies [to those who could pay].

It is obvious, however, that the primary obligation to feed the people of Roumania rests upon the Roumanian Government . . . the efforts of the United States, France and Great Britain to assist the people of Roumania cannot be successful unless the Roumanian Government also applies to the same object such resources as it has available. . . .

I regret that at the present time I do not appear to have the cooperation of the heads of the Roumanian Government in this task. In making impossible the plan for accepting private remittances from the United States the Roumanian Government is obviously refusing to avail itself of a resource which may be translated into a considerable volume of foodstuffs. To this day, so far as I can find, the Roumanian Government has made no serious effort to export its oil, either to . . . [the Banat in Yugoslavia] where foodstuffs may be purchased, or to Western Europe, where exchange might be created. As yet no reply has been made to the request of the United States Treasury that Five Million Dollars in United States Treasury drafts . . . [must] be applied in payment of foodstuffs. ·

Under these circumstances, I regret that I cannot recommend to the Treasury the providing of credits for food supplies for the months of May, June and July. . . .

HERBERT HOOVER

I received no reply.

In April, 1919, a great crisis arose in Armenia, where we had transferred Captain Green and part of his staff to take charge. With General Pershing's approval, we enlisted Colonel William N. Haskell of the American Army and some twenty-five American officers to take charge in Rumania. Among the staff were Lieutenant Colonel L. G. Ament, whom we placed in charge of the children's relief, assisted by Captain Albert A. Schaal and Lieutenant Aime N. Fregeau.

On April 25, Robert Taft of our staff sent Colonel Haskell a copy of my letter to Bratianu, asking him to show it to the Rumanian Cabinet Ministers in Bucharest. Some passages of Taft's letter illuminate the situation:

From the beginning we have had an entire lack of cooperation from the Roumanian officials here in Paris and their whole attitude has been that of doing us a favor rather than asking for assistance. They seem to be wholly out of touch with the situation in Roumania, as reported by all our telegrams from there, and care very little whether food reaches that country or not. . . .

. . . I think it would be a good idea if you would show Minister Constanescu [sic] the enclosed letter. . . . The British are taking the same position as ourselves. . . .

On May 4, the Colonel telegraphed back:

. . . Your statement that the Roumanian officials in Paris show a lack of cooperation with you . . . is exactly the attitude that I find in Bucarest. . . . They have no inclination to exert themselves and in all matters large and small we have to beg them over and over to do those things which are evidently essential for the relief of the country. . . .

. . . I showed Mr. Hoover's letter to Premier Bratiano with the in-
closures to Minister Constantinescu and it had the effect of dropping a
bomb shell on him. I think it will help us considerably out here and no
doubt will react in Paris. . . .

Things in Rumania were partly improved after that, but not fully.
Haskell found that a whole cargo of food had been divided among
Rumanian officials for resale in the black market for their personal
benefit—netting them more than $300,000. Their pleasant justifica-
tion was that they simply had to have some money. Haskell demanded that the entire lot be returned and put under the control of
his men for distribution to the people. Under threat of exposing to
the world this piece of graft and stopping all further relief, Haskell
recovered 90 per cent of the goods.

It is easy to condemn weakness in such governments as Rumania;
it is easy to denounce corruption; it is not difficult to understand the
reasons for the all-consuming hates and thirst for vengeance. But I
sometimes wonder whether Americans would not be more violent if
they had gone through what Rumania suffered at the combined
hands of the Germans, Hungarians, Bulgarians, and Austrians.

GENEROUS SUPPORT FROM THE BRITISH

The British, after a good start in January and February, 1919,
shortly lost interest in Rumania for the same reasons that troubled
our staff. But there were special reasons why they should have assumed the major load. The Far East and Australia were the obvious
sources of food for Rumania. The British and French were regularly
bringing supplies from those areas through the Suez Canal and
thence through the Mediterranean to their home ports. The Mediterranean and Atlantic parts of these voyages covered about two thousand miles. It was a complete absurdity for the United States to ship
supplies in the other direction over these same two thousand
miles.

The British had appointed a new representative on food matters in Paris, Sir William A. M. Goode,[1] an old friend of mine. Therefore, I took up the question with him in the following note:

PARIS, 29 April 1919

MY DEAR GOODE:

The most critical food situation on the whole face of Europe today is the situation on the South, East and West sides of the Black Sea. It seems to me . . . a pity that Australian cargoes should be . . . [going through] the Mediterranean when, even if we had the shipping it is such a dreadful waste for us to . . . [ship] on this overlapped journey.

. . . Do you not think it is possible to divert the 20,000 tons of Australian cargoes up to this sorely distressed center?

HERBERT HOOVER

Sir William secured the full and generous co-operation of the British.

FINANCE OF RUMANIAN RELIEF

The Rumanians did not have a penny with which to pay for supplies. Under the law, our organization had to receive payment from somewhere, except for children's relief. In the early deliveries I have mentioned, we relied on using a part of the President's $5,000,000 allotment to me from his emergency fund, pending settlement of Rumania's right to loans from the United States as an Allied Power. I have related the troubles with Secretary of the Treasury Carter Glass over her eligibility in the previous volume.[2] Secretary of State Lansing finally ruled that Rumania was eligible.

From the beginning Secretary Glass had little enthusiasm for making loans to Rumania. Just as we had secured co-operation from the British, he concluded—from reports of his own agents in Rumania—that American financial aid should slow down. We in the American relief agencies were not too happy over the conduct of Rumanian officials yet with the generous British program, we felt it imperative

---

[1] Sir William A. M. Goode was the British liaison officer with the United States on food matters, British director of relief missions, and member of the Supreme Economic Council.

[2] *An American Epic*, Vol. II, Chap. 37.

that we also do our part. Above all, we were representing the American people in preventing mass starvation.

I therefore wrote Mr. Davis, our Treasury representative in Paris, as follows on May 1, 1919:

MY DEAR DAVIS:

Roumania. This situation is much more acute than we originally anticipated and these people really need ten million dollars worth of food per month for April, May, June and July. We are making every possible effort to secure help from other directions and have, as you know, induced the Canadians to deliver them five million dollars worth of food. I have now some hopes of inducing the Australians to do the same. The British have already furnished approximately five million dollars worth. Despite this, if we are to save this population from actual starvation we should need all five of the Treasury advances of five million dollars each, and if possible we ought to have the use of the five million Treasury bills in addition. You, however, appreciate as well as I do the attitude of the officials which dampens one's sense of service a little, but I think we must dissociate the official classes entirely from the suffering humanity which receives little consideration from them. . . .

. . . I have sent out word to each one of the . . . governments that are under relief to the effect that the Food Administration will bring its entire operations in Europe to a termination with the forthcoming harvest, and that any arrangements beyond that date must be matters for direct and renewed arrangements between themselves and the American Government in Washington.

As I have often expressed to you, it seems to me absolutely essential from a national point of view that we take advantage of next harvest to get a complete cut-off as an eleemosynary institution. . . .

HERBERT HOOVER

Rumania possessed the greatest oil fields in Europe outside Communist Russia. They were largely owned by British and French corporations. The Germans and Bulgarians had destroyed the derricks in their retreat, but, with the former British and French staffs, the Rumanians steadily recovered production from the wells. Since oil was wanted all over Europe, one of our complaints against Rumania was that profits from its export were not applied to the purchase of food supplies. We had other complaints about their petroleum products. We desperately needed them to keep the railways and other public services in operation in Eastern Europe, and our only alternative in Rumania was to import petroleum products from the United States with relief money. The Rumanians wanted to export their oil to cash-paying countries.

We appointed Captain Lisle S. Powell to our Rumanian staff to negotiate sales on credit or for the inflated currencies of the needy neighboring states. The negotiations were interminable, but our mission managed to squeeze out enough to keep the wheels moving through the rest of Southeastern Europe.

PROBLEMS OF TRANSPORTATION

Except along the Danube, our inland transportation in Rumania was paralyzed because of the railway equipment plundered by the German and Hungarian armies. I have already described our mandate from the Big Four to manage the railways of Eastern Europe in the previous volume.[3] But Rumania needed more than management. Under the Armistice agreement, the Germans were to surrender 5,000 new locomotives to the Allies. General Pershing received a part of them. Immediately upon my application to him he gave us 150 of these locomotives for Rumania, and the French also made an allotment from the same source. We also negotiated the sale, on credit, of 400 locomotives and 4,000 cars from American Army surplus in France. The British, having furnished most of Rumania's prewar locomotives, furnished spare parts and repair crews for the few the Hungarians left behind.

At best we could effect only a meager restoration of traffic. Finally, the Rumanians took the matter in hand by demanding the return of their railway equipment and other loot from the Hungarians. Receiving no satisfactory reply, their army crossed the Hungarian frontier on May 2. This, however, got no results, for the Allies ordered them to stop. I continue the story of the Rumanian railway reprisals in a later chapter of this volume.[4]

[3] *Ibid.*, Chap. 43.
[4] Chap. 45.

THE REHABILITATION OF CHILDREN

When the Congressional appropriation of $100,000,000 was available, we quickly set in motion the canteen system of an extra meal a day for debilitated children, expectant mothers, and the aged. The essential paragraphs of my directions to Captain Green were:

MY DEAR CAPTAIN GREEN:

Reports of special investigators and from many other sources confirm the . . . very serious condition in Roumania due to lack of . . . food for children. All investigations indicate that in the cities and industrial centers not only is it impossible . . . to obtain the food which is required to maintain their children . . . but the mortality amongst these children is reported to be so large as to warrant the sympathy and active aid of the entire civilized world. . . .

. . . The American Relief . . . must also look to the . . . Roumanian people for substantial financial support . . . certain . . . [items] suitable for children . . . will be imported into the country by the American Relief . . . and distributed gratuitously for the purpose indicated.

. . . shipments . . . of cocoa, sugar and milk, white flour and certain of the fats suitable for children have already arrived at Constanza. . . . We look to the Roumanian Government to provide us with rail transportation for supplies. . . . We must also look to the Roumanian people to provide the necessary facilities . . . [by] supplying . . . kitchens, dining rooms, fuel and other equipment necessary. . . .

HERBERT HOOVER

On April 26, I wrote to Colonel Haskell, who had succeeded Captain Green, advising him of the children's relief:

PARIS, 26 April 1919

DEAR COLONEL HASKELL,

The problem of special feeding for undernourished children is one which not only do we want to accomplish in an efficient way for its intrinsic necessity, but for the evidence of American sentiment. . . . You may take it . . . that the precise limits set upon expenditure can be exceeded on your own authority. . . .

There is one feature of this problem and . . . [of relief as a whole] that is . . . we must prepare for a termination of this entire effort and the withdrawal of our entire staff. With the forthcoming harvest in Europe . . . all of our financial resources expire. . . .

I wish to take this occasion to express the appreciation we all have of the labor being carried on by . . . [our] men at the front.

HERBERT HOOVER

The social organization of the Rumanian people made this children's project most difficult. The dominant class consisted of old families and landlords who formed an elite, with no consequential middle class between it and an oppressed peasantry and working people. Colonel Haskell reported on June 10:

> . . . The people in the country have no notion of charity and will not furnish ox-teams, kettles, wood, or even axes to chop the wood for the establishment of canteens in their own villages to feed their own children. It is a most remarkable country. . . .

For all these reasons he had none of the usual foundations upon which to build the children's relief. The Queen of Rumania organized a few charity groups, but in the main, we were dependent upon municipal and local authorities, which required much more extensive supervision by Colonel Ament and his staff than was required when we could organize devoted women, as in other countries. In fact, we had to place a larger American staff in Rumania than in any other liberated country.

By the time the Peace was signed, the staff had the work under way. They had established 530 canteens providing an extra meal a day to 200,000 practically prostrate children. The total number of meals served exceeded 24,515,000. We shipped 1,432 tons of special food at a cost of $414,286—a gift from the American people.

CLOTHING

We secured 4,735 tons of clothing from United States Army surplus, and another 82 tons were contributed by the Jewish Joint Distribution Committee. To this the British added 11,100 tons, making a total of 15,917 tons. The Red Cross provided some additional clothing.

AID TO RUMANIA FROM OTHER NATIONS

A considerable part of the burden of Rumanian relief fell upon the British, who provided 99,788 tons of supplies valued at $15,428,688. However, the United States provided 127,087 tons valued at $38,938,571. The French contributed some supplies, but we have no record of the amount.

AID FROM THE AMERICAN RED CROSS

In September, 1917, about five months after the United States entered the war, the Red Cross sent a strong medical mission to Rumania. With the Rumanian surrender six months later, the Red Cross was compelled to withdraw to a small segment unoccupied by the enemy in the neighborhood of Jassy. During this time, it furnished food to 40,000 people daily, maintained an orphanage, and ran two hospitals with dispensaries attached.

After the Armistice, the Red Cross expanded its medical aid over all of Rumania by providing physicians, surgeons, hospitalization, and increased child care and protection against infection. The Red Cross accounts show an expenditure of $809,322 in Rumania up to the Peace. Its records show an additional fund to the Balkans, but we could not determine how much of it Rumania received, if any.

AID FROM THE JEWISH JOINT DISTRIBUTION COMMITTEE

The Jewish Joint Distribution Committee was active in Rumania both before and during the Armistice. Prior to the Armistice, this group acted through its Jewish committees in other parts of Europe to give protection and aid to the persecuted and to refugees. After the Armistice, it turned its energies to rehabilitation in agriculture and industry and to children. The J.D.C., in co-operation with the

A.R.A., delivered food, clothing, and soap amounting to 382 tons at a value of $256,000.

AID FROM THE SOCIETY OF FRIENDS OF ROUMANIA, INC.

Early in the Armistice period, this organization was created under the auspices of William Nelson Campbell. The only indication of its activities is a note in the files of the American Relief Administration concerning funds covering the distribution of literature to the war and civilian blind: $7,935 raised up to March 31, 1919.

AID FROM THE ROUMANIAN RELIEF COMMITTEE

The Roumanian Relief Committee was founded in 1917. The executive officer was T. Tileston Wells. Through this group some funds were sent to Rumania to be disbursed by the Queen, but no amounts can be discovered.

TOTALS

It is reasonable to estimate the total expenditures of American charitable agencies in Rumania, aside from the children's relief conducted by our organization and the J.D.C. contribution to the A.R.A., at $1,000,000 prior to the Peace.

THE END

By the first of May, 1919, food, medicine, and clothing problems in Rumania began to clear up. Haskell was able to advise that his staff were getting better results in distribution and that with the inflow of American and British supplies the crisis was rapidly passing, the crop prospects were favorable, and the dangers of a Communist insurrection had been greatly lessened. He added: "However, Communism is still the chief topic of conversation."

TOTAL SUPPLIES TO RUMANIA
FROM THE ARMISTICE TO THE PEACE *

	Food	Clothing & Misc.	Total	$ Value
American Relief Administration:				
Children's relief	1,432		1,432	$ 414,286
General relief	102,942		102,942	23,438,339
Army surplus	17,596	4,735	22,331	13,012,689
Jewish Joint Distribution Committee	300	82	382	256,000
Other American charitable contributions †	(quantities unknown)			1,000,000
British Empire	88,688	11,100	99,788	15,428,688
	210,958	15,917	226,875	$53,550,002

* In tons.
† Total includes some contributions prior to the Armistice.

American Government supplies, except for children's relief and charitable contributions, were in the form of loans to the Rumanian Government. For the reasons which I have stated in the Introduction to this volume, the whole of these loans was also a gift. What the British may have recovered from their loans we have no record, but it was probably not very much. The dramatic events in Rumania after the Peace are described in a later chapter of this volume.

RUSSIA, SIBERIA, AND THE AREAS BEHIND THE "WHITE" ARMIES

CHAPTER 17

THE RELIEF OF RUSSIA AND SIBERIA

A short account of events in Russia is necessary for an understanding of her relief problems. On July 31, 1914, the Germans sent an ultimatum to Russia demanding that she cease preparations for war on the German frontier. They received no reply and, on August 1, 1914, declared war on Russia. On August 6, 1914, Austria declared war on Czarist Russia. This declaration was provoked by the action of the Russian Government a few days previously in deciding on a general mobilization against Austria. That act was, in the minds of most observers, including myself, due to the Czar's resorting to the old Machiavellian doctrine of diverting internal discontent by war.

I had practiced my engineering profession in various parts of Russia for six years—1909–1915—under the Czarist regime and was a witness to its cruelties and the general weakening of the monarchy. The hammer blows of the German Army contributed to the further weakening of the Czarist regime, but there were other forces which added to the Czar's difficulties. He was not able wholly to suppress the revolutionary ferment; there was little semblance of food administration; and the people in the cities were hungry, while there were large supplies of food in the interior.

Early in March, 1917, strikes, riots, and mutinies in the armed forces broke out in St. Petersburg (renamed Petrograd at beginning of the war). Nicholas II abdicated in favor of his brother, Michael, who, in turn, abdicated in favor of the provisional government under

159

the leadership of Alexander Kerensky. The Kerensky Government was recognized by the United States on March 22, 1917, fifteen days before we came into the war. The Communists seized the government from Kerenski on November 7, 1917, and signed a peace treaty with the Germans at Brest-Litovsk on March 3, 1918.

The Allies, including the United States, had furnished huge military supplies to Murmansk, Archangel, and Vladivostok to assist the Czarist and Kerensky governments. To prevent these stocks of munitions from falling into the hands of the Germans, the British landed in Murmansk in June, 1918, followed by a joint Allied landing at Archangel. In August, 1918, Japanese and British forces landed in Vladivostok.

THE AMERICAN RED CROSS

In August, 1917, four months after we entered the war, a political mission, of which Elihu Root was chairman, arrived in Petrograd. Accompanying it was an extensive Red Cross mission comprising 17 physicians, surgeons, nurses, and sanitary and civil engineers. It brought huge quantities of medical supplies, 125 ambulances, condensed milk which supplied 25,000 infants in Petrograd, and clothing and food—to a total value of $1,560,000. That Red Cross mission finally despaired of accomplishment under the Communists and left for the United States in October, 1918.

In the meantime, however, another Red Cross mission of thirteen representatives was dispatched to Archangel in the summer of 1918 with 4,200 tons of food and medicine to alleviate the distress of the population and to provide military relief for Allied troops and "White" Russian forces. It supplied civilian hospitals in and around Archangel and opened a hospital which was later turned over to the Russian Army. Medicines worth 1,000,000 rubles were sent to the various district zemstvos. Russian prisoners of war, returning from Germany through the Bolshevik lines to North Russia, were also cared for. Before leaving Archangel, the Red Cross provided rations for needy civilians for an additional two months and shipped the balance of supplies to the Baltic States.

THE NEAR EAST RELIEF COMMITTEE

This committee provided great aids to the Russian provinces in the Caucasus. This will be discussed in the chapters on Armenia, Georgia, and Azerbaijan.

AMERICAN FRIENDS SERVICE COMMITTEE

In September, 1917, six women of the American Friends Service Committee arrived in the province of Samara. Here they joined with British Friends in providing medical care, workshops for refugee women, and aid for orphans and distributed corn, seed grain, clothes, and books. This project closed in October, 1918, partly because of the return home of Russian doctors and partly because the Bolshevik upsurge made their relief work impossible. One American worker made her way to Moscow with an English colleague and there took charge of five hundred undernourished children in three colonies in the surrounding countryside until August, 1919. Three women went to Siberia, where they worked alongside the American Red Cross. Quaker expenditures during this period amounted to $64,716.

THE JEWISH JOINT DISTRIBUTION COMMITTEE

The Jewish Joint Distribution Committee or its predecessor organization aided religious compatriots from the beginning of the war. An estimated 800,000 Jews were uprooted from their homes in the combat zones. Some of them, regarded as enemy subjects, from the Austro-Hungarian provinces of Galicia and Bukovina were permitted only basic relief.

The local activities of the J.D.C., through its Russian agent, EKOPO, aided in evacuation, transportation, and the creation of orphanages and workshops. Its expenditures from the beginning of its work to the Communist Revolution in 1917 were $3,680,300.

After the Revolution, the contacts of the J.D.C. and the EKOPO gradually weakened, and the administration of even basic relief became impossible. The J.D.C. did return, however, at the time of the great famine of 1921–1923, and I shall discuss this later.

THE YOUNG WOMEN'S CHRISTIAN ASSOCIATION

In March, 1917, the Young Women's Christian Association was asked by a group of representative Russian women to aid Russian girls. By November, 1917, about 150 Russian girls were registered for classes in Petrograd, and a canteen was later opened for them. The Y.W.C.A. secretaries were forced to leave this work early in 1918 because of the Communist situation.

THE RELIEF OF SIBERIA

After the Bolshevik Revolution, a resistance movement against the Communists sprang up in Siberia. It centered partly around the Czechoslovak armies of 70,000 men who had seized the railways in their retreat from the Eastern Front after the Communist Revolution and partly around the organization of a "White" army under Admiral Alexander Kolchak.

As I mentioned, the Japanese landed troops in Vladivostok on August 11, 1918, partly to protect Allied stocks of munitions there and partly to encourage Kolchak. The American Government landed troops on August 15 and 16 for the multiple purpose of protecting munitions, aiding the evacuation of the Czech armies, and helping Kolchak.

On November 18, 1918, the Admiral declared himself the Supreme Ruler of Russia. He advanced his army into Eastern Russia, capturing Perm and Ufa, but the Communists drove him back into Siberia.

After two years of effort, Admiral Kolchak gave way to the Communists in December, 1919, and was later captured and executed by them. The Japanese continued to occupy Vladivostok until October 25, 1922.

THE AMERICAN RED CROSS

A Siberian commission of the American Red Cross established headquarters at Vladivostok in July, 1918. It provided aid to the American forces, to the Czechs still fighting the Communists, and to the Kolchak "White" armies. The Red Cross also provided medical aid to the civilian population over a vast area in Siberia.

To reach the needy, the Red Cross operated relief trains as far west as Omsk, where Admiral Kolchak had his headquarters. Each train with Red Cross supplies—averaging some 220 tons—took about two months to make the trip into Siberia and out again. In addition to the general relief trains, there were three others for sanitary supplies and one for dental supplies. Hospitals on wheels, with a capacity for handling 1,500 patients, covered a total distance of 18,000 miles. Also, an American Red Cross anti-typhus train shuttled back and forth between Vladivostok and Perm, disinfecting 105,000 people and 1,000,000 pieces of clothing and issuing 500,000 new garments.

With Admiral Kolchak's defeat in December, 1919, the American troops were withdrawn, and the American Red Cross completed the liquidation of its work early in 1920. From the beginning to the end of its work in Siberia, the Red Cross expended $14,965,409.

JEWISH JOINT DISTRIBUTION COMMITTEE

In April, 1920, the Jewish Joint Distribution Committee joined with twelve other voluntary bodies to form the Siberian War Prisoners Repatriation Fund, furnishing both money and supervisory personnel for this effort. Its financial records show an expenditure for Siberia, from the beginning to the end of its work, of $475,768.

SIBERIAN WAR PRISONERS REPATRIATION FUND

This organization was established to raise funds to return Austrian and Hungarian prisoners to their homelands. Felix M. Warburg was chairman of the fund, and it expended $3,000,000.

YOUNG MEN'S CHRISTIAN ASSOCIATION

By the end of 1919, the Y.M.C.A. had nineteen representatives assisting in Siberian prison camps where Germans and Austrians were being held by Russia. It provided books, music, kitchens, soap, and endless services until the Peace—despite the Communist Revolution. Financial records of the Y.M.C.A. show expenditures of $254,404 on prisoners of war in Siberian camps.

The Y.M.C.A. provided its usual services of huts, recreation, and supplies for Russian and Allied armies wherever accessible throughout the war. Its accounts show expenditures for Allied armies in Siberia (and also Murmansk and Archangel) of $7,932,210. (This figure cannot be broken down for Siberia alone.)

YOUNG WOMEN'S CHRISTIAN ASSOCIATION

During the summer of 1919, Y.W.C.A. representatives assisted stranded refugee Russian women and children at the port of Vladivostok. They also assisted American soldiers through hostess houses and worked with the American Red Cross in aiding civilians.

My colleagues and I in the American relief agencies believed that any concept of humane action required an attempt to provide food, medicine, and clothing for the starving in the larger cities and towns of Communist Russia. We had hopes that such action might soften the situation in order to permit some workable relationship with the Peace Conference. We made such an attempt but failed. The details and documents are fully set out in my book *The Ordeal of Woodrow Wilson* [1] and need not be repeated here.

[1] *The Ordeal of Woodrow Wilson* (New York, McGraw-Hill Book Company, 1958), pp. 115–23. A more condensed account also appears in my *Memoirs* (New York, The Macmillan Company, 1953), Vol. I.

CHAPTER 18

RELIEF
BEHIND THE "WHITE" ARMIES

Four "White" armies had sprung up in Russia and Siberia soon after the Communist Revolution of November, 1917. None of them was dedicated to the purpose of restoring the Czarist regime. They were determined to establish constitutional government and fundamental personal liberties.

General A. I. Denikin's "White" army, with British support, was fighting in an area northeast of the Black Sea, with his headquarters at the port of Novorossisk.

General P. N. Wrangel, with the support of the French, was fighting in an area to the northwest of the Black Sea, with his base at the port of Odessa.

General N. N. Yudenich, with British support, attempted an invasion from the port of Narva on the Baltic.

Admiral Kolchak was holding an area in Siberia, which I have described separately in the previous chapter.

Also, Allied armies were holding small areas at the ports of Murmansk and Archangel on the Arctic Ocean in order to protect the military supplies intended for the use of the regimes prior to the Communist. They engaged in very little fighting.

The Supreme Council requested me, as Director General of Relief and Reconstruction, to supply the armies and civilians in the areas of the four "White" armies. Since only our official American relief agencies had supplies, it meant that my organization had to undertake these jobs from the only funds available—the $100,000,000

Congressional appropriation. Congress had never intended this appropriation to be used to feed armies. I therefore insisted that they should be supplied by their sponsors but that where necessary we would aid the civilians behind their fronts as part of our humane purpose.

BEHIND GENERAL DENIKIN'S FRONT

At my direction, Howard Heinz, chief of our mission at Constantinople, sent Major Edward R. Stoever, a member of his staff, to report on the food situation behind the Denikin and Wrangel fronts. A condensation of Heinz's account of this report concerning General Denikin's area, dated February 22, 1919, is as follows:

. . . [Major Stoever] states that food is plentiful enough but exceedingly high in price, money is plentiful enough but exceedingly cheap in value being for the most part the product of Bolchevist printing offices. He reports the people as being apathetic and inclined to be influenced by Bolchevist propaganda of which there is a great deal and which is likely at any time to overturn the present civil Government. There appears to be an unwillingness on the part of the people there to export grain or to sell it for any available . . . [currency], but presumably . . . grain might be obtained in exchange for merchandise. The volunteer army under General [Denikin] . . . [has food but is] in great want of clothing of all kinds as well as munitions. . . . the officials have stated to Major Stoever that there is great need . . . [in the civil population for] tea, coffee, rice, pepper, shoes for women and children, textile materials of all kinds, buttons, thread, paper for printing and for correspondence and . . . agricultural implements. . . .

. . . there is a reasonable prospect of barter in all this country from Odessa east to the Kuban, taking out such merchandise as tobacco, wine and seed grain, principally the latter, in exchange for such material as we may desire to offer. . . .

. . . I wish to record a belief that there will be no demand for American . . . [food] in any Black Sea port, either North or South, east of the ports in Rumania and Bulgaria. . . .

In spite of the fact that Denikin's area had a large surplus of grain, there was some suffering in the towns because the peasants would not part with food in exchange for the inflated currencies. The British had established their military mission with headquarters at Ekaterinodar, some seventy miles northeast of Novorossisk. They urged that our organization supply that city with food shipped from the United States.

Such food had to be sent 2,000 miles through the Mediterranean and Black seas, while at the same time the British were shipping cargoes from the Far East and Australia over this same route. I refused and recommended that they send some trading goods to their mission with which to barter for food from the peasants. The British representatives in Paris appealed over my head to the Supreme Council, which requested us to do the job. In consequence, Mr. Heinz sent a member of his staff with 394 tons of food, costing us $86,680, which he found amply filled the need. Our staff secured obligations from Denikin's government to pay for these supplies, but since it was obvious that these obligations were worthless, we wrote them off as a gift—and called it a day.

RELIEF TO CIVILIANS BEHIND GENERAL WRANGEL'S ARMY

We were provisioning the civilian population behind General Wrangel's forces. However, the French, in March, 1919, insisted that we furnish food to Wrangel's army, which included French regiments. They threatened to withdraw from Russia if we did not do so. Heinz telegraphed a reminder to our office in Paris that there was a surplus of food in Denikin's area which the French could get from the peasants in exchange for trade goods. I offered one of our cargo ships returning from an Armenian relief mission to transport such food. The matter became academic when the French regiments mutinied and Wrangel was compelled to retreat to Constantinople. In a press statement, the French general in command blamed his troubles on my organization. We made an appropriate reply, likewise in a press statement.

RELIEF TO CIVILIANS IN THE UKRAINE

During the Armistice period, the Ukraine was a sort of independent Communist state with Soviet Government connections. The Ukrainians wanted certain supplies from the Western countries. The diplomats in Paris developed a theory that the American relief agencies could divorce the Ukrainians from their Communist link through a relief action. The Ukrainians reportedly had some surplus of grain which they could exchange for their needs of clothing, medical supplies, and trucks. We arranged a sale from the Army surplus stocks totaling 5,550 tons, the value of which was $8,500,223. The Ukrainian representative in Vienna agreed with our organization to provide us an equivalent value in wheat. We proposed to distribute the wheat in Czechoslovakia and Austria. The Ukrainians never delivered a ton of wheat, and they did not pay a dime of their obligations to the Army Liquidation Commission. Nor did they ever enter into the expected divorce proceedings with Moscow.

THE VOYAGE OF THE *KICKAPOO*

We decided that we could obtain food for civilians behind the "White" armies in South Russia and possibly for Armenia by undertaking to trade goods to the Russian peasants north of the Black Sea. We chartered the ship *Kickapoo* and loaded it with Army surplus supplies of tools, hardware, cooking utensils, and clothing.

The *Kickapoo* did not arrive in the trading area until after the termination of all our official operations at the Peace. However, great use of her cargo was made by our organization through trading it for food for the Armenians. I continue this story in the chapter on the relief of Armenia.

RELIEF BEHIND GENERAL YUDENICH'S ARMY

In March and April, 1919, a group of White Russian officers in Finland and Estonia had organized an army under General Nicholas Yudenich, who proposed to take Petrograd (St. Petersburg) from the Communists. The nucleus of his forces consisted of the White Russians who had fought the Communists alongside the Finns, Estonians, and Letts. Yudenich was furnished arms, munitions, and food for his army by the British and French governments. British General Sir Hubert Gough was assigned as his adviser.

Yudenich established a provisional government at Narva, inside the Russian frontier, and invaded an area comprising about 400,000 civilians. We sent Captain John C. Miller, a member of our Baltic mission, to report on the civilian needs. His report was a terrifying document. The Communists, in their retreat before Yudenich, had plundered the district of what little food and livestock there was and had machine-gunned resisting peasants. Thousands were dying of starvation.

Yudenich began his attack in May, 1919, but because the promised British and French armies had not arrived, he was compelled to retreat, holding onto a small area. He began his renewed attack on September 28, 1919, and was joined by the small Estonian Army; the Finns refused to join him. Yudenich was within twenty-five miles of Petrograd on October 22. The revolt he had expected in Petrograd failed. He never stood a chance, and by November 7, 1919, he was in full retreat into Estonia, where his troops were disarmed. On February 2, 1920, Estonia made peace with Communist Russia.

The United States Department of State urged that we relieve the population behind Yudenich's advance and that we prepare a sufficient food supply for Petrograd when taken by Yudenich. To aid us in this relief, the State Department diverted a cargo of 5,000 tons of food, costing, with freight, $1,550,000, which was originally intended to support the Allied armies holding Murmansk. Since Yudenich was failing, we discharged this cargo at Viborg in Finland.

Our American relief agencies under Captain John Thors furnished 19,000 tons of supplies to the civilians. We secured on "credit" from United States Army surplus 200 tons of clothing and 510 tons of miscellaneous supplies, mostly medical, which were distributed to civilians by our organizations.

In the period of the American Relief Administration's activities, we not only had fed many of the adult population but had established canteens and were rehabilitating about 9,000 children.

At Yudenich's retreat, we were faced with two problems: his demoralized army and a mass of Russian refugees who had fled into Estonia. Fortunately, we were able to provide food for them from the Viborg stocks.

IN SUMMARY

All these operations behind the "White" armies were snuffed out by their defeats, but it can be said of these activities that they preserved the lives of many hundreds of thousands of human beings, at least temporarily.

TOTAL SUPPLIES TO RUSSIA AND SIBERIA
FROM THE ARMISTICE TO THE PEACE *

	Food	Clothing Medical & Misc.	Total	$ Value
American Relief Administration:				
Children's relief	1,241	21	1,262	$ 373,874
General relief				
Northwest Russia (Yudenich's army) ...	17,950		17,950	4,465,465
Freight				52,188
Denikin's army	394		394	86,680
Army surplus				
Northwest Russia (Yudenich's army) ...		710	710	428,299

TOTAL SUPPLIES TO RUSSIA AND SIBERIA FROM THE ARMISTICE TO THE PEACE (*continued*)

	Food	Clothing Medical & Misc.	Total	$ Value
Ukraine		5,550	5,550	8,500,223
American Red Cross †				
Supplies shipped, August, 1917		(quantities unknown)		1,560,000
Relief of Siberia		(quantities unknown)		14,965,409
Jewish Joint Distribution Committee †				
Relief of Russia to 1917 ...		(quantities unknown)		3,680,300
Relief of Siberia		(quantities unknown)		475,768
American Friends Service Committee †		(quantities unknown)		64,716
Young Men's Christian Association †				
Allied prisoners		(quantities unknown)		254,404
Allied armies		(quantities unknown)		7,932,210
Young Women's Christian Association †		(quantities unknown)		313,860
Siberian War Prisoners' Repatriation Fund		(quantities unknown)		3,000,000
United Kingdom Kouban district		100	100	10,472
	19,585	6,381	25,966	$46,163,868

* In tons.

† Total includes some contributions before the Armistice.

THE RELIEF AND PROTECTION OF THE CHRISTIAN AND JEWISH MINORITIES IN THE MOSLEM STATES

CHAPTER 19

THE RELIEF OF MINORITIES
IN THE MOSLEM STATES

The burden of relief and protection of the Christian and Jewish minorities in the Near East, except for some American government aid to the Armenians, fell upon three great American charitable institutions: the Near East Relief Committee, the Jewish Joint Distribution Committee, and the American Red Cross.

The Near East Relief Committee began its service in September, 1915, the Jewish Joint Distribution Committee in November, 1914, and the American Red Cross began direct relief in 1918. All of these organizations maintained their services until the signing of the Peace and thereafter to 1923. The American relief agencies under my direction entered the Near East in 1919 and continued operations until 1921.

The magnitude of the service by all these charitable and government agencies to all of the Near Eastern countries is indicated somewhat by their expenditures. From the beginning of their work to 1923 the totals were:

Near East Relief Committee	$ 51,658,903
American Red Cross	27,461,383
Jewish Joint Distribution Committee	8,674,413
American Friends Service Committee	44,398
Other religious and charitable organizations	3,000,000
American official relief agencies and the new American Relief Administration	17,259,248
	$108,098,345

However, money statements are a poor indication of the suffering prevented, the persecution abated, the human lives saved, and the devotion of the hosts of Americans who served. Many Americans died that these peoples might live.[1]

This section is devoted to the eleven Moslem states in the Near East. There were four states in which there were majorities of Christians—Greece, Georgia, Armenia, and Abyssinia. These I discuss in other sections of this volume.

The reader will be less confused if I give the account of the protection and relief in each state from the beginning—in 1914—to the end of 1923, at which time many of these activities ceased. The main reason for not dividing the narrative of these countries at the Peace is that the relief organizations were continuous in these areas both before and after the Peace.

THE POLITICAL SITUATION

Certain major political events in the Near East bear upon relief activities. After the Communist Revolution in Russia, the Russian provinces of Georgia, Azerbaijan, and Armenia declared their independence and established themselves as republics. They maintained their independence until 1922, at which time they were snuffed out by Soviet conspiracies and invasions.

In the course of the war, the British-Indian armies landed at the Fort of Fao on the Persian Gulf, moved up the Tigris and Euphrates rivers, and finally completed the occupation of Mesopotamia (Iraq). Other British forces based in Egypt, under General Edmund Allenby, advanced over the Arab states until the Turkish Empire surrendered to the British in October, 1918.

RELIEF

I have, in Volume II of this memoir, already given a brief account of the origin and organization of all of the major American charitable

[1] I discuss the relief of Greece in Part Two of this volume. However, I have included in this table the expenditures for this nation and also Armenia from 1914 to

agencies giving protection and relief. However, the events and problems that arose in these different states require a much more extensive record. It is presented here.

1923 to illustrate, through this financial yardstick, the magnitude of relief activities in the Near Eastern countries.

CHAPTER 20

MESOPOTAMIA, PALESTINE, AND SYRIA

MESOPOTAMIA (IRAQ)

Mesopotamia was principally the territory between the Tigris and Euphrates rivers, and at the time of the war, her population was about 2,850,000. On November 7, 1914, two days after the declaration of war between Great Britain and Turkey, a contingent from the Anglo-Indian Army under the command of General Charles Townshend landed at Fao in Southern Mesopotamia and on November 22 occupied Basra. On March 11, 1917, Baghdad was captured by Sir Stanley Maude. When General Maude died of cholera, General Sir William R. Marshall succeeded him and at the time the Turks surrendered to the Allies in October, 1918, Marshall had occupied the whole of Mesopotamia. On April 25, 1920, the Supreme Council gave a mandate over Mesopotamia to the British; it was formally established with the signing of the Treaty of Sèvres on August 20, 1920.

In 1918, the Near East Relief Committee, through one of its representatives, E. W. McDowell, joined with a British relief agency. This joint committee organized a tent camp for 50,000 Persian refugees near Baghdad and provided self-support for some 3,000 of them through cloth- and garment-making enterprises. Another 50,000 Persian refugees at Mosul were given aid. One thousand unclaimed youngsters were cared for and given training in ten orphanages. This committee continued its service in Mesopotamia until 1923.

178

The committee's accounts do not permit separation of expenditures in Mesopotamia from those in Persia. One statement gives its total expenditures from 1915 through 1923 for Mesopotamia and Persia as $7,541,959.

PALESTINE

Palestine was part of the Turkish Empire. The Syrian boundaries during this period extended from the Mediterranean to the River Jordan.

Under the command of General Allenby, the British armies based in Egypt occupied Jerusalem on December 9, 1917. Because of demands elsewhere, the British temporarily abandoned this offensive for ten months, resuming it in September, 1918. The Turks surrendered the following month. Until July 1, 1920, the country remained under a British military administration.

The Balfour Declaration of November 2, 1917, sought to recognize the interests and aspirations of both Arabs and Jews. The Jews interpreted the declaration as a promise of an independent Jewish state. The Arabs have never abandoned their objections to this interpretation. In 1920, the Supreme Council in Paris established a British mandate in Palestine. The British military administration tried to reconcile the conflict, to keep the peace, and to revive economic life. However, it added to the fire by introducing Hebrew as a third official language. On July 1, 1920, the military government was replaced by a civilian administration, with Sir Herbert Samuel as High Commissioner.

In May, 1921, there were more Arab riots. On September 1, there was promulgated a constitution providing for a partly elective legislative council, but the power remained in the hands of the High Commissioner. Because the Arabs refused to co-operate in the council, Palestine was ruled by executive decree.

Amid all these conflicts, relief was a ray of sunlight. Three great American charitable organizations participated in service, not only to the Jews, but also to the Arabs.

THE JEWISH JOINT DISTRIBUTION COMMITTEE
IN PALESTINE

As I have related in Volume II, the Turkish decree of early 1915 expelling all Christian and Jewish minorities from the Empire exempted the Jews in Palestine. However, those Jews living in the Empire who had come from other places were dumped into Palestine. The organized relief of the Jews originated from an appeal by American Ambassador to Turkey Henry Morgenthau, Sr., in 1914. Through him, two American Jewish committees distributed $90,000. In late 1914, these committees were merged into the Jewish Joint Distribution Committee.

The J.D.C. operated in Palestine through a committee set up in Jerusalem under the chairmanship of the American Consul-General. The committee purchased food and distributed it to the destitute through kitchens, schools, hospitals, and orphan asylums. It also provided homes to start employment enterprises.

With the British occupation, the problems of persecution were ended. And with the surrender of the Turks to the Allies in October, 1918, the activities of the J.D.C. were transformed into long-range objectives and in time mostly to other areas. However, it continued the support of 4,000 war orphans and financed a malaria-eradication drive. From a 1919 peak of $1,329,130, the J.D.C. spending in the Holy Land dropped to $416,599 in 1923.

The total expenditures of the J.D.C. from the beginning of its work in 1915 through 1923, were $6,401,039.

THE NEAR EAST RELIEF COMMITTEE IN PALESTINE

The Near East Relief Committee began aid in Palestine in late 1915. It operated through a local committee under the chairmanship of Bishop McInnes of the Anglican Church in Jerusalem. This committee's effort was, directly, mostly to the relief and protection of the Christian minorities in Palestine, largely in Jerusalem and Jaffa. It provided food and care for the destitute and for orphans. At the surrender of Turkey, the Red Cross assumed part of the load from the Jewish Joint Distribution Committee, and after the Peace, the Near East Relief Committee took over the Red Cross work.

The Near East Relief Committee combined its expenditure accounts for Palestine with Syria, and they cannot be separated. The total for both countries from 1915 to December, 1923, was $9,837,687.

THE AMERICAN RED CROSS IN PALESTINE

Prior to the British occupation of Jerusalem in 1918, the American Red Cross served through contributions to the Near East Relief Committee. In June, 1918, a Red Cross mission of fifty members was sent to Palestine under Dr. John H. Finley. The mission included physicians, surgeons, nurses, and sanitary engineers. They brought with them 300 tons of medical supplies and food and established their headquarters at Jerusalem. By October, 1918, they had set up a general dispensary, a children's clinic, and a hospital, were managing two orphan asylums at the government's request, and had begun a program of industrial service work, furnishing employment in weaving, knitting, and sewing. The mission was withdrawn at the signing of Peace.

Red Cross records show that during the period of its operation in Palestine, it shipped 800 tons of supplies from the United States. The records also show that an estimated $1,000,000 was expended by the Palestine commission during its operation.

SYRIA

The Turkish province of Syria included Syria, Palestine, and the people in the area comprising present-day Lebanon. Syria, including present-day Lebanon, was kept under Turkish domination throughout the war. It had a population of about 3,000,000, embracing considerable minorities of Jacobite Christians, Maronite Roman Catholics, and the Christian Armenians.

The British Army, under General Allenby, assisted by Arab forces directed by Thomas Edward Lawrence ("Colonel Lawrence of Arabia"), began an attack on Syria in September, 1918, and occupied Damascus in early October. Turkey surrendered to the Allies a few days later.

It is unnecessary to give a narrative of the political events in Syria after the surrender of Turkey except to state that the French insisted that Syria was in their sphere of influence. They were given a "mandate" by the Peace Conference at San Remo, and this was confirmed by the League of Nations on July 24, 1922.

During the war the Christian and Jewish minorities were dependent, for their protection and relief, upon aid from the Near East Relief Committee, the American Red Cross, the Jewish Joint Distribution Committee, and the American Friends Service Committee (the Quakers).

THE NEAR EAST RELIEF COMMITTEE IN SYRIA

The Near East Relief Committee carried the burden of support of the Christian and Jewish minorities during the war. Its usual organization in other Arab states was a formal "Committee of American Residents" recruited from the American institutions in the Near East. However, the Military Governor of Syria, Jemel Pasha, decreed that any member of a foreign organization giving food in Syria was subject to arrest. Thus, the relief of the Christian minorities was accomplished under great difficulties, since all action had to be taken by the non-foreign staffs of American-founded institutions, such as the university at Beirut, the American colleges, hospitals and orphanages, and the Presbyterian missions. These staffs created kitchens in refugee camps, enlarged hospitals and orphanages, and established a clothing factory to give employment to women. Their problems were greatly increased by the Turkish Government's action in dumping some 500,000 Armenians from other parts of the empire into Syria.

In January, 1919, the Near East Relief Committee was able to install open administration of its work in Near East countries, including Syria. The Committee set up an administrative staff, together with additional sanitary and economic staffs. It expanded the existing hospitals, clinics, orphanages, and trade schools and imported some food for their support. It undertook agricultural and industrial reconstruction.

In an analysis of accounts, it is impossible to separate the Near East Relief Committee's expenditures in Syria from those in Palestine. Its reports show that for Syria alone the Committee appropriated $2,659,760 prior to the Peace. From July 1, 1919, to July 1, 1923, appropriations for Syria and Palestine amounted to $4,460,362. Its reports also show a total appropriation of $9,837,687 for Syria and Palestine from 1915 to 1923.

THE AMERICAN RED CROSS IN SYRIA

Prior to the surrender of Turkey, the Red Cross gave no direct aid to Syria, but it did make large contributions to the Near East Relief Committee for its work. At the Turkish surrender, the Red Cross began medical relief on a large scale. It sent a mission comprising physicians, surgeons, sanitary staff, and nurses. It expanded hospitals, clinics, and medical aid on a large scale, not only to the hosts of refugees and orphans, but to the whole population. At the Peace, it reduced its operations and finally turned over its work to the Near East Relief Committee, to which it made large contributions.

From the Red Cross accounts it is impossible to separate its expenditures in Syria alone. The accounts show that during the Armistice period it appropriated to the Near East $4,763,155, a considerable part of which was used in Syria. Its accounts show an expenditure of $870,369 in the Near East and Palestine from the Peace to 1923. From 1914 to 1923, its records show an expenditure of $9,-681,765 in the Near East. Of this amount, approximately $6,000,000 was given to the Near East Relief Committee for its work in Syria, Palestine, and other Near Eastern countries.

THE JEWISH JOINT DISTRIBUTION COMMITTEE

The J.D.C. gave some service to its co-religionists and the other minority groups in Syria from 1914 to 1923. Its records do not give the details of these services, nor do its accounts permit the separation of its expenditures in Syria alone from those in neighboring states. Its records show that for Greece, Turkey, Serbia, and Syria from 1914 to 1923 its expenditure was $1,366,178.

AMERICAN FRIENDS SERVICE COMMITTEE

The American Friends Service Committee established a relief mission in Syria under Daniel Oliver, who had the aid of fourteen local workers. Direct expenditures by the Committee for Syria from June, 1920, through May, 1924, totaled $44,398.

THE OFFICIAL AMERICAN GOVERNMENTAL RELIEF AGENCIES

The official American governmental relief organization, under my direction, took little part in the relief of Syria. However, Howard Heinz, the Chief of our mission in Constantinople, on my instructions, sent Lieutenants W. O. Goodrich, Jr., and Norman S. Buck of his staff to Syria to inquire if the work of the Near East Committee there required any support from us. They reported on May 8, 1919, that the Committee was taking care of the situation effectively. At the request of the Committee, we purchased and transported to Syria a total of 15,176 tons of supplies with a value of $2,276,400, for which it reimbursed our cash outlay. Our staff costs were our contribution.

CHAPTER 21

TURKEY

The narrative of Turkey's persecution of the Christian and Jewish minorities in her Arab provinces is ample demonstration of her governmental attitudes prior to her surrender. But these actions in the truncated Turkish Empire did not cease when Turkey quit the war on October 30, 1918. It was not until the Treaty of Lausanne in July, 1923, that she agreed to end these activities.

At the time of Turkey's surrender to the Allies in October, 1918, she apparently did not wholly demobilize her armies. The Turkish nationalists, under Mustapha Kemal, reorganized and strengthened their forces and on November 1, 1922, overthrew the government of the Sultan. In my narrative of Greek relief,[1] I have given an account of the Greek-Turkish War, the result of which was the expulsion of about 1,000,000 Greeks from Turkish territory.

During the First World War, the Near East Relief Committee, the Jewish Joint Distribution Committee, and the American Red Cross had carried on the protection and relief of the Christian and Jewish minorities in Turkey itself, as well as in the Arab states under Turkish rule described above.

THE NEAR EAST RELIEF COMMITTEE IN TURKEY

The Near East Relief Committee began its work in Turkey in the fall of 1915. The Turkish surrender gave no assurance that persecu-

[1] See Chap. 47.

tions would cease. The Committee reported that a large number of Armenians and Greeks required continued aid.

The Near East Relief Committee opened headquarters at Constantinople in January, 1919, under an administrative committee, headed by Major Davis G. Arnold, in charge of all its activities outside Russia. A sub-director was appointed to take charge of orphanage educational programs, as was a medical director to supervise medical personnel, hospitals, clinics, and public health.

The services of the Near East Relief Committee included the care of orphans and the establishment of rescue homes for former captives of Moslem harems and their children. The Committee set up industrial enterprises to teach trades and encourage self-support among the rescued women and orphans and provided medical and sanitary relief.

It is impossible at this writing to separate the expenditures of the Committee for Turkey alone. One account's heading shows that from the Armistice to the Peace, the Committee appropriated a total of $2,301,000 to Turkey. All but $40,000 of this sum was for work in Constantinople. There were, however, further expenditures which cannot be broken down.

THE AMERICAN RED CROSS IN TURKEY

Constantinople was chosen in December, 1919, as the headquarters for the Red Cross in Southeastern Europe. Major C. Claflin Davis was appointed director.

Following the collapse of General Wrangel's "White" army in November, 1920, a great exodus of his soldiers and some Russian civilians took place from the Black Sea area to Constantinople; there were probably more than 200,000 persons. The only agency able to meet this crisis was the Red Cross. It provided the necessary food, clothing, and medical service. In July, 1922, an arrangement was made by the terms of which the League of Nations, the American Relief Administration, and the American Red Cross undertook to finish the task of evacuating the refugees from Constantinople.

Red Cross financial records show that from 1914 to June, 1923, it expended $6,627,889 in Turkey. The records also show that from the Peace until 1923, the Red Cross expended $6,531,316 in Turkey, almost all of which went to aid the Russian refugees.

THE JEWISH JOINT DISTRIBUTION COMMITTEE IN TURKEY

This Committee gave protection and relief to its co-religionists in Turkey from 1914 to 1923. Its records do not give details of its service in Turkey. No breakdown of its expenditures in Turkey alone is available. Its records show that from 1914 to November, 1918, the Committee expended $693,484 for "Turkey, Greece, Serbia and Syria," and from 1914 to 1923 its expenditures for these countries were $1,366,178. The specific sum recorded for Turkey alone is $705,771 from 1919 to the end of 1923.

THE AMERICAN RELIEF ADMINISTRATION IN TURKEY

Four months after the surrender of Turkey to the Allies, this organization, under my direction, established a mission at Constantinople under Howard Heinz and a competent staff to conduct our operations in the Eastern Mediterranean and Black Sea areas.

We were limited by the Lodge amendment to the use of the $100,000,000 Congressional appropriation in the relief of Turkey except to give relief to the non-Moslem population, namely, the Armenians, the Syrian Christians, and the Jews. While this legislation was in progress, I cabled our Washington office:

PARIS, 19 January 1919
It would be unfortunate if Turkey were eliminated for . . . [a large] Christian . . . population is sprinkled throughout the country and have in no way been the cause of Turkey's action. The present Bulgarian Government is comprised of men who have opposed the war. . . . I do hope we shall be permitted to assist in these situations. Bulgarians and Turks

will pay in commodities, but we require working capital pending realization. Henry White cabling Lodge above effect.

HOOVER

When the bill came out of the Senate, I also protested to President Wilson:

PARIS, 27 January 1919

DEAR MR. PRESIDENT:

The Senate amended our $100,000,000 Relief Bill excluding Bulgaria, Germany, Austria-Hungary and the Mahomedan population of Turkey from the provinces of the Bill. These populations have to be fed if the prime objective of . . . [our] action is to be secured. The Bill goes into conference and I am wondering if you could send a cablegram to Mr. Glass asking him to represent you in requesting that these exceptions should be taken out. . . .

The fact is that three of these countries have established democratic governments and are really making an honest struggle towards respectability. The men in charge of each country are men who have been against the war, and it must be desirable from a political and a humane point of view that they should be supported. The Turkish situation is one of complexity as it will be almost impossible to sort out the Christian population from the rest, and in any event we do not look for a very large expenditure of money in this direction as . . . [they] have commodities ready to export and it becomes a matter of trade rather than international finance.

The Bill as passed by the House was in the form that we hoped. . . . The large majority by which it passed . . . the House would seem to indicate some hope of getting it reviewed in conference without too much of a struggle.

HERBERT HOOVER

However, the Lodge amendment prevailed.

At the time of our appointment of Howard Heinz as head of our mission in Constantinople, I gave him a letter of instruction, some paragraphs of which throw light on our problems in that area:

PARIS, 26 January, 1919.

MY DEAR HEINZ:

We are yet so undetermined as to the exact organization that it is almost impossible for me to give any precise directions. You are appointed the head of the American . . . [Relief Administration] Mission at Constantinople. You will necessarily be the American member of the Allied Commission which will sit at that port to deal with the provisioning problems covering Turkey, Bulgaria, Greece, and that portion of Serbia available from Salonica, and you will undoubtedly be a halfway station to Roumania. . . .

I then described the separate functions of the American Relief Administration, the United States Grain Corporation, and the Allied councils at Constantinople, adding:

. . . [Thus] you have three functions. First, that you are the head of the American Food Mission and, as such, establish the necessary official relations with . . . such governments as we deal with. Second, you are the Director of the . . . [American] Relief Administration in your territory. Third, you are the agent for the . . . United States Grain Corporation at Constantinople.

I then stated that the Grain Corporation would set up stocks in Constantinople and continued:

There will be various private reliefs in Turkey, such as the . . . [Near East Relief Committee in Armenia and Syria]. We wish to give . . . [them] every possible encouragement. You are authorized to sell foodstuffs to that Committee ad lib, as against their undertaking to pay in Washington in American dollars. . . . You can also sell foodstuffs from the Grain Corporation to anyone else who will pay you American exchange. Your only reserve needs to be that you should retain such foodstuffs as are necessary to support the destitute as against buyers of less need. . . .

You will . . . [need] local currency with which to support your organization, to pay storage, discharging of steamers, etc. You are authorized to sell enough food to local merchants for local currency to keep you thus supplied. I would be glad if you would discuss with the normal commodity exporters from Turkey to the United States as to whether . . . they will . . . pay you American exchange in return for foodstuffs . . . they undertaking that there shall be a just distribution of this food. I am anxious that the normal commercial trade shall be re-established as fast as possible. . . .

The theory of this whole business is that the British, French and Italians are also going to provide foodstuffs for the area in . . . some proportion with us, which proportion is not as yet determined, and it may be necessary for you to arrange with them that they relieve certain places and you undertake others which you can do under the law, but bear in mind you can accept no Turkish Government obligations. You can accept obligations of municipalities or institutions in Turkey, as I interpret the law, provided the people fed are those described in the law itself, i.e., Christian, Jewish and Greek. . . .

HERBERT HOOVER

I have recorded elsewhere the relief in Armenia, Bulgaria, Yugoslavia, and Rumania conducted under our Constantinople organization.

THE WORK OF OTHER CHARITABLE ORGANIZATIONS IN TURKEY

Under the law, the American Relief Administration could sell food for cash to any country. Mr. Heinz arranged to sell 20,278 tons of American flour for $4,369,404 to a group of responsible merchants in Constantinople. The merchants resold it on a ration basis to the whole population of the city. It was sufficient to meet the situation, and the price of bread dropped 50 per cent overnight.

In 1921, when General Wrangel's "White" army was defeated, some 1,200 soldiers from his army—mostly engineers—reached Constantinople. This group appealed to me for assistance in getting to the United States. We called upon American engineers for both financial help in bringing them to the United States and for job placement assistance on their arrival. The engineers created a committee and immediately raised a fund of $25,000 to which the American Relief Administration contributed $5,000. This committee initially found jobs for the Russian engineers as mechanics and draftsmen, but as soon as they learned English, they rose rapidly in the engineering profession.

It is interesting to note that the Russian quota of emigrants to the United States was at this time exhausted. But Secretary of State Kellogg declared Bessarabia, then unsettled as to its ultimate destination, to be a part of original Russia, and thus created an additional Russian quota which covered these 1,200 refugees.

Early in March, 1922, the Laura Spelman Rockefeller Memorial Fund provided the American Relief Administration with $100,000 for Russian refugees who had fled to Constantinople. Since we had closed our Constantinople office prior to this time, we sent Arthur Ringland of our staff to Constantinople on March 22, 1922. As a result of his efforts, an agreement was drawn up whereby the League of Nations would provide funds for the evacuation of these refugees and the A.R.A. (on behalf of the Laura Spelman Rockefeller Memorial) would undertake to feed them during the period of evacuation. This program was begun in July, 1922, and ended May 1, 1923. The A.R.A. fed 11,407 refugees and helped with the evacuation of 22,000. The funds expended were $98,622; we returned the balance to the donors.

The Young Men's Christian Association, the Young Women's Christian Association, along with other religious groups, came to the support of the suffering minorities in Turkey. Most of these groups performed their services through the other larger relief organizations—the Near East Relief Committee, the Jewish Joint Distribution Committee, and the American Red Cross.

On June 7, 1919, the Y.W.C.A. opened a service center in Constantinople for homeless girls of the Greek and Armenian nationalities. A month after the opening, 147 girls had been enrolled in English classes, and there was a general membership of 300. Other service centers were opened later.

For the women released from harems, the Near East Relief Committee provided homes and the Y.W.C.A. sent teachers. The homes were located in Asia Minor, Turkey, and Armenia.

CHAPTER 22

PERSIA

When the First World War came, Persia already had suffered great damage to her independence from the Russian-British agreement dividing the exploitation of her resources into spheres. During the war, the Russians, Germans, Turks, and British—each at some period—had placed troops in her territory, which further limited her independence. One purpose of these occupations was to keep the supply route to Russia open. The Communists withdrew the Russian troops soon after their revolution, and the Turks withdrew at their surrender to the Allies.

The Persians sent a delegation to the Paris Peace Conference in 1919, demanding an abrogation of the various treaties which trespassed on Persia's sovereignty, but the delegation was refused a hearing. The British military forces were withdrawn in January, 1921.

THE RELIEF

There had long been minority groups of Christians in Persia (Nestorians, Armenians, and Assyrians), and with the Communist Revolution came a large group of Russian refugees. Most of these groups were concentrated in the Urmia and Tabriz districts bordering on the Turkish provinces of Kurdistan and on Russian Armenia.

The Persians had been more tolerant than the other Moslem

states, American missionary efforts having been carried on since 1811—over a hundred years. At the outbreak of the war of 1914, there were American medical, educational, and religious institutions in Persia, with about 75 Americans on their staffs. These Americans joined with the staff of the American Legation and created a relief committee for minorities and refugees under the chairmanship of the United States Consul-General Gordon Paddock. Almost the sole support of the committee, aside from its own resources, was the Near East Relief Committee.

This American relief committee has a great record of accomplishments in Persia, including the feeding of 15,000 Persian Christians in a mission compound at Urmia for five months of 1915 during a Turkish occupation in that area. To the hundreds of thousands of refugees in Teheran and Hamadan in 1918 it furnished monthly rations. Refugees were given tools, animals, and seed to encourage their return home. The committee maintained some orphanages, but its major operation was to give the refugees and destitute minorities work on constructive public improvements. These workers widened impassable streets in Tabriz, Teheran, and Hamadan; rebuilt and paved highways; built dikes to protect Tabriz from floods; and, with the aid of the Americans, who arranged contracts with the British Army, established workrooms which took on contracts for manufacturing stockings and underwear for the Army.

In the summer of 1918, a thirteen-man American commission of specialists under Dr. Harry P. Judson, President of the University of Chicago, undertook an organized attack on typhoid, typhus, and cholera epidemics. The epidemics were not very severe, and the commission reported a few months later that its work was accomplished.

It is impossible to segregate relief expenditures for Persia from those of the surrounding states. The accounts of the Near East Relief Committee show $7,541,959 for Persia and Mesopotamia from 1914 to 1923. The Jewish Joint Distribution Committee shows a total expenditure of $38,717 from 1914 to 1923. The American Red Cross records an expenditure of $6,618 in Persia from 1914 to the Armistice.

CHAPTER 23

EGYPT, SAUDI ARABIA, TUNISIA, ALGERIA, MOROCCO, AND AZERBAIJAN

EGYPT

Egypt was under British influence during the war and served as a base for British military operations against Turkey. The country maintained its low standard of living from its own production, aided by expenditures of the British armies and profits realized from exports—chiefly cotton.

The accounts of the Jewish Joint Distribution Committee show an expenditure of $56,342 for relief of refugees in Alexandria from late 1914 through December, 1918. Total expenditures up to December, 1923, are given as $58,851. The accounts of the Near East Relief Committee show that total appropriations for Egypt from late 1915 through December, 1923, were $18,474.

SAUDI ARABIA

This province of the Turkish Empire had a varied political history during the war. A part of this province revolted against Turkey on June 5, 1916, and on October 29, 1916, united with the British forces against the Turks. The British military authorities furnished food and medical aid of which we have no record. Nor is there a record of persecution of religious minorities in this area.

194

TUNISIA, ALGERIA, AND MOROCCO

The only American charitable institution interested in these North African Moslem states was the Jewish Joint Distribution Committee, which contributed $9,000 for support of Jewish refugees.

AZERBAIJAN

There were no official governmental organizations providing relief to this nation. The voluntary organizations gave relief to the Caucasus in general, but we do not have a specific financial figure for Azerbaijan.

ARMENIA, GEORGIA, AND ABYSSINIA

CHAPTER 24

ARMENIA PRIOR TO THE PEACE, GEORGIA, AND ABYSSINIA

In the second volume of these memoirs,[1] I have described the organization and purpose of the Near East Relief Committee. I may recall that the Committee originated from an appeal in September, 1915, of Ambassador to Turkey Henry Morgenthau, Sr., stating that "the destruction of the Armenian race in Turkey is rapidly progressing." While the Near East Relief Committee performed great service in saving Christian minorities in the Moslem states, its greatest burden was the Armenians.

There were estimated to be about 2,000,000 Armenians in the Turkish Empire, about 1,500,000 in the Russian provinces of Armenia, Georgia, and Azerbaijan, and about 500,000 elsewhere—or about 4,000,000 Armenians in peril. During the hideous persecutions by the Turks, more than 400,000 fled to Russian Armenia, increasing this group to about 2,000,000. In previous chapters on the relief of minorities in the Moslem states, I have recited the efforts of the Near East Relief Committee and the American Red Cross for relief of Armenians in those areas.

During the first three years of the war, prior to the Bolshevik Revolution, the Russian Government had given rations to the Armenians. The whole scene shifted with the Communist Revolution. At this time, the three Caucasian provinces of Armenia, Georgia, and Azerbaijan declared their independence and established themselves as separate republics. For a time they were protected from

[1] *An American Epic*, Vol. II, Chap. 22.

Communist invasion by the Germans after their defeat of Communist Russia.

In March, 1918, the German Army secured a supply of oil, seized control of the port of Batum on the Black Sea, and took over the railways and pipelines to the great oil field of Baku on the Caspian Sea. With the defeat of Germany, the British seized the German positions to secure oil supplies. The northern boundary of the Armenian Republic lay some miles to the south of these operations, and aside from these protections from Communist invasions, all three of the Caucasian republics were for a time assured by General Denikin's "White" army, which was operating against the Communists to the north of them.

The Georgians had no particular love for the Armenians. The Azerbaijans, being Moslems with sympathetic ties to Turkey, were a persistent enemy—with a bad habit of border raids on the Armenian villages.

THE ECONOMIC AND POLITICAL SITUATION
OF ARMENIA

With the lifting of the curtain over Armenia at the Armistice, the situation of these people came into the full light of day. Prewar Russian Armenia had a sparse agriculture but managed to provide further supplies of food by exports of manufactured goods. However, the harvest of 1918 was devastated by a drought. Four months later, at the Armistice, with the huge burden of the host of refugees, the Armenians were eating their meager seed grain. The only access for relief supplies to Armenia from overseas was the Baku-Batum railway, from which a branch line extended south to Erivan, the capital of Armenia. Up to the Armenian borders, the railways were in Georgian territory; the distance to Batum was about 400 miles. At the Armistice, the Armenians had only 32 live locomotives and 1,704 useful cars.

The government of Armenia was a problem in itself; it was only a shadow of a government. Prime Minister Khatisian was an honest man whose governmental experience had been gained through the mayorship of Tiflis. His ministers had never had an atom of administrative experience. All of them, including the Prime Minister, were stunned and helpless in the face of their disasters. If anyone wants material for a treatise on human woe, intrigue, war, massacre, and governmental incompetence, he can find ample sources in the mass of reports from relief officials in Armenia during 1918–1919.

RELIEF

Russian Armenia, Georgia, and Azerbaijan were ruled by the United States Treasury as ineligible for Government loans. Thus the saving of Armenia was dependent on public appeals for charity. The Near East Relief Committee, under the leadership of Dr. James Barton and Mr. Cleveland Dodge, made the word "Armenia" known to virtually every American school child. The association of Mount Ararat and Noah, the staunch Armenian Christians who were massacred periodically by the Mohammedan Turks, and the Sunday School collections to alleviate their miseries—all accumulated to impress the sufferings of the Armenians on the American mind. Added to this was the existence of a considerable group of American citizens of Armenian descent. Under our stimulus of freedom, they had shown great qualities in business, literature, art, and public service. They gave generously to their race in the Near East.

The Committee decided in December, 1918, to launch an appeal to the American people for an addition of $30,000,000 to its funds. On January 6, 1919, Edgar Rickard of our Washington office cabled me as follows:

. . . It is obvious . . . that their [Near East] proposed drive for $30,000,000 scheduled to commence January 12, will fail completely without your endorsement . . . A statement from you to effect the Armenians . . . have no funds, cannot secure Government's loans, and must depend upon American generosity, adding such other humanity appeal as you may care to authorize, would largely assist committee. . . . An early reply is urgently requested. In meantime I have, in your name, endorsed the request to Secretary of the Navy for space on naval vessel to carry over about two hundred special field workers composed chiefly hospital units . . . also about two hundred tons of medical supplies and miscellaneous groceries more particularly adapted for hospital needs. . . .

I naturally complied with this request, but the result of the appeal fell very short of the needs for the Committee's work. The appeal brought in only $19,485,000 for the year 1919.

The Near East Relief Committee established its organization for the Caucasian states of Armenia, Georgia, and Azerbaijan under President J. H. T. Main of Grinnell College, Iowa, with a staff of thirty members. A medical service was established; physicians, surgeons, and nurses were delegated to Armenia. The Committee supplied food and clothing and set up orphanages, hospitals, clinics, trade schools, and new industries to aid in employment.

The Near East Relief in the early months of 1919 informed my organization (the official American governmental relief agencies) that it could carry the financial load of Armenia but that we could be of help if we purchased and transported these supplies to Batum. Before the end of February, we delivered over 7,000 tons of supplies for which it paid. We were unable to contribute to Armenian needs until the Congressional appropriation to our organization was available at the end of February.

On February 10, when it was evident that the $100,000,000 appropriation for our organization would pass in Congress, we informed Howard Heinz, our director in Constantinople, that we would help in Armenia if the Near East Relief ran short of resources. On February 22, Heinz replied to this suggestion:

The representatives of this organization here including Dr. Barton and Mr. Hatch are not of the opinion that much . . . [American Relief Administration supplies] can be utilized by them at any time, partly because of lack of funds and partly for economic reasons it being their belief that Eastern Armenia can be fed with material obtainable near-by at much less cost. It would also appear that their funds have been so extensively invested in clothing, hospital supplies and general operations that they will of necessity have to forego the purchase of much food material anywhere, other than seed grains . . . So far as they and I can see, this arrangement will constitute practically our entire dealing with these people except so far as may be of assistance in getting seed grain for them out of Southern Russia and the Kouban district in exchange for reclaimed quartermaster supplies, farming implements, etc. . . .

In April, 1919, however, Mr. Heinz began to receive most disturbing reports of the inability of the Near East Relief to meet the situation in Armenia. He dispatched Captain Abraham Tulin and Lieutenant Reuben Horchow of his staff to investigate. Their report was appalling. Some sentences were:

The condition of all these people is horrible beyond belief. They are daily dying of starvation by the hundreds. In the district of Alexandropol alone, where some 110,000 people are concentrated, the mayor of the town told me on April 17 that 140 persons had died of starvation the day before and 168 the day before that, and that the district had for some time averaged around 150 deaths from starvation per day. The truth of this statement was only too plainly borne out by what I myself saw, and was attested by everyone to whom I talked, both British and Armenian. In and around Erivan, Etchmiadzin and Igdir, all of which are large concentration points for refugees, I observed the same fearful conditions, while at Shusha and other places, which are off the route of travel, things are, according to British reports even worse, if possible. It was stated to me by British officers, and also by Americans on the ground, that cannibalism had in some places been resorted to and that human dead were being disinterred from fresh graves and eaten. I saw some of the horrible evidences of the latter at Igdir. Grass and roots dug up in the field have been the general diet for some time now, and the state of the people is such that, to quote the opinion of Dr. Usher (medical) of the Near East Committee at Erivan, an opinion which he gave me for quotation, "Unless relief on an extensive scale is rushed in at once, by the time that it is brought in the majority of the people will have died."

It was obvious from Captain Tulin's report that we would have to take over responsibility for supplies to Armenia.

Mr. Heinz left immediately for Armenia to examine the situation personally. Without waiting for his report, we directed from Paris that certain cargoes of supplies en route continue to Batum and begin loading further supplies from our stocks in Constantinople.

Before he left for Armenia, Mr. Heinz urged that we send an experienced staff to take charge of food distribution and official relations with the government. We directed Colonel William N. Haskell, who was in charge of our operations in Rumania, to send quickly Captain Joseph Green of his staff (and an old C.R.B. hand), together with adequate assistants, to Armenia.

Mr. Heinz' report is worthy of preservation as an appraisal of famine at its worst. He said:

. . . I found the most distressing situation all through this country . . . [where] starvation and misery actually beggars description. . . . [the] people are literally dying from lack of food and from diseases caused by malnutrition. There are 500,000 refugees who are in need of food and of these, the estimate that 200,000 to 250,000 are at the starvation point, is a reasonable one. . . .

The lack of food among . . . [them] is so serious that the women actually go into the fields and obtain grass roots which they cook into a kind of a broth and serve as boiled greens, occasionally getting a bit of rice to mix with it, and this constitutes the principal diet of many. The little children, naturally, get the worst of this situation because they cannot eat such material and it is among the children that the death-rate is the highest.

It is difficult to make comparisons as to the degree of destitution and distress existing in different districts or towns, but I think the worst situation that came to my knowledge was in Igdir where there is a larger proportion of sickness and a higher death rate than either Erivan or Alexandropol.

Regarding reports of cannibalism which have come out of this district from time to time I have been forced against my will to believe these reports to be true. I saw with my own eyes mutilated remains of corpses which had been exhumed from newly made graves and was informed by the Director of one of the Armenian orphanages that he had met a woman carrying a human arm and when asked what she was going to do with it she replied "I have no other food!" I did not see anybody who had actually witnessed the eating of human flesh, but there is so much circumstantial evidence of this in and around Igdir that as I have said I personally came to believe it true.

Typhus has been epidemic during the winter and has taken away thousands but with the moderation of the weather it is now decreasing but cholera is making its appearance and the outlook is threatening. Every condition is favorable to its spread. The people are clad in vermin infested rags with no possible change or chance of improvement, because there is no clothing of any kind or textile material available at any price even if the people had the money with which to buy it.

Very few crops have been planted in the district because of lack of agricultural implements, but mainly because of lack of seed. . . .

. . . Unquestionably most of these people have to be fed for another year. Many of them, as you doubtless understand are refugees from Turkey and these all desire to get back to their homes to till the land they have left, but when they get back I am sure, from what I know of conditions, that they will find very little. The Turk has despoiled everything and they will have nothing on which to commence, neither houses, furnishings or tools and implements. . . .

Orphanages. . . . the Near East Committee . . . had been doing considerable work in Russian Armenia which extends down to the cities of Erivan, Alexandropol and Kars. In these districts they have been conducting orphanages which have saved the lives of thousands of children, and while I was there they decided to take over all the orphanages in operation by the Armenian Government which had neither the personnel, food or medicinal supplies to properly run such institutions. I believe there will be no less than 70,000 children under the roofs of these Near East Committee Orphanages and think that they will be able to do one of the greatest pieces of constructive relief work ever accomplished.

Hospitals. This committee has also opened one or two hospitals and has established several hospital units with physicians and trained nurses. They are not however sufficiently well equipped as yet to take on the awful problem of epidemic diseases in this vast country. . . .

. . . [*Food*] *Distribution.* I have made arrangements with the British Military Authorities to assume responsibility for unloading our . . . [food] at Batoum and for taking this to the interior in one or two solid trains of twenty cars each per day under British military guard. . . . as the Georgian railroad is limited best arrangements will not permit to exceed from 1000 to 1300 tons per week . . . [of food] distribution to the Armenian interior. . . . What will happen after your program is finished I do not know. [Our financial authorities expired June 30.] Certainly the . . . [Near East Relief Committee] has not at present funds with which to continue an extensive program of feeding so many people. I accordingly wish to recommend to your consideration the possibility of finding funds to send some additional cargoes over and above the 20,000 tons that you have planned to supply. I believe storage facilities could be found for any additional . . . [food] that you may be able to furnish to take the population through some of the fall months. . . .

Our supplies and the devotion and skill of Captain Green's staff quickly brought a stop to mass starvation. The Near East Relief Committee carried on efficiently the burden of the orphanages, hospitals, clinics, and medical aid. We shipped from Constantinople the food needed for these orphanages and hospitals, and Captain Green established canteens for the special feeding of other children.

The devoted leaders of the Near East Relief Committee are not to be blamed for the failure to realize the impending disaster or to organize to meet it. They were a religious organization staffed with religious men who knew nothing about mass starvation or its stealthy approach.

We had still other troubles. Despite the fact that the Georgians had sufficient food, their government demanded of Captain Green, for the use of its railway, a free supply of 2,000 tons of food a month, which we promptly refused, but that did not silence them.

On June 20, the British notified us that they were withdrawing their military contingent from the Caucasus. The same day, I wrote President Wilson asking his aid in delaying the withdrawal of British troops, which meant both our protection from highway robbery by Georgia and Azerbaijan and efficient operation of the ports and railways. After describing the attitudes of the Georgian Government, I took the occasion to inform the President of the situation in Armenia:

. . . Our people estimate that there are already 200,000 deaths from starvation and that unless we can have a rigid control of this railway under the British authorities and unless we can stop the piracy of the Georgian Government, and unless we can have no interruption by military change, we shall certainly lose another 200,000 lives.

I do not wish to burden you with the heart-breaking details of the whole Armenian situation. The daily reports that we have not only through all our own agencies at work here but as well through the British agencies are of the most appalling that have yet developed out of the war.

I need only mention that the eating of the dead is now fairly general. We have large stocks of foodstuffs lying in Batoum and I am confident that everything has been done both on our part and on the part of the British authorities that could have been done so far, but these impending interruptions can mean nothing but total breakdown.

With the arrival of harvest about the end of August, the situation will be much ameliorated. [Due to our provision of seed grain.]

If it were possible for you to discuss this matter with your colleagues it might be that some arrangement could be made that the change in armies could be delayed and that the British authorities could take a more emphatic and rigid control of the railways than they now hold, and that emphatic notice be given the Georgian government. . . . The matter is of the most urgent order.

HERBERT HOOVER

The President obtained British agreement to remain a while, and, as usual, they were most co-operative.

During the month prior to July 1, 1919, in preparation for the end of the official American relief agencies, we ordered several cargoes en route and the balance of our stocks in Constantinople shipped to Armenia and, if necessary, stored in Batum. This would provide two or three months' supplies after the Peace, during which time a new organization could be established.

My colleagues and I did not believe that America should abandon the Armenians, for it was obvious that the Near East Relief Committee had neither the resources, the trained staff, nor the political weight to do the job. Also, it was obvious that if the Armenians were to be saved from their fierce neighbors on every side, there would have to be more than supplies. It was essential that there be an exhibition of Allied power, and there had to be a man of iron nerves with enough American Army personnel not only to distribute relief but to train an Armenian army. Since these problems concerned Armenia after the Peace, I take up this subject in Part Two of this narrative.

In summing up the American official relief agencies' contributions to Armenia before the Peace, I give a table showing the amounts of supplies which were distributed by them.

TOTAL SUPPLIES TO ARMENIA
FROM THE ARMISTICE TO THE PEACE *

	Food	Clothing & Misc.	Total	$ Value
American Relief Administration				
Congressional loan	45,312		45,312	$ 8,028,412
Freight				47,688
Near East Relief				
Committee	17,444	15,207	32,651	9,222,894
American Red Cross ...		754	754	258,600
United Kingdom				71,400
(freight)				
	62,756	15,961	78,717	$17,628,994

* In tons.

The American Government received notes from the Armenian Government for the Congressional loan, but as I have stated in the Introduction to this volume, we were never paid and thus this was a gift—as were the contributions of the Near East Relief Committee and the Red Cross.

GEORGIA

The relief activities in Georgia were mainly carried on by the Near East Relief Committee's support of Armenians. From the beginning of its work in 1915 until 1923, this committee's records show an appropriation of $18,288,877 for its work in the Russian Caucasus. However, it is impossible to estimate how much of this was designated for Georgia.

ABYSSINIA

The Jewish Joint Distribution Committee expended $11,908 in relief of refugees who had fled to Abyssinia.

THE APPROACH OF PEACE

CHAPTER 25

WINDING UP AMERICAN PARTICIPATION IN INTER-ALLIED ECONOMIC ACTIVITIES

The problems of settling American relations with various inter-Allied councils, committees, or commissions created for the war, the Armistice, or peace purposes included those listed below.

First, there were more than sixty wartime or Armistice inter-Allied commissions, boards, or committees of which we Americans were members or with which we had relations. Many of them died automatically with the signing of the Peace. In any event, our representation on them ended with the legal expiration of our authorities and appropriations on July 1, 1919.

Second, there were economic agencies set up solely among the Allies, which they might continue after the Peace. We Americans were particularly interested in ending this category—that is, the joint British, French, and Italian wheat, fats, meat, and sugar purchasing agencies and shipping controls through which they might affect the postwar American economy. I proposed to the Supreme Economic Council on May 31, 1919, that these Allied agencies be dissolved with the signing of the Peace. The Allied members of the Council refused. However, these agencies quickly went out of existence anyway, as they proved unable to control free markets in the rest of the world.

Third, there were countries which would still need relief after the Peace. In my memorandum to the Supreme Economic Council, I reviewed the prospective economic situation—the possible countries where aid could be discontinued. I said:

. . . Obviously, such a liquidation depends upon three factors: (a) the consummation of peace prior to this harvest, (b) upon there being sufficient food supplies in the world during the next harvest year to meet the world's needs, and (c) a sufficiency of shipping to handle the world's trade. As to (a) we must assume that we shall have peace before the end of July. As to (b) I am convinced from a critical study of the world crop prospects that there will be a sufficiency of supplies [for the world as a whole]. As to (c) I am informed that with the constantly increasing volume of shipping and the completion of repatriation, there will be a much greater mobility of food shipping than any time during . . . [recent] years.

. . . As to Germany, I should propose that within a few days of peace no further ships should be loaded . . . [and] that the Germans should be informed that they must instruct their own agencies abroad to arrange their [own supplies]. . . .

. . . the liberated or ex-enemy [controlled] States, Finland, Esthonia, Lavonia, Lithuania, Poland, Roumania, Bulgaria, Greater Serbia, Czecho-Slovakia, Austria and Belgium have been under relief administration in which credit purchase, transportation, and to a large extent internal distribution have been . . . administered [or guided] by [The American Government relief agencies and] the Agencies of the Associated Governments. In their political and economic situation no other measures could have saved wholesale starvation, and could have laid the foundations for stable government. With the coming harvest their food resources will be greatly expanded. In fact, Bulgaria, Roumania . . . [Yugoslavia], and old Turkey, outside of Armenia, will have sufficient of the principal staples and enough in surplus to exchange for their other food necessities [to care for their adults]. Belgium, Czecho-Slovakia, Poland, Austria and the Baltic States will require a margin of food imports throughout the next year.

I have been strongly convinced, however, that a continuation of exterior administration for even these latter States after peace and harvest will only undermine their initiative and self-reliance. They should rely upon themselves for purchase, transport, and administration of supplies and thus reduce the problem in relation to the Allies to one of finance only.

Some two months ago, I advised each of these Governments that while

I considered the first step in . . . [this direction] the upbuilding of their own Food Ministries, that the second step in progress seemed to me to call for . . . [each of them to create their own] Economic Commission[s] with representatives at the principal centers of the world who could not only administer the purchase and transportation of foodstuffs and raw material, but could also negotiate for credits and mobilize the marketing of exports and exchange, and that the work of these Commissions should also involve the stimulation of private trading to the point of the third step, i.e., normal commerce. Some of them have taken such steps.

The *fourth* category was the representation of the United States in the many organizations created by the Peace Treaty. They were considered by the President's Committee of Economic Advisers early in April. We did not agree on all points, for my colleagues had not been through my experience of the previous six months. I gave a condensation of my views in a letter to the President:

11 April 1919

DEAR MR. PRESIDENT:

Your economic group has had before it the question of whether the United States should continue membership in the various commissions set up under the peace treaty. I should like to lay before you my own views on this subject.

I feel strongly that any continuation of the United States in such an Allied relationship can only lead to vast difficulty and would militate against the [independence and] efficiency of the League of Nations. My reasons are as follows:

I. These commissions are primarily to secure the enforcement of reparation and other conditions imposed upon the Central Empires. As the United States is not calling for any form of reparation . . . our presence on these commissions would appear to be for one of the following purposes.

(*a*) To give moral and political support to the Allied Governments. . . . It cannot be conceived that in the prostrate condition of the enemy that the Allies will require any physical assistance to the enforcement of their demands. . . .

(*b*) Another objective might be that we should remain in these commissions with a view to securing justice and moderation in the demands of the Allies against the Central Empires. We would thus be thrust into the repulsive position of the defender of our late enemy, in order to secure what we would conceive to be constructive and statesmanlike rehabilitation in Europe. Our experience during the last three months has shown us bitterly that we thus subject ourselves to complaint and attack from the Allied Governments. . . .

II. If our experience in the last four months counts for anything, the practical result always is that the Allied Governments . . . ask for more than they expect to get, and that we find ourselves psychologically . . . on the side of the enemy in these negotiations. . . . I am not attempting to dispute the righteousness of any Allied demand, but merely to set up the fact that our viewpoint is so essentially different. . . .

III. If we continue to sit in the [commission for] enforcement of this peace, we will be in effect participating in an armed alliance in Europe, where every change in the political wind will affect the action of these commissions. We will be obliged to participate in all [sorts of] European questions. . . .

IV. This whole matter has a very practical relationship to the League of Nations. If we can bring to an early end our whole relationship to these political combinations in Europe, which grew up before and during the war and can lend our strength to the League of Nations, that body will gain a stability and importance which it could not otherwise attain. . . . If, on the other hand, we can again secure our independence, we can make of the League that strong and independent Court of Appeal that will have authority.

V. I am convinced that there has grown up since the Armistice the policy, perhaps unconscious but nevertheless effective, of dragging the United States into every political and economic question in Europe. . . . These objectives and interests may be perfectly justified from their point of view. . . . For instance, I don't see how we can remain in these enforcement commissions unless we participate in the military enforcement with its enormous cost and risk. . . .

VI. I have the feeling that revolution in Europe is by no means over. The social wrongs in these countries are far from solution and the tempest must blow itself out, probably with enormous violence. Our people are not prepared for us to undertake the military . . . [policing] of Europe while it boils out its social wrongs. I have no doubt that if we could undertake to police the world and had the wisdom of statesmanship to see its gradual social evolution, that we would be making a great contribution to civilization, but I am certain that the American people are not prepared for any such a measure and I am also sure that if we remain in Europe with military force, tied in with an alliance which we have never undertaken, we should be forced into this storm of repression of revolution, and forced in under terms of co-ordination with other people that would make our independence of action wholly impossible.

VII. It grows upon me daily that the United States is the one great moral reserve in the world today and that we cannot maintain that independence of action through which this reserve is to be . . . [sustained] if we allow ourselves to be dragged into detailed European entanglements over a period of years. In my view, if the Allies cannot be brought to adopt peace on the basis of the 14 points, we should retire from Europe lock, stock and barrel . . . we should lend to the whole world our economic and moral strength, or the world will swim in a sea of misery and disaster worse than the dark ages. If they cannot be brought to accept peace on this basis, our national honor is at stake and we should have to make peace independently and retire. I know of nothing in letter or spirit of any statement of your own, or in the 14 points, that directly or indirectly ties the United States to carry on this war through the phase of enforcement or the multitudinous demands and intrigues of a great number of other governments and their officials. . . .

HERBERT HOOVER

The President agreed except on the question of our continuing on the Reparations Commission. His reply was:

PARIS, 15, April 1919

MY DEAR MR. HOOVER:

I am very much impressed by your objection to the United States continuing to supply members to the various commissions which are to be set up under the Peace Treaty and am ready to say at once that I agree with you.

I am afraid that we cannot escape membership on the Financial Commission on Reparation because that commission will undoubtedly need an umpire, and I am afraid we must take the necessary risks in that matter.[1] But with regard to most of the others, you may be sure I shall fight shy.

WOODROW WILSON

[1] The problem of American representation on this commission died with the failure of the Senate to ratify the Peace Treaty.

CHAPTER 26

CONTINUED AMERICAN ECONOMIC
CO-OPERATION AFTER THE PEACE

Continued American co-operation with the Allies in European and world-wide economic problems was supported by the President's "Committee of Economic Advisers" and by the leaders in our American relief activities. Our immediate difficulty was that our experienced American leaders in these economic fields were volunteers who wanted to return to their professions at home, and in any event, we had no appropriations with which to maintain such a staff.

Among the economic proposals to stem the miseries which the European nations were suffering, or anticipating, there were many extensive commitments involving the United States. Prime Minister Lloyd George's active mind furnished most of these ideas, and the President usually referred them to his "Committee of Economic Advisers."

Since the Committee kept few minutes, Vance McCormick's diary and our actual reports to the President compose most of the record. An entry by McCormick in his diary for January 21, 1919, says:

. . . [The President informed me he had] heard from reliable sources the Allies want to pool the total expense of the war and have us pay our proportionate share of the whole. This, of course, is not to be considered, and the President was considerably exercised over this proposal and wanted me to tell the other advisers not to get mixed up in any of their committees by discussing this subject at this time; but we were to confine ourselves only to our own . . . financial or other problems in which the

216

enemy countries are involved, thereby keeping clear of embarrassing discussions which have nothing to do with Germany. . . .

On April 23, Lloyd George addressed a long letter to the President proposing a plan to provide Europe with working capital after the Peace Treaty was signed. The plan called for a joint guarantee by the United States, Britain, France, and Italy of six and one-half billion dollars in German, Austrian, and Hungarian bonds, the proceeds to be used to rehabilitate European industry. The President referred the matter to the "Advisers" Committee.

An entry in McCormick's diary for April 24 states:

At 10.00 went to meet Hoover at Davis' room to discuss new proposal of British for international bond issue to relieve financial distress in Europe and to use U.S. credit to guarantee bonds of bankrupt nations. . . .

We advised the President to have nothing to do with the proposal. The next day, Lloyd George proposed another financial plan to the President whereby all Allied debts would be consolidated, with the United States participating in their joint guarantee. McCormick's diary on April 25 recorded its fate:

All advisers busy today discussing new financial scheme of British to consolidate debt and have all Allies guarantee interest and principal. That means the United States would guarantee all the bankrupt nations. The more the plan is studied the less enthusiastic our people become. . . . We will have to help but I don't believe in quite that way.

In response to requests from newspapers back home, I issued a statement on Europe's economic outlook. The Associated Press summary of its pertinent paragraphs (*The New York Times,* June 10, 1919) was as follows:

"This sort of economic delirium tremens will end with peace," said Herbert C. Hoover . . . today, discussing the situation in Europe and the need of financing different nations. Asked for a statement as to the financial requirements of Europe from the United States during the next year, he said:

"Any statement is premised upon peace and the return of Europe to work. I do not take it we will finance any more wars in Europe, directly or indirectly, nor that we will provide money to enable the people of Europe to live without work, or to work part time, as at present all over Europe. . . ."

Lloyd George had still another idea which he proposed to Mr. Wilson. On June 13, McCormick's diary recorded:

. . . I was called upon the phone and told the President wanted to see economic advisers at 10.00 A.M., before the 11.00 o'clock meeting of the Big Four, now the Big Five, as the Japanese joined Council this morning. When we, that is, Baruch, Hoover, Davis, Lamont and I, arrived the President told us Lloyd George was . . . arguing importance of Allied control of all purchases of foodstuffs, otherwise prices would get too high and European countries ruined. President, of course, opposed to principle, but wanted our opinion and practical arguments against same. We strongly advocated no price control and no Inter-Allied combination. The President said he thought Allies would do collective buying in any event and wondered how we could break it. Baruch and I did not think it would last as it would defeat itself. Hoover said that Lloyd George should be told that if they attempt to control and lower food prices the production would fall off seriously, and he feared the result. The President said Lloyd George never argued from real hard facts, but depended on his eloquence. He said he made him mad by intimating we were not willing to join because we wanted higher prices for our food. He said he and Lloyd George had a hot argument and Lloyd George later apologized for his insinuation.

In late June, McCormick told me the President had informed him that Lloyd George had still another financial idea: the Prime Minister now wanted to pool the total expenses of the war. Mr. Wilson was much exercised and wanted all his advisers to oppose it.

At the request of the advisers, I sent a note to the President expressing their views—all negative. I may stress here that none of us was averse to organized and properly controlled financial aid to Europe from the United States after the signing of the Peace.

The first concrete proposal of the Allies for a continuing organization to deal with European economic problems was that we continue our membership in the Supreme Economic Council. Vance McCormick's diary contains the following entry for June 23:

Just as I was going out [from the President's house] Herbert Hoover was coming in and he asked me to remain. We discussed the question of maintaining Supreme Economic Council after signing of peace treaty. President agreed with us it should be abolished and agreed he would have to go to the U.S. to talk with Department heads before discussing any new Inter-Allied organizations. . . .

On June 27, I introduced in the Supreme Economic Council the following statement, which my colleagues on the Committee of Economic Advisers had approved:

The American Delegates on the Supreme Economic Council, being as they are, officials for the period of war only, have felt that the establishment of some form of international conference on economic matters must rest for decision, so far as the United States is concerned, with the permanent departments of the Government. In conference with the President on this matter, he has taken the same view and feels that on his own authority alone he could not establish such an American representation in a body of this character as would make it an effective organ from the American point of view. The matter therefore requires to be laid before the leading officials in the Government at Washington and their views obtained. It is my understanding that this will be undertaken. I also understand that the present Council in any event continues until the end of July pending the signature of peace. . . . It seems to the American Delegates undesirable that the present Council should continue after such a date lest it should give the impression to the world of an economic block of the Governments who have been aligned in war.

At this same meeting, in reply to questions from Lord Robert Cecil regarding the kind of international body the American members thought could be worked out, Norman Davis and I told him that all of us were necessarily going out of office, and we recommended that the Allied leaders send their most important cabinet ministers to join the members of the American cabinet in a conference on the subject in Washington.

THE CONTROL OF AMERICAN LOANS TO EUROPE

Another phase of international action was often discussed at meetings of the President's Committee of Economic Advisers during our last days in Paris. It was certain that there would be an enormous demand for loans and credits from the United States—either from our private institutions or our Government. The applicants would no doubt offer high interest rates to American bankers. We felt that there might be unwarranted loans. Further, we believed there should be some organization in the United States to direct these activities into proper channels in order that the world's meager financial resources could be directed to safe and constructive purposes.

Since the President was soon leaving for home, I sent him the following note on June 27; McCormick, Davis, and Robinson of the President's "Advisers" staff, then present in Paris, had approved it:

MY DEAR MR. PRESIDENT:

. . . I am deeply impressed with the necessity for coordinated action within the United States in connection with the granting of private and public credits . . . [to supply] raw material and food to various countries in Europe. That is, it would seem to me to be a disaster if we allowed our merchants and bankers to expend either American private or public credits to Governments in Europe who did not maintain stability, who did not cease hostilities and who do not busy themselves with sound economic reconstruction and return to production. I would like to lay before you for consideration whether it would not be desirable to set up some sort of an economic committee in the United States representing the different departments of the Government and such other persons as you might select . . . who would in a general way pass upon the policies to be pursued by the American Government and [American] people in these matters. . . . I have discussed this matter with Mr. Davis who will no doubt take it up with you [further] on the steamer enroute home.[1]

[1] I may complete the account of this problem here, although it remained alive and its consequences persisted over several years.

Upon my return home I repeatedly recommended that there be some control of private loans or there would be huge losses to American people. Especially was this

As a basis for consideration of future setups, the President's "Advisers" suggested to me early in May that our relief and reconstruction organization of skilled Americans in thirty-two countries make a report on the economic and social situation in Europe. When the report was completed, the "Advisers" suggested that a copy of it

---

the case of all former enemy countries, where the reparations took priority over any repayment of loans, whether public or private.

In January, 1920, and again in April, I made public statements on these questions. I insisted that private credit was needed, that it should be organized to prevent fraud, waste, and loss.

A committee of the American Bankers Association consulted me on this subject and finally called a meeting in Chicago on December 10, 1920, to consider the problem. I was the principal speaker. The purpose of the meeting was to organize a corporation through which these credits could flow, with proper checks against speculative, wasteful, and bad loans. Congress, some years before, had authorized such corporations. By an organization of this kind a safer and larger volume of credit for constructive purposes could be provided. I said in part:

". . . It is far better that these problems be solved by the process of business and individual initiative than that . . . [solution] be attempted by our government. The resort to direct loans by our government to foreign governments to promote commerce can lead only to a dozen vicious ends. . . . Our government would be subject to every political pressure that desperate foreign statesmen can invent and their groups of nationals in our borders would clamor at the hall of Congress for special favors to their mother countries. Our experience in war shows that foreign governments which are borrowing our money on easy terms cannot expend [it] with the economy of private individuals and it results in vast waste. Our government cannot higgle in the market to exact the securities and returns appropriate to varied risk that merchants and banks can and will exact. Finally, the collection of a debt to our Treasury from a foreign government sets afoot propaganda against our officials, against our government and there is no court to which a government can appeal for collection of debt except a battleship. The whole process is involved in inflation, in waste and in intrigue. The only direct loans of our government should be humane loans to prevent starvation. . . ."

I added a note of warning:

"The world is not alone in need of credit machinery. It is in need of economic statesmanship. . . ."

"The world must stop this orgy of expenditure on armament. European Governments must . . . balance their budgets . . . [They must cease] publishing paper money if exchange is ever to be righted. . . .

I spoke on the subject again to the Merchants' Association of New York on January 24, 1921. But after a promising start, the movement fell apart.

In view of the host of bad loans, as Secretary of Commerce, in 1921, I again took up the question. At my suggestion, President Harding called a White House conference of Secretary of State Hughes, Secretary of the Treasury Mellon, representatives of responsible banking and investment firms, and myself in February, 1922.

At this meeting it was pointed out that loans being made at a rate as high as 7 per cent were an indication of the undue risks being taken by the ignorant investors and that any loans to former enemy countries, whether by private firms or municipalities or governments, were subordinate to reparations, which themselves amounted to more

should be given to the Supreme Economic Council. This I did on July 3, 1919, although I had many misgivings regarding the value of economic lectures to distraught people. The following are the pertinent paragraphs:

The economic difficulties of Europe as a whole at the signature of peace may be almost summarized in the phrase "demoralized productivity". The production of necessaries for this 450 million population . . . has never been at so low an ebb as at this day.

A summary of the unemployment bureaus in Europe will show that 15 million families are receiving unemployment allowances in one form or another and are in the main being paid by constant inflation of currency. A rough estimate would indicate that the population of Europe is at least 100 million greater than can be supported without imports and must live by the production and distribution of exports . . . their situation is aggravated not only by lack of raw materials imports but by low production of European raw materials. Due to the same low production, Europe is today importing vast quantities of certain commodities which she formerly produced for herself and can again produce. Generally . . . production [is] far below even the level of the time of the signing of the armistice. . . .

Even prior to the war these populations managed to produce from year to year but a trifling margin of commodities over necessary consumption or to exchange for deficient commodities from abroad. It is true that in pre-war times Europe managed to maintain armies and navies, together with a comparatively small class of non-producers, and to gain slowly in physical improvements and investment abroad, but these luxuries and ac-

---

than these countries could ever repay; further, many of these loans—both to former enemy and other states—were being used for non-reproductive purposes and for increased military expenditures.

The firms present expressed the desire that some steps be taken. We suggested that legislative control would constitute an invasion of government into private business and therefore proposed that we set up a cabinet committee from the Departments of State, Treasury, and Commerce to which the lending houses should submit their proposed loans for advice. To this they agreed. Most of the lending houses co-operated fully in refusing loans when we pointed out the undue risks involved or lack of reproductive purpose.

This arrangement worked successfully until certain financial houses broke away. After this informal control broke down, the State and Commerce departments continued to give advice to those who asked for it. These addresses and actions were prophetic; the sad end of it was the loss of at least a billion dollars by the American people, directly or indirectly, through the failure of their banks.

cumulations were only at the cost of a dangerously low standard of living to a very large number. The productivity of Europe in pre-war times had behind it the intensive stimulus of . . . [private enterprise] and of a high state of economic discipline, [yet] . . . the density of population at all times responded closely to the resulting volume of production. During the war the intensive . . . [restriction of] consumption, the patriotic stimulus to exertion and the addition of women to productive labor largely balanced the diversion of man power to war and munitions. These impulses have been lost.

It is not necessary to review at length the causes of this decrease of productivity. They comprise in the main . . . :

The industrial and commercial demoralization arising originally out of the war . . . [the] continued . . . struggle for political rearrangements during the armistice, the creation of new governments, the inexperience and [the] friction between these governments in the readjustment of economic relations.

The proper and insistent demand of labor for higher standards of living and a voice in administration of their effort has unfortunately become impregnated with the theory that the limitation of effort below physical necessity will increase the total employment. . . .

There is a great relaxation of effort as the reflex of physical exhaustion of large sections of the populations from privation, mental and physical strain of the war. . . .

During some short period, it may be possible for the Western Hemisphere, which has retained and even increased its productivity, to supply the deficiences of Europe. Such deficiences would have to be supplied in large degree upon credits; but aside from this the entire surplus productivity of the Western Hemisphere is totally incapable of meeting the present deficiency in European production if it is long continued. . . .

The [long view] solution . . . of the problem . . . does not lie in a stream of commodities on credit from the Western Hemisphere, but lies in a vigorous realization of the actual situation in each country of Europe and a resolute statesmanship based on such a realization. The . . . [people] of Europe must be brought to a realization that productivity must be instantly increased.

. . . Growing out of the yearning for relief from the misery imposed by the war, and out of the sharp contrasts in degree of class suffering, especially in defeated countries, the demand for economic change in the status of labor has received a great stimulus leading to violence and revolution in large areas and a great impulse to radicalism in all others. In the main these movements have not infected the agricultural classes but are essentially a town phenomenon.

In this ferment Socialism and Communism . . . [have] embraced to . . . [themselves] the claim to speak for . . . the downtrodden, to alone bespeak human sympathy and to alone present remedies, to be the lone voice[s] of liberalism. Every economic patent medicine has flocked under . . . [these banners]. Europe is full of noisy denunciation of private . . . [enterprise] as necessarily being exploitation. . . . Its extremists are loud in assertion that production can be maintained by the impulse of altruism alone, instead of self-interest. . . . The Western Hemisphere . . . still believes that productivity rests on the stimulus from all the immutable human qualities of selfishness, self-interest, altruism, intelligence and education. It still believes that the remedy of economic wrong lies not in tampering with the delicate and highly developed organization of production and distribution, but in a better division of the profits arising from them. . . . The Western Hemisphere's productivity is being maintained at a surplus over its own needs.

. . . *No economic policy will bring food to those stomachs or fuel to those hearths that . . . [do] not secure the maximum production. . . . [It is useless to shed] tears over rising prices; they are, to a great degree, a visualization of insufficient production.*

During the period of reconstruction, and recovery from reduced productivity . . . [reduced] consumption of non-essential commodities is more critical than any time during the war. . . . [the increased consumption shows] in . . . beverages and articles de luxe in many countries, even above a pre-war normal. Never has there been such a necessity for the curtailment of luxury [in Europe] as exists today.

The universal practice in all the countries at war of raising funds by inflation of currency is now bringing home its burden of trouble and in extreme cases the most resolute action must be taken, and at once. . . .

The stimulation of production lies in the path of avoidance of all limitations of the reward . . . [for] the actual producer. In other words, attempts to control prices (otherwise than in the sense of control of vicious speculation) is the negation of stimulation to production. . . . All attempts at international control of price, with view to benefitting the population in Europe at the cost of the producer elsewhere, will inevitably produce retrogression in production abroad, the impact of which will be felt in Europe more than elsewhere. A decrease of 20 per cent of

Western Hemisphere wheat would not starve . . . [America], it would starve Europe. . . .

It must be evident that the production cannot increase if political incompetence continues in blockade, embargoes, censorship mobilization, large armies, navies and war.

There are certain foundations of industry in Europe that no matter what the national or personal ownership or control may be they yet partake of the nature of the public utilities in which other nations have a moral right. For instance, the discriminatory control of ships, railways, waterways, coal and iron in such a manner as to prevent the resumption of production by other states will inevitably debar economic recuperation and lead to local spats of economic chaos with . . . [their] ultimate . . . [effect] abroad, to say nothing of the decrease in productivity. These misuses are already too evident.

The question of assistance from the Western Hemisphere during a certain temporary period, and the devotion of its limited surplus productivity to Europe, is a matter of importance and one that requires statesmanlike handling and vision. . . . It is a service that the Western Hemisphere must approach in a high sense of human duty and sympathy. . . .

After the President had returned to the United States, Norman Davis and I were the only Americans who attended meetings of the Supreme Economic Council. In those meetings, the Allies proposed an elaborate plan for a joint food purchase, which was to include the United States and which they proposed to submit to the President. The views of Norman Davis and myself are indicated by the cable I sent to the President:

2 August 1919

. . . At Supreme Economic Council today France, England, Italy, produced and adopted in principle a plan providing for . . . co-operation in purchase of foodstuffs.

We took the attitude that we had no authority to even discuss the matter, but advised them that it was not in the world interest to use such powers to the detriment of the farmers of the world or they would stifle the world's production and starve themselves, but that they should seek to place it on a basis of co-operation with the United States or otherwise they would create in the mind of the American producer the impression of such combination against him—further that if the impression of such combination was to gain currency it would destroy the hopes of Allied credits in the United States. We stated that the American people would sympathize with any constructive method of dealing with speculation and profiteering.

It was finally decided by the other Governments to propose to you for acceptance a plan to be further amplified by a Committee upon which we decided we would not be represented.

Hoover

So far as I am aware, the President made no reply to this proposal.

When the Allies followed up the matter of our proposed meeting with the cabinet in Washington to perfect economic aid and co-operation, they suggested sending only economic delegates and not their cabinet members. Apparently, the President decided that a meeting of this sort would be useless, because he dropped the matter.

CHAPTER 27

SOME EXPRESSIONS
OF APPRECIATION

It is appropriate to record the evidences of appreciation to the American people for their aid in the relief and reconstruction of Europe. Of the mass of such expressions, I give a few abbreviated extracts.

THE PREMIER OF FRANCE

As you are about to leave France, I wish to tender you all the thanks of the French Government for your great and untiring efforts to feed the Allies and all of Europe.

You know, however, that the task is not yet completed. . . .

The reconstruction of the ruins of war, the re-establishment of broken economic equilibrium, the creation, in a word, of a world of times of peace, require the immense effort which we are ready to give. . . .

I therefore hope soon to have the pleasure of seeing you back among us.

G. CLEMENCEAU

THE PRIME MINISTER OF GREAT BRITAIN

At the moment when you are relinquishing your official duties to return to the United States I wish to express to you on behalf of the British Government their warm thanks and their great appreciation of the work you have done for the Allied and Associated Powers. The ability and energy which you have shown in directing the economic relief of the population stricken by . . . [famine] has been of inestimable value. They have earned for you the lasting gratitude of the people of Europe.

DAVID LLOYD GEORGE

227

THE PRIME MINISTER OF POLAND

. . . The Polish people are not forgetful, their sense of gratitude is very strong and you may be certain that your thoughtfulness and generosity will always be remembered. . . .

. . . In behalf of the Government, I beg to offer you most sincere thanks, and with deepest personal gratitude, I remain,

Devotedly yours,

I. J. PADEREWSKI

THE MUNICIPAL COUNCIL OF WARSAW

The . . . members of the Municipal Council . . . of Warsaw . . . wish . . . to express its homage and gratitude. . . .

. . . the entire Polish Nation unite with Warsaw in transmitting to you our deep thankfulness for all you have done for the suffering humanity. . . .

. . . your helping hand reached Poland and saved thousands of human beings in the most critical moment. . . .

The President of Warsaw
P. DVREWIECK
The Vice-President
K. I. JERISKY

THE POLISH CABINET

. . . The Polish Government hereby asks the American Relief Mission to kindly forward to the Government and the citizens of the United States its heartiest thanks. . . .

The President of the Ministers Council
S. WOJCIECHOWSKI
The Minister of Labour and Public Welfare
G. L. IWANOWSKI

THE PRIME MINISTER OF CZECHOSLOVAKIA

. . . I understand perfectly the voluntary and intensive work carried on so long by your associates and by your organization. We cannot thank them enough for their energy and for the zeal with which they have put into execution the generous project of the American people having for its purpose the material assistance and the moral regeneration of the peoples which have suffered during the war. . . .

EDUARD BENEŠ

THE FOOD MINISTER OF CZECHOSLOVAKIA

. . . Bohemia, deprived . . . of all its foodstuffs . . . the Americans first took an interest in our distress. . . . They acted without any political motives, from a real altruism and friendliness to our Republic. They had to cope with innumerable obstacles which interfered at every step with their actions. . . . [They] secured the financial credit for our Republic, they opened the route through Trieste for the transport of foodstuffs. . . . each train had to be forwarded under the protection of American soldiers. . . . [By] the energetic intervention of the United States . . . [there is now a food route open] via . . . the Elbe to Bohemia. . . .

We have to thank . . . the American people with sincerity and gratitude for having saved our life in the critical time. . . .

Dr. B. Vrbensky
Minister of Food

THE FOOD MINISTER OF FINLAND

. . . After completing the greatest and most humanitarian act that anyone has ever performed, please permit me, as a member of the people of little Finland, to express my heartiest thanks for the fact that you, through your undertaking, have saved the Finnish people from outright starvation. . . .

. . . I saw with horror what the people of Finland had to face during the . . . winter . . . You, esteemed Sir, have saved Finland. . . .

Aksell Rauanheimo
Food Minister

THE MINISTER OF FOREIGN AFFAIRS OF FINLAND

. . . As I had experienced considerable difficulties to get interviews with your leading statesmen in order to hasten our recognition, you . . . in a memorandum . . . put the entire case before them. When the following Saturday, May 3rd, the question of recognition of Finland's independence was discussed at the Peace Conference, your memorandum . . . was the document which formed the basis of the discussion. It was then that the American and British Governments decided immediately to take definite steps to guarantee to Finland her place among the sovereign States of the world.

. . . When once the true history of the struggle of the Finns for political freedom will be written, your memorandum will be one of the most conspicuous documents in that connection. . . . Now, when after a waiting of several hundreds of years, at last the moment for our full freedom had come, your political action to our everlasting benefit will remain an outstanding feature. . . . We who belong to the present generation will soon disappear, but the moral greatness of the Associated Governments when recognizing Finland's independence will never vanish in the memory of the Finnish people nor [will] the name of him who through material and moral assistance helped Finland through grave difficulties to the maintenance of internal peace and to the final obtaining of eternal freedom. . . .

RUDOLF HOLSTI
Minister of Foreign Affairs

COMMITTEE OF KORPISEEKA PARISH, FINLAND

While the hunger and want were at the greatest, the knowledge that the American people had started to help the poor of the suffering peoples in Europe . . . was conveyed to the farthermost backwoods corners of the land. Now, when that the knowledge has become a reality . . . [words] are insufficient to describe the joy of these mothers and children when they, after years of suffering caused by hunger, again were able to eat clean bread made of pure grain. . . .

THE PRESIDENT OF DALMATIA

. . . Permit me to give expression to my feelings of gratitude. The names of your nation will remain engraved in golden letters in the annals of our towns and our province. Requesting you to be the interpreter of my feelings to your superiors, I express to you the deepest esteem.

DR. I. TARTGILA

QUEEN MARIE OF RUMANIA

[I] am exceedingly grateful for the generous help you are extending. . . . Thank you most heartily for all the splendid help you are giving my people.

MINISTER OF FOREIGN AFFAIRS OF ARMENIA

The Armenian National Congress . . . unanimously resolved to record its most grateful thanks to the United States Government and people for the generous and prompt assistance they are rendering to mitigate the terrible situation there. . . .

G. NORADOUNGHIAN

THE PUBLISHER OF THE LONDON TIMES

. . . I should like, as one Briton, to express my gratitude for the very great part you played in the stabilizing of the world. . . .

NORTHCLIFFE
Publisher of the London *Times*

ADMIRAL MARK L. BRISTOL

I desire to take this particular opportunity to express to you my great satisfaction at the support that you have given me in my work here in Constantinople. I appreciate this more than can be expressed by merely thanking you. The fact of your support assisted me wonderfully when at times things appeared to be going all wrong. It has been a pleasure to do anything I could for you and your people working in the Near East. I want to state that I have found your representatives to be most able and congenial collaborators.

MARK L. BRISTOL
Rear Admiral, U.S. Navy

THE AMERICAN PEACE DELEGATION

With the completion of your work with the American Commission to Negotiate Peace, we, the Commissioners, desire to extend to you, on behalf of the Government which we represent, as well as personally, our warm thanks for the important services which you have rendered your country while on duty here. The task of making peace has been great and arduous, and our country is indebted to those who, like you, have rendered such valuable service to the Government.

ROBERT LANSING
HENRY WHITE
E. M. HOUSE
TASKER H. BLISS

GOOD-BYE TO PREMIER CLEMENCEAU

My last call before leaving Europe was upon Premier Clemenceau —to express my appreciation for his undeviating support. He was in a gloomy mood, saying, "There will be another world war in your time and you will be needed back in Europe." [1] We would not have agreed on the methods of preventing it, so I did not pursue the subject. But to lighten the tone of our parting, I said, "Do you remember Captain Gregory's report on the decline and fall of the Hapsburgs?" He laughed, pulled out a drawer in his desk and produced the original telegram, saying, "I keep it close by, for that episode was one of the few flashes of humor that came into our attempts to make over the world." He was still chuckling when we parted.

[1] The Prime Minister was fairly accurate on both counts. The Second World War began twenty-one years after the end of the first one. I was back in Europe in 1946 to co-ordinate world food supplies to meet the terrible famine arising from that War.

PART TWO

AFTER THE PEACE

SECTION X

ORGANIZATION BEHIND THE FRONT

CHAPTER 28

THE WORLD SCENE AT THE PEACE

I have no need to elaborate here the many unhappy events in the Peace Conference which extended long tentacles of trouble after the Peace.[1] At the Peace, the British, French, Italians, and Belgians had expanded their territorial possessions and had high anticipations of reparations from the Germans. But they, in fact, emerged from the war appallingly impoverished. And they were faced with the continuing burdens of military establishments to enforce the Peace, with vastly increased national debts, with the endless responsibility of care for disabled veterans, widows, and orphans, with dislocated foreign trade and widespread unemployment. The cynical fact was that while the enemy countries had depleted their resources during the war, they practically wiped out all national and private debt by inflation, and they were not allowed to have much of a military burden.

All of Europe not already under parliamentary government had adopted that form of freedom. But the parliaments of the new nations were made up of many splinter political parties. With no major party in control, they could agree upon little but negative action.

The Poles, the Czechoslovakians, the Yugoslavs, and the Rumanians emerged from the Peace with the inclusion of foreign populations which they could not assimilate.

The Allied blockade against the Neutrals, the former enemy na-

[1] See *The Ordeal of Woodrow Wilson.*

tions, and the newly liberated countries during most of the Armistice suspended economic recovery in those countries—since they could not import raw materials or export goods.

All of the combatant countries involved in the war emerged at the Peace with demoralized economies. Only the Neutral states or those with a nominal participation in the war emerged at the Peace as the gainers from war.

In the midst of the war came a new aggressive force in the world, born of the Communists' seizure of Russia. It was to plague the whole earth with conspiracies, violence, and a determined purpose to dominate the world.

In all nations a hideous aftermath of the war was the loss of talent and manpower. The Allied and enemy armies had expanded during the war to more than 65,038,810 men, of whom 8,538,315 had died. In addition, there were 37,508,686 casualties, with millions of crippled men to be a burden upon every nation. And not least of the aftermath were the millions of undernourished and diseased children who, unless restored to health, would leave a burden of dwarfed bodies and stunted minds to infect the well-being of the world.

On the American scene, President Wilson left Paris for home immediately after the signing of the Peace, intent upon securing Senate ratification of the treaty, with its provision for the League of Nations. Under Secretary of State Frank Polk became the United States diplomatic representative in Paris and, with General Tasker Bliss, sat in the meetings of the Supreme War Council. Of the President's Committee of Economic Advisors, only I remained in Paris, and by invitation of the Allies, I continued to sit with the Supreme Economic Council and to undertake many political or other missions.

On either July 1, 1919, or upon the signing of the Peace, according to the United States law, the authority of the Treasury to make loans to Europe and the use of the $100,000,000 Congressional appropriation with which to purchase supplies came to an end. Moreover, our control over food movement, finance, imports, and exports to and from the United States also ended.

The daily echo of the continuing wrangles and conflicts in Europe coming to the American people and the Congress, plus home problems of readjustment and recovery, had driven our people to disgust with all Europe. In this murky atmosphere, the one hope to preserve stability in governments, to prevent mass starvation, and to check sweeping pestilence was to mobilize American charity through voluntary agencies.

CHAPTER 29

AN APPRAISAL OF
THE EUROPEAN FOOD SITUATION

At the Peace, most of Europe was faced with continued need for food, medical supplies, and clothing from overseas. Before any relief could be devised, it was imperative that we appraise the food prospects after the 1919 harvest. Our appraisal had to include the 1919 ground-crop prospect, the surviving food-producing and work animals, and the ability of these nations to provide financial resources to pay for overseas imports and to provide transportation.

As for the food prospects, I telegraphed our missions in the thirty-two countries of Europe to make an appraisal; we could not include Communist Russia because no facts on that nation were available. I also secured reports from our co-operating American charitable agencies in other countries. I consolidated the information in a report, on June 2, 1919, to President Wilson. The following is a summary of that report:

. . . We estimate the total prospective European yield of wheat and rye, outside of Russia, as of . . . [June] first, after deducting seed, at 1,550 million bushels. This indicates a crop of about 77 per cent pre-war normal. The pre-war consumption, outside of seed, was about 2,500 million bushels, indicating a net import need of about 950 million bushels if consumption were normal next year. The somewhat diminished populations and diminished buying power . . . [will reduce] full normal consumption, but the least possible consumption with the maintenance of public health we estimate at 2,250 million bushels, or an import necessity on a minimum basis of about 700 million bushels. . . .

The present stocks and crop conditions in the . . . [overseas] exporting countries would indicate that there would be in the coming harvest year an export surplus of wheat and rye of from 870 million to 970 million bushels, but of this other countries than Europe require about 100 million bushels, leaving a supply of from 770 millions to 870 millions available for Europe [or a sufficient supply of bread grains]. . . .

The European production of sugar will be apparently about 35 per cent of the pre-war normal, and before the war imports averaged 2,250,000 tons per annum. The [decreased] buying power of the people so greatly [affected] the consumption of this commodity that no estimate of probable import demands can be forecast. The crops of potatoes, peas, beans, cabbage and other vegetables promise to be above the pre-war normal.

Our survey of the food animals shows that, compared to pre-war conditions, there is a net decrease of 18,400,000 cattle from 98,300,000 pre-war herds; a decrease of 39,500,000 swine from 69,300,000 and a decrease of about . . . [86,000,000] sheep from the pre-war 190,800,000. The horses are also greatly diminished. . . .

As to feed crops in Europe for animals, it is too early to forecast crop prospects. To all appearances, about 75 per cent of the . . . [pre-war] yield will result. . . .

The use of vegetable oils largely of tropical origin for human consumption has greatly expanded during the war. There has been an enormous extension of the oleomargarine and substitute lard manufacturing capacity. . . .

Taking all factors together, every evidence points to continued large imports of animals products, provided the resources can be found to pay for . . . [them]. . . .

. . . unless some untoward catastrophe happens to the world's harvests [outside Europe], there . . . [are] enough . . . [supplies] to meet the world's essential needs. . . .

With peace, all European states can manage their own transportation and distribution, therefore a continuation of the world food control as it exists today is unnecessary. In fact, each of the new governments has under our encouragement not only established its own food administration but they are now also establishing their buying commissions abroad in preparation for handling their own buying and transport problems the moment peace is signed. . . .

A month later we re-examined the prospects and found them somewhat less favorable. Recovery from a famine and demoralized agriculture is a slow process. In any event, we drew up some conclusions.

First, those countries which would have their own supplies or the ability to finance imports for both adults and children were:

Britain	Holland
France	Denmark
Italy	Sweden
Belgium	Norway
Portugal	Switzerland
Greece	Azerbaijan
Bulgaria	Georgia
	Spain

Second, those countries whose harvests plus ability to finance imports were at least sufficient for their adult population included:

Finland	Lithuania
Estonia	Rumania
Latvia	Yugoslavia

Third, those countries which would require aid to provide for their adult population were:

Poland	Czechoslovakia
Hungary	Armenia
	Austria

Fourth, those countries which would require financial aid and special food imports for continued rehabilitation of their children consisted of:

Finland	Czechoslovakia
Estonia	Austria
Latvia	Hungary
Lithuania	Yugoslavia
Poland	Rumania
Germany	Armenia

In addition, the needs for medical aid, clothing, and reconstruction materials extended not only over these twelve countries but over many others among the forty-five famine nations.

THE CONDITION OF THE CHILDREN

I requested Colonel Carlson, who had charge of our canteen system for children, to make an analysis of our experience, both administrative and medical. The following is a condensation of his rather hard-boiled report of June 27, 1919: [1]

There is a decreased resistance to disease in all cases of marked starvation. . . . the prolonged starvation by millions of people in Europe during the present war is demonstrating anew the fact that the individual, weakened by lack of food, falls an easier prey to all infectious diseases, and we have thus in a starving society an increased incidence of infectious diseases and an increased death-rate, quite apart from deaths due to actual starvation. . . .

There is nearly always an increase of gastro-enteric diseases—diarrhoea, dysentery, etc.—in a starving society, because starving peoples are forced to consume spoiled or unsuitable foods and food substitutes. . . .

A notable effect in the starving child and young person is the appearance of rickets, or faulty growth and nutrition of the bones. . . . an epidemic . . . disease practically unknown before the present war.

Prolonged and marked starvation may cause atrophy of important organs and functions. In girls and women this may appear in the stunting of the ovaries and suppression of fertility. . . .

Prolonged under-feeding induces a type of dropsy that has been called "War edema" or "Hunger edema." It appears that this malady has never before been so prevalent as during the present war in several of the starving nations. . . . The dropsy appears when starvation approaches the point of danger to life, and ends in death unless suitable foods can be provided. . . .

Starvation leads to death of many individuals already weakened by disease. This is not a serious loss to the race. Starvation is also very hard on elderly persons. They become prematurely senile, shrivel up, and die. Again, this is no serious loss to the race.

To the extent that starvation intensifies and spreads tuberculosis in

[1] To any curious person who wishes more detail, I recommend *American Food in the World War and Reconstruction Period*, written by Frank Surface and Raymond Bland of our statistical staff and published by the Stanford University Press in 1931.

the old and young, the evil effects of starvation are more or less permanent, because the cure of tuberculosis is an uncertain and long-drawn-out process and the conditions requisite for cure, (among other things, an abundance of good food) are such that they cannot be fully provided . . . in most of the starving nations. The increase of tuberculosis by starvation not only affects the tubercular person, but each new tubercular individual produced by starvation acts as . . . [a] focus for the further spread of the disease.

Rickets in the young is more than likely to affect the individual permanently in rendering him a cripple, or at the best, a physical and mental weakling. . . . We may sum up the whole matter by stating that starvation kills the weak and maims the strong. . . . It should also be added that the physical and mental weaklings produced by starvation are likely to beget their kind, (physical and mental weaklings) to the detriment of the next generation. . . .

To diminish or check the permanent injuries to child life . . . particular . . . emphasis . . . [must be] laid on the permanency of the Child Relief . . . initiated by the American Relief Administration in the starving countries. The starved, the subnormal, the dwarfed and the tubercular child can perchance be reclaimed, cured, and rendered useful members of society. . . . If this is not done, the injury to the race . . . will in many countries be more severe than that due to the loss of vigorous manhood on the field of battle.

. . . The extent of the damage varies not only in the different [acute famine] countries, but in different sections of each state. In some regions 90% of the children under ten years of age are seriously starved, and 10–25% stunted. . . . 30 to 60% among the adult population have lost on the average 30 to 35% of their normal body weight. . . .

The food supplied through the American Relief Administration has in every case been sufficient to check the starvation progress. . . . as regards the children, the recuperative powers of youth are so great that a large majority of the starved and stunted ones can be "salvaged" and this alone is a sufficient reason for every American Relief Administration officer in the field to carry on.

Prior to the Peace, we had completed rehabilitation of 2,500,000 children. But on July 1, when our authorities and appropriations ended, we had 3,950,000 children, expectant mothers, and orphans in our canteens, and many millions more were in need.

CHAPTER 30

THE CREATION OF THE NEW
AMERICAN RELIEF ADMINISTRATION

With the end of American official relief operations at the Peace, the great charitable agencies—such as the American Red Cross, the Jewish Joint Distribution Committee, the Near East Relief Committee, and the American Friends Service Committee—were determined to continue their beneficent services. But it was not their field or within their resources to undertake the great burden of continued food or clothing supplies and the many other services imperative to save millions of lives from starvation. Moreover, my colleagues and I could not bear the idea of America's deserting the millions of children to whom we were giving supplies or the devoted women who were carrying on that service. In our own consciences and for the good name of America, we determined to set up a new organization so that we might discharge these obligations. The experience of witnessing a wilted child restored to health and joyous chatter was itself an impelling reason for our continuation.

We were confronted with other great food problems. The Food Administration had outstanding guarantees of prices to the farmers covering many commodities which would extend for many months after the Peace, and an organization to carry out these guarantees had to be maintained. Also, we had a mass of outstanding agreements with other nations in the name of the Food Administration Grain Corporation which had to be settled.

As a first step to solution of these problems, I addressed the following letter to President Wilson in June, 1919. I quote this letter

243

at some length, for it was to become the charter of a great enterprise in American compassion. The important paragraphs were:

PARIS, 6 June 1919

DEAR MR. PRESIDENT:

As you are aware, under your approval I set up very early in this general relief work in Europe a plan and organization for special feeding of children sub-normal because of under-nourishment. In this matter, we defined sub-normal children as those already showing the disease effects. . . . It appeared at the time, and has since been demonstrated, that the furnishing of rough staples to large massed populations under the difficulties of distribution in weak governments was more or less a hit or miss as to whether the children, especially of the poor, would [survive]. . . . in order to bring them back to normal they required special types of food which no available finance could provide for the population as a whole.

I then described our canteen system of free food, medicine, and clothing conducted by committees of women under experienced American supervision. I pointed out that at the moment we had 3,950,000 children in the canteens, which represented a much larger number to whom we had been of service. I continued:

. . . Some of the money has been found by public charity in the United States and locally; we have found some from the residue of the Five Million Dollar fund which you have placed at my disposal, and I have found some from the Hundred Million Dollar appropriation of Congress. We also have a contingent fund in the Grain Corporation which I will describe later, on which I am expecting to draw for some of this cost.

As you are aware, the Hundred Million Dollar appropriation ceases to be effective and will, in fact, be exhausted on the 30th of June and there seems little hope of getting this great mass of child life back to anything like normal for some months yet. . . . I feel that it must go on . . . after the broad relief measures of Europe have been relaxed [by] . . . the harvest. I am, therefore, greatly concerned over the question of finance, as it represents an expenditure of [many] . . . Millions of Dollars. . . .

In the course of our [United States Government relief] operations in Europe, we have been constantly faced with the possibilities of large losses if there should be a breakdown in the political situation . . . [because of our] enormous stocks of food afloat and in warehouse. We have, therefore, in the sale of these foodstuffs, provided a small margin for insurance to cover such an eventuality, thus having gradually built up the contingent fund . . . referred to. We are approaching the end of our large shipping campaign, and I now have hopes that we will get through without such a loss. . . .

I mentioned his previous approval of my public declaration that none of the official American relief agencies would make profits out of the famine. I also mentioned the agreements I had made with each government: [1] that the residue of the contingent fund should be applied to continued rehabilitation of children. I pointed out the wholesome effect the work had had on public opinion in Europe and continued:

. . . It is obvious that no single country in Europe is going to obtain what its politicians want, and that there will be, until they awaken to more rational sense than most of them display at the moment, a tendency for them to blame the United States for failure to secure each and every one his objectives against the other.

Beyond all this . . . is the infinitely more important . . . question of the saving of child life by such widely organized and wholesale methods as will meet the necessities of Europe at the present time.

HERBERT HOOVER

I received the following note in the President's handwriting:

MY DEAR HOOVER:
    I entirely approve the proposal you make here.

WOODROW WILSON

The name "American Relief Administration" was known to hundreds of millions of people all over Europe and was on the walls of every canteen, along with an American flag. In order to retain the good will already created by this established organization and the continued full functioning of its staff, we decided, with this approval of the President, to set up a volunteer successor under the same name. Under his authority I had, as stated above, already arranged for some resources for the new organization. On June 22, 1919, I sent the following letter to him in Paris asking for further aid:

[1] *An American Epic*, Vol. II, Chap. 40.

MY DEAR MR. PRESIDENT:

In accordance with your request to the Treasury of December 16th, [1918] five million dollars from your National Security and Defense Fund was paid on that date to the Food Administration Grain Corporation for the purpose of paying the expenses of the Food Administration's relief activities in Europe, partly for administration, and partly for the furnishing of supplies.

On February 13th [1919] you approved my proposal that this fund be turned over for administration to the . . . American Relief Administration. This fund has been practically indispensable in meeting emergency situations in Europe. . . .

It is impossible at present to determine what amount of this fund may be reimbursed, but to avoid any misunderstanding, I now propose that such balance of the fund as there may be, should be disposed of . . . to cover the expenses of administering such relief work in Europe as may be necessary after June 30, 1919. . . .

My final report will of course include the details of these expenditures, as of those previously made.

I should be indeed pleased if you could indicate your approval of this expenditure.

HERBERT HOOVER

[Approved and authorized:
WOODROW WILSON]

ORGANIZING FOR THE TASK OF CHILDREN

On July 7, 1919, I sent the following cable to our New York office, requesting it to take the necessary steps to set up the new American Relief Administration:

PARIS, 7th July, 1919

In order to meet all the various complexions of the problem of winding up the Government's relief measures and of continuing the children's relief . . . we believe it is critically necessary that we should at once set up a new and wholly private organization which we propose to call the American Relief Administration. . . . we wish to . . . [hold] continued American interest in European welfare . . . and . . . it is desirable to maintain the established prestige [of the name]. I propose that the new organization should have a committee in the United States comprising the leading men of . . . [our former organization] such as Barnes Flesh Glasgow Taft Rickard Whitmarsh Hallowell Heinz White Taylor Colonel Logan Colonel Barber Boyden and such other names as you would suggest of these groups. I would suggest that . . . a meeting . . . be held in New York at the earliest possible moment at which officers will be elected and of which I think I should be chairman. You can, as soon as you have made the necessary steps announce to the Press . . . that it is a private charitable organization and the funds will be provided in cooperation with the various governments in Europe and private charity . . . [from] the United States, that it is proposed to carry on the present large program of feeding children in Europe until conditions are more normal. . . . it is expected that the various committees of nationals of these countries in the United States will co-operate to support the organization.

In a second cable sent the same day to our New York office, I stated:

. . . we are anxious to expedite the launching of this organization as quickly as possible . . . and we suggest you register it as a charitable organization under the laws of New York. We propose Walter Brown to be the director in Europe with Headquarters in London . . . retaining a staff of two or three members in . . . [various countries]. If you agree with the above principle we will start operations here. . . .

Also on July 7, I sent to our staff in Europe a memorandum of what we proposed to do and asked for their co-operation.

My colleagues in New York responded at once. On July 12, they formed the new American Relief Administration, which was registered as a non-profit corporation, and elected the following officers:

HERBERT HOOVER, *Chairman*

DIRECTORS

ALVIN B. BARBER	HOWARD HEINZ
JULIUS H. BARNES	VERNON L. KELLOGG
R. W. BOYDEN	JAMES A. LOGAN
EDWARD M. FLESH	EDGAR RICKARD
WILLIAM A. GLASGOW	ALONZO E. TAYLOR
JOHN W. HALLOWELL	JOHN B. WHITE

THEODORE F. WHITMARSH

A large number of the members of our relief organizations wished to join, and we designated them "members," with the authority to select future officials and to determine our policies. I appointed Edgar Rickard our director in New York and Walter Lyman Brown director in Europe.

As a second step in solution of our major domestic food problems after the Peace, we had, with the President's approval, determined to continue the Food Administration Grain Corporation to carry out the guarantees. Being a Delaware corporation of which the President was the sole stockholder, it did not necessarily go out of existence at the Peace. Since the new American Relief Administration would be its largest customer for the surplus arising from the guarantees, I secured the President's approval that it should act as the purchasing, transporting and accounting agency for the new organization. Inasmuch as the directors of the two organizations were largely identical and had no personal financial interest, there was no difficulty in coordinating the organizations.

To carry out our relief work we had to assemble for Walter Brown a staff to administer the work in the various countries. I called for volunteers, and a sufficient number of our former staff agreed to make the sacrifice of further service. I give their names and positions under the nation-by-nation narrative of this work.

The task we had undertaken proved far greater than the single problem of children's relief in some twelve countries in Central and Eastern Europe which we had anticipated at the Peace. Originally, we had expected to end our labors with the harvest of 1920, but we were compelled to continue the children's relief in some countries until 1923. We were also compelled to find large amounts of relief for adults in these states and to undertake a huge relief for the great famine in Communist Russia. Beyond all this, we were compelled to undertake a great number of what I describe as "extracurricular activities," some of which involved large expenditures and the raising of large sums for that work.

CHAPTER 31

FINANCE OF THE RELIEF

For an understanding of the financial resources of the new American Relief Administration, I give the amounts secured from various sources during its entire life. The final settlement of our accounts and our liquidation stretched over many years—in fact, until 1937.

First, the official American relief agencies operating during the Armistice had on hand, at the moment Peace was signed, supplies in warehouses and cargoes en route amounting to 17,585 tons of food, medical supplies, and clothing valued at $6,625,051. The President authorized me to transfer these supplies to the American Relief Administration to complete their distribution.

Second, the residue from the National Security and Defense Fund transferred to the new American Relief Administration by the President amounted to $1,660,573.

Third, I have described [1] the system by which the Grain Corporation, in providing supplies to the different countries during the Armistice, added to prices at which supplies were sold a small margin to cover losses and other contingencies. We had contracted with the countries of Central and Eastern Europe that any balance in this fund should be used for general European children's relief, in which they would participate. The amount paid over to the new American Relief Administration from its inception until the end totaled $25,-109,989.

[1] *An American Epic,* Vol. II, Chaps. 13 and 38.

Fourth, in our official governmental relief activities during the Armistice [2] we had set up a system of monetary remittances for Americans desiring to aid friends and relatives in Europe as an added relief. The system proved very difficult to operate. However, out of this experience, we devised a much improved system.

The American Relief Administration inherited the warehouses which its predecessor had established in many countries in Europe. The new method was to sell, "food drafts" to individuals through American banks; the drafts, in denominations of ten to fifty dollars, could be sent by the purchaser to friends in Europe, and the food designated could be obtained from our warehouses. We also devised a "bulk draft" system whereby other American charities could obtain supplies from our warehouses when and where they needed them. The latter procedure freed them from maintaining their own purchasing and transporting facilities. The total amount of all food drafts sold was $24,302,916.

Fifth, in 1920, we organized the American Council for the Relief of European Children, which made a public appeal for funds and received a total of $29,556,071. The American Relief Administration received $15,669,899 of this total.

Sixth, we undertook the relief of intellectuals in Central and Eastern Europe. For these purposes we raised $2,556,251 outside our own contributions. These funds were partially duplicated by the purchase of food drafts.

Seventh, we joined with the Young Men's and Young Women's Christian associations in the organization of the relief of students. Their contributions, outside our own funds, were $273,244.

Eighth, in January, 1920, it was evident that certain countries— Armenia, Austria, Czechoslovakia, Hungary, and Poland—could not get through the months of April, May, June, and July (prior to the harvest of 1920) without relief for adults. As I have mentioned, the Grain Corporation had earned a considerable profit from trading with Neutrals during the war (this was not the "margin" recorded above). On March 30, 1920, with the support of President Wilson, I secured authorization for the Grain Corporation to sell flour to

[2] *Ibid.,* Chap. 37.

these countries from its profits, which amounted to $57,782,118.

Ninth, on December 22, 1921, being aware that there still remained in the Grain Corporation treasury a part of its profits from trading with Neutrals, we secured authority from Congress to use this money for Russian relief. It amounted to $18,662,180.

Tenth, on January 20, 1922, we secured authority from Congress for the War Department to furnish us surplus medical supplies for Russia and Armenia; this amounted to about $5,000,000. I give more details on the funds for Russia in the chapters devoted to that country in this volume.

Although the American taxpayer was not called upon for taxes to pay for these appropriations from the Grain Corporation or the surplus medical supplies, all of which amounted to $81,444,298, these sums were, in reality, a gift. Part of this amount was given in the form of loans, but, as explained in the Introduction to this volume, these were never repaid—making the entire amount a gift.

Eleventh, at the request of the Supreme Council, we undertook to battle the typhus epidemic which was sweeping westward from the old Russian trenches. For this purpose we had obtained anti-typhus equipment from the American, British, French, and German armies, the original cost of which was estimated by American Army officials at $60,000,000. It was not received until after the Peace. The American Army and the American State Department contributed the pay of our staff in this undertaking—amounting to at least $2,000,000.

Twelfth, in our operations in Central and Eastern Europe, we undertook purchase, transportation, or organization for other agencies as follows:

In the Baltic States:	World Student Christian Federation
In Poland:	American Friends Service Committee
	The Commonwealth Fund
	Jewish Joint Distribution Committee
	World Student Christian Federation
In Germany:	American Friends Service Committee
	General Allen's Committee for Relief of German Children

In Austria:	American Friends Service Committee
	The Commonwealth Fund
	Jewish Joint Distribution Committee
	World Student Christian Federation
In Czechoslovakia:	The Commonwealth Fund
	World Student Christian Federation
In Hungary:	The Commonwealth Fund
	World Student Christian Federation
In Armenia:	Near East Relief Committee
	The Commonwealth Fund

Thirteenth, we took part in the relief of refugees going from Russia into Poland, Turkey, and Constantinople, for which we received a total contribution, aside from our own funds, of $300,622.

Fourteenth, we received gifts in supplies and/or in cash from many of the governments in whose countries we worked. These donations were (from after the Peace to 1923):

	Tons of Supplies	$ Value	Cash	Total
Finland	936	$195,949	....	$ 195,949
Estonia	1,693	298,445	....	298,445
Latvia	479	60,880	....	60,880
Norway	7	3,960	....	3,960
Poland	52,684	7,659,375	....	7,659,375
Germany	16,833	2,392,021	$18,010,219	20,402,240
Austria	12,703	1,364,656	....	1,364,656
Czechoslovakia	5,248	888,830	....	888,830
Rumania	2,327	1,024,322	....	1,024,322
Yugoslavia	2,634	533,677	....	533,677
Hungary	1,733	265,807	....	265,807
Russia	554	30,026	11,357,325	11,387,351
Total	97,831	$14,717,948	$29,367,544	$44,085,492

Fifteenth, in later chapters, I relate the relief of the great famine in Communist Russia from 1921 to 1923. Aside from funds for this purpose already mentioned above we had need to raise supplies and services amounting to $40,213,563.

CHAPTER 32

BUILDING OUR ORGANIZATION

In the last chapter—"Finance of the Relief"—I mentioned some of our undertakings which need amplification. And the "front line" story of each nation's relief will be clear only if the reader understands our "behind the front" organization. I will therefore elaborate on the following activities: the food-draft system, co-operation with other charitable organizations, the relief of intellectuals, food and clothing for students, and the Food Administration Grain Corporation.

THE FOOD-DRAFT SYSTEM

The evolution, from our experience during the Armistice, of money remittances into the food-draft system was one of the great resources of the American Relief Administration. There were three types of these: individual drafts, family drafts, and "bulk" drafts for our affiliates. Purchased in the United States, each draft for an individual, or family, represented in value a definite amount of staple foods in four alternative combinations of specific quantities, to be delivered to a relative or a friend abroad. Since the recipients could "cash" the draft in exchange for food from any American Relief Administration warehouse in Europe, we arranged that the post-office parcel-post services in each country would present the drafts and deliver the food to those living at a distance from the warehouses. I appealed to the American banks to sell the drafts without charge. More than five thousand banks generously responded.

The drafts sold to individuals or families called for the following alternative combinations of food:

<table>
<tr><td>

Package A
$10

24½ lbs. flour
10   lbs. beans
 8   lbs. bacon
 8   cans milk

</td><td>

Package B
$10

24½ lbs. flour
10   lbs. beans
 7½ lbs. cottonseed oil
12   cans milk

</td></tr>
<tr><td>

Package C
$50

140 lbs. flour
 50 lbs. beans
 16 lbs. bacon
 15 lbs. lard
 12 lbs. corned beef
 48 cans milk

</td><td>

Package D
$50

140 lbs. flour
 50 lbs. beans
 45 lbs. cottonseed oil
 48 cans milk

</td></tr>
</table>

The bulk drafts included any amount of different foods desired by other charitable organizations. These drafts proved a great help to them, since they were relieved of the chore of purchasing, shipping, and warehousing food on their own—and they could obtain their supplies delivered on the spot at less cost than if they had managed it themselves.

In November, 1920, because of the decrease in the cost of food, each ten-dollar package was augmented by two and one-fifth pounds of sugar and one pound of cocoa and each fifty-dollar package by thirteen pounds of sugar and three and one-third pounds of cocoa, in addition to the commodities listed.

When we undertook the relief of Communist Russia, we had to change the method of food-draft deliveries; this is described in the chapters devoted to Russia.

We charged a small margin on all of the drafts to cover uninsured risks and changing food prices. This margin supplemented our charitable funds. Every draft sold, whether individual or bulk, meant that somebody in the United States was paying for food for somebody in Europe. It therefore constituted just as much "relief" as any other method of organization.

The deliveries of food by food drafts from the inception of the new American Relief Administration until we stopped selling them in June, 1923, were:

Country of Destination	Tons	Value
Austria	11,795	$ 3,330,636
Czechoslovakia	1,376	433,433
Danzig Free City	232	71,086
Estonia	293	146,556
Germany	9,347	2,820,420
Hungary	1,629	527,939
Latvia	84	15,686
Poland	15,559	2,539,650
Communist Russia	89,236	14,417,510
Total	129,551	$24,302,916

CO-OPERATION WITH OTHER CHARITABLE ORGANIZATIONS

As I have said, we originally expected to continue the American Relief Administration until the European harvest of 1920, and our finances were sufficient for these purposes. But from a survey of European crop prospects, it became evident that we would need to extend our efforts in support of the children over the winter of 1920—and even longer. At this time the American Relief Administration was carrying a load of more than five million children. Actually, we had served far more who cannot be counted because they had moved out of the canteens upon their recovery and upon the ability of their families to care for them.

In June, 1920, I called a preliminary meeting of some of the leaders of American charitable relief agencies. They decided that I should call a formal meeting on September 27, 1920. I presided at this meeting, which was attended by Edgar Rickard, representing the American Relief Administration; Dr. Livingston Farrand, Chair-

man of the American Red Cross; Felix M. Warburg, representing
the Jewish Joint Distribution Committee; Dr. Rufus M. Jones, Chairman of the American Friends Service Committee; James A. Flaherty,
representing the Knights of Columbus; Michael J. Slattery, representing the National Catholic Welfare Council; Dr. Arthur J. Brown,
representing the Federal Council of the Churches of Christ in America; Charles V. Hibbard, representing the Young Men's Christian
Association; and Miss Sarah S. Lyon, representing the Young Wom-
en's Christian Association.

We organized the European Relief Council. An executive committee was named, and the following officers were elected:

> HERBERT HOOVER, *Chairman*
> FRANKLIN K. LANE, *Treasurer*
> CHRISTIAN A. HERTER, *Secretary*

The board of directors was made up of the representatives of the
nine co-operating organizations.

It was agreed that we would launch a nation-wide appeal for help.
All organizations wished to accept the offer of the American Relief
Administration to purchase and transport their supplies to destination and also to accept the offer of the American Red Cross to purchase their medical supplies. The American Relief Administration
agreed to provide transportation of medicine and clothing to any
destination in our food ships free. We agreed that all gifts earmarked
for any particular organization should be turned over to it and that
we should set up a committee to divide the unearmarked funds.

We launched our joint public appeal in December, 1920, with a
statement from President Wilson. One of our most useful ideas was
to hold a series of public dinners under the title "The Invisible
Guest," who was to be symbolized by a lighted candle at the center
of the head table. The dinners were to be comprised of the menus
in use at our children's canteens in Europe (with second helpings).
They were served by volunteer college girls and nurses' organizations.

The most fruitful of these dinners was in New York. General
Pershing and I presided. It was announced that the leading artists

of the Metropolitan Opera would give their services free. We sold
1,000 tickets for $1,000 each. During the course of the dinner, a gen-
tleman (whose name I never learned) arose and declared that an
appeal for still greater contributions should be made on the spot. I
explained that we could not do this because the dinner announcement had stated that we would ask for no contributions beyond the
initial $1,000. The gentleman demurred and put a motion to the
guests, which was carried unanimously. The waiters placed a slip of
paper before each guest. When these were collected, we had an
additional $1,000,000 in pledges. At this point, Mr. John D. Rocke-
feller, Jr., arose and stated that he would like to bring the total up
to $3,000,000, which he did.

Similar dinners in different cities were held, with $100 and $500
tickets, and I spoke at many of them. The results of the appeal and
major sources of contributions were as follows:

American Relief Administration state committees and sundry remittances to headquarters	$10,645,510.40
American Red Cross	5,000,000.00
American Relief Administration (directly)	3,200,000.00
Literary Digest	2,516,000.00
Jewish Joint Distribution Committee	2,200,000.00
John D. Rockefeller, Jr.	1,000,000.00
The Rockefeller Foundation	1,000,000.00
Laura Spelman Rockefeller Memorial	1,000,000.00
American Friends Service Committee	861,022.31
Commodity contributions	351,440.51
Cleveland Community Fund	300,000.00
Detroit War Chest	200,000.00
Contributions of Securities	192,487.50
Cincinnati War Chest	179,180.82
Motion Picture Campaign	169,187.76
Rochester Patriotic and Community Fund	149,100.00
Twenty-four other community funds	112,000.00
The Commonwealth Fund	100,000.00
School children, New York City	100,000.00
Interest received on contributed funds	88,092.52
Young Women's Christian Association	52,204.52

National Polish Committee	50,000.00
Miami County (Ohio) War Chest	35,000.00
American Express Company collection	29,845.56
Youngstown Community Fund	25,000.00
Total contributions	$29,556,071.90

More than 3,000 persons gave their time and energies to the appeal, and we estimated that 7,000,000 individuals contributed. The entire cost of the appeal was 2.31 per cent, as against the usual 20 per cent cost of public solicitations.

The committee on allotment assigned the funds among the several relief organizations as follows:

American Relief Administration	$15,669,899.59
American Red Cross	10,000,150.00
Jewish Joint Distribution Committee	3,000,000.00
American Friends Service Committee	861,022.31
National Polish Committee	25,000.00

We in the American Relief Administration undertook to look after the European outlays of the minor member organizations. Later, the Red Cross contributed a large part of its allocation to the American Relief Administration for medical supplies to the Russian Relief of 1921–1923.

THE RELIEF OF INTELLECTUALS

If civilization was to survive, it was imperative to prevent starvation among the intellectual groups in several European countries, particularly in Poland, the Free City of Danzig, Austria, Hungary, and Czechoslovakia (and, later on, in Communist Russia). These were the destitute students, schoolteachers, professors, physicians, surgeons, artists, scientists, engineers, lawyers, clergymen, and their widows and orphans.

For Central and Eastern Europe, we sought the aid of Mrs. Stephen V. Harkness, who had established a great benevolent trust—

The Commonwealth Fund. Mrs. Harkness was most sympathetic and through this source gave the American Relief Administration $1,318,753 for this purpose. (She also gave us $100,351 for our general relief funds and $746,107 for Armenian children's relief. In all she contributed to us a total of $2,165,211.) The Jewish Joint Distribution Committee contributed $250,000 to us for this relief.

Our method of aiding these groups was to organize special free kitchens and to give free food drafts to individuals or bulk drafts to committees. They were also given a large amount of clothing sent from the United States.

We had the same problem of special aid to intellectuals in our relief of Communist Russia. For them we raised and expended $1,206,037.

Thus the contributions to our intellectual fund totaled more than $3,500,000.

The number of intellectuals served through the American Relief Administration was estimated as follows:

Austria	222,377
Czechoslovakia	19,671
Free City of Danzig	3,351
Hungary	25,000
Poland	96,087
Communist Russia	1,821,000
Total	2,187,486

However, many "intellectuals" who received relief through food drafts purchased individually by people in the United States cannot be traced from our accounts.

FOOD AND CLOTHING FOR STUDENTS

The Young Men's and the Young Women's Christian Associations had organized the "World's Student Christian Federation." They had joined in our public appeal for funds under the European Children's Relief Council. When that drive was completed, it was agreed that the American Relief Administration would furnish $80,000, an amount which was equal to their estimated earmarked funds, and we provided an additional $16,756 for purchases of clothing and materials. These organizations contributed $273,244 from their own funds. The food was purchased from our warehouses, and our staffs, assisted by the World's Student Christian Federation, managed the distribution of both food and clothing. The students given aid were:

	Max. No. of Students Fed	Value of Food
Austria	9,500	$ 95,147
Czechoslovakia	2,819	23,512
Estonia	600	1,271
Hungary	3,385	28,300
Latvia	1,000	8,498
Lithuania	745	927
Poland	11,695	115,589
A.R.A. contribution for overhead, general purposes and clothing	......	96,756
Total	29,744	$370,000

THE FOOD ADMINISTRATION GRAIN CORPORATION

One of our most important "behind the front" organizations was the Food Administration Grain Corporation. I have fully described this United States Government agency in Volume II of this memoir. I may recall that the Corporation, of which the President was the sole stockholder, had been organized during the war to market food commodities, the price of which had been guaranteed to the farmers by the Congress.

During the Armistice, upon my recommendation to the President, the Corporation had continued to provide the supplies to overseas nations and in so doing had carried on the purchasing, transportation, contracting, and accounting for the old American Relief Administration.

At the Peace, although the Food Administration was ended by law, the President, upon my recommendation, continued the Corporation to serve the new American Relief Administration by purchasing, transporting, and accounting for its supplies.

The Corporation had a further relation to our relief arising from marketing overseas the current surplus of American food products. I may also recall that the Corporation's total purchases and sales of food during its lifetime were $7,466,581,025. When its work was completed, it had $226,384,291 in cash assets. Of this sum, the Corporation returned to the United States Treasury the $150,000,000 capital which had been furnished by the Congress. It then still had in hand $76,444,298 of cash assets, most of which had come from profits earned by trading with the Neutral nations, to whom it made a charge for its services.

I have already mentioned the authority of March 30, 1920, given the Corporation by the Congress, upon my recommendation, through which our relief was aided with food to Europe to the value of $57,-782,118. This authority was again extended, upon my recommendation, by the Congress in December, 1921, to apply the residue of these profits to the relief of Russia. This amounted to $18,662,180.

Thus the Corporation was a vital part of the new American Relief Administration. There was good co-ordination between the organizations because the directors of each were almost identical, and none of them had any personal interest—except saving human life.

CHAPTER 33

THE EXTRACURRICULAR ACTIVITIES OF THE NEW AMERICAN RELIEF ADMINISTRATION

We had organized the new American Relief Administration primarily to restore health to millions of debilitated and diseased children, of whom we were already caring for more than 3,950,000. But we were urged from many sources to undertake matters far beyond these tasks.

I have hesitated to delay the narrative, but clarity in the following record requires this interruption of the text. Moreover, these activities disclose many new sidelights on the history, events, and personages of the times. A bare list of the A.R.A.'s extracurricular activities indicates the extent of them. Such a list includes the following:

(1) President Wilson had assigned to me several political and administrative jobs to be completed, such as winding up our relations with the inter-Allied economic organizations.

(2) President Wilson and Prime Minister Ignace Paderewski had requested that I make a good-will visit to Poland.

(3) Premier Clemenceau, President of the Supreme Council, had requested me to remain for advice and action on both political and economic questions, and these missions increased during the months following the Peace.

(4) The Supreme Economic Council requested me to continue as a member, although I no longer had official status.

(5) We had sent hundreds of American technical advisers to the

new Eastern European republics, and their services had to be demobilized or reorganized.

(6) We had to complete and demobilize our management of the Eastern European railways, waterways, and coal mines.

(7) We were confronted with a problem in sugar supplies for the American people.

(8) At the direction of the Supreme Council, we were involved in political questions, such as the rise and fall of Communist Bela Kun's dictatorship in Hungary, the Rumanian invasion of Hungary, the rise and fall of Archduke Joseph's usurpation of dictatorship in Hungary, and their subsequent revolutions.

(9) We were asked by the Supreme Council to take a hand in a conflict between Poland and Germany over territorial and coal problems.

(10) We were requested by the Supreme Council to help solve the internal military conflicts in the Baltic States.

(11) We were still involved in the relief of the Russians behind Yudenich's army, which was operating from the Baltic States.

(12) We had not completed one task assigned to us—demobilizing the Russian prisoners of war in Germany and the Hungarian and German prisoners in Siberia.

(13) We had, during the Armistice, only laid the foundations for the fight against the sweep of typhus in Eastern Europe.

(14) We had to settle our accounts with each of the thirty-odd nations for supplies and services during the war or the Armistice.

I deal with some of these problems topically, but where these activities were confined to a particular country, I deal with them in the chapters devoted to that country.

ORGANIZATION OF SPECIAL STAFF

In order to manage these extracurricular duties, it was necessary for me to obtain further voluntary service from leading members of our Armistice staff. These men responded willingly for this continued volunteer service. They included:

COLONEL JAMES A. LOGAN, *our Chief of Staff in Paris*

ROBERT A. TAFT, *in charge of our Paris office*

LEWIS L. STRAUSS, *my secretary*

EDWARD M. FLESH, *in charge of our London office and the European operations of the Grain Corporation*

CAPTAIN PAUL S. CLAPP, *to continue our telegraph system in Europe*

COLONEL ANSON C. GOODYEAR, *to liquidate our Eastern European coal operations*

COLONEL W. B. CAUSEY, *to liquidate our Southern Railway Administration*

COLONEL ALVIN B. BARBER, *to liquidate our Northern Railway Administration*

COLONEL H. L. GILCHRIST, *to continue the battle against typhus in Eastern Europe*

WILLIAM B. POLAND, *to wind up our relief and charitable activities in Belgium and Northern France*

In addition, it was imperative that certain of our experienced heads of missions in countries where we had political assignments should continue their service. They were:

> COLONEL JOHN C. GROOME, *the Baltic States*
> COLONEL WILLIAM R. GROVE, *Poland*
> CAPTAIN T. T. C. GREGORY, *Vienna and Budapest*
> EDWIN SHERMAN, *Germany*

We were, however, able to release most of the four thousand Americans engaged in the official American relief agencies during the Armistice period.

Upon my return home I received a plaintive letter from a young Army officer who checked the railway rolling stock crossing the border between Poland and Germany (our organization had guaranteed its return to its proper home). The young man asked how long I thought he ought to continue that duty. He had been overlooked when, two months before, we sent out orders releasing our men. I wrote him a personal apology and a strong recommendation to anybody who wanted a faithful associate. He undoubtedly ranked with the original "forgotten man."

There was little chronological sequence in our extracurricular tasks; many were in motion at the same time. Those which need to be dealt with topically are: the great battle against typhus, liquidating our technical advisers in the Eastern European countries, the world shortage of sugar, and settlement of our accounts for Armistice supplies with thirty-two countries. I have devoted separate chapters to the European coal chaos and the repatriation of prisoners of war—Russian prisoners in Germany and German and Hungarian prisoners in Siberia.

THE GREAT BATTLE AGAINST TYPHUS

In Volume II [1] of this memoir I have described the events which led up to the Supreme Council's request that our organization should organize the great battle against typhus because the Red Cross Societies in Europe had declined the task as being too great for their resources. I also described in Volume II the preparations which we had made prior to the Peace by our appointment of Colonel H. L. Gilchrist of the Army Medical Corps with a large staff of Army officers, including 200 tough sergeants. I described the manner in which we had obtained the anti-typhus equipment of the American, British, French, and German armies which our American officers estimated to have cost over $60,000,000. Of this amount, $40,000,000 came from the American Army, as did a huge amount of used clothing from the United States Army Liquidation Commission.

The actual battle, however, occurred almost entirely after the Peace, and the operation had to be financed and its supplies shipped by the new American Relief Administration. I may recall here that this hideous epidemic was sweeping westward out of the old Russian trenches from the Baltic to the Black Sea. The infection was transmitted by lice, and the hovels of war ruins in which the people lived were one of its stimulants.

Since this battle was one of the most notable accomplishments of medical science and the work of great medical leaders, it warrants a place in this record. Colonel Gilchrist drew a battle line hundreds of

[1] Chap. 46.

miles long in front of the major typhus areas—this was to be a "sanitary cordon." With the aid of local police of each nation, traffic was stopped at this line. When the line was established, Colonel Gilchrist's staff, with the aid of all national health departments and local police, village by village, deloused, disinfected, and reclad the people. In addition, the Colonel established hospitals for the care of the afflicted. Gradually, in a general movement eastward, the pestilence was driven out.

On one occasion I sent Dr. Vernon Kellogg to the typhus front to find out what more our organization could do. He got inside the cordon, and when he was returning by automobile, he was stopped by a stern American sergeant who ordered him to be deloused. His hair was cropped and his clothes baked while he waited—all in spite of his expostulations. In the end, the Doctor's high sense of humor triumphed over his feeling of indignation, and for many years he proudly exhibited his certificate.

After the Peace, the huge amount of used clothing which we had arranged to get from the United States Army Liquidation Commission arrived on the scene, together with the immense amount of anti-typhus equipment which we had secured from the armies. The total weight of all this was more than 166,000 tons. The A.R.A. paid the costs of its transportation, as well as the incidental expenses of the staff, which came to more than $950,000. The American Army paid the salaries of the uniformed staff, and we arranged that the civilian staff be placed temporarily upon the salary rolls of the United States Foreign Service. The cost of the entire operation possibly amounted to over $100,000,000. But the dollar mark is a poor interpretation of the service to the millions of persons whose health was restored and whose lives were saved.

In addition to the battle conducted under our organization, the American Red Cross successfully attacked many local outbreaks of typhus, the account of which appears in later chapters relating to the relief in each special country.

On July 26, 1919, I received an inquiry from Premier Clemenceau with regard to the progress of the typhus battle. In my reply, on July 30, I narrated the steps taken by the Supreme Council and its decision that the Red Cross offers were insufficient and that our organization should take on the task. I also related that the Council had requested the American, British, and French armies to provide some of the equipment and supplies. I continued:

. . . the President of the United States and the Secretary of War delegated personnel from the American Army to be placed at my disposal . . . at the expense of the American Army. With the intervention of the President I also arranged with the American Liquidation Board to sell several million dollars worth of supplies and material at a nominal figure to the Polish Government and I undertook for the Relief Administration to . . . [pay] the expenses of transportation. . . .

The principle underlying these arrangements has been in accordance with policies of the Council in all of its measures; that is, to build up and strengthen existing government departments among the new governments rather than to impose authority over them. Any other measures must be short lived and the only hope of permanent solutions is by the development of local efficiency.

As a matter of record I enclose herewith copies of the more essential documents that have passed in this connection.

HERBERT HOOVER

On October 24, 1919, after I had returned to the United States, I received the following letter from the Polish Minister of Health in Warsaw concerning the progress of the campaign and requesting that Colonel Gilchrist and his staff remain over the winter of 1920:

DEAR MR. HOOVER:

The work initiated by you has borne rich fruit. We are in the possession of practically all the material which we have obtained through your friendly intermediary . . . Colonel Gilchrist with his unit are at work with us rendering us invaluable . . . [services]. Field operations have been going on for some time now in spite of the somewhat late season of the start but the time is rapidly approaching when they will have to cease on account of the inclemency of weather. New spheres of activities are however opening up in the same line for the coming winter while in the spring all the splendid material now in our hand will have to be set in motion for field operations on a really effective scale. The services of the Gilchrist Unit have been timed by the American Government to continue for four months from the day the respective units . . . [land] in Poland which would mean that they would have to commence with-drawing before long. This I feel would be a calamity for us and I have to address the enclosed letter to the Secretary of War requesting the permission for the Gilchrist Unit to stay with us throughout the next year, the strength . . . being reduced to an establishment suggested by Colonel Gilchrist. I am sure that your powerful support will not be refused by you on this occasion as indeed it never has been before whenever the needs of relief work demanded from us that we should seek your help.

The selection which you have made by suggesting Colonel Gilchrist as Commanding Officer of the Unit could not have been a happier one. We found in him a friend of whom we are verily proud and on whose complete loyalty I can count absolutely. I should be indeed very grieved if my Ministry were to be deprived of his further cooperation during the very critical winter months that are ahead of us and if his command failed us in the coming spring when field operations will be restarted as we hope . . . on a truly grandiose scale.

I am perfectly content to leave the matter in your hands believing that the happy issue of your negotiations with the War Department cannot be doubted.

I arranged with the War Department in Washington that this be done.

The Colonel and his men had to stay on until March, 1920, but they performed the most herculean task ever known in public health —and they did it with magnificent courage and ability. They did more than save lives and mitigate suffering; they saved Europe from an immense calamity.

•

LIQUIDATING OUR TECHNICAL SERVICES IN THE EASTERN EUROPEAN COUNTRIES

During the Armistice, we had been confronted with governments in Eastern and Southern Europe whose leaders were able revolutionists but had had little practical experience in governing. They were saddled with huge problems in food supply, rationing, currency, finance, railways, public health, and farm and coal production. We furnished them some one thousand technical advisers. Some of the advisers were officers from our Regular Army; many were prewar civilians we had recruited from the military forces. And there were some civilian specialists. The political intentions of Americans were not suspect, and as far as I know, American advisers were sought exclusively through our organization.

Several governments expressed a wish that we continue our technical services after the Peace. Before making any such arrangements, I wrote to the President, describing the problems and asking for his approval. The President replied:

PARIS, 25 June 1919

MY DEAR MR. HOOVER:

What you propose in the enclosed letter, which I take the liberty of returning with this answer, meets with my entire approval, and I am glad that you thought of so interesting and serviceable a scheme.

WOODROW WILSON

I informed the governments who wished to retain these men that they had served without remuneration, except for the small pay of our military forces, that they wanted to go home to re-establish their livelihoods, but that I thought we could find some among them who would stay for a year or two if the positions were made attractive. The answer in each case was that I should set the amount of the salaries to be paid in dollars.

We did not fully escape from worry by this method. The men who remained stipulated that their salaries be remitted to our New York office for distribution to their families or to named repositories. And we were also called upon to supply new men to replace those leaving for home. We set up a small unit in our office to administer these matters.

This entire arrangement was a tribute to American disinterestedness, intelligence, and technical skill—all so badly needed. These men formed the co-ordinating link in the operation of the railways, coal mines, and river traffic between states whose relations with each other were otherwise not too good. They advised in government finance, budgets, and currency. They brought new ideas into agriculture. They belong in the record of the reconstruction of Eastern Europe.

THE WORLD SHORTAGE OF SUGAR

When the United States Food Administration was ended by law at the Peace, we were left with continuing responsibilities through the Sugar Equalization Board, and we were at once faced with a world shortage in sugar, which greatly affected the United States.

The Sugar Equalization Board, of which I was chairman, had agreed to buy the West Indian sugar crop of 1919, the delivery of which would extend for six months after the Peace. The Board had stabilized the price of sugar at about nine cents per pound to the American people during the war and the Armistice. It handled, for both our own country and the Allies, 6,944,773 tons of sugar. The expenditure for sugar directly purchased by the Board amounted to $835,701,210.50. We returned its initial capital to the Treasury and earned a profit of $40,404,833.95, mostly from its foreign operations. Its total overhead was less than six-tenths of one per cent of its expenditures. We failed to persuade the Congressional committees to assign this profit to the new American Relief Administration.

Two months before the Peace, it became evident that the Western European nations would not recover their prewar beet-sugar acreage. The controls on imports imposed by the blockade would end at the Peace, and shipping would be decontrolled. With the shortage, the many countries which did not produce sugar would be seeking more of it, thus increasing the demand. It was obvious that higher prices and speculation were inevitable unless action was taken.

On May 17, 1919, I warned the Sugar Equalization Board of these probabilities, and on June 4, I proposed to President Wilson that the Board accept an offer of the Cuban sugar growers to sell their entire 1920 crop to us at the same price as before. Since the Allied governments were participants in these purchase contracts, they, as well as the American people, would enjoy certainty of reasonable supplies at the controlled price levels. The President, however, was overwhelmed with peace negotiations and decided to defer action until after he returned home.

On July 24, 1919, I cabled the President, again predicting a world shortage, and urged the purchase of the Cuban crop. I repeated these recommendations either directly or through the Sugar Equalization Board on August 2, August 14, and September 18. But the President was then engaged in his great crusade to secure the ratification of the Treaty of Versailles and American membership in the League of Nations. Then came his stroke. Since prices and speculation were increasing daily, the Congress took a hand and passed a law on October 25. My telegraphic advice to the Sugar Equalization Board was: "The Sugar Law is complete political bunk."

It is needless to pursue this subject further. The price of sugar rose to 25 cents a pound, or a penalty at that price of $30,000,000 a month on the American people. Thousands of retailers had bought their sugar at this high price. When the bubble burst, many of them had huge losses, and some were bankrupt. It was a bitter pill to swallow in later years, when we were blamed for these tragedies. But American consumers cannot be expected to remember the details of our activities on their behalf.

SETTLEMENT OF OUR ACCOUNTS FOR ARMISTICE SUPPLIES WITH THIRTY-TWO COUNTRIES

The settlement of our official American Government relief accounts under our contracts with each European government for supplies delivered prior to the Peace was a long, drawn-out operation, and we were not able to abolish our organization for many years. Among our duties was to secure for the United States Treasury the documents of obligation for future payment (which proved mostly valueless). And we had to settle our American Government relief agencies' accounts with the United States Treasury, which action also required years.

The activities of the American Government relief and reconstruction agencies in providing supplies for European nations extended over six years—from our entry into the war in April 1917 until September 1923. The activities of the American Relief Administration extended from June 30, 1919, to the end of September, 1923. All of this involved chartering a multitude of ships and establishing financial contracts with forty governments and twelve private associations. Out of these transactions there arose a host of claims—amounts due us and claims of foreign governments for spoilage or underdelivery on contracts. We had claims for insurance against delivery losses at sea. Considerable litigation arose over various matters, and all accounts had to be audited by responsible firms of accountants.

It was indeed a tedious business, even involving appeals to the United States Supreme Court by some claimants. The burden of these settlements of the accounts of the official American Government agencies fell upon the new American Relief Administration and the Grain Corporation. We were unable to conclude all the affairs of the Government agencies and receive quittance certificates from our auditors until 1937.

The liquidation of the new American Relief Administration stretched over several years. There were long delays in settlement of claims for insurance damages and our accounts with the many European countries, arising from the contracts we had made with them during the Armistice period, which provided certain residues or margins in prices. The members of our organization were, in fact, partners, not corporations, and we had to retain reserves to meet claims which might be made against them. We had established state and local committees to collect funds for our charitable activities, and the accounts with them also had to be settled.

CHAPTER 34

THE EUROPEAN COAL CHAOS

With the Peace, the coal supplies of all Europe fell into complete chaos. During the Armistice, my organization, under a mandate from the Supreme Council, had directed the production and distribution of coal in Eastern Europe. With the Peace, this authority ended because our official American organizations were disbanded. The resulting chaos affected the countries where the new American Relief Administration was striving to save lives and stabilize governments.

The German treaty had so reduced Germany's coal supply that, if Germany was to maintain her public services, there was insufficient coal to keep the people warm. Further, Austria, Yugoslavia, Albania, and Hungary were without coal or money with which to buy it.

A small war broke out between Poland and Germany over the possession of some of the Silesian coal fields. On August 1, 1919, in an effort to restore the situation, I recommended to the Supreme Council that it set up a "European Coal Council," with every coal-producing state in Europe represented. I hoped it could restore coordination of production and distribution and would recognize the impossible restriction on Germany—and would amend it.[1]

My memorandum to the Supreme Council regarding the coal commission was as follows:

[1] Germany later took back her major coal fields by violence.

I desire to again raise to the Council the coal situation in Europe.

Under the direction of the Supreme Council . . . my Administration undertook . . . so far as possible to control the distribution of coal during the Armistice in Central and Eastern Europe. A considerable staff has been employed upon this labor and numerous agreements and undertakings entered upon, involving the old States of Austria, the Balkans, Poland and to some extent Germany. While the result could not be ideal . . . [it has] at least served to maintain sufficient supplies for the transportation of municipal and domestic services necessary to maintain life. With the ending of the Armistice (and this authority) . . . the supervision which we have exerted must necessarily cease.

Colonel A. C. Goodyear and Colonel W. G. Atwood of our staff have compiled a summary . . . of the 1913 production and consumption of the principal countries in Europe (excluding Russia and the Balkan States) and have also conducted a careful inquiry into the probable production during the year 1919, based upon the experience of the first six months of the year. The net result shows that . . . the production in these States has fallen to a rate of about . . . 65% of normal production. The consumption cannot be decreased in this ratio (35%) upon certain vital consumers, such as transportation and municipal and other essential services, so that a shortage for manufacture and household use must be on a far greater ratio. Beyond this the very natural tendency of productive countries to reserve a larger degree of their normal consumption will and does result in . . . [reducing] the non-producing countries far below . . . 35%. . . . Furthermore, the summer accumulation against winter use has not been in progress and therefore the hardships of the coming winter are even further increased.

I then enumerated the various political and economic causes of this degeneration in production and continued:

. . . All these causes are operating to varying degree in different localities but their summation is shortage of production below the living necessity of the population of Europe. . . .

I urgently recommend that some form of coal control should be set up in Europe with view to the stimulation of production and to secure a distribution that will maintain the essential services upon which economic and political stability must rest. The problem cannot be solved for any one European country alone but the energies of all must be enlisted and the position of all must be considered. It is purely a domestic problem for Europe.

HERBERT HOOVER

I also proposed to the Big Four a resolution by which the Reparation Commission for Germany, the Teschen Commission, the Plebiscite Commission for Silesia, and the various commissions charged with matters of internal transport should all be instructed to co-operate with the proposed coal commission and assist in its work to the full extent of their powers.

General Bliss reported to the Secretary of State in Washington on the meeting of the Big Four at which this resolution was taken up. After repeating my proposals, his report included the following quotation from the minutes of the meeting:

Mr. Loucheur [for France] proposed that the United States should be represented upon the Commission [and that coal should be shipped from the United States to Europe]. Mr. Hoover stated that American representation had been omitted because it was felt that this matter was a domestic problem of Europe. The United States was faced with a crisis at home, and at best, for various reasons, could only ship to Europe about 500,000 tons [monthly]. This assistance was negligible. Under the authority of the Council he had managed the coal production in Central and Eastern Europe. The Reparations Commission set up under the treaty was now taking charge of the mines and his own work was therefore coming to an end.

Mr. Balfour [for Britain] inquired whether the Commission would take charge of all coal fields—would it attempt to regulate the conditions of production in England.

Mr. Hoover explained that the Commission would give advice as to ways and means and the best methods of co-ordination.

Mr. Loucheur [for France] suggested that if an American member could not be appointed to the Commission, Mr. Hoover's agents should at least be allowed to continue their work in Poland and Czecho-Slovakia.

Mr. Tittoni [for Italy] suggested that Mr. Hoover might at least continue his activities for the first six months of the operations of the Commission.

It was decided that Mr. Polk, Mr. Hoover and Mr. Loucheur should confer regarding American representation on the Commission.

We conferred, and I stated that there was no one in the United States with the authority to name an American member and that it was unlikely Congress would provide funds to support him and his necessary staff. However, the Big Four agreed, in principle, to establishing the coal commission, but when it was handed over to their governmental agencies for organization and administration, disunity prevailed and they soon buried it.

I here give an account of the dispute between Poland and Germany over coal questions in certain districts of Silesia, since it is a facet of the history of those times, as well as one of the problems of the American Relief Administration.

The Peace Treaty provided for a plebiscite of Upper Silesia to determine the boundaries between Poland and Germany. Silesia was historically German. Through the long years of development of the Silesian coal industry, the Germans had imported Polish labor, and the Poles gradually became a substantial majority in certain regions. After the war, as part of the French drive to dismember Germany, there evolved the idea of separating those parts of Silesia which were Polish in majority and annexing them to Poland. The Big Four had appointed a commission, with Polish and German representatives, to supervise a plebiscite among the inhabitants so that they could decide to which country they wanted to belong.

When I arrived in Vienna on August 18, 1919, en route back from a visit to Poland, I began to receive reports of fighting which had flared up between the Poles and the Germans in the Upper Silesian districts. I directed Colonel Anson Goodyear, who headed our Coal Administration during the Armistice, to see if he could do anything to stop it, as the outbreak included coal districts which he knew well and it was stifling coal production. I feared that a prairie fire had been started which might well spread all over Eastern Europe.

Some paragraphs of Colonel Goodyear's report, dated September 10, 1919, are as follows:

On the afternoon of August 19, 1919, under directions from Mr. Hoover . . . I arrived in Kattowitz. . . . Reports had been received by Mr. Hoover in Vienna to the effect that German troops had occupied certain Polish towns and Polish troops had in turn occupied German towns. These reports proved to be incorrect, but there had been an insurrection or rebellion commenced in Upper Silesia on August 17th, and at the time of our arrival in Kattowitz this insurrection was . . . [serious].

We went immediately to a conference with Dr. Williger, the President of the Mine Owners' Association of the Kattowitz district and secured from him information as to the causes of the outbreak and the situation as it then existed. Following the meeting with Dr. Williger I went to the offices of the [German] Military Commander, General von Pessow, and received additional information from him and from Colonel Hoffmann. General von Pessow agreed, at my request, to stop all executions [of so-called rebels] in his sector, and also in writing agreed not to enter Polish territory with his troops. At this time fighting was going on in the vicinity of Schoppowitz and Janow. . . . We left Kattowitz early the following morning and went to Sosnowice, where we met a committee, consisting of Dr. Diamond, and Monsieurs Pospiech, Rymer, and Sosinski, the three latter members of the Polish Diet, and formerly members of the German Reichstag. This committee stated that it had come to Sosnowice with the approval of . . . [Prime Minister] Paderewski. I had been notified of the time of its arrival by a telegram from Mr. Gibson [American Minister to Poland]. The committee made several statements regarding outrages in Upper Silesia and requested permission to enter Upper Silesia. We had no authority to give them such permission, but promised to investigate the matters they complained of. We then went to Milowitz and saw there a house that had been hit by a German shell and a child killed by fire from a German air plane. From Milowitz we crossed the border to Shoppowitz, then in the hands of the [Polish] insurgents. We talked there with the insurgent leader, August Kopek. It was evident at this time that the insurgents could not hold out much longer. We returned to Kattowitz and followed the German forces in their occupation of different towns, including Shoppowitz.

The following day the German troops had occupied nearly all of the territory of Upper Silesia; the insurgents being driven out had taken with them into Poland over two hundred [German] hostages. These persons had been turned over to the Polish military authorities and by them removed to Krakow. On the morning of August 21st, I was requested by Colonel Hoffmann, commanding the German troops in Kattowitz, to undertake the return of these persons. I agreed to do so on condition that executions [of Polish insurgents] in all of Upper Silesia were immediately stopped and were not resumed. Dr. Williger, who was present at the conference, at once telephoned to General von Friederburg, in command of the 6th Army Corps. General von Friederburg agreed to stop all executions until the following morning at seven o'clock. At the same time Dr. Williger telephoned to Berlin, notifying the government there of the conditions proposed.

I then went to Zabkowice in Poland, the headquarters of General Modelon, commanding the 2nd Division of Haller's [Polish] Army, and from there telephoned to General Haller at Krakow, making an appointment with him at Zabkowice. I returned to Kattowitz and arranged for an extension of the period during which executions would be stopped, and on the following day met General Haller. I had in the meantime received word from Berlin that the German Government had ordered all executions stopped permanently, as demanded.

While in conference with General Haller, two German officers arrived and delivered to General Haller an ultimatum, requiring the immediate return of the German hostages, with a statement if this were not done two Poles would be seized for every German held and other retaliatory measures would be adopted. A reply was required at 12 noon, failing which action would be taken by the Germans. This ultimatum was not delivered until 1:30 P.M. It was entirely contrary to my understanding with the Commander of the [German] 6th Army Corps and the Berlin Government, and, therefore, I requested permission of General Haller to see the German officers, which he granted. I suggested to these officers that they should withdraw the communication, as I was convinced it was not authorized; they stated they could not do so as they were under positive orders to deliver it. I suggested that they request General Haller to hold the communication and not forward it to Warsaw until they could have an opportunity to return to Kattowitz and secure further information. After some argument this was agreed to. I then continued my conference with General Haller and he agreed to recommend to Warsaw that the [German] hostages be returned under certain conditions. I returned to Kattowitz that afternoon; I was invited to a meeting of military and civil authorities, at which were present Generals von Groener, Commander-in-Chief of the German Army, von Friederburg, von Hoeffer and von Pessow. I at once stated what had happened regarding the ultimatum and it was very evident that its delivery was a surprise to all of the German authorities. The officers who had delivered the ultimatum were in the room and it developed that they had delivered it on a verbal order from the Assistant to the State Commissioner, Hoersing. I further stated that the delivery of this ultimatum, of course, made it impossible for me to act further, and I considered its delivery as an act of bad faith on the part of the Germans. The officers delivering the ultimatum were strongly criticized by their superiors at the meeting and General von Groener stated that while he had no authority to withdraw the ultimatum, he would immediately take the matter up with Berlin and secure a decision not later than the following day. On the following day the ultimatum was withdrawn.

There followed several days of adjustment of various difficulties between the Poles and the Germans. For example, the German airplanes had made several raids across the Polish border, or had fired on Polish towns from the German side of the border. These raids on our demand were stopped. Polish insurgents were at the same time making raids across the German border, and while these raids were not entirely stopped, the Polish military authorities, at our request, took steps toward stopping them.

We also investigated various reported cases of atrocities and interviewed a large number of refugees in Poland. There were reported to be from fifteen to thirty thousand refugees. We also commenced negotiations with the German authorities as to the granting of an amnesty to the insurgents. In the meantime we had also been in communication with the Warsaw Government through Minister Gibson and finally secured authority for the return of the German hostages. We went to Krakow and interviewed the hostages [Germans] taking their statements in writing, arranged for a train for them and delivered 220, as well as 157 other Germans held in the same camp, to the German authorities at Herby in Upper Silesia. For our action in this matter we received the thanks of the 6th Army Corps [German].

In the meantime it had seemed most desirable to have an Inter-Allied Commission come to Upper Silesia immediately, and the Supreme Council at Paris had [by Mr. Hoover's intervention] ordered [Allied] Generals du Pont, Malcolm and Benoivenge from Berlin as a Commission, of which I should become a member upon its arrival in Upper Silesia. Prior to this by arrangement with the German Government another Commission, of which Lt. Colonel Tidbury of the British Army was Chairman, had been appointed. This Commission included, in addition to Lt. Colonel Tidbury, one British, three French, two Italian and one Japanese officer. It arrived at Breslau on August 24th. Its authority was too limited to accomplish the results desired and, therefore I requested [of Mr. Hoover] the appointment of the other Commission. This other Commission finally arrived in Kattowitz on September 2nd. This Commission by its presence did a great deal toward re-establishing order and restoring calm. The Commission made a preliminary report to the Supreme Council under date of September 5th. I left Kattowitz on September 6th and returned to Paris, via Prague, arriving in Paris on September 9th. Work has been resumed in practically all of the mines in Upper Silesia and production is now approximately the same as before the insurrection. A large force of German troops is occupying the district and disorders had been stopped before I left Kattowitz. The situation is outwardly calm, but below the surface there is the strongest feeling of unrest and dissatisfaction. The recommendations of the Commission to the Supreme Council should be acted upon promptly, otherwise there are certain to be renewed outbreaks, which, of course, contain possibilities of war between Poland and Germany.

I arrived back in Paris and was called in by the Supreme Council on August 22 for a report. General Bliss (who was still in Paris), in a dispatch to the Secretary of State in Washington, stated on August 23, 1919:

Mr. Hoover read a telegram from his representative in Silesia concerning the German-Polish disorders there and Colonel Goodyear's efforts to solve them and Mr. Hoover went on to suggest that Colonel Goodyear be attached to the [Plebiscite] Commission . . . the Council approved instructions [as to the Coal War] for the Allied representatives in Berlin prepared by Mr. Hoover, Mr. Loucheur and General Weygand. . . . The essence of these instructions was that the Commission should work to re-establish order, ensure coal production and keep [the] Peace Conference informed.

Mr. Polk's report to the Secretary of State on August 23 was more extensive. A summary of it is:

The Council then heard Mr. Hoover on the coal situation in Central Europe and the position in Upper Silesia. . . . There were three coal fields from which the major supply for this section of Europe was drawn. One, in Upper Silesia now affected by strikes; one in Teschen under dispute between the Czecho-Slovaks and the Poles and one in Poland. The total output from these three fields was from 5 million to 6 million tons per month and they constituted the very heart [coal supply] of Central [and Eastern] Europe. If their production was not kept up it would be impossible to maintain the transportation and municipal services. . . . In Upper Silesia it would only be a matter of days before all mines would be disabled beyond repair [from these conflicts]. . . . He said that Colonel Goodyear was trying to effect a reconciliation. . . . Mr. Hoover . . . had learned from Mr. Markensen a German member of the Armistice Commission on the Eastern Front that the German Government was not fully in control of Grenzschutz troops and were trying to replace them by regular troops. . . . Mr. Hoover believed military occupation all the more necessary because of the contradictory currents among the Germans themselves, and because of a point which racial animosities had reached. . . . At Teschen the Polish Trade Union Leaders had informed Mr. Hoover that they would not help to increase production until they knew to whom the mines would fall. They were unwilling to work for the Czechs. . . . There were two questions: The political question of restoring order and the economic question of stimulating production and getting the necessary output . . . Mr. Hoover expressed the belief that a Coal Commission [referred to in the previous chapter] should appoint a sub-Committee to control all three districts with the authority of the Peace Conference. He suggested that this be done immediately and expressed hope that the Coal Committee enter upon its duties with . . . [that] prestige. . . . Mr. Hoover suggested that the Coal Commission be strengthened by a German member and even by a Czech and a Polish member and believed that if they should be disposed to obstruct business they could be controlled by the [Supreme War Council]. . . .

Mr. Balfour and Mr. Pichon (the British and French members) disagreed with this program:

. . . Mr. Balfour suggested that Mr. Hoover go to Berlin on behalf of the [Supreme] Council and negotiate on this matter. He believed that Mr. Hoover was the most suitable representative and that he had better hopes for success than anyone else. . . .

Certain draft instructions for Mr. Hoover authorizing him to negotiate with the German Government (one) for the immediate dispatch of a high Inter-Allied Administrative Commission to Silesia (two) for the acceptance of immediate inter-Allied occupation in Silesa, were approved in principle and it was agreed that Mr. Hoover after consultation with his colleagues on the Coal Commission should report on the following day whether he was able to undertake the mission and whether any alterations to the draft instructions appeared desirable. The instructions also directed Mr. Hoover to place himself in contact with General DuPont in Berlin and also instructed him to inform the German Government that the Council had no political interest, only in the very important material interests of Central Europe.

I greatly appreciated the compliment, but by this time Colonel Goodyear's action had produced a "calm" in the worst fighting areas. And I did not think it my duty to take on more European quarrels than I already had.

CHAPTER 35

REPATRIATION OF PRISONERS OF WAR

RUSSIAN PRISONERS IN GERMANY

The American organization under my direction had been called upon during the Armistice to furnish food to the Russian prisoners of war in Germany. These prisoners had not been repatriated to Russia; the French had objected to their repatriation on the ground that they would join the Communist armies.

The problem was still unsolved at the Peace, and at the request of the Supreme Council, I submitted to it the following memorandum on July 15, 1919:

PARIS, July 15, 1919

It will be recollected that the Allied Governments made certain agreements with the Germans for the retention of Russian prisoners in Germany, and made undertakings for the support of these prisoners by the Allied Governments. Their food supply and support has been carried out through the French Government, the British Red Cross, the American Red Cross, with a personnel of some 800 Allied officers, doctors, etc., under the general direction of the Inter-Allied Military Mission at Berlin.

I then recounted our organization's participation in supplying food to the prisoners, stated that our Congressional appropriations had come to an end, and continued:

. . . In any event, it is necessary to provide at once some measures for food, clothing and personnel to supervise [its] distribution pending re-

283

patriation. . . . This latter operation will require some months, but they must be repatriated before winter.

I understand the German Authorities are demanding the immediate repatriation of these prisoners, as it requires a force of some 18,000 German troops to guard them. The prisoners themselves are demanding their repatriation. I understand that their boots and clothing are in such condition that they cannot be marched to any destination and, in any event, they would probably indulge in brigandage unless repatriated under military supervision. The points therefore to be decided are:

1. Are the prisoners to be repatriated at once?
2. Are they to be repatriated to the nearest Russian point through Poland?
3. Are they to be repatriated by sea to Black Sea ports?
4. If either of these alternatives, who is to pay for the cost thereof, and who is to undertake it?
5. Who is to furnish the food and personnel for their care in the meantime?

I would like to emphasize that . . . [our] relief agencies . . . have now practically exhausted their resources and cannot take part in this matter, so that other arrangements must be set up at the earliest possible moment.

On July 18, the Supreme War Council passed the following resolution:

It is agreed:

(1) That upon the failure of the supplies already provided for the feeding of Russian prisoners now in Germany, they shall be fed and supplied by the military authorities of the Armies of Occupation until repatriated.

(2) That the means of repatriation of Russian prisoners now in Germany and maintenance at the cost of the Allies, shall be referred for consideration to the Military Representatives at Versailles with whom the Naval Advisors shall associate themselves for this purpose.

This undertaking met the usual bureaucratic delays, and General Bliss therefore took a hand at speeding it up in a letter to Under Secretary of State Polk:

PARIS, 15 August, 1919

DEAR MR. POLK:

I hand you herewith a report from General George H. Harries, who is the American Representative on the Inter-Allied Commission in Berlin on the Repatriation of Russian Prisoners of War.

As you know, some days ago the Council of Five adopted a resolution to the effect that the German Government should be immediately informed that the Allied and Associated Powers removed all restrictions which they had previously imposed on the repatriation of these Russian prisoners of war, the burden of the maintenance of these prisoners thereby falling upon the German Government from the moment of receipt by them of the notification above referred to.

Nevertheless, there is a moral responsibility in this matter which still rests upon the Allied and Associated Powers. As a matter of fact, the latter have not removed all of the restrictions imposed upon the repatriation of the Russian prisoners of war. At this moment there is an insuperable obstacle to their repatriation in the fact that the Polish and other governments east of Germany refuse permission for the passage of these prisoners through their territories. These Russian prisoners were captured by the Germans when the former were fighting in the Allied cause.

I suggest that you present this matter to the Council with a view to one of the following solutions:

a) Immediate permission to be obtained from the Polish and Lithuanian Governments for the passage of these prisoners by rail through their territories to some interior point in Russia.

b) If the foregoing is not considered desirable, repatriation by rail or sea to South Russia.

c) If neither of the foregoing can be done, promptly represent the facts in the case to our respective governments with a view to securing the necessary appropriations of money for the proper support of these prisoners.

TASKER H. BLISS

These permissions were secured, and most of the Russian prisoners in Germany made their way home. However, from such information as came to me, I concluded that, for safety's sake, most of the non-Communists joined their Communist fellows on the way home.

THE GERMAN AND HUNGARIAN PRISONERS
IN SIBERIA

The 200,000 German and Hungarian prisoners in Siberia were fed as long as they were in the hands of the Allied or Russian White Army authorities, but this support was coming to an end. The problem was far afield from our relief province, but we became involved through a request for advice. Secretary of State Lansing cabled Mr. Polk in Paris urging that prompt action be taken. Secretary Polk asked for my advice. On July 26, 1919, I prepared a memorandum as follows:

It appears that there are some 200,000 German-Austrian and Hungarian prisoners in Siberia, and that these prisoners are suffering greatly and are a constant menace to the [White] Siberian Government. There are also certain Polish prisoners and civilians now scattered all over the world who will require more systematic assistance at repatriation, but there is an entire deficiency of funds with which to pay the incidental expenses. There are probably also other odd lots of expatriates of various nationals as the result of the war, who need systematic repatriation. It would appear to me that this problem requires definite organization, and I should like to submit the following plan in the matter for action by the Council.

First, that a Commission, comprising a British, French, American and Italian military officer, should be set up and undertake the management of this repatriation. That this Commission should communicate their appointment to the Austrian, Hungarian and Polish and other Governments, and that they should offer to undertake the repatriation, provided funds are placed to their credit in advance by each of the Governments concerned. It would appear to me that if such a body is set up under capable officers that they would be able to work out a solution in this manner and to secure from the Allied Governments the necessary shipping and other services. . . . They could invite a delegate of each of the Governments concerned to sit with them in respect to the matters which concerned such a Government and they could engage the necessary staff to carry on the work. They would probably need to appeal to the various Allied Governments and to charitable societies for some assistance in respect to prisoners originating from quarters unable to supply these funds, but, in any event, they would create a center around which all effort of this kind could be directed.

With the repatriation of the Allied troops nearing completion, it would appear to be an appropriate moment for the erection of such a body. I attach two memoranda on the subject indicating the volume of the problem involved, the first from the British Authorities on "Prisoners in Siberia," the second from the Polish Office for Repatriation.

HERBERT HOOVER

Secretary Polk reported to Washington as follows:

21 August 1919

SECRETARY OF STATE, WASHINGTON

The question of the repatriation of German and Austro-Hungarian prisoners of war in Siberia was considered by the Supreme Economic Council at its meeting in London on August first.

He then quoted my memorandum and continued:

It appeared that the Austrian Government had offered to provide funds for the repatriation of their nationals. The Hungarian Government had stated that they were unable to contribute to the expense, but it was believed that this matter would be reconsidered if a responsible and recognized Hungarian Government were established. It was also believed that Germany would contribute the necessary funds for the repatriation of her prisoners of war.

The British and French objected to the Hoover plan in that it would seem to commit the Allied Governments to furnish the shipping necessary for repatriation purposes. Finally it was agreed that Hoover's report should be forwarded to the Supreme Council with a communication pointing out that considerable difficulties might arise with respect to the shipping arrangements and suggesting that the repatriation commission, if appointed, should be directed to take under careful consideration Allied needs with respect to the transport of Allied troops.

The report of the Supreme Economic Council has not yet come before the Supreme Council but I shall take steps to have it put on the agenda at a very early date and shall urge the necessity of action on this matter as suggested by Department 2852.

I believe that the chief difficulty in this matter will be the furnishing of the necessary ships and I should appreciate being advised as to how far the United States is prepared to go in providing the necessary shipping.

POLK

On August 22, John Foster Dulles, Secretary Polk's assistant, informed me that his office was urging that the matter be taken up by the Supreme Council while I was still in Paris. I replied to him as follows:

PARIS, 26 August 1919

MY DEAR DULLES:

I have asked to have my plan for handling prisoners placed on the Supreme Council agenda and, as I may possibly have to go from Brussels direct to London and not return here until the middle of next week, I would be glad if you could see the matter through.

My plan is simplicity itself. . . . I do not propose that any of the Allied Governments should incur any expense, but that it should say to the German . . . [and other Governments] that if they want their prisoners home they may pay their money to this commission, who would for that purpose add a German officer to their body, and would then proceed to make the necessary arrangements.

I would earnestly suggest Colonel Logan for the American member of such a commission, as he will be attached to the Peace [Mission]. . . . The entire expense for conducting such organization ought to be supplied . . . [by] the various Governments. Some appropriation by Congress is probably necessary to help the Poles, Czechs, and various friendly countries, to get their people back.

HERBERT HOOVER

Ultimately, my plan prevailed, in principle. The prisoners got home with the assistance of the Allies, their own governments, and some charitable contributions.

All this prisoner business is a tedious recital of a minor incident in world history, but possibly I am warranted in giving this information to historians as an answer to much misinformation from later German and Hungarian sources.

FINLAND, THE BALTIC STATES, POLAND, AND THE DANZIG FREE STATE

CHAPTER 36

FINLAND

The American Government's official agencies had saved Finland during the Armistice, and her independence had been ratified by the Allies shortly before the Peace. During a century of Russian oppression at its worst, the Finns had preserved their intellectual life, with a determination to restore their representative government, which they had instituted centuries before. With independence and the Peace, a great spirit of hope and initiative swept over the nation. One of our purposes in founding our new American Relief Administration had been to give Finland aid in her continuing difficulties.

The Peace finally freed her from the Allied blockade and enabled her to put her small fleet of cargo ships to work and to start exports of wood products in exchange for imports of raw materials and food. The Finns' grain harvest of 1919, although much better than that of 1918, was still below normal. Their total of about 3,100,000 food animals before the war had decreased to about 2,000,000 at the Peace. Because of the lack of feed during the war and the Armistice, these animals were much below normal in production of meat, fats, and dairy products.

Major Ferry K. Heath remained head of our mission in Finland until August 1, when Lieutenant Angus I. Ward succeeded him. Ward carried on until December, 1919, when he was succeeded by Joseph F. Feit, who, with Ivar W. Wahren, continued until the end.

At the Peace, Lieutenant Ward appraised the Finnish situation in regard to products other than grain as follows:

. . . It is estimated that the soap and sugar cards will be done away with shortly. . . . This is a great improvement over the ration during the past winter. . . . Meat is still very scarce and the people have to depend mostly upon fish for this portion of their diet. . . .

The sum of their food situation was that they could supply their adult population; the difficulty was the expensive special food required for the weak children, the sick, and the aged.

Our new American Relief Administration continued the canteen system, established before the Peace, until July 1, 1920. During this period we provided for a total of 192,000 children, expectant mothers, and elderly people, the maximum load at any one time being 127,770. The canteens served 35,000,000 meals. The Finnish Government furnished the A.R.A. with 936 tons of food for the canteens valued at $195,949.

We provided fifty-six tons of clothing materials, having a value of $201,826, as follows:

> 63,344 yards of 54-inch woolen cloth
> 47,374 pairs of children's boots
> 40,002 pairs of woolen stockings
> 40,000 needles
> 172,800 buttons
> 8,000,000 yards of thread

From these materials the devoted Finnish women made and distributed a host of children's clothes.

Among Finland's other burdens were about three thousand absolutely destitute refugees from Ingermanland; moreover, when General Yudenich's army was defeated in its attack on Petrograd, his destitute soldiers flooded into Finland and Estonia. The Finns looked after the adults, and we undertook the care of the children.

The A.R.A. furnished 35 tons of special overseas food for the canteens, purchased 350 tons of local food for these purposes, and received a donation of 936 tons from the Finnish Government. This, together with 56 tons of clothing, made a total of 1,377 tons of supplies and an expenditure of $449,816.

Aids to Finland after the Peace also came from two other American organizations. The Jewish Joint Distribution Committee gave some help, but it is impossible to break down its expenditure for Finland alone. The National Lutheran Council expended $49,338 in Finland between 1919 and 1923.

TOTAL SUPPLIES TO FINLAND FROM THE PEACE TO 1923 *

	Food	Clothing & Misc.	Total	$ Value
American Relief Administration				
Children's relief	35	56	91	$216,205
Expenditures for local purchase	350		350	37,662
Finnish government donation	936		936	195,949
National Lutheran Council ..	(quantities unknown)			49,338
Jewish Joint Distribution Committee	(quantities unknown)			Not available
	1,321	56	1,377	$499,154

* In tons.

CHAPTER 37

ESTONIA

Before I begin the narrative of post-Peace relief in Estonia, I will include some introductory comments concerning all three of the Baltic States—Estonia, Latvia, and Lithuania.

The signing of peace at Paris—and thus recognition of the independence of Estonia, Latvia, and Lithuania—did not bring peace to these little nations. It did bring the removal of the blockade, from which removal came rapid expansion of their foreign trade and their industries.

I have related the agonies of their struggle for independence and recovery in Part One of this volume. But trouble continued to plague them from many directions after the Peace. They had set up governments on the British parliamentary pattern, but instead of the British tradition of a majority political party, their membership was divided into a dozen political parties among whom little constructive action could be agreed upon. However, at the time of the Peace, all of their political parties were united on three determinations: they would hold their separate independence, they would divide the land among the peasants, and they would resist the Communists.

After the Peace, they were involved in both internal and external wars. The Balt and Russian overlords in control of their lands and industries were slow to realize the power and determination of these nationalities, whom they had dominated for a thousand years.

With the harvest of 1919 and the resumption of exports and imports, they were able to meet most of the needs for their adult population. But huge problems of debilitated children, the ill, the old, and the destitute fell upon the American Relief Administration. Moreover, our staff was compelled to deal with many economic and political problems. Colonel John C. Groome continued to head our mission to all three states for some months after the Peace.

POST-PEACE RELIEF IN ESTONIA

Estonia was at peace, except for an attack she made on Latvia. The 1919 harvest and end of the Allied blockade enabled her, by export of goods, to provide fairly well for her adult population. The unsolved problem was the subnormal children and others requiring expensive special food from overseas.

During the relief of children prior to the Peace, it was not possible to set up an efficient canteen system, and they had to receive their special food in the homes. This method was most difficult for our able Estonian women's committees, and it did not produce the physical results for which we were striving.

Captain John C. Miller was appointed chief of our Estonian staff at the Peace and served from March, 1919, to July, 1920. His assistants were Angus I. Ward, who served from August, 1919, to April, 1920 (when he succeeded Captain Miller), and Captain John Thors, Jr., who served from August, 1919, to August, 1921.

Captain Miller, reporting on the condition of Estonian children when our new organization took over the work, stated:

Owing to the . . . fact that the little ones had been without proper nourishment in many cases over a period of years, almost all the needy children were backward in physical and mental development. . . .

. . . Tuberculosis was prevalent to an alarming extent, owing to the crowded conditions of the houses and the fact that throughout the long winter the children had been confined indoors because they did not have sufficient clothing to keep them warm. Rickets, too, the result of under feeding and improper foods, appeared among [the children]. . . .

. . . on July first it was announced that on and after the fifteenth of the month children over six years of age, except those who were sick, would be fed at . . . [canteens]. The children under six years of age continued to receive food at their homes. The sick, upon presentation of a doctor's certificate by the mothers, also received their ration away from the . . . [canteens].

It was . . . [amusing] and yet a pathetic sight to see the children who first came to the . . . [canteens] after the issuance of this order. Many of them did not have proper clothing, but the food was of paramount importance, and they borrowed the clothing of their parent, or if they couldn't borrow, simply took it, in order . . . [not to miss] their daily food allowance.

The new American Relief Administration established our canteen system at the Peace and carried on for three years—until August, 1922. We cared for 126,000 persons and provided them 35,935,350 meals. The maximum number provided for at any one time was about 84,000.

The shortage in clothing was almost as bad as the shortage in food. In preparation for the cold winter of 1919–1920, we made the following shipment of clothing materials valued at $199,352:

> 60,636 yards of 54-inch woolen cloth
> 50,012 pairs of children's boots
> 52,426 pairs of stockings
> 35,000 needles
> 139,600 buttons
> 818 pounds of thread

As was the usual procedure in our work, our staff organized workrooms where clothing was made by devoted women.

A report of the mission prepared by Captain John Thors, Jr., stated:

. . . The difficulties of the selection of the needy children to whom clothing was to be issued, were immense. Practically no clothing could be bought in Esthonia and parents of all classes made application for these outfits. . . . Every parent who wished to make application registered his child, and the investigators personally looked into the claims of all. . . . attendants who were fitting shoes and stockings early complained that the kiddies had not been given an opportunity for bathing. After the second day of distribution a protest appeared in the Reval newspapers, and within a week a public bath . . . was opened. . . .

MEDICAL CARE

Medical inspection of the children in the canteens was carried on by volunteer Estonian physicians. In the first months, the children were examined every fortnight and records made of their improvement. After that, the intervals were increased to once a month. We received the following report on the physical progress of the children:

. . . Teachers and physicians throughout the nation . . . testified to the effectiveness of the Administration's work. And to those who watched the children from day to day the success . . . was plainly written on the faces of the . . . [children]. Faces which had been pale and shrunken filled out. . . . Skin once yellow regained a natural color. Arrested growth sprang up and during the summer and fall seemed to make up for the . . . difficult winter of 1918–19.

. . . Teachers told how children who, the year before, had been hopelessly backward because they were too poorly nourished to study, were . . . making excellent progress. As the months wore on . . . the good results showed increasingly on every side.

. . . The children were encouraged in bodily cleanliness by the word and example of the leaders in the work, and new standards of personal sanitation were held up for [them] . . . to follow.

In the records of the health office, however, are found the most eloquent testimony of the effectiveness of the work. The child mortality rate, which had been constantly increasing since the outbreak of the war . . . in 1914 soon began to decline and before the mission was ready to announce its withdrawal these statistics had returned to more or less [pre-war] normal. . . .

RUSSIAN REFUGEES

Because of the failure of Yudenich's army in its attack on Petrograd, a mass of refugees crossed the Estonian border. There were about 10,000 of them, with many children. Our organization furnished all their food, free to both adults and children, and assigned 5,000 clothing outfits to them, for they were almost naked. The Estonian Government found them shelter somewhere among a population already destitute of housing from the war.

Estonia made remarkable progress in economic recovery from the war and the blockade. Captain Miller reported:

. . . Whereas . . . when the Administration began its work, there was no food or manufactured commodities in the shops of Reval or the other large towns; now the stores are filled with articles of all sorts. . . .

The American Relief Administration, including food drafts, furnished a total of 2,124 tons of supplies valued at $669,485. The Estonian Government contributed to us 1,693 tons of supplies valued at $298,445, making the total of our distribution 3,817 tons with a value of $967,930.

In closing the mission in August, 1922, after three years work by the new American Relief Administration, supplies were left in the hands of the Estonian committees, which would carry them some months.

AIDS FROM OTHER AMERICAN CHARITABLE SOURCES

The American Red Cross established an extensive medical service in Estonia. Its work included attacks on raging epidemics, mostly typhus and smallpox, the creation and support of clinics, special services for children, aid to hospitals, and medical service generally.

The Red Cross expenditures are given under one heading: "Western Russia and the Baltic States." We have estimated the amount expended in Estonia, partly from Red Cross accounts and partly from information in the A.R.A.'s files, at a total of $1,158,952. So far as we can find from Red Cross records, there is no enumeration of the quantities of medical supplies.

In December, 1919, we forwarded 531 packages of clothing and clothing materials (about 100 tons) collected for us by the Red Cross (value estimated at $186,323).

THE JEWISH JOINT DISTRIBUTION COMMITTEE

The records of the Jewish Joint Distribution Committee show a special expenditure of $1,500 for medical aid, and an additional $58,872 was given in medical aid to the three states. We have credited one-third of the latter sum (or $19,620) to Estonia—making a total of $21,120.

THE NATIONAL LUTHERAN COUNCIL

The division of the land in Estonia in 1921 deprived the German Balts of their estates, and there arose considerable poverty among them. The Balts had been the prime supporters of the Lutheran Church. The National Lutheran Council established relief for retired pastors, widows, and orphans of pastors—and for rebuilding the Lutheran churches. Its financial records show that from the Peace to 1923, it spent $32,573.

THE YOUNG MEN'S CHRISTIAN ASSOCIATION

Thousands of Russian refugees fled to Estonia during the Russian Revolution of 1917. Among these there were hundreds of Russian children, 60 per cent of whom were orphans. The Estonian Government at that time appealed to the Y.M.C.A. for aid. The records show little detail of its work in that period, but in the summer of 1920, the Y.M.C.A. opened fifteen schools in Estonia. An athletic program for the Estonian Army was also undertaken. A rough estimate from its records indicates an expenditure of about $200,000.

The Northern Baptist Convention and the Student Friendship Fund also did work in Estonia, the details of which have not survived.

TOTAL SUPPLIES TO ESTONIA FROM THE PEACE TO 1923 *

	Food	Medical, Clothing, & Misc.	Total	$ Value
American Relief Administration:				
Children's relief	1,771	60	1,831	$ 522,929
Food drafts	293		293	146,556
Estonian Government donation	1,693		1,693	298,445
American Red Cross	(quantities unknown)			1,158,952
Jewish Joint Distribution Committee	(quantities unknown)			21,120
National Lutheran Council	(quantities unknown)			32,573
Y.M.C.A.	(quantities unknown)			200,000
	3,757	60	3,817	$2,380,575

* In tons.

Our mission reported:

. . . In bidding good-bye to the members of the American Relief Mission sincere regret . . . [was] shown by the Esthonians of all political parties. . . .

The . . . government . . . presented . . . a richly illuminated script thanking the United States of America for stretching its hand of relief toward Esthonia in time to save thousands of starving children.

CHAPTER 38

LATVIA

Peace may have been made in Paris, but there was no indication of it in Latvia, which, at the Peace, was in complete military, political, and economic chaos. There were four armies on her soil:

(1) The forces of General von der Goltz, which the Allies had stipulated, to the Germans, should be retained in the Baltic States to maintain order;

(2) A small army of Latvians;

(3) An army, called the *Landeswehr,* composed mostly of the Balts; and

(4) The Estonian Army, which on one occasion invaded the Latvians.

Von der Goltz, with the aid of the Landeswehr and a small contingent of Latvians, had expelled the Communists from Riga a month before the Peace and was still in control of the city at the Peace. The Estonians, fearing both von der Goltz' army and the Landeswehr's intentions to expand to permanent control of the Baltic States, attacked them a few days after the Peace. A report from Captain William H. Foreman, approved by Colonel Groome, chief of our mission in the Baltic States, indicates the situation:

July 3

Esthonian armored trains opened bombardment on the famished city of Riga yesterday afternoon at 4 o'clock in an effort to expel German and Baltic Landeswehr troops which have held the strong fortifications of the city against more than 20 infantry and machine gun attacks by the superior Esthonian forces during the last few days. Poison gas is being used by both sides, neither of which is sufficiently equipped with gas masks, one third of the Baltic troops are reported casualties and at least 30 civilians including women have been killed.

Although the Germans under General von der Goltz are in control of the city, the people have been supplied with nothing to eat except food from the American Relief Administration which has staved off starvation ever since the evacuation of Riga by the Bolsheviki late in May. The American food, which is under guard and is being distributed to civilians and especially to children, is the only supply other than military rations within the city. Members of the German Eisner or Iron Division Military Police yesterday afternoon arrested Lieutenant Nixon, of the American Relief Administration, Lieutenant Cawn and an American sailor, both of the American food ship U.S.S. Lake Tulare, which was hailed with great joy when it sailed into port. The arrests were made on a crowded boulevard, without provocation. All the Americans had official passes to carry on their work. They have now been released.

Colonel Du Parquet, of the French Military Mission, crossed the firing line yesterday afternoon in an attempt to arrange an armistice, but the last report at 8:30 last night stated that firing continued.

Colonel John C. Groome . . . is continuing the supply of food for the civilians who are in such dire need . . . Colonel Groome is rushing another food ship to Riga and it will arrive there Friday. The plight of the people is desperate and their only hope against . . . [starvation] is this supply of American food. The red terror of Bolshevism left the population wan and wizened, wandering the once splendid streets in a ghastly sort of way. The city was then saved from starvation by a trainload of American white flour which arrived under fire from retreating Bolshevist patrols. 90% of the children in the city have been estimated by the American Relief Administration medical experts to be undernourished. During this week the happy results of American rations were beginning to become apparent and the work of supply and distribution is continuing.

. . . The Latvians had asked the Esthonians to aid in driving out the Germans and the Baltic Barons.

Colonel John C. Groome reported:

2 July 1919.

. . . I have seen dead civilians including women in streets and burning houses in center of city . . . Firing reported from armoured train and

Estonian ships off Denamunde. Recommend immediate and drastic action to stop bombardment.

Our relief staff at Riga now undertook to arrange an armistice between the Estonians and von der Goltz, who was in command of both the Landeswehr and his own troops. The only force which could be appealed to was the Allied Military Mission in the Baltic, of which British General Gough was the head. The report of Colonel Groome on this undertaking was as follows:

. . . Sunday night . . . Lieutenant Harrington came through the lines in a motor car from Riga and . . . described the situation to me. I immediately notified the British and French Representatives in Libau, and called a meeting in my office at 11:00 A.M. Harrington described conditions in Riga . . . and while they apparently doubted his statements, he was able to answer all their questions and convinced them that all his accounts of the situation were true. The Allied [Military] Mission then decided that an armistice should be arranged immediately to prevent further blood-shed, and Harrington returned that night . . . to Riga, taking Colonel Du Parquet of the French Mission with him to inform Colonel Fletcher, Commanding the Balts, who were defending Riga, that the Allies insisted upon an armistice. . . . On Tuesday, July second, word was gotten to General Laidoner, Commanding the Estonian Army, and an armistice was signed that evening. . . . Lieut. Harrington deserves the greatest credit for his actions . . . he . . . was alone responsible for forcing the British to insist upon an armistice. . . .

A cabinet for Latvia was agreed upon, to be headed by Karl Ulmanis as President.[1]

The situation in Northern Latvia at this time was certainly desperate. Riga's prewar population of 600,000 had decreased to 250,000. Of these, 19,000 were destitute and ill, and 3,000 children were in 26 different orphanages, asylums, and children's hospitals without food. Typhus and other infectious diseases were rampant.

Riga was devoid of food except for that supplied by the American Relief Administration. The Communists had stripped what food there was in their retreat to Russia, and, with the requisitions by von der Goltz and the Landeswehr, the peasants were almost foodless. One of our reports stated:

[1] See Chap. 5.

. . . There is a daily, almost continuous, procession of peasants and citizens, trudging for the most part barefoot, over the roads to and from the outlying districts, carrying small bundles of food on their backs, in baskets or on such small handcarts or carriages as they possess. Many of these people cover great distances in a day in their quest for food, thus depleting their already enfeebled energies and rendering themselves utterly fatigued and exhausted. . . .

The August, 1919, monthly report of our staff stated:

. . . The effect of only a few days of full bread rations soon began to be noticeable in the city's spirit. Although there was nothing to be bought in the shops and very little in the markets, the streets became well filled with people, especially in the parks and boulevards. Within a week the grass was being cut, gardens being cared for and more cafes and restaurants opened every day. . . . Both German and Russian theatres were running and concerts being given in various halls. . . .

On the other side of the scene one found the four large hospitals of the city filled to overflow with patients of all ages suffering from diseases caused by mal-nutrition. Spotted typhus and rickets, both due to lack of proper food, raged among children, many of whom are never likely to recover from the effects. . . . conditions slowly improving while medical supplies given by the American Red Cross were rushed forward by ship. . . .

In five boroughs in North Latvia, there were 157,000 buildings before the war. Of these

59,314 buildings or 37.75% are entirely demolished
38,982   "   or 24.81% are partially demolished
58,824   "   or 37.44% exist without having suffered much

Other sentences from our reports on the situation in Latvia read:

. . . in Libau . . . [physical] examinations . . . [of children revealed] an immense amount of gastrointestinal distress caused by bad hygienic environment plus restricted and poor foods; great numbers of skin diseases; a lot of hitherto hidden tuberculosis; many cases of epilepsy; numbers of cases of feeble-mindedness of various degrees that are at present acting as a drag upon whole families; many cases of marasmus; all sorts of other ailments of childhood. . . .

Libau . . . city of 65,000 inhabitants, of these about 19,500 are chil-

dren from 1–16 years of age. About 5,000 are under 7 and absolutely destitute. It was determined best to begin with this place. . . .

The children came in great crowds, so many of them displayed evidences of physical disability that necessity occurred to me for securing
some idea as to the extent and kinds of physical disabilities in these
children. . . .

. . . large percentage . . . [had] tuberculosis. . . .

. . . Observation of the children *in Riga* in July 1919 showed a patent
lowered tone in both physical and mental condition—apathy and malnutrition being very apparent.

. . . [In] Lettgallia . . . conditions all through that area were fright-
ful; typhus was raging as well as other disease complexes. . . .

The knowledge of the pathological ring surrounding Latvia especially
to the North and East—e.g. Typhus, Small-pox, Venereal diseases, all of
which prevailed to an alarming extent in those areas, made it wise to . . .
[supplement] the regular feeding and clothing programs with some kind
of medical supervision of our children.

The situation in South Latvia (Courland) was somewhat better.
There was little fighting and the peasants had brought in a fair crop.

Von der Goltz's army was ordered out by the Allied governments
in August, 1919, at my request, but the Germans plundered all the
food they could carry away. We were compelled to hold most of our
staff of American Army officers to meet these emergencies until late
in August. In the meantime, we placed Captain Thomas J. Orbison
(formerly in charge in South Latvia) in full charge of all children's
relief in Latvia, with Lieutenant T. D. Howard as his assistant.

The situation of the children is illustrated by the fact that under
normal conditions there should have been in Latvia more than
535,000 children under ten years of age, whereas there were, in
August, 1919, actually less than 250,000.

Our organization, prior to the Peace, had started canteens and
was caring for 41,000 children, expectant mothers, and aged in South
Latvia. With the Communist retreat, the work was at once expanded
over all Latvia. During the whole period, 121,500 persons were cared
for in the canteens, which provided a total of 39,616,000 meals.

CLOTHING

We delivered clothing of a value of $198,764 as follows:

> 80,564 yards of 54-inch woolen cloth
> 48,736 pairs of children's boots
> 45,049 pairs of woolen stockings
> 50,000 needles
> 140,832 buttons
> 1,000,000 yards of thread

The devoted Latvian women made up the clothing and distributed it. They made from 29,687 yards of the woolen cloth alone 6,465 overcoats and 5,053 warm dresses.

Our staff found it necessary to establish free clinics in the canteens, of which the following is the record of the children treated up to July, 1920:

Dental clinic	9,222
Eye clinic	4,198
Internal disease	371
Total	13,791

That our Latvian children's canteens had an international complexion is indicated by the nationalities among 22,857 children canvassed:

Latvians	9,531
German-Balts	4,910
Jews	2,711
Russians	2,696
Poles	1,778
Lithuanians	1,036
Estonians	162
English, Turks, French, Austrians, Swedes, Gypsies, and Brazilians	33

Our organization also distributed food for 1,000 destitute students in high schools and colleges in co-operation with the Y.M.C.A. and the Y.W.C.A. student movement.

The American Relief Administration distributed 4,129 tons of food, mostly special food for our canteens, valued at $769,556. The Latvian Government contributed to us 479 tons of food valued at $60,880. The Norwegian Government donated seven tons of cod-liver oil for the children's relief at a value of $3,960, making the total distribution 4,615 tons valued at $834,396. The value of about $180 a ton for our supplies was due to the very special sorts of food for children, which comprised condensed milk, fats, meat, cocoa, and medicine.

THE AMERICAN RED CROSS

As I have stated, after the Peace the American Red Cross established a commission to the Baltic States and Western Russia comprising physicians, surgeons, and nurses. In Latvia, the Red Cross established clinics and dispensaries; it furnished medical and surgical supplies. During the spring of 1921, it inaugurated a special child-health program which was operated by special clinics in A.R.A. canteens. The Red Cross also set up milk stations, training classes for personnel, and bathing establishments to accommodate several thousand children daily.

Of the sixty-four dispensaries which were in operation in the Baltic States at the end of June, 1921, thirty-four were in Latvia. Dental clinics were also set up. The Red Cross organized workshops for Latvian women to manufacture children's clothing and paid the workers. During April, 1921, alone, these workshops distributed clothing to thirty-one thousand children.

An epidemic of dysentery which broke out in the Latvian towns of Dvinsk, Reschitza, and Libau was stopped with the assistance of Red Cross sanitary units early in September, 1920.

By May, 1922, every one of the child-health stations established by the American Red Cross in the six large cities of the Baltic States was taken over and operated by local personnel, supported by the governments of their respective states.

From July 1, 1919, to June 30, 1923, the Red Cross expended

$3,068,286 in Western Russia and the Baltic States. Our estimate was that $1,022,762 of this was expended in Latvia.

THE JEWISH JOINT DISTRIBUTION COMMITTEE

This committee set up two subcommittees to co-operate with the American Relief Administration after the Peace. One committee directed medical aid, and the other was concerned mostly with the care of orphans. The total expenditure of these subcommittees in Latvia was $436,273. In addition, our estimate of their general expenditure in medical aid in Latvia was $19,630—making a grand total of $455,903.

THE NATIONAL LUTHERAN COUNCIL

The National Lutheran Council expended $49,405 in Latvia for the reconstruction of Lutheran churches and support of pastors, their families, and congregations.

THE YOUNG MEN'S CHRISTIAN ASSOCIATION

In 1920, the Premier of Latvia asked the Y.M.C.A. to undertake work with the Latvian troops. The Y.M.C.A. set up athletic and educational programs. By December, 1921, there were five centers for these purposes.

OTHER CHARITABLE ORGANIZATIONS

The Northern Baptist Convention contributed to the relief of Latvia after the Peace, but we were unable to discover the details of its work.

TOTAL SUPPLIES TO LATVIA FROM THE PEACE TO 1923 *

	Food	Medical, Clothing, & Miscellaneous	Total	$ Value
American Relief Administration:				
Children's relief	3,962	58	4,020	$ 752,076
Food drafts	109		109	17,480
Latvian government donation	479		479	60,880
Norwegian government donation	7		7	3,960
American Red Cross	(quantities unknown)			1,022,762
Jewish Joint Distribution Committee	(quantities unknown)			455,903
National Lutheran Council	(quantities unknown)			49,405
	4,557	58	4,615	$2,362,466

* In tons.

CHAPTER 39

LITHUANIA

Lithuania did not have the problems which plagued her sister states after the Peace. Von der Goltz' army remained in occupation and lived on requisitions for about two months after the Peace. Relieved of the blockade, Lithuania was able to export such goods as her minor industries produced; she had an abundant harvest which provided for her adult population. The problem after the Peace was a minor number of debilitated children in small towns.

We appointed Captain James T. Scott Chief of Mission; he served from July to September, 1919. He was succeeded by Richard H. Simpson, who served from September, 1919, to June, 1920. Simpson's assistants were Frank H. Holden, who served from September, 1919, to February, 1920, and Durrell L. Noyes, who served from January to May, 1920.

We continued our canteens until May, 1920, when improved conditions warranted our withdrawal. However, in the winter of 1920–1921, we again resumed and continued relief until the harvest of August, 1921. A total of about 40,000 children and other persons were cared for.

There was the usual need of clothing for the children. For the winter of 1919–1920, we distributed the following through the municipalities at a cost of $61,466 to our organization:

Shoes	13,939 pairs
Shoelaces	12,528 pairs

Woolen stockings	12,588 pairs
Woolen cloth (54" wide)	19,044 yards
Thread	2,500,000 yards
Needles	15,000 number
Buttons	49,680 number

We also established a small service of free food to students, which amounted to $927. Our total expenditures were $111,988.

THE AMERICAN RED CROSS

The American Red Cross undertook a large program of eradicating typhus and other contagious diseases, of supporting orphanages, hospitals, and clinics. It expended a considerable part of the total of $3,068,286 carried in its accounts as "Western Russia and Baltic States." Our estimate of its total expenditures in Lithuania after the Peace is $1,178,952.

THE JEWISH JOINT DISTRIBUTION COMMITTEE

There was a considerable population of Jews in Lithuania. During the times their country had been occupied by the German armies, they had been under great persecutions, but their liberation came with the Armistice. The Jewish Joint Distribution Committee provided medical service, care for orphans, and aid to refugees and the destitute.

The expenditures of the Committee in this state after the Peace to the end of relief in 1923 amounted to $568,279. In addition, Lithuania participated in the Committee's medical fund for the three Baltic States. For statistical purposes, we have assigned one-third of this, or $19,624, to Lithuania—making a total of $587,903.

THE NATIONAL CATHOLIC WAR COUNCIL

This organization expended $6,211 in Lithuania after the Peace.

THE NATIONAL LUTHERAN COUNCIL

The National Lutheran Council records show an expenditure of $4,343 for rebuilding churches and schools after the Peace.

TOTAL SUPPLIES TO LITHUANIA
FROM THE PEACE TO 1923 *

	Food	Clothing & Misc.	Total	$ Value
American Relief Administration:				
Children's relief	174	13	187	$ 111,061
Students' relief	8		8	927
American Red Cross	(quantities unknown)			1,178,952
Jewish Joint Distribution				
Committee	(quantities unknown)			587,903
National Catholic War				
Council	(quantities unknown)			6,211
National Lutheran Council ..	(quantities unknown)			4,343
	182	13	195	$1,889,397

* In tons.

EPILOGUE

Throughout the years after the relief period, I received invitations from a score of countries in Europe to become their guest as a mark of appreciation for services during the war. Some of these invitations came from Finland, Latvia, and Estonia. In response, in March, 1938, I visited these countries, where great courtesies were shown me.

I found that the three Baltic States were enjoying the highest standard of living of any place in Europe. Their ambitions for representative, constitutional government of free men had not, however, altogether succeeded. The multitude of factional political parties in their parliaments had produced only compromise or opposition, with collapsing ministries—and a man on horseback. By the time of my visit, all had Fascist governments with mild but resolute dictators.

THE RISE AND FATE OF ULMANIS

The greatest leader in the Baltic States—Ulmanis—at one time had been voted out of his office as President by his unmanageable parliament. A few years prior to my visit, with the aid of the Latvian Army, he had taken over the government and transformed it into a Fascist state.

In 1940, after the beginning of the Second World War, the Baltic States were seized by the Communists. Ulmanis was taken prisoner and liquidated in a Russian prison.

Hope of independence again rose high among these peoples at the announcement of the Atlantic Charter by Churchill and Roosevelt in 1942, but these men later condemned the Baltic States to slavery by their agreements with Stalin at Yalta and Potsdam.

Under Communist domination, there has been an era of liquidation, deportations to Siberia, and colonization of Russians on seized farms. The restoration of these states to freedom may possibly come again because their nationals abroad are unceasing in their determination. Peoples whose mores have survived a thousand years of foreign domination do not easily perish.

CHAPTER 40

POLAND AND THE DANZIG
FREE STATE

The situation and problems confronting Poland at the Peace may be summarized as follows:

(1) The people were still hungry. The country had been ravished, looted, and destroyed until, at the Armistice, there were no reserves of consequence in Poland. As great as our effort had been through the United States governmental relief agencies, we had not been able to supply more than the bare margins upon which these 28,000,000 people survived, although we, our affiliates, and other charitable organizations provided over 419,162 tons of supplies at a cost of more than $134,191,223 in relief.

(2) The country was still in the grip of the greatest typhus epidemic ever known in history.

(3) The continued blockade by the Allies against import of raw materials and export of goods during the Armistice had left Polish industries unrecovered and unemployment rampant.

(4) Poland's railways were miserably deteriorated, despite all the efforts we had made during the Armistice to rehabilitate them.

(5) Her currency continued to consist of the German marks, Austrian kronen, and Russian rubles in use prior to her independence. These countries were printing more of it and using it to purchase and export whatever commodities they could find in Poland.

(6) Politically, the country was in turmoil. The conflict between Paderewski, the Prime Minister, and Pilsudski, the chief of state, had become even more bitter. Paderewski was striving to establish

a constitutional government of free men; Pilsudski was endeavoring to establish himself as dictator of Poland. Paderewski was holding the nation by sheer force of his personality and eloquence. The Polish people knew little of his immense service and sacrifice, which had made possible the independence and greatness of Poland. Pilsudski had gained wide popularity through his welding an army from Polish recruits in the three partitioned provinces and establishing a reunited Poland.

Added to Paderewski's difficulties was the fact that in the parliament he had assembled there were seventeen political parties, from which no constructive majority could be formed. Beyond this, Paderewski and his chief aide at Paris—Roman Dmowski—had extended Poland's new frontiers to take in too many unassimilable nationalities, including about 3,800,000 Ruthenians, 500,000 Germans, and nearly 300,000 people of other nationalities.

The Prime Minister's difficulties became so great that he resigned in December, 1919, and Pilsudski became, in fact, the dictator of Poland. Pilsudski and his supporters dreamed of further expansion—with the borders of Poland as they were in 1772. In April, 1920, he made war on Communist Russia and, with the aid of the French, won a large part of the territory he wanted—and more unassimilable races.

The impoverishment of the Polish people by their oppressors during 150 years and the destruction of the advancing and retreating armies during the war could not be cured in the six months of the Armistice. Such was the political, economic and military tumult when the new American Relief Administration again undertook to save the country from mass starvation and the sweep of typhus from the east. We had hoped that with the harvest of 1920 or 1921, our tasks could be completed. But we were compelled to continue until the harvest of 1922.

STAFF ORGANIZATION

Prior to the Peace, we had in Poland a strong organization of more than twenty Americans. Our staff was comprised largely of American Army officers who had joined us immediately after the Armistice, and they naturally wanted to return home. But the following members of the directing staff devotedly continued with us:

Chief of Mission

WILLIAM R. GROVE	January–November, 1919
W. PARMER FULLER, JR.	November, 1919–August, 1920
JOHN C. MILLER	March–June, 1921
CYRIL J. C. QUINN	July–December, 1921
PHILIP S. BALDWIN	December, 1921–July, 1922

Chief of Children's Activities

MAURICE PATE	July–August, 1919
WILLIAM R. NELLEGAR	August–November, 1919
PHILIP S. BALDWIN	July–August, 1920, and March–December, 1921
GEORGE F. HOWARD	August, 1920–March, 1921

Except for Colonel Grove, all of these men had served as lieutenants or captains during the war.

FOOD FOR ADULTS

Although the primary purpose of the new American Relief Administration was the restoration of health to the subnormal children, Poland, despite some improvement in the 1919 harvest, presented an enormous problem of food for adults. We met this problem from many directions.

FOOD DRAFTS AND BULK SALES

Most of the supplies from food drafts went to adults. Poland received food from this system amounting to 15,559 tons valued at $2,539,650. The Polish Government contributed 7,720 tons at a value of $864,562 through purchases from our warehouse in Danzig.

The relief of students, in association with the Y.M.C.A. and the

Y.W.C.A., provided 11,695 students with food valued at $115,589. The money was used to purchase food drafts and is therefore included in the $2,539,650 total above.

A part of adult relief was accomplished by our relief of intellectuals. The Commonwealth Fund contributed $401,532 to our organization for this purpose. All of the Fund's expenditures were for food and bulk draft purchases, except for clothing valued at $57,532. The Jewish Joint Distribution Committee also donated $50,000 to the A.R.A. for the care of intellectuals.

Another important source for adult relief was the Congressional appropriation of March 30, 1920. From this we provided 202,564 tons of wheat flour valued at $24,353,591. The British provided overseas transportation for this food at a cost (to them) of $8,102,558. Through our total work for adults we estimated that we had provided the necessary margin to maintain life for 10,000,000 adults. I have already given an account of our battle against the typhus epidemic—for which many adults were employed.[1]

CHILDREN'S RELIEF

When the new American Relief Administration took over from the official United States agencies at the Peace, we were feeding more than 500,000 persons in our canteens and giving aid to orphans and waifs. After the Peace, we rapidly expanded this service until May, 1920, when 1,315,500 children were being cared for. At that time meals were being served in 6,289 canteens and in 1,361 children's institutions—making a total of 7,650 feeding centers. The program decreased somewhat at the 1920 harvest, but the load increased to 1,246,900 by April, 1921. From then on, the number was gradually reduced until the harvest of 1922, when we were able to retire and the Polish Government took over the work. The total number of meals provided in our canteen system was estimated at 640,000,000; a total of 1,973,000 persons had been cared for.

We provided free clothing, mainly for children but also for many

[1] See An American Epic, Vol. II, Chap. 46.

adults. This amounted to 1,915 tons at a value of $4,689,625. Some of the items provided were:

      2,154,193 yards of 54-inch woolen cloth
      1,058,137 pairs of children's shoes
         32,931 ready-made coats
      1,059,170 pairs of woolen stockings
    145,808,800 yards of thread
      1,238,000 needles
      5,411,805 buttons

The Polish women established workshops where these materials were made up and distributed to more than 750,000 children.

The finance for our children's relief program and the distribution of supplies fell to our organization. The money expended after the Peace totaled $23,785,193. The Polish Government donated $6,742,316 and the Jewish Joint Distribution Committee $273,555, which amounts are included in the above total.[2]

THE RELIEF OF REFUGEES

The relief of refugees coming into Poland, mostly from Russia, was an added burden for which we had need to raise special funds. On July 12, 1920, we received the following message from Hugh Gibson, the American Minister in Poland:

Thousands destitute refugees coming into Poland as result Bolshevik advance. Great need food relief, especially warehouse packages. General relief food drafts almost exhausted. Cannot some philanthropic organization be persuaded to help in this emergency?

The emergency was further emphasized by cables such as this one of July 24 from our Warsaw office:

Freight cars in train loads reach our eastern feeding stations filled with refugee families, frequently days without food. Crowded into same cars

[2] Our children's relief program was begun before the Peace—during the Armistice period. Contributions for this were included in the chapter on Poland prior to the Peace.

are several families with such belongings as they could rescue, often including cow, pig, or few chickens.

We immediately advanced A.R.A. funds to help the children, issued an appeal to the public for support, and asked other organizations for assistance. The total funds gathered for this purpose were:

A.R.A. general funds	$125,000
National Polish Committee	50,000
Jewish Joint Distribution Committee	25,000
Edward W. Harkness	75,000
William Bingham II	27,000
Total	$302,000

We set up special kitchens for the refugees and from these funds purchased food from our warehouses. More than 2,000 such kitchens were established; food packages were prepared in our warehouses for those who could not be served by the kitchens. We had no record of the actual number of refugees, although the number of the children in the group was estimated at 150,000 and the total meals provided for them at 2,892,572. In Warsaw alone, as many as 10,000 refugees were fed daily. We distributed 810 tons of food costing $302,000.

The new American Relief Administration—from its own funds, food drafts, donations to us from the Polish Government, and the Congressional authority—provided 331,249 tons of supplies valued at $51,683,315 from just after the Peace until the end of its work for adults and children. To this might be added $35,000,000 expended in the fight against typhus.

OTHER AMERICAN CHARITABLE AGENCIES GIVING AID TO POLAND AFTER THE PEACE

These organizations were:

The American Red Cross
The Jewish Joint Distribution Committee

The Young Men's Christian Association
The Young Women's Christian Association
The American Friends Service Committee
The National Lutheran Council
The Methodist Episcopal Church, South

THE AMERICAN RED CROSS

The American Red Cross established its service in Poland during the Armistice and continued after the Peace for nearly three years until the end of June, 1922. It established new hospitals and clinics with American medical staffs; it supplied medical equipment, including ambulances, to the Polish hospitals; it established centers to combat local outbreaks of typhus and cholera. The Red Cross built new orphanages and rebuilt old ones. In 1921, it undertook, in cooperation with the American Relief Administration, a child-health program. Through canteens, it provided dairy and milk supplies for children, gave child-health educational aid to mothers, and distributed instructive literature. It provided canteen services for General Haller's army and aided the return home of 12,000 Americans in his army—and also aided refugees with transportation and food. Among its many services, the American Red Cross gave aid to 750,000 orphans.

Red Cross annual reports show that more than $18,040,398 was expended in the service of Poland. Never before in all history has such assistance in medical aid been extended from one nation to another in time of peace.

THE JEWISH JOINT DISTRIBUTION COMMITTEE

The huge Jewish population of Poland had been a concern to this committee from 1914 because of their persecution and poverty during the war. I have already given some account of the Committee's great service in the years prior to the Armistice.[3] At the Armistice,

[3] *An American Epic,* Vol. II, Chap. 23.

the persecution ended, and the Committee was able to undertake a huge program of rehabilitation.

After the Peace, the Committee continued its rehabilitation to co-religionists by placing them on farms, by opening trade schools, and by aiding them in resuming business undertakings. It established and supported orphanages and homes for the aged. It gave full co-operation to the new American Relief Administration. Records show the sum of $273,555 covering 537 tons of relief supplies of milk and soap for our organization's work in the relief of children. It sub-scribed $50,000 to the American Relief Administration for aid to the intellectuals.

The J.D.C.'s service in Poland is indicated by its expenditures from the Peace until 1923, which were $8,972,015. Included in this sum was $323,555 given to the new American Relief Administration.

THE YOUNG MEN'S CHRISTIAN ASSOCIATION

During the war, Y.M.C.A. representatives worked with the Polish Legion of France. Upon the Legion's return to free Poland in April, 1919, the Y.M.C.A. followed with its usual "huts" and services.

In the Russian-Polish War of 1920, some 200,000 Russian prisoners taken by the Poles were aided by the Y.M.C.A.

The Y.M.C.A. also conducted educational work, theater programs, canteens for social purposes, and movies in the cities. It established a recreation program, and by April, 1920, a total of 40,000 men and women were participants.

Y.M.C.A. expenditures in Poland after the Peace were $1,366,826.

THE YOUNG WOMEN'S CHRISTIAN ASSOCIATION

A month after the Peace, the Y.W.C.A. dispatched the first unit of twenty "Grey Samaritans" to Poland. They were American girls of Polish descent trained in the United States for welfare service. A second unit arrived in Poland in January, 1920. They gave medical aid to children, they helped in the operation of soup kitchens and milk depots, and they assisted in the American Relief Administration's distribution of children's clothing.

In October, 1919, the Y.W.C.A. sent eight American representatives to Poland; they established a clubhouse for Polish women in Warsaw, set up recreation rooms, and conducted classes in languages and health education. In October, 1920, Polish nurses took over the club's management.

The Y.W.C.A. established a hut and canteen to serve the units of women enlisted as soldiers in the Polish Army. There were, in August, 1920, four thousand women in the ranks.

Y.W.C.A. expenditures after the Peace were $161,002.

THE AMERICAN FRIENDS SERVICE COMMITTEE

After the Peace, the American Friends Service Committee cooperated with the British Friends Service Committee in Poland. They were largely occupied with relief for refugees returning from Communist Russia, for whom they provided food, clothing, and occupational training. They distributed 107 tons of food drafts valued at $50,000 and 633 tons of cottonseed meal valued at $30,291 —or a total of $80,291 worth of supplies. These were turned over to the American Friends by the American Relief Administration. The Friends built sawmills to provide housing for displaced families and set up a training school for orphan boys. Their expenditures in Poland, aside from the American Relief Administration contribution, were $107,000, plus $100,000 worth of gifts in kind—or a total of $207,000.

THE NATIONAL LUTHERAN COUNCIL

After the Peace, the National Lutheran Council sent to Poland 508 tons of clothing and undertook other services. The Council's expenditures in Poland after the Peace were $303,266.

THE METHODIST EPISCOPAL CHURCH, SOUTH

The Woman's Missionary Council of the Methodist Episcopal Church, South, conducted a campaign for food and clothing for children and adults in Poland. One million garments were shipped to Poland. Included in the clothing shipments were five thousand blankets.

The Council set up three soup kitchens in Warsaw which fed three thousand persons daily and established several new orphanages and a sewing room where young Polish girls made clothes for orphans. Our estimate of the value of clothing and cash outlays is $1,017,000.

OTHER CHARITABLE ORGANIZATIONS

There were other charitable organizations, about which, after more than forty years, we have been able to find only scraps of information. They include:

	Funds	Officers
National Polish Committee of America, September 1, 1920–February 28, 1922	$351,770	J. F. SMULSKI, *President*
Polish Children's Relief Fund, November 8, 1918–February 6, 1920	34,000	C. A. BARNES, *President*
Paderewski Fund for Poland, December, 1919–December, 1920	34,065	I. J. PADEREWSKI, *Chairman*

Our research also disclosed the following organizations, all of which contributed aid to Poland, but we have no detailed information:

> The Northern Baptist Convention
> The Presbyterian Church in the U.S. (South)
> Friends of Poland
> Polish National Department
> Polish Reconstruction Committee
> Polish Victims' Relief Fund

We estimate that the total expenditures in kind and cash of these "other organizations" probably exceeded $1,000,000.

TOTAL SUPPLIES TO POLAND
FROM THE PEACE TO 1923 *

	Food	Clothing & Misc.	Total	$ Value
American Relief Administration Children's relief	57,327	1,915	59,242	$16,769,322
Polish Government donation	45,611		45,611	6,742,316
Jewish Joint Distribution Committee	506	31	537	273,555
Food drafts and bulk sales . .	15,517	42	15,559	2,539,649
Polish Government (donation of flour)	7,073		7,073	917,059
Commonwealth Fund (clothing)		30	30	57,532
Congressional Authority of March, 1920	202,564		202,564	24,353,591
American Friends Service Committee	633		633	30,291
American Red Cross	(quantities unknown)			18,040,398
Jewish Joint Distribution Committee (not through A.R.A.) .	(quantities unknown)			8,648,460
Young Men's Christian Association	(quantities unknown)			1,366,826
Young Women's Christian Association	(quantities unknown)			161,002
American Friends Service Committee (not through A.R.A.) .	(quantities unknown)			207,000
National Lutheran Council		508	508	303,266
Methodist Episcopal Church South	(quantities unknown)			1,017,000
Other charitable organizations .	(quantities unknown)			1,000,000
	329,231	2,526	331,757	$82,427,267 †

* In tons.
† In addition, I have estimated that the Typhus Commission expended about $60,000,000 on medical equipment and supplies for Poland.

The United Kingdom furnished relief to Poland. Our only record is for transportation of our supplies amounting to $8,102,558.

A VISIT TO POLAND

Prime Minister Paderewski had urged President Wilson to visit Poland, stating that despite all we had done for that country during the Armistice, the people were still in despair from unemployment, disease, short rations, and war with the Communists on their frontiers. This was indeed true. Paderewski said that Poland was an easy prey for Communist conspiracies and added that the tide of discouragement could be turned by showing the Polish people that their friend—America—stood with them and with him.

The President had to go home to present the ratification of the Treaty of Versailles to the Senate. Paderewski asked him if I could go as his representative. The Prime Minister added that the Polish Government greatly wanted my advice on its economic and governmental problems.

The situation was indeed discouraging for the Polish people. Aside from the poverty resulting from the war and its many invasions, the Red Army was still attacking on the Galician frontier during my visit. General Haller's army, made up of Poles who had served in the Allied armies and of recruits from the United States, had set up a stout defense.

Our party arrived in Warsaw by a special train from the Swiss frontier on August 12, 1919. I was accompanied by several American generals and admirals and their aides and by Robert Taft and Commander George Baker of my staff. When we arrived in Warsaw (at nine o'clock at night), the great barn of a station was filled with people and was gaily decorated with Polish and American flags. The platforms were lined with troops. Massed bands were playing the American and Polish national anthems—and they continued to play them.

We Americans lined up alongside our train, with our silk hats clasped to our bosoms if we were civilians or our right hands frozen to our caps if we were military. The Polish officials were likewise lined up, including Chief of State Pilsudski, Prime Minister Paderewski and his cabinet ministers, the Mayor of Warsaw, and various generals and officials, all likewise frozen in salute during the American national anthem. But the bands were not disposed to allow the salute to thaw out.

Finally, after a seeming year of embarrassing minutes, the Mayor stepped forward and presented me with the traditional Polish welcome of bread and salt. This time it was a round loaf eighteen inches in diameter, with a great salt crystal in the dome, and all of it resting upon a specially carved wooden platter. The Mayor spoke English, but because the bands played on, I did not hear a word. With my right hand freezing my silk hat to my breast, I took the platter in my left hand, with appropriate remarks, which he, in turn, could not hear because the bands played on. Quickly my left wrist began to wobble under the weight, and I just managed to pass it over to the left hand of the admiral next to me. His arm quickly began to wobble, and he passed it to the left hand of the general next to him. I watched it go all down the line to the last sergeant. The crowd applauded this maneuver as a characteristic and appropriate American ceremony.

Hugh Gibson was now Minister to Poland, and accompanied by him, Pilsudski, and Paderewski, I was taken to the American Embassy for the night, leaving the enthusiastic bands still playing national anthems.

Thereafter followed a week of strenuous visits from city to city and talks with delegations from labor, industry, agriculture, and the universities. We attended banquets, mass meetings, and reviews of troops and delivered speeches in many places. One of the most important meetings took place at Kosciuszko's tomb at Cracow. I was to speak first, and Prime Minister Paderewski was to translate. I had incorporated into my remarks the sentiments he wanted, and he had a copy in advance. My speech was about eight minutes long. There were probably not five hundred out of the massed audience of 30,000 who understood English. After the Prime Minister had devoted about forty-five minutes to the translation, I asked my Polish aide what he was talking about. My aide replied: "Oh, he is making a *real* speech."

Also at Cracow, our hosts put on a gala performance at the opera —which was opening its doors for the first time since the Independence. The best of all Polish talent was assembled. I was escorted to the Opera House by the revived Kosciuszko Regiment, in uniforms styled like those of 150 years before. It had been arranged that I should arrive after the play opened and be taken to Prime Minister Paderewski's box. He was already there with Madame Paderewska. As I entered, he motioned me to the front of the box; the orchestra and the artists on the stage stopped instantly while Madame Paderewska kissed me energetically and audience and performers applauded—to my intense embarrassment.

The Prime Minister convened a meeting of his ministers in Warsaw to discuss their economic problems with me. There was not a man among them who, during the oppression years, had been allowed a day's experience in the down-to-earth problems of government administration. Our technical advisers to the government had all left for home, except for Colonel Barber. He and the men of the American Relief Administration, together with Hugh Gibson, briefed me in advance of the meeting on the problems and personalities.

I have already stated that the Poles had inherited three currencies in the pre-Armistice segments of Poland, with no resources behind them and that their ancestor countries continued to print more and more of them to buy commodities to take out of Poland. We urged the Minister of Finance, as an immediate measure, to put a stop to this activity by stamping the currency at every post office, to disqualify all notes not thus stamped, and eventually to replace these three currencies with a new issue, with some kind of security (if any). The Minister was a former banker, and his reply was a sign of the men lacking experience whom the Prime Minister was compelled to recruit. He replied: "Currencies are living things in the minds of people; we must not abandon them." However, Prime Minister Paderewski followed our advice.

On August 17, at the request of one of the cabinet members, I submitted a note on problems of organization, in the drafting of which

I was aided by our American officials in Warsaw, including Minister Hugh Gibson. It recommended the appointment of a minister of economy, with a staff of experienced American administrators to work out the organization of their departments. At Prime Minister Paderewski's request and by his undertaking to pay their salaries, I recruited for him a new staff of six able administrators for the departments of railways, public health, food, mining, commerce, and finance. These advisers remained for more than a year and contributed greatly to the reconstruction of Poland. Hugh Gibson was always a tower of strength.

I received many marks of appreciation from the Poles—a square named for me in Warsaw, streets in Cracow and other towns, a statue in the park at Warsaw,[4] and degrees from all the universities. Letters, telegrams, and resolutions from officials, public men, and public bodies came at birthdays and Christmas for many years afterward. A touching form of these compliments was scores of elaborately bound volumes containing hundreds of thousands of signatures of children whom we had fed in our canteen systems, all illustrated by their own hands.

It is not inappropriate to add here the most profoundly touching incident of my visit to Poland. A reception was organized at the former Warsaw race track by the Polish women who ran our canteens. An estimated 50,000 youngsters had been brought in trains and buses to be reviewed by me in a march in front of the grandstand. Ranging in age from five to eleven years, clad often in rags, all carried a paper flag with the American and Polish national colors. Some also bore banners with inscriptions to me. They paraded for hours—chattering, laughing, squealing, trying vainly to look sober while the women were attempting to maintain some sort of marching order. A rabbit tried to run through the line. That was too much for live kids. They fell upon it in a mob. Having captured the rabbit, they insisted upon bringing it to me. The frantic efforts of the

[4] In 1938, I visited Warsaw on relief matters. An eyewitness told me the Germans had blown off the head of the statue with a hand grenade. In any event, I found I was headless at that time—and no doubt continue so under the Communist regime.

women supervisors to restore the line provided a much-needed bit of relief.

The march began early in the afternoon, and they had not all passed by at dark, when the review had to end. I marvel yet at the capacity of those women who had thought of everything, including where every out-of-town group of youngsters was to sleep that night.

General Henrys, the head of the French Military Mission to Poland and a commander in great battles during the war, stood near me with tears coursing down his face until finally, overcome, he left the stand, saying in parting, *"Il n'y a eu une revue d'honneur des soldats en toute histoire que je voudrais avoir plus que cette qu'est vous donné aujourd'hui."* ("There has never been a review of honor in all history which I would prefer for myself to that which has been given you today.")

These are the happier memories of my Polish visit in 1919, but our troubles in that hapless country did not end. The defeat of Paderewski, the continued needs of hungry people and undernourished children were to haunt us until we were able to withdraw in 1923 at Poland's economic recovery.[5]

THE DANZIG FREE STATE

Simply because of its neighborhood and the occasional use of the port by the Poles, I have attached the narrative of the Danzig Free State to the narrative of Poland. It hardly constitutes a chapter in itself.

The Peace Conference had set up Danzig as a free state. The population was German. The purpose of creating a free state was twofold: to reduce the potency of Germany in any future war and to give greater assurance to Poland of a more secure outlet at the Baltic end of the Polish Corridor through Germany. The Poles

[5] I was to return again to Poland in 1946 on another relief mission after the even more terrible Second World War. The barbarity of Hitler's armies presented unspeakably horrible sights, and after the retreat of the Germans, the people were enslaved by the Communists.

promptly built a rival port nearby, and Danzig, having lost its seaport business and having no agricultural area, became dependent on American charity as the alternative to starvation.

The American Friends Service Committee gave aid to Danzig until April, 1921. At that time the Friends were serving about 3,000 children in their canteens. However, they wanted to devote themselves to refugee relief in Poland and requested the American Relief Administration to take over the relief task, which we conducted under our staff in Poland. Also, at their suggestion, we reimbursed them for their outlays to date in order to increase their funds for relief to refugees. Our work in Danzig was concluded in April, 1922, during which time we had cared for about 10,000 persons, having furnished 957,374 free meals.

The Commonwealth Fund provided relief for the intellectuals of the Danzig Free State from 1921 to 1923. It purchased food drafts from the A.R.A. amounting to $14,752 for this purpose. (This amount is included in the food-draft total of the table below.)

The Jewish Joint Distribution Committee came to the aid of refugees, upon whom they expended $10,012.

The chief of our mission was John H. Lange, who served until January, 1922, when he was succeeded by Luigi Sorieri, who served to the end. Sorieri's principal assistant was Leo B. Tyson.

Expenditures in the Danzig Free State were as follows:

	Food (Tons)	$ Value
American Relief Administration:		
Children's relief	108	$ 17,750
Food drafts	233	71,085
Reimbursement of the American Friends Service Committee	158	30,291
Danzig Government donation of fats, milk, etc.	74	8,574
Jewish Joint Distribution Committee		10,012
	573	$137,712

GERMANY, CZECHOSLOVAKIA, ALBANIA, AUSTRIA, HUNGARY, AND YUGOSLAVIA

CHAPTER 41

GERMANY AFTER THE PEACE

Germany came out of the Peace Conference at Versailles a mangled and shackled nation. The suffering of the European Allies from the four years of German attack had left an imprint of hatred and vengeance which dominated the Peace. Great as were the German outrages, there was scarcely an American at the Peace Conference who believed that signed papers would hold the sick giant that was the German race. And we were in despair over the dragon's teeth from which would grow the evil jinn of the future.

Although more than 1,215,216 tons of food valued at $282,421,665 had been delivered during the Armistice, the food outlook in Germany at the Peace was grim. A large part of her "breadbasket" had been given to Poland, and the 1919 grain crops in truncated Germany were only about 64 per cent of the normal production. Sugar production was about 30 per cent of prewar averages. The cattle and calves had decreased by 11 per cent and the swine by 80 per cent. In addition to the decrease in numbers was the decrease in weight and products of the food animals because of the lack of feed.

Because of the Lodge amendment, which prevented the use of any Congressional appropriations for relief in enemy countries, we were able, during the Armistice, to give only partial aid to the rehabilitation of the German children. In our agreed program at Brussels in March, 1919, my colleagues and I had stipulated that there should be included 70,000 tons of fats and condensed milk per month. This milk and some extra fats had served to stem the tide of degeneration somewhat, but when peace came, a multitude of children were still deteriorated in body and mind.

At the Peace, we in the new American Relief Administration were determined to extend to Germany our canteen system for children, nursing mothers, the sick, and the aged. We had assumed the great burden of children's relief in many other nations, and we were short of administrative staff. The American Friends Service Committee—the Quakers—had been engaged in a minor children's-relief operation in Germany. They had a two-hundred-year-old tradition of relief in every great disaster and war; they were able administrators. I asked for their administrative help. Their major personnel were, of course, known to me because at one time I had been an official of the Committee. I had a further purpose in inviting the Quakers to aid: I believed they could make a more effective appeal to the Americans of German descent than we who had been officials on the Allied side during the war. I also felt that they would bring the healing message of the Good Samaritan to the hearts of German women, where the fires of hate burned with frenzy from their long watch over their wilting children.

The Friends responded as I had expected. We of the new American Relief Administration agreed to deliver free supplies to the doors of their canteens and to furnish them expert advisers on organization and methods. We extended our food-draft system to Germany, and in order to operate it and to supply the Quakers, we established warehouses at important points. To establish full co-operation with the German Government and people, both for our operations and those of the Quakers, our representative in Berlin arranged, through President Ebert, to set up the "German Central Committee for Foreign Relief," through which his government would furnish free internal transportation and German staff for the work.

The Friends did an admirable job of organizing and operating the canteens, and we furnished them 28,720 tons of special food supplies amounting to $6,728,989. Of this amount, $5,031,582 was a direct contribution from the A.R.A., $861,022 was from the American Friends Service Committee's participation in the 1921 European children's relief appeal, and a further $836,385 was available to them from a fund which they sponsored among Americans of German descent. In addition, the A.R.A. received from the German Government a donation of 16,833 tons of food valued at $2,392,021, which was turned over to the Quakers for distribution.

During their work in Germany, the Friends, under the direction of J. Henry Scattergood, served 293,000,000 meals in their canteens to 1,026,656 subnormal children, expectant mothers, and the aged. They rehabilitated 5,350,000 children.

In July, 1922, the Friends withdrew from Germany, believing their service was needed more in the appalling famine in Russia. Upon the Friends' withdrawal, General Henry T. Allen, who had commanded the American Army of Occupation in Germany, proposed to me that he would organize a new committee, to be called the "American Committee for Relief of German Children," to continue the children's relief if we would give him our support and services. We endorsed his public appeal, and to help get his drive started, we furnished him $50,000.

Dr. Kellogg, attached to our Paris office at this time, arranged for the German Central Committee to operate General Allen's canteens. The American Relief Administration handled General Allen's purchasing and transportation matters and also provided him with the services of our staff for inspection. The General's committee contributed $4,320,000.

The relief of children was not our only service in Germany. Our food-draft system supplied 9,347 tons of food valued at $2,820,420. And another important aid to Germany after the Peace arose from the settlement of our accounts with her in respect to our gold and various services throughout the Armistice. During this period, the Federal Reserve Bank of New York had advanced to us 92 per cent of the estimated value of the gold it held, pending its accurate determination of value after melting it. On August 26, 1919, in Paris, I settled an agreement with Herr von Bergmann, the German Under Secretary of State, in regard to the 8 per cent residue owed the German Government. The essential paragraphs of this agreement were:

(1) Confirming my conversation, I wish to outline the basis on which I propose that the final accounting be made between the German Govern-

ment and myself for food supplied from the United States Food Administration Grain Corporation and from the Commission for Relief in Belgium.
This settlement must, of course, be made in accordance with the agreement entered into between the German Government and the Associated
Governments at Brussels on March 13th and 14th, 1919 [which I
quoted]. . . .

(2) The final form of account will be as follows:

. . . (a) The bags deposited in the Belgian and Holland Banks, pre-
sumed to contain 730,000,000 gold marks, have been transferred to the
Federal Reserve Bank of New York, as previously advised. The Federal
Reserve Bank is now in preliminary examination and count of the gold at
the various banks in Belgium and Holland. As this preliminary examination proceeds, the bank is paying to the Grain Corporation and the Commission for Relief in Belgium 92 percent of its estimated theoretical value,
and this 92 percent is estimated to realize about $159,000,000. It is too
early to determine what the further realization will be from the reserved
8 percent, but it is my impression that a sum of money somewhere between Eight and Twelve Million Dollars will be available.

(b) The amount of payments and exchange made on behalf of the
Grain Corporation and the American Relief Administration are now in
course of determination and will be credited as above.

(c) The prices at which foodstuffs have been invoiced to the German
Government by the Grain Corporation are based upon the American Shipping Board rates, and as the rate charged to the Grain Corporation by the
Inter-Allied Maritime Council for German ships is at a lower rate, we propose to credit the German Government with the difference between the
two rates on all foodstuffs delivered to Germany in German bottoms.

(d) We have no desire to take advantage of the rigid interpretation of
the Brussels Agreement and will be glad to receive from the German
Government any claims that can be substantiated for shortage or deteri-
oration. Some of these claims, at least, we should be able to collect from
the carrier and from insurance.

(e) The invoiced value of provisions furnished by the Commission for
Relief in Belgium will, I am informed, be in condition for agreement by
both parties within the next few days. The total of this account will, I understand, be approximately $45,000,000. This material having been de-
livered in Rotterdam and the invoices agreed there, there will be no
further adjustments.

(f) As to the Grain Corporation invoices, I propose that the basic sum will be settled on the footing of the invoiced prices and the approximate amount will apparently be about $114,000,000. This sum, however, will be subject to the items mentioned in (c) and (d) which do not apply in the case of the Commission for Relief in Belgium. In order to centralize the settlement of account, I propose, after complete payment to the Commission for Relief in Belgium, to consider that all of the other items on credit and debit side should revolve through the Grain Corporation.

(g) This item will comprise the interest on the value of foodstuffs delivered over the period from the delivery of those foodstuffs during the time that the gold was held as security for payment, and that claims for interest cease at the time the gold was released for realization.

(h) The balance due to the German Government after deducting E F G and A B C D will be held subject to the order of the German Government for purchase of food from any source they may desire, and will comprise the final amount due to the German Government.

(3) The prices upon which the Grain Corporation invoices were based under 2F above, have been calculated as nearly as possible to cover cost and risk of delivery, and these foodstuffs form in fact a part of a general operation of provisioning Europe. The operation has been carried on en bloc for all of the countries served, and there may be some final margin after all accounts are settled. It is the desire of the President that no profits should be earned by the Relief Administration agencies. All of the Governments of Europe have profited by the en bloc character of these operations, the better control of buying and shipping and of price levels, and while the prices have been based on the same foundation with calculated difference of freight levels to different ports, it might prove if analysis of the costs were possible that some of the Governments would not be entitled to any participation in margins of profits. Any such margins as will be found would, in any event, be the result of the voluntary service of the American staff. The price levels established as the basis of invoices were in themselves below commercial levels. The whole of the directing staff of over one thousand members, throughout the Food Administration, the Relief Administration and the Grain Corporation, were volunteers or were furnished by the War and Navy Departments of the United States without charge.

It would not, in any event, be possible to calculate the precise distribution of any sum that might remain in hand, should it prove to exist, nor will all expenditures and claims be settled for some months. I have approached the other Governments in Europe concerned in these operations and have received their approval and direction to me to pay any such margin, if it develops as available to the "American Relief Administration European Children's Fund," of which I am the Chairman, to assist in carrying on the special feeding of undernourished children during the forthcoming winter. Any such margin represents in some sense of measure of voluntary service and is a contribution of such service to this purpose. If such margin does develop and I can secure its being made available, it will be added to those funds which may be raised by public subscription or from other sources and expended in each country.

I would propose to pay such sums as were available to German children to such charitable organizations in Germany as your Government may approve, or to such organizations in the United States as may be interested in the relief of German children, in order to provide for the import of special foodstuffs for this purpose. There is, of course, no obligation, nor do I wish to alter the basis of settlement as set out in Paragraphs (1) and (2) and I have as yet to arrange the execution of the above proposals, but, before I undertake the matter, I should be glad to know if it meets the approval of your Government and if you will give to me a direction to devote the margin, if any should develop, to the above purposes. Any such fund would not be available until the accounts can be settled, nor until ratification of peace.

I received confirmation the same day; the important paragraph was:

PARIS, August 26, 1919

MR. HERBERT HOOVER
American Relief Administration
Dear Sir:

I beg to state that the German Government finds itself in accord with the propositions laid down in your memorandum of August 26th and hereby authorizes you to pay to the "American Relief Administration European Children's Fund" any margins of profit which may develop as between the invoiced price of foodstuffs and the actual cost and outlay that you may determine to have been expended thereon, and described in Paragraph 3 of the above memorandum. . . .

VON BERGMANN

The final settlement of these accounts proved to be a long and tedious labor. The Federal Reserve Bank did not complete the melting of the gold for some months, and there were many insurance, ship-loss, and other items to settle. It was not until March, 1920, that

I was able to send the German Government a final statement of our accounts. The statement was:

	Dr.	Cr.
Gold Deposit in Bank of Belgium	$100,000,000.00	
Proceeds of Gold Deposits with Federal Reserve Bank U.S. Grain Corporation	19,923,106.52	
Proceeds of Gold Deposits with Federal Res. Bank Commission for Relief in Belgium	50,000,000.00	
Proceeds of Gold Deposits with Federal Res. Bank [to] U.S. Grain Corporation	2,541,903.17	$172,465,009.69
Credit for Difference in Freight Rates on Shipping Board and German Tonnage, as per Schedule I.	3,292,063.10	
Credits for Sundry Payments and Exch. Remittances .... $377,682.43 Steamer disbursements as per Schedule II. ...... 284,562.98 Sundry cash payments, as per Schedule III. 79,511.75	741,757.14	
Credit for Shortages not previously allowed	112,884.21	4,146,704.45
Charges for Foodstuffs shipments by U.S. Grain Corporation, as per Schedule IV	113,672,030.84	
Charges for Foodstuffs Shipments by Commission for Relief in Belgium ..	44,530,021.74	
Interest @ 6% on Value of Foodstuffs delivered by U.S. Grain Corporation from date of sale to June 17, 1919 ..	399,441.62	
Payments to Guaranty Trust Co. for account of Government of Germany [for food]	3,500,000.00	
Balance	14,510,219.94	
	$176,611,714.14	$176,611,714.14
Balance due to Government of Germany		$ 14,510,219.94

A few days later, I was advised by the Embassy that the German Government had given me a final receipt as follows:

The German Government has received your statement of account showing Fourteen million five hundred ten thousand two nineteen dollars and ninety four cents due the German Government from the seven hundred and thirty million gold marks released to you for the purpose of making payment for the food supplied to the German Government from the United States Food Administration Grain Corporation and from the Commission for Relief in Belgium. The German Government acknowledges that the above amount represents the final and complete settlement of your account with the German Government in strict conformity with the [agreements]. . . .

Thus the finance for additional food under this settlement is represented by the amounts $3,500,000 and $14,510,219, or a total of $18,010,219. The shipments covered by this sum totaled 81,210 tons.

THE TOTAL OF AMERICAN RELIEF ADMINISTRATION RESPONSIBILITIES IN THE RELIEF OF GERMANY

The total of American Relief Administration service to German relief from its own funds, its food drafts, the settlement of gold balances, those agencies for which we provided purchase and transport, plus the donation of the German Government, amounted to $34,271,649.

OTHER AIDS TO GERMANY AFTER THE PEACE

The American Red Cross furnished some medical aid to Germany after the Peace, but the details of this direct service are not available from its published records. However, its records do show that it expended $1,652,634, primarily on the German prisoners of war in the Allied countries and Russia, and that an additional $25,000 was contributed to the German Red Cross in 1922. Its total expenditures on behalf of Germany for the post-Peace period were therefore $1,677,634.

After the Peace, the Y.M.C.A. continued its work with Russian prisoners still in German camps. Its representatives provided comforts and services to these prisoners and expended $359,908 in their work.

The Jewish Joint Distribution Committee's records show expenditures of $624,185 in Germany from the Peace until 1923. The Committee contributed to the new American Relief Administration and to other American charitable organizations working in Germany, and its representatives served on the staffs of these organizations. It provided for orphans and, through trade schools and agricultural settlements, gave effective aid to its co-religionists.

After the war, Archdeacon Nies, Rector of the Episcopal American Church in Munich, initiated a relief movement for Germany among American Episcopalians. The major part of their aid was a supplement to the American Relief Administration's work for children. About $1,500 was expended.

The National Lutheran Council expended $457,702 in Germany after the Peace, mostly for relief of its co-religionists and the reconstruction of Lutheran churches. It also shipped about thirty-seven tons of clothing to Germany during 1920 and 1922.

The Church of Jesus Christ of Latter-day Saints contributed used clothing to needy Germans. In the Church's General Board minutes of December 12, 1923, it was reported that the drive for used clothing for German co-religionists had been very successful and that it was estimated that over three carloads of clothing had been sent to Germany.

American Homes for Children in the Rheinpfalz was established by Dr. William Scharsmith of New York. The organization gave aid to German institutions for children. Our research showed that $13,330 was raised.

The president of the American Relief Committee for German Children was A. Barton Hepburn, and the treasurer was James Speyer. So far as our research shows, its funds, stated at $500,000, were donated to the American Relief Administration, the American Friends Service Committee, and other organizations.

TOTAL SUPPLIES TO GERMANY
FROM THE PEACE TO 1923 *

	Total	$ Value
American Relief Administration		
Gold settlement	81,210	$18,010,219
Food drafts	9,347	2,820,420
American Friends Service Committee (A.R.A. donation)	23,611	5,031,582
General Allen's Committee	20,187	4,320,000
German government donation	16,833	2,392,021
American Friends Service Committee (their own funds)	5,109	1,697,407
American Red Cross	(quantities unknown)	1,677,634
Y.M.C.A.	(quantities unknown)	359,908
Jewish Joint Distribution Committee	(quantities unknown)	624,185
Protestant Episcopal Church	(quantities unknown)	1,500
National Lutheran Council .	(quantities unknown)	457,702
The Church of Jesus Christ of Latter-day Saints	(quantities unknown)	($ value unknown)
American Homes for Children in the Rheinpfalz ...	(quantities unknown)	13,330
	156,297	$37,405,908

* In tons.

CHAPTER 42

CZECHOSLOVAKIA AND ALBANIA

Because of an attack on Slovakia in May, 1919, by Bela Kun, the Communist dictator of Hungary, Czechoslovakia suffered an economic setback which affected the 1919 harvest and her recovery. The Allies gave Kun an ultimatum to retire on June 13, 1919. On June 24, an armistice was concluded between Bela Kun and the Czech Government, but the evacuation was not complete. Our staff reported on this war:

The military operations in Slovakia have had a very disastrous effect upon economic conditions in Czecho-Slovakia. Not only were men diverted from useful pursuits, but food was expended in feeding the army. A large amount of railway material was used in the services of supply, which extended between Trencin-Tepla and Iglau thus producing a shortage of cars and engines which had its effect upon movement of all kinds of goods, especially coal. Had there not been this war . . . Czecho-Slovakia would be in far better shape to withstand the winter of 1919–1920.

However, Bela Kun ignored the armistice and continued his attack until his government fell on August 1, 1919, whereupon the Czechs not only recovered their invaded territory, but, in reprisal, annexed further areas from Hungary.

Our mission was originally headed by Lincoln Hutchinson. Captain John T. Shaw was director of child relief, and Arthur C. Ringland was assistant director. We put Captain A. R. Wheeler in charge of feed allocations, Lieutenant P. S. Platt in charge of investigations, Lieutenant W. Nolan in charge of requisitions, and Early Osborn in charge of the warehouse.

Captain Shaw became head of the mission in August, 1919, and was succeeded by Arthur C. Ringland, who served until October, 1920. Ringland was succeeded by John C. Miller, who served until January, 1921. At this time Ringland returned to head the mission and served until the end in July, 1922.

RELIEF OF ADULTS

A consequence of the Hungarian invasions was insufficient food for adults. Under the Congressional authority of March, 1920, our organization provided 23,809 tons of flour at a value of $2,873,238.

We extended our food-draft system to Czechoslovakia, which resulted in 1,376 tons of supplies valued at $433,433. Through these food drafts we provided relief for intellectuals. This program gave aid to 19,671 Czech teachers, doctors, and other professions at a cost of $82,501. The funds were provided to us by The Commonwealth Fund of New York. We also provided for 2,819 students at a cost of $23,511 through food drafts.

In addition to the supplies from the Congressional appropriation, the Czech Government purchased, for adults, 1,264 tons of flour and milk from our warehouses at a value of $174,549, and the Czechoslovakian State Fat Institute made a further purchase of twenty-eight tons of pork products from our supplies.

RELIEF OF CHILDREN

During the Armistice we had begun our canteen system with funds from the $100,000,000 Congressional appropriation.[1] At the Peace our staff reported:

The need for the continuance of relief for the children is very great. Deprived of essential food values for four or five years, there has been a

[1] See Chap. 11.

considerable development of tuberculosis, scrofula and Rachitis, while many children in the impoverished sections are far below normal in stature and health.

The new American Relief Administration continued the canteen system until the end of 1921. After the Peace, it provided for 697,500 individuals with 151,522,000 meals. The maximum load was in December, 1919, with 465,000 in daily attendance. We distributed 4,784 tons of food and 211 tons of clothing at a value of $1,906,945. The Czech Government gave us a donation for the canteens of 3,956 tons, mostly sugar, of which they had a surplus, valued at $693,099.

For the Czech children, we provided 211 tons of clothing material valued at $516,128. It included the following:

>   211,904 yards 54-inch woolen cloth
>   101,296 pairs of shoes
>   99,488 pairs of woolen stockings
>   100,000 needles
>   537,408 buttons
> 20,096,000 yards of thread

The Czech women organized volunteer workshops and made the cloth up into children's outfits, which were distributed through the schools.

The A.R.A., from its funds, food and bulk drafts, Congressional appropriation, intelligentsia relief, sales to the Czech Government, and the donation of the Czech Government, distributed, after the Peace, 35,428 tons of supplies at a value of $6,102,446.

AIDS TO CZECHOSLOVAKIA BY OTHER AMERICAN CHARITABLE ORGANIZATIONS

The Red Cross undertook its usual medical and surgical aid and supplies to hospitals. It established health centers and conducted vacation camps for children. And it conducted a nursing school and eliminated, through aids, local typhus outbreaks and other epidemics. Its accounts show expenditures of $1,161,542 from the Peace to 1923.

The Jewish Joint Distribution Committee gave medical and child care, established orphanages, and aided in placing persons in occupations. Its records show an expenditure of $596,927.

The National Lutheran Council's records show that one and one-half tons of clothing were sent to Czechoslovakia in 1920. The Council's expenditures from the Peace to September, 1923, were $45,518.

From the Peace to 1923, the National Catholic War Council expended $28,683 on relief in Czechoslovakia.

The Y.M.C.A. had carried on extensive service to the Czech Army when it was fighting on the Allied side during the war. This army was returned to Czechoslovakia at the Armistice, and the Y.M.C.A. continued with its services, establishing the usual huts or foyers for aid to the troops. The expenditures of the Y.M.C.A. from the Peace until the end of its work in March, 1921, were $1,159,808.

President Masaryk's daughter, Alice, enlisted the Y.W.C.A. to provide experienced American women to conduct a school for the training of Czech welfare workers. Its expenditures after the Peace were $189,354.

In 1921, the Methodist Episcopal Church, South carried on relief work among students at the University of Prague. It also provided food for refugee Ukranian and Russian students and care for Russian refugees in Prague. The cost of its work is not known.

In 1921, the Northern Baptists distributed some clothing to Czechoslovakia, and the Presbyterian Church contributed funds to aid in rebuilding the Protestant churches of Czechoslovakia, but the amount of these expenditures is not available.

The United Kingdom carried on relief in Czechoslovakia. The only information we have on expenditures is for transportation of our food from the Congressional appropriation amounting to $952,362.

TOTAL SUPPLIES TO CZECHOSLOVAKIA
FROM THE PEACE TO 1923 *

	Food	Clothing & Misc.	$ Value
American Relief Administration:			
Children's relief	4,784	211	$1,906,945
Czechoslovakian government			
donation	3,956		693,099
Food drafts and bulk sales	1,355	21	433,433
Congressional Appropriation,			
March, 1920	23,809		2,873,238
Sale of food to Czech govern-			
ment	1,292		195,731
American Red Cross	(quantities unknown)		1,161,542
Jewish Joint Distribution			
Committee	(quantities unknown)		596,927
National Lutheran Council	(quantities unknown)		45,518
National Catholic War Council	(quantities unknown)		28,683
Y.M.C.A.	(quantities unknown)		1,159,808
Y.W.C.A.	(quantities unknown)		189,354
	35,196	232	$9,284,278

* In tons.

ALBANIA

The little country of Albania, with a population of about one million people, had suffered greatly during the war. The American Red Cross initiated some relief to the Albanians during the Armistice, expending a total of $23,312 prior to the Peace. However, this operation disclosed conditions that required strong measures.

After the Peace, the Red Cross undertook the construction of hospitals, orphanages, and clinics. It furnished medical and hospital supplies and the services of physicians, surgeons, and nurses. It provided food for children and destitute adults; it gave relief to refugees; it established workrooms to make over the clothing which it imported. Generally, the Red Cross ran the gamut of relief measures. Its total outlays from July 1, 1919, to June 30, 1923, were $656,412.

AUSTRIA

The peacemakers had left Austria in such a state that it was impossible for her to support herself. As I have said,[1] there were 6,500,000 people in the country—more than 2,500,000 concentrated in Vienna—with little agricultural or natural resources. The official American relief organizations under my direction had expended or initiated in barter nearly $100,000,000 during the Armistice to keep Austria's people alive.

The peace treaty with Austria stipulated that there should be no joining between Austria and Germany. That, as a matter of fact, was the only possible constructive settlement, since Germany would have given Austria economic and political protection. I protested this settlement to President Wilson, and my final note to the "Big Four" before I left for home in 1919 sums up my view of Austria's future:

It is obvious to the most superficial observer that the present economic resources of . . . Austria are incapable of supporting the population of . . . [six] and one-half million people. . . . A large part of this population has for generations lived on the empire with its centralization of political life, finance, economic and educational institutions, and a population has been thereby created totally incapable of supporting itself when denuded of its hinterland. Its future lies not only in full production of such resources as exist, but also in . . . migration. To restart the established industries involves credits, reorganized currency, raw material, etc. . . . the very in-

[1] See Chap. 12.

sistent fact stands out that to prevent sheer starvation the population will need to be fed and furnished raw materials on credit continuously. The food production of this year's [1919] harvest in Austria would not, even if it could be uniformly distributed, last the population more than three months. As the peasant population will undoubtedly retain its twelve months' supply, it means that the probable food intake to the city populations from the state itself does not exceed six or eight weeks. . . .

The Austrian Government was living on its printing presses, and inflation was rampant. Austria printed more than five billion kronen which in the last year of our work had a value, in terms of the old kronen, of about 15,000 to 1. Further, the Reparations Commission had impounded all of Austria's realizable assets, and she therefore had little basis for foreign credits.

It seemed to me at the Peace that there was no possibility of saving these people except through unified action by the former Allies. I sought to initiate some action from them through our Secretary of State in a letter on July 11, 1919:

My dear Mr. Lansing:

As you are aware, we have been for many months providing large food supplies for the State of German-Austria. The financial cycle that we have set up between Allied and Associated Governments for this end will have exhausted itself by the end of August, with the provision of about $80,000,000 of supplies. Austria must receive continuous relief in food thereafter and it must also be provided with raw materials during the whole of the next year. The conditions of the treaty are such that the entire financial resources of Austria are placed at the disposal of the Reparations Commission. It is therefore utterly impossible to arrange any credits or finance to Austria except by the activities of this Commission.

It is also necessary to give some assurance to Austria at the earliest moment that further food is going to be provided or that Government is likely to collapse before the Treaty can be signed. The Supreme Economic Council therefore yesterday directed me to lay before the Council of Five the suggestion that a communication should be given to the Austrian Delegates in Paris to somewhat the following effect:

"In respect to the Request laid before the Supreme Economic Council from the Austrian Delegates that provision of further food supplies should be immediately undertaken by the Allied and Associated Governments, this request has been laid before the Council of five and the Council wishes to state that as food and raw materials for Austria during the forthcoming year are fundamental to her recuperation and her ability to make reparation, the method of provision of such food and raw material will be one of the first considerations of the Reparations Commission."

For the information of the [Supreme] Council . . . I enclose herewith, first, a note from myself on the economic situation of Austria; and, second, copy of the communications to the Supreme Economic Council from the Austrian delegates in respect to this matter.

HERBERT HOOVER

However, all of our efforts to secure support for Austria by unity of action among the Allies failed. The burden then fell upon the American charitable agencies and, to a lesser extent, upon the British.

THE AMERICAN RELIEF ADMINISTRATION STAFF

Fortunately, Captain T. T. C. Gregory, who had headed our mission during the Armistice, volunteered to stay on until we could organize such relief as we could command. After Captain Gregory was compelled to return home in August, 1919, Gilchrist B. Stockton succeeded him. In September, 1920, Gardner Richardson took over from Stockton and continued until he was succeeded in August, 1922, by Russell W. Bell, who served until the end. Elmer G. Burland and John A. Sellards served as assistants during a part of this period.

Our staff reported that of the food supplies imported by us during the Armistice period, only one month's supply remained. The reports of our staff further showed that the forthcoming harvest of 1919 would not, after the farmers' requirements, supply the country for more than three months.

The health situation in Vienna and other cities was terrible. There had been, since prewar days, an appalling increase in death rates and a decrease in births.

RELIEF OF ADULTS

Under the Congressional authority of March 30, 1920, the A.R.A. provided Austria with 200,825 tons of flour (at a cost of $24,055,709) for her adult relief. The British undertook the transportation of these supplies at a cost, to them, of $8,032,992. We set up our food-draft system, which resulted in 11,726 tons of food, and in addition, we provided seventy tons of clothing, the total amounting to $3,330,635 for adults.

Under the food- and bulk-draft program we steadily expanded our relief to the intellectuals, who comprised 222,377 teachers, professors, doctors, scientists, engineers, musicians, and other professional men. The Commonwealth Fund of New York contributed $691,333 and the Jewish Joint Distribution Committee $200,000 to the relief of intellectuals in Austria, mostly through food drafts.

The American Relief Administration contributed $95,147 in food drafts to the Student Relief Fund, which was conducted by the Young Men's and Young Women's Christian associations.

RELIEF OF CHILDREN

We had organized our canteen system for children and others in Austria during the Armistice, and at the Peace we were serving 213,600 persons. We continued this system for three years—until July 1, 1923. The number being served in the canteens increased until June, 1921, when a maximum of 356,214 persons were given aid. A total of about 550,000 children, aged, and expectant mothers were helped, and more than 200,000,000 meals were served to them during the course of our relief after the Peace.

During the winters of 1919, 1920, and 1921, we shipped to Austria the following clothing materials. They weighed 862 tons and cost $1,504,523. Some of the items were:

> 721,713 yards of 54-inch woolen cloth
> 347,475 pairs of boots

350,649 pairs of stockings
664 woolen sweaters
19,884,000 yards of thread
3,096,288 buttons
202,200 needles

The Commonwealth Fund contributed thirty-two tons of the above clothing materials valued at $62,475, and in addition, we shipped a huge amount of used clothing into the country. Workshops employing hundreds of Austrian women were organized in different cities . to make up the clothing—and their wages, where necessary, were paid by the American Relief Administration.

There were so many children in need of clothing that the A.R.A. was compelled to issue the following stipulations:

(1) Advance lists of the names in each locality must be submitted;

(2) Only the neediest children are to be considered; and

(3) Children who have received clothing from any other organization are not eligible.

In addition to food and clothing, our organization imported substantial medical supplies for the physicians who served our canteens. In all, the A.R.A. distributed 25,963 tons of food and clothing to children, amounting, in value, to $6,695,693. We also obtained from the Austrian Government its accumulated cash balances in the United States, with which we provided 12,703 tons of supplies for children at a value of $1,364,656.

COMMODITY EXCHANGE

The A.R.A. staff initiated some commodity exchanges with neighboring countries amounting to 893 tons of food. No money was involved in these exchanges.

TOTAL AMERICAN RELIEF ADMINISTRATION SUPPLIES

The total supplies distributed from the American Relief Administration funds, food drafts, Congressional appropriation, and Austrian Government donations were 252,212 tons of a value of $35,509,168.

AIDS TO AUSTRIA BY OTHER AMERICAN CHARITABLE ORGANIZATIONS

The American Red Cross conducted a major service to Austria, co-ordinating its work with our organizations. It provided physicians, surgeons, medical supplies, and clinics—acting mainly through the existing hospitals. It joined in the fights against the epidemics; it established schools for nurses. At times it furnished food and clothing, and it gave aid to Russian refugees in Austria.

Red Cross accounts show an expenditure in Austria, from the Peace to 1923, of $4,473,985 and some part of a special fund, entitled "Vienna and Budapest," of $310,651. If one-half of this be assigned to Austria, the total Red Cross expenditures were $4,628,310.

The Jewish Joint Distribution Committee had given important relief prior to the Peace. It continued its work of relief to orphans, relocation of its co-religionists to agriculture, shops for training in trades, and some medical supplies. Its total expenditures in Austria from the Peace to September, 1923, were $1,145,208. Of this amount, $200,000 was spent to purchase American Relief Administration bulk drafts for the intellectuals.

The Commonwealth Fund not only contributed to the American Relief Administration but also undertook directly the organization of relief of special groups of intellectuals and children. It also set up convalescent homes. Its expenditures through the American Relief Administration for intellectual relief were $691,333, and other expenditures on its own efforts were $187,232, making a total of $878,565.

The American Friends Service Committee, in conjunction with the British Friends, began work in Austria in August, 1919. Among their services was the establishment of a factory for making small houses, the importation of two thousand dairy cows, and the creation of tuberculosis treatment centers. They also set up centers to support children under six years of age and subsidized land resettlement projects. Their total expenditures in Austria after the Peace were $483,086.

The National Lutheran Council handled most of its distribution through the pastors of the Lutheran faith. It included clothing and some food. The records, as far as we can discover, show expenditures of $83,720 after the Peace.

The Northern Baptists, in November, 1921, loaded a "Ship of Fellowship," part of which cargo went to Austria.

The American Episcopalian journal *The Living Church* acted as treasurer for American Episcopalians. The Church gave substantial contributions for children's aid.

The Federal Council of Churches issued appeals for funds for Austrian relief, urging aid to the various Protestant denominations. So far as our research can discover, the subscriptions sent directly to the Federal Council for Austria, as of December, 1923, totaled $2,868.

Our research disclosed the following committees, about which we find only the following information:

American Relief Committee for Sufferers in Austria—Chairman, Frederic C. Penfield, former Ambassador to Austria. This group collected $50,610 worth of goods and cash amounting to $25,394—a total of $76,004.

Vienna Children's Milk Relief—Chairman, Mrs. Fritz Kreisler; Treasurer, Dr. Ernest Meyer. This organization collected $203,538 as of December 31, 1921, but no further details of its work exist.

TOTAL SUPPLIES TO AUSTRIA
FROM THE PEACE TO 1923 *

	Food	Clothing & Misc.	$ Value
American Relief Administration			
Children's relief	25,133	830	$ 6,695,693
Austrian government donation ..	11,028	1,675	1,364,656
Food drafts and bulk sales	11,726	70	3,330,635
Congressional appropriation,			
March, 1920	200,825		24,055,709
Commodity exchange	893		
The Commonwealth Fund			
clothing		32	62,475
American Red Cross	(quantities unknown)		4,628,310
Jewish Joint Distribution	(quantities unknown)		945,208
The Commonwealth Fund (additional money not spent through A.R.A.)	(quantities unknown)		187,232
American Friends Service Committee	(quantities unknown)		483,086
National Lutheran Council	(quantities unknown)		83,720
Federal Council of Churches	(quantities unknown)		2,868
American Relief Committee for Sufferers in Austria	(quantities unknown)		76,004
Vienna Children's Milk Relief	(quantities unknown)		203,538
	249,605	2,607	$42,119,134

* In tons.

THE BRITISH CONTRIBUTIONS

The British carried on some relief work in Austria after the Peace. However, we have no record of British expenditures, except for the transportation of the flour which we purchased through our Congressional appropriation of March 30, 1920. The British expended $8,032,992 for this.

EXPRESSIONS OF GRATITUDE

We received many evidences of appreciation from the Austrian Government and from Austrian cities. Our files are filled with touching expressions of gratitude from the children and from individual citizens. Our staff also received many personal expressions.

The astronomers of the observatory in Vienna named a newly discovered planet for me. Protests from some world astronomical organization against naming planets for living persons removed me temporarily from that glory, but the Vienna astronomers later corrected this hardship, and I still have a planet.

CHAPTER 44

HUNGARY

The record of events in Hungary at the time the new American Relief Administration was striving to bring relief to the Hungarian people is a necessary background for the narrative of that country. These documented events also have some historical importance.

THE DECLINE AND FALL OF BELA KUN

I have related, in Chapter 13, the Communist seizure of the government of Hungary on March 22, 1919, by Bela Kun, a Russian-trained former Hungarian war prisoner in Russia. I have also related that with the approval of the Big Four, our official American relief organization was supplying a limited amount of food to Kun's government in order to keep the railway lines operating to neighboring states during the Armistice. Kun paid for the food in gold which he had seized from the National Bank.

We also continued to supply our children's canteens and the children's hospitals in Budapest. Our American staff, whose headquarters were in Vienna, traveled in Hungary freely, and thus we were well informed of what was going on. Kun had ordered the confiscation of all private property and had introduced the Russian form of the "Red Terror," arresting as many as two thousand persons daily and executing a large number of them.

When our American Government official relief agencies came to an end on July 1, 1919, Kun was in considerable trouble. The Rumanians had, during the previous May, moved troops across the Hungarian border but had been stopped by orders of the Big Four. Kun had made war on the Czechs, and the Allies had declared a blockade on Hungary except for our limited supplies.

I was asked to attend the Supreme Council meeting of July 5, 1919, and I can give no better description of the situation in Hungary after the Peace than that which can be drawn from the minutes of the meeting. I quote some of the more important paragraphs here:

M. CLEMENCEAU asked Mr. Hoover to explain the economic position in Hungary.

MR. HOOVER said that the problem was that of the economic re-habilitation of Central Europe. As matters stood, there was no hope of removing and distributing the . . . harvest [in the neighboring states] unless the Danube and the railways across Hungary were reopened for traffic. The question, therefore, was not merely an internal Hungarian question. It was one of external economic relations. . . . Further, the withdrawal of the German Armies from south-eastern Europe had left behind it in Hungary a large quantity of rolling stock and river craft [needed by the surrounding states]. In order . . . to set the economic life of . . . [Eastern] Europe going again, it was necessary to have control of these essential means of transport. The third aspect of the question was largely political. [Communist] . . . ideas were impregnating the working classes throughout the area. Unless some means could be devised of abating the infection, the economic regeneration of Central and South-Eastern Europe would be difficult. Bela Kun's government was spending a great deal of money on sending . . . [Communist] missionaries to industrial centers outside Hungary. . . . Moreover, the military power of the Hungarian Government was growing. . . . It was not likely that Bela Kun would . . . [spread] his theories outside the borders of Hungary by the help of this military force. The next probable victim after Czecho-Slovakia was Austria. . . . [He would observe that] executions had increased, which indicated that opposition was growing in the country and that . . . red terror . . . [was] being resorted to. Previously, it might have been possible to treat the Hungarian revolutionary party with indulgence. Now . . . [that it is overflowing] its frontiers, it must be considered as an economic danger to the rest of Europe.

M. CLEMENCEAU asked Mr. Hoover what he thought of the Szegeden group [who were opposing Kun].

MR. HOOVER replied that this group appeared to him to be . . . without any notable intellectual capacity. For instance, their deliberations of late had been devoted to the question of the resumption of the right of duelling. He did not expect much help from that party. It appeared, however, that discontent with the Bela Kun Government was growing among the working classes. Information from [our own and] British sources had been received . . . that the Trade Unions would gladly see the Government upset. Communism would not appear to have penetrated very deeply into the population . . . [but] Government was becoming, like that in Russia, a [red] tyranny. . . . Another difficulty applying to any solution that might be suggested was the obvious duplicity of Bela Kun. In support of this, Mr. Hoover quoted the following [intercepted] messages . . . between Lenin and Bela Kun:

1. *Message sent by Lenin from Moscow to Bela Kun at Budapest on 19th June, 1919, includes following:*

"It is necessary to make the fullest possible use of every opportunity to obtain a temporary armistice of peace, in order to give the people a breathing space. But do not trust the Entente Powers for a moment. They are deceiving you, and only attempting to gain time in order to be able to crush you and us. Try and organize postal communications with us by aeroplane."

2. *Message sent on June 21st by Bela Kun . . . to Lenin (Moscow) in reply to his telegram of June 19th.*

"I thank you very much for your telegram in which you approve of my foreign policy. I am very proud of being one of your best pupils, but I think in one point I am superior to you, namely, in the question of 'mala fides.' I think I know Entente very well. I know that they will fight us to the end. In this war, only a state of Armistice can occur, but never peace. This is an out and out fight. Once more I thank you for your note."

The authenticity of these messages . . . [is] supported by the fact that they had been received first by British sources and subsequently intercepted by Austrian wireless. Of the various solutions proposed in the memorandum he had submitted (Appendix A), no doubt the military occupation of Budapest would be . . . welcomed by the population, but it was no doubt beset with difficulties. [One] . . . alternative . . . to this policy [was] . . . a more or less mitigated recognition of the Bela Kun

Government. . . . [However his suggestion] was that the various Inter-Allied Commissions working in the neighborhood should establish . . . relations with the Hungarians. There need be no direct recognition by the Governments, but by this side entrance it might be possible to obtain the opening of the river and the setting in motion of the means of transport and thereby the distribution of necessary supplies. He admitted that this might possibly strengthen Bela Kun's Government, but, on the other hand, Bela Kun was supporting himself . . . with the working class [by blaming the] . . . blockade. All the hardships of the situation were attributed to the blockade. By removing it, the Powers would deprive him of this argument and he might find it more difficult to plead his case. Whether this would neutralize the advantage of semi-recognition, he did not know.

M. CLEMENCEAU asked what was being done to re-victual Hungary.

MR. HOOVER replied that nothing at all was being done [except as above]. At the time when Bela Kun came to power, [his organization] . . . was about to re-victual Budapest, as the situation . . . was . . . urgent. The Communist Government . . . [had] made a stringent search for all supplies and had, by careful re-distribution, managed to feed [Budapest] . . . tolerably well. It appeared clear that they would reach the next harvest without starvation. . . .

M. TITTONI said that the question of Hungary was one of the most difficult the Conference had to deal with. The Bela Kun Government was a serious threat to the neighboring countries, including Italy. There had been two periods in this movement. In the first a peaceful revolution had been brought about. The effect of this stage had been the most dangerous. The Russian Revolution had been represented to the people of Europe as being accomplished by carnage and general destruction. . . .

MR. BALFOUR said . . . the Powers were bound to do to Hungary what they would have done to Germany had she broken the armistice. To carry this out it would be necessary to organize the Roumanian, Czecho-Slovak, Serbian and French troops at hand. . . . By this means the evil of giving credit to Bela Kun, which Mr. Hoover had shown was to be feared, would be avoided. At the present time Vienna was in danger and perhaps Roumania. This could be stopped by prompt military action, which would be justified by Hungary's flagrant breach of the armistice.

M. CLEMENCEAU said that he would like to state his opinion, though he feared it would not be a very clear one. He had agreed thus far with all the speakers. The situation reminded him of the La Fontaine fable in which a gathering of rats decided to hang a bell round a cat's neck. All

agreed this was desirable but no one knew how to do it. He thought that
the situation had been accurately described by Mr. Hoover. He acqui-
esced in all M. Tittoni had said. . . . But how were the Powers to do
what he proposed? France was demobilizing and could not stop the
process. At the end of October there would be but three classes with the
Colours; that was to say the Army would be on a peace footing. . . .

The annex referred to in the minutes was the report of an inspection
tour made July 9 by two members of the A.R.A. staff, Lieutenant
Emery Pottle and Dr. E. Dana Durand, who were accompanied by
Captain Bernath Weiss of the American Army, who spoke Hungarian. The importance of the report lay in the evidence of rising discontent in all groups, including peasants and workmen. One paragraph of their report reads:

. . . [The peasants] object to having to sell their crops for worthless
paper money or to being absolutely robbed of them. Within the few days
before we were in Budapest there had been several massacres of peasants
who had attempted to resist the requisitioning . . . Where such resistance arose the Terrorist troops shot down many of the peasants, made
prisoners of the people of entire villages, condemned selected persons to
be hung, levied huge money fines on the people and carried off all of
their grain and livestock. . . .

At the July 5 meeting of the Supreme Council, it was agreed that
there should be no military action. The Council wished to see the
situation develop further. But on July 10, the Council directed Marshal Foch to advise whether the Allies should occupy Hungary with
troops and, if so, what kind of army was needed. He made a recommendation regarding the troops required, proposing that an American contingent be sent with the other Allied troops. I strongly advised Secretary Polk that the United States should not join in any
new military ventures in Europe, that it was not necessary because
I now believed there was another alternative by offering decent
treatment to Hungary if she would throw off the Communist yoke.

Also on July 10, Captain Weiss advised that Bela Kun had imported, from somewhere, 100,000 rifles and 40,000,000 rounds of
ammunition and indicated that they had been furnished by the Italians. I mentioned this to my Italian colleagues on the Supreme Eco-

nomic Council. Being honorable men, they at once denounced such a transaction and agreed to investigate.

General Boehm, a member of the old Imperial regime who had gone over to Bela Kun as the commander of Kun's army, resigned on July 16 and came to Vienna, where he proposed to Captain Gregory and other Allied officials that he should organize a counterrevolution, with the understanding that he would be the new "head of state."

On July 23, I protested, to our American Legation in Paris, the furnishing of arms by Italian military officers. Following are the important paragraphs of my letter of protest:

With regard to Italian assistance to the Hungarian Government. This matter has been up several times before the Supreme Economic Council but we did not directly give any formal or informal hints to the Italians as to what we might do in the matter. What we did do was to point out that assistance was proceeding from Italy to Bela Kun and gave some authentic instances of it. The Italians, as usual, promised to investigate rigorously, but, beyond ventilating the fact that we were well aware of what was going on, we have taken no action whatever.

. . . In one instance, the Italians received 3,000,000 gold kronen, and upon ventilation of this matter they assured us that they had not exported any goods against it, and after some discussion agreed to deposit it to the credit of the Allies for disposition under reparation. Another instance of some nine carloads of nitrates from Trieste which were hooked on to our food trains, they, as above, agreed to investigate. . . .

I was called to attend a Council meeting on July 26. There was some discussion regarding General Boehm. I protested that the Allies could not persuade the people of Hungary to revolt against Kun by recognizing General Boehm. The subject was dropped, and I instructed Captain Gregory to have nothing to do with Boehm.

In the course of the discussion, I posed the following question:

. . . Would it not be possible to make a public declaration of policy . . . ? Such a declaration might take the form of a statement to the effect that economic assistance would be given to a properly constituted government, and that such a statement would not bind the Conference to subsequent military action.

MR. BALFOUR . . . asked . . . whether the conclusion of the Council was that whether military action should be taken or the situation allowed to remain in its present state. He asked, in conclusion, how the declaration could be made public.

M. CLEMENCEAU replied that it could be published in the press. . . .

M. CLEMENCEAU said . . . He believed Mr. Hoover held the key to the situation. The offer of food in return for good behaviour would be a very effective weapon. . . .

. . . The action exercised by Mr. Hoover would therefore have, he thought, greater chances of success than military intervention. . . .

MR. BALFOUR pointed out that there was no inconsistency between the points of view of Mr. Hoover and Marshal Foch. In a public notification it could be stated why the Allies could not deal with Bela Kun, and what kind of person they would consent to deal with.

(It was therefore decided that Mr. Balfour and Mr. Hoover should confer in the preparation of a public notification to be sent to Hungary, and that it should be presented to the Council at the afternoon meeting.)

At the afternoon meeting, Mr. Balfour and I submitted our proposed statement—in the ponderous phraseology of the British Foreign Office. The minutes state:

After some further discussion it was decided to issue in the Press and by wireless the following declaration:—

"The Allied and Associated Governments are most anxious to arrange a Peace with the Hungarian People and thus bring to an end a condition of things which makes the economic revival of Central Europe impossible and defeats any attempt to secure supplies for its population. These tasks cannot even be attempted until there is in Hungary a Government which represents its people, and carries out in the letter and the spirit the engagements into which it has entered with the Associated Governments. None of these conditions are fulfilled by the administration of Bela Kun: which has not only broken the Armistice to which Hungary was pledged, but is at this moment actually attacking a friendly and Allied Power. With this particular aspect of the question it is for the Associated Governments to deal on their own responsibility. If food and supplies are to be made available, if the blockade is to be removed, if economic reconstruction is to be attempted, if peace is to be settled it can only be done with a

Government which represents the Hungarian people and not with one that rests its authority upon terrorism.

"The Associated Powers think it opportune to add that all foreign occupation of Hungarian territory, as defined by the Peace Conference will cease as soon as the terms of the armistice have in the opinion of the Allied Commander-in-Chief, been satisfactorily complied with."

I telegraphed the statement to Captain Gregory, who communicated it to the trades union and other leaders in Hungary.

On August 1, after 131 days of power, Bela Kun was overthrown by the Hungarian trade-union leaders, who brought about a revolt in his army. Kun fled, and some of his assistants committed suicide. A government comprised largely of trade-union leaders assumed power, with the usual liberal proclamations. This was Hungary's third revolution since the Armistice.

With Bela Kun's fall, we in the A.R.A. immediately began further measures to provision Budapest. We increased shipments for the children's canteens and hospitals. Captain Gregory arranged for a large shipment of pork and dairy products from stocks of the Chicago packers at Trieste and Vienna. They were paid for from the remnants of Hungarian gold.

At the meeting of the Supreme Council on August 4, I proposed that the blockade on Hungary be taken down and the Danube opened to traffic. The minutes read:

M. CLEMENCEAU suggested that Mr. Hoover should furnish a draft.

MR. HOOVER then suggested a draft, which after some amendments suggested by M. Tittoni, was adopted in the following form:

"It is agreed that instructions should be sent to the representatives of the various Allied Governments at Vienna and to the Blockade Commission and to General Franchet d'Esperey that the Blockade on Hungary shall be lifted at once and that the Danube shall be opened and shall remain opened so long as the present Hungarian Government gives practical evidence of its intention to comply promptly with the conditions of the Armistice."

General Bliss reported to Washington on the presentation I made at this August 4 meeting as follows:

In view of the new situation brought about by the fall of Bela Kun, Mr. Hoover recommended a relaxation of the blockade against Hungary, the opening of the Danube, and the supply of foodstuffs to Hungary from the Banat. The new government, though very radical, represented the trade unions. Trade-unionism was an instrument used to upset Bolshevism. . . . the Hungarian Government should be encouraged as a very important reaction might result on Russia. The Council adopted a resolution which followed Mr. Hoover's advice on opening the Danube and lifting the Hungarian blockade.

THE RUMANIAN INVASION OF HUNGARY

The troubled life of the Magyar people was not brightened with the abdication of Bela Kun. Now the American Relief Administration was to be an eyewitness to the invasion of Hungary by the Rumanian Army.

In May, 1919, the Rumanians had advanced their army over the Hungarian border but had been stopped by orders from the Supreme Council. On August 1, immediately upon the fall of Bela Kun, the Rumanians began an invasion with their army. By August 5, they had occupied Budapest. Then began a regime which was less bloody than Bela Kun's, but it was a full revival of the medieval practice of looting the vanquished. They claimed this right, with some justification, because of the hideous plunder of Rumania by the Hungarian Army during the war and in its retreat at the Armistice. The Rumanians proceeded at once to recover railway rolling stock, of which they had been almost totally denuded. Before they left, they had carried away industrial machinery, farm animals—in fact, everything movable, some of which Bela Kun had collected in preparation for shipment to Russia. They looted the banks, the art galleries, many homes, and even the hospitals. These actions were described in the meeting of the Supreme Council on August 4 by the American representative, Frank Polk. The minutes state:

MR. POLK said that the latest news, received [from Captain Gregory] was to the effect that the Roumanian advance guard had reached Budapest and that the Trade Union Government feared an occupation of the city by the Roumanians and a further invasion by the Czecho-Slovaks. These fears would doubtless rouse nationalist feelings. At two o'clock the news was that 600 Roumanian cavalrymen were to the west of Budapest, where they had cut all communications with Vienna. Looting was said to have begun in the suburbs. To avoid worse trouble the Hungarians suggested that an inter-allied police force should be sent immediately to Budapest.

The Council decided to tell the Rumanians to stop the advance. The Council also decided to send a military mission of four generals representing the major Allies to Budapest.

Also on August 4, Mr. Polk, on behalf of the American Government, notified the Rumanian Government that we would have no further economic relations with Rumania until she had withdrawn her troops from Hungary.

At the Council meeting on August 5, the following was recorded:

M. CLEMENCEAU asked Mr. Polk if he had any news of Budapest.
MR. POLK read the following telegram:—
"HOOVER, *American Relief*, Paris

August 5th, 1919
"Last night there were 15 or 20 people killed in Budapest which I have definitely verified. It is absolutely necessary that the Roumanians be taken out of this situation as rapidly as possible and pending their departure General Gorton should act for the rest of the Commission. I was sure that these conflicts would take place. They also demand hostages and threaten definitely to kill 5 persons for each one who is injured in Budapest, naturally after their starting the killing further difficulties are apt to occur. The railroads are all tied up with machine-guns on the bridges. The Police Force has been dispossessed and whole city in absolute military control. This condition cannot continue and the movement to re-organize Hungary succeed.

GREGORY"
MR. HOOVER said that half an hour before the meeting he had received a message for M. Clemenceau, from Lt. Col. Romanelli:—
"BUDAPEST, August 4th. 1919
"I have the honor to inform you that I communicated your orders to the High Command of the Roumanian Army but the Roumanian troops

have advanced in spite of this. . . . At the present time they have occupied the city of Budapest, have cut communications, taken hostages and made prisoner one member of the new Government. The Serbians also are advancing from the South and pillaging. The situation makes it impossible for the new Government to . . . [support] itself."

M. CLEMENCEAU said that under the circumstances it might be desirable to send a more threatening message than the one sent on the previous day.

Also on August 5, the Supreme Commander of the Rumanian armies announced the conditions upon which the Rumanians would retire from Hungary. They included reduction of the Hungarian Army to 15,000 men; delivery to Rumania of all war materials in the possession of the Hungarian troops and state, as well as transfer of all munition factories; 50 per cent of all rolling stock; 30 per cent of Hungary's livestock and animals of all kinds; 30 per cent of all agricultural machinery; 20,000 carloads of wheat; 10,000 carloads of corn; and 50 per cent of all river craft. The time for reply was set on the same day. If Hungary failed to reply, the Rumanian Supreme Commander stated, the Rumanian Army would carry out these conditions by force. Telegrams from our relief staff in Budapest stated that the Rumanians had begun these seizures the same day.

On August 6, I addressed to Premier Clemenceau a letter which, after referring to the events given above, continued:

. . . I cannot refrain from remarking that this must mean a great setback in the evolution of self government in Hungary . . . it is my duty to advise you that I cannot recommend either to my own government or to the allied governments, for whom I act, that they should incur any expenditure or effort in endeavoring to provision the city of Budapest in the face of these demands and the existing situation.

The Allied and Associated Governments have expended upwards of $38,000,000 in the provisioning of Roumania within the last six months, and the advices we have from the Allied Food Mission in Roumania are that the harvest now in course will produce a surplus of food for Roumania for the forthcoming year. Therefore, the immense food requisitions by the Roumanian Army upon Hungary amount to a form of indemnity, the rights and wrongs of which in the face of the necessities of the Hungarian population and of the previous suffering of the Roumanian population are not matters for my determination. . . .

HERBERT HOOVER

At the meeting on August 4, I protested that the Yugoslavs were refusing to deliver food to Hungary and other neighboring states from their surplus in the Banat. Some of it had been paid for in gold by the Hungarians prior to the rise of Bela Kun and was not yet delivered. A long discussion followed. The minutes record that I stated I had prepared a draft telegram to be addressed to the Serbian Government which might perhaps be too strong but which might form the basis of a second draft. I then read the following:

"The Council is informed . . . that there is a very considerable surplus of foodstuffs now lying in the Banat and surrounding counties and that with the impending favourable harvest in Greater Serbia there is now no reason for the reservation of these supplies from general distribution through Central Europe. The continuation of provisioning of Vienna is absolutely dependent upon the free shipment of these supplies . . . and the recent over-turn of Government in Budapest makes it of prime interest to the Allies and to all hope of stability in Central Europe that the City of Budapest should be given every facility for the purchase and export of foodstuffs from these counties.

"Therefore, the Council wishes to urge upon the Serbian Government in the strongest terms that not only will the greatest contribution be made by Serbia towards the re-establishment of order and stability in the counties adjacent to her borders, but that the dictates of humanity demand that no obstruction of any character shall be placed in the way of food exports from the Banat to the surrounding counties and that, in fact, the Serbian Government is requested to join with the Allies and through their various agencies in promoting the export and distribution of these supplies. The Council hopes for an early and favourable reply to this representation, the importance of which it cannot over-emphasize, and it trusts that the Serbian Government will realize that unless the Allies can receive co-operation in the labors they have undertaken for the restoration of stability in Central Europe that it is impossible that the Allied Governments should continue the economic support which they have given and expect to continue giving to the Greater Serbian Government."

. . . M. CLEMENCEAU said that he approved Mr. Hoover's policy. . . .

M. Clemenceau suggested that a re-draft of Mr. Hoover's proposal should be made. He asked M. Berthelot to make a draft.

The re-drafted message was equally emphatic.

At the meeting of the Supreme Council on August 6, instructions were issued to the military mission. The minutes of the meeting stated:

M. Clemenceau suggested that the Council should proceed to draft the text of a telegram to be sent to the Roumanian Government, stating that the Allied and Associated Governments would not admit her right to conclude an independent armistice with Hungary; that such an armistice would not receive recognition, particularly as it was intended to take away large quantities of material, the joint property of all the Allies and not of Roumania alone.

Mr. Balfour said he had prepared a draft telegram.

(After a short discussion, the following draft telegram was approved:)

"Supreme Council have learned that Roumania Military Authorities at Budapest have imposed Armistice on Hungarian Government, to be accepted at a few hours' notice. Terms of this armistice render it impossible for Hungarian Government to fulfill armistice concluded with Allied Powers on November 15th. Moreover, terms in themselves pay no regard to the rights of reparation of other Allies. Supreme Council desire formally to record their refusal to recognise right of Roumanian Commander-in-Chief to impose any armistice without authority of Allied and Associated Powers."

THE RISE AND FALL OF ARCHDUKE JOSEPH

At this point I must interrupt this narrative of Rumanian invasion and plundering to record the usurpation of another dictatorship over Hungary by Archduke Joseph (a Hapsburg). On August 6, the Archduke, with ten policemen, arrested the members of the Trades Union Ministry. However, the Rumanian Army had surrounded the Ministry building with machine guns—pointed directly at it.

The Archduke's action was an ironic consequence of a war which had been directed toward putting the Hohenzollerns and Hapsburgs out of business. At once all of the surrounding new states began to shiver in their boots. They raised to Paris a cry of "No return of the Hapsburgs!"

Our relief organization was now confronted with three problems in Hungary: the looting by the Rumanian Army, the return of the Hapsburgs to power, and food supply.

On August 12, I left for Poland on the mission arranged by President Wilson. From Vienna, on August 18, on my way back to Paris, I sent Mr. Polk a telegram in which I recited certain disturbances between the Poles and the Germans in Upper Silesia (which I take up later) and continued:

> . . . what is your policy with regard to Archduke? Is he going to be recognized by the Conference? If not why do they not . . . at once . . . demand the . . . [formation] of a Coalition Ministry eliminating the Hapsburg element? His recognition and encouragement by British General Gorton is the worst thing that has been done in three . . . [weeks]. Did the British authorize this? . . . If [the] Military Commission would demand Archduke's retirement and the formation of a ministry representing labor and . . . middle classes and peasants it could be done easily. If the present line continues another three . . . [weeks] the Hapsburg element will be strong enough to hold on and enforce their position by terrorism and control . . . [of] elections. . . .

Also on the same date, in a second telegram, I said:

> A word from the Peace Conference that no Hapsburg will be recognized or dealt with if sent properly to various representatives at Buda Pest and communicated to Archduke would settle him, especially as powerful labor and social democratic group refuse to assist his government.
>
> HOOVER

On my arrival in Paris, Mr. Polk requested that I attend a meeting of the Supreme Council on August 21. The pertinent part of the minutes of this meeting read:

> MR. POLK asked that Mr. Hoover be heard on the situation in Hungary.
> MR. HOOVER said that the staff of the Relief Organisation had been in Budapest and other parts of Hungary during the past ten days. . . . Up to 10 am. on the previous Monday, the Roumanians were still requisi-

tioning food all over the country. . . . Trains carrying the requisitioned supplies were passing out of the country as fast as possible. . . . Two of his officials, Captains in the American Army, had themselves seen the Roumanians take sixteen wagon loads of supplies from the Children's Hospitals and eleven deaths had resulted therefrom within twenty-four hours, for there was no way of replacing these supplies. He did not think that any action by the Roumanians could be secured unless the military Mission were instructed to send agents to frontier points to stop the Roumanians from shipping out any more of the requisitional material until its disposal could be decided by the Council. In his own opinion the [food] supplies requisitioned should be turned back to Budapest to feed the population of that city. He would like to call attention to another point which threw a sidelight on the situation. While the *coup d'état,* by which the Archduke Joseph's Government had been installed was not entirely a Roumanian affair, nevertheless Roumanian troops had surrounded the meeting place of the Ministry and had turned their machine guns on the building in which they were. This event had had an immediate repercussion throughout Poland and Eastern Europe and the Bolshevists were making much of it and claiming that the . . . [Allies were] trying to re-establish reactionary government in its worst form and this had done more to re-habilitate the Bolshevist cause than anything that had happened for a long time. The social democrats had refused to have anything to do with the new Government and . . . the leader of this group . . . thought that if things were allowed to continue as they were, the old reactionary party would be well established in ten days and the Allied and Associated Powers would have to be prepared to see the House of Hapsburg begin to re-establish itself throughout all its former . . . [dominions]. . . .

. . . Very energetic action was required. He thought the Generals in Budapest should summon the Archduke and tell him clearly that he would never be recognized, and that he had better resign. . . .

Prior to the meeting of the Council on August 22, Mr. Balfour requested me to draft a telegram to be sent to the Archduke. He made some minor changes at that meeting. The telegram was authorized. The important parts were:

The Allied and Associated Powers . . . are most anxious to conclude a durable peace with the Hungarian people, but they feel that this cannot be done while the present Hungarian Government is in power.

That Government has been brought into existence, not by the will of the people but by a *coup d'état* carried out by a small body of police, under the protection of a foreign army. It has at its head a member of the house of Hapsburg, whose policy and ambitions were largely responsible for the calamities under which the world is suffering, and will long suffer. A peace negotiated by such a Government is not likely to be lasting, nor can the Allied and Associated Governments give it the economic support which Hungary so sorely needs.

. . . In the interests, therefore, of European peace the Allied and Associated Governments must insist that the present claimant to the headship of the Hungarian State should resign, and that a Government in which all parties are represented should . . . [be elected by] the Hungarian people. The Allied and Associated Powers would be prepared to negotiate with any Government which possessed the confidence of an Assembly so elected.

There was some discussion as to how the telegram was to be delivered. Finally, rather than acting through the commission of four generals, I was directed to send the telegram over our wires to Captain Gregory for delivery in person.

On the following day (August 23), I received Captain Gregory's reply, expressed in the effective slang code which our men had adopted in amplification of *en clair* language:

Archie on the carpet 7 p.m. Went through the hoop at 7:05 p.m.

I had this code message translated into more formal language and sent to Prime Minister Clemenceau. Our messenger showed the Old Tiger the original. The Prime Minister, having been a reporter on a New York newspaper, needed no translation but seized the original as a "memento" of the war.

A new and representative ministry was set up in Hungary. This was the fifth Hungarian revolution in eight months.

THE RUMANIAN INVASION AGAIN

I must now return to August 12. On that date I forwarded a telegram from Captain Gregory to the Supreme Council. The important paragraph was:

. . . [the Roumanians] have been stripping the country, grabbing railroad transportation and lining everything up to move it out. Have taken . . . [machinery] from the fields, food and medical supplies from the hospitals. And flour and sugar from the warehouses. . . .

At the meeting of the Supreme Council on August 22, they sent the following telegram to the military mission at Budapest:

"The Supreme Council learns that the Roumanian troops of occupation continue to make requisitions of every kind in Hungary, and to send the goods so obtained to Roumania.

"The Council begs the Inter-Allied Commission to report on the practical possibility of sending officers to the frontier posts between Hungary and Roumania to prevent the export of goods requisitioned to the detriment of the Allies, and in diminution of their common security.

"Should the Commission regard this suggestion as feasible, Supreme Council authorises it to act accordingly."

At the meeting of the Supreme Council on August 25, the following agreement was reached:

It was agreed . . . that the export of all supplies to Roumania should be stopped from the United States, Great Britain, France, Italy and Japan, until further orders. It was further decided to send the Roumanian Government, through the French Chargé d'Affaires at Bucharest, a reminder that a reply to telegrams was expected.

Even after the Rumanian seizure of Hungarian railway material there was still left in Hungary an inordinate proportion of railway rolling stock belonging to other neighboring states. As one of my last acts in Europe, on September 3, I recommended to Premier Clemenceau, as Chairman of the Big Four, that the Hungarians' excessive holdings of railway rolling stock be distributed to the proper owners in other Eastern European states:

PARIS, 3 September 1919

YOUR EXCELLENCY:

The great number of reports, which have come to my hands through the engineers who have been acting . . . in the co-ordination of railway operation in South Eastern Europe, indicate that the amount of railway rolling stock in locomotives and wagons in Hungary is much larger than was originally surmised. This rolling stock includes equipment formerly belonging to the Galician railways, and therefore due to the Polish Government; belonging to the Bohemian railways and therefore due to the Czecho-Slovak Government; belonging to the East Prussian railways and therefore due to the Polish Government; belonging to the Alsace-Lorraine railways and therefore due to the French Government; a considerable number of wagons and cars belonging to the Trentino railways and therefore due to the Italian Government; and, of course, a number of locomotives and cars formerly belonging to the Roumanian railways and therefore due to the Roumanian Government.

Under all these circumstances, it seems to me imperative that the Peace Conference should at once direct that the distribution of this railway rolling stock should be taken up systematically on behalf of all of the Governments concerned, and I would like to recommend that the Communications Section of the Supreme Economic Council be at once authorized to undertake the immediate control of all of this railway rolling stock, subject of course to the Allied Mission at Budapest, and that they should authorize a preliminary distribution of this railway rolling stock on the basis of the actual identification of the material.

The Communications Section, as you are aware, is comprised of eminent engineers representing the French, British, American and Italian Governments, and would therefore seem to me to be the appropriate body to at once undertake this matter. A decision on the above lines on your part would allay the very considerable amount of feeling now existing in Poland, Czecho-Slovakia and elsewhere, with regard to the large diversions now being made to Roumania.

HERBERT HOOVER

The Premier gave the necessary orders, and the other states benefited—but it was lame rolling stock.

There were two subsequent echoes of this sorry episode after I left Europe on September 15. On September 23, the Big Four ordered a blockade of Rumania until her army withdrew from Hungary and accounted for its plunder. The Rumanians withdrew, but I doubt that there was any accounting for the plunder. In any event, the Rumanians had, in their theory and practice of reparations, considerable justification for their actions, particularly with regard to animals, agricultural implements, household furniture, and railway rolling stock which the Hungarians had plundered from them.

SYSTEMATIC RELIEF

In the midst of all this tumult, we established fairly systematic relief for the Hungarian people. The Archduke had gone away, and a good ministry had been installed temporarily.

Captain Gregory continued as head of our mission to Hungary and Austria until mid-August, 1919. He was succeeded for a short time by Captain Charles N. Leach. In October, 1919, Captain Leach was succeeded by Gardner Richardson, who served until July, 1920. We then appointed Carlton G. Bowden, who served until August, 1921, and he was succeeded by Russell W. Bell, who served to the end in February, 1922.

The Yugoslav Government now sent Banat supplies to the Hungarians for gold. However, the Rumanians having plundered a part of the 1919 Hungarian harvest and the Banat supply becoming exhausted, the adult population was again in great need by April, 1920.

Under the Congressional authority of March 30, 1920, we supplied 14,114 tons of flour valued at $1,685,836 on "credit." We extended our food-draft and bulk-sales system to Hungary, providing 1,630 tons of supplies valued at $527,939. Under our organization for intellectuals, $126,994 was expended on about 25,000 individuals— the gift of The Commonwealth Fund. This sum was used to purchase food drafts from our organization. With our affiliated committees, we provided for 3,385 students at a cost of $28,300 (included in food-draft and bulk-sales total).

RELIEF OF CHILDREN

We established our canteen system for debilitated and diseased children. A report from Dr. Leach of our staff, dated August 18, 1919, stated:

. . . There are about 75,000 children under 15 years of age in Budapest. . . .

The mortality rate among children has already doubled and as the winter approaches their conditions will naturally become much worse. In the City Children's Hospital the percentage of deaths among infants increased to 135% in July, as against 28% for June, and the figure for August will be very much higher. . . .

We organized the usual nation-wide committee of women, who, in turn, operated the canteens, and did it magnificently.

By November, 1919, nearly 45,000 Hungarian children, expectant mothers, orphans, and aged were being given care. This number gradually increased to about 110,000 in April, 1920, then decreased to about 8,000 after the September, 1920, harvest. By January, 1921, however, needs again increased, the number of people needing care rising to 47,000. We had served a total of 28,500,000 meals to 225,000 individuals.

We furnished 230 tons of clothing and materials for children. Some of the items were:

> 258,778 yards 54-inch woolen cloth
> 103,797 pairs of children's shoes
> 103,637 pairs of stockings
> 55,000 needles
> 9,808,000 yards of thread
> 937,296 buttons

The material was made up into children's outfits in workshops established by the Hungarian women.

The A.R.A., from its own funds, through food drafts and bulk sales, from our Congressional appropriation, from our relief of intellectuals, and from a gift of food from the Hungarian Government, distributed 21,075 tons of supplies valued at $3,797,057.

OTHER AMERICAN CHARITABLE AIDS TO HUNGARY

In June, 1920, the American Red Cross established a full organization of physicians, surgeons, and sanitary engineers. It gave medical supplies to the hospitals and established schools for nurses.

Red Cross accounts show $3,599,173 expended in Hungary. These records have under one item, "Vienna and Budapest," the sum of $310,650. They also show an item of $6,339,702 for Russian refugees in Greece, Turkey, Austria, Yugoslavia, and Budapest. What came to Hungary from the last two items can only be an estimate, but, judging from the character of Red Cross work elsewhere and our own information, we estimate about $155,325 from the first and $425,000 from the latter, making a total of $4,179,498.

The Jewish Joint Distribution Committee had been continuously active in the protection of its co-religionists from 1914 until the Peace. Its accounts show an expenditure of $581,966 from the Peace to December, 1923. The Committee engaged in general rehabilitation, supported orphans, and furnished some food supplies.

The National Lutheran Council's accounts show an expenditure of $75,013, but we can find no information regarding the kind of work undertaken.

For the American Presbyterian Church, our research uncovers only one item—from April, 1920, to August, 1921—of $14,000 for restoration of churches.

The American Relief Committee for Hungarian Sufferers was of great importance, but in our research we have been unable to find any extensive account of its operations. It was apparently organized after the Peace under Bertalan Barna, President, and Rudolph Oblatt, Treasurer. Its record, so far as we can find, reveals that the funds raised amounted to $923,052.

TOTAL SUPPLIES TO HUNGARY FROM THE PEACE TO 1923 *

	Food	Clothing and Miscellaneous	$ Value
American Relief Administration			
Children's relief	3,368	217	$1,292,157
Hungarian Government donation	1,733		265,807
Food draft sales	1,619	11	527,939
Surplus clothing		1	791
Congressional Appropriation			
(March, 1920)	14,114		1,685,836
The Commonwealth Fund			
(Clothing)		12	24,527

TOTAL SUPPLIES TO HUNGARY FROM THE PEACE TO 1923 (*continued*)

American Red Cross	(quantities unknown)	4,179,498
Jewish Joint Distribution Committee	(quantities unknown)	581,966
National Lutheran Council	(quantities unknown)	75,013
Presbyterian Church	(quantities unknown)	14,000
American Relief Committee for Hungarian Sufferers	(quantities unknown)	923,052
	20,834 241	$9,570,586

* In tons.

The totals in the above table do not include the barter in a large amount of food which our staff brought about with Czechoslovakia and Yugoslavia because we have no accurate record of them, but the Hungarians certainly secured another 60,000 tons of food as a result of the intervention of the American Relief Administration officials. Nor do these totals include the voluntary services of all charitable-organization staffs or the free services given by business firms over the world.

The British made a notable contribution to Hungarian relief by transporting our food, at a cost to them of $564,562, which was paid out of the Congressional grant. They also extended other aid to Hungary, but we do not have these records.

CHAPTER 45

YUGOSLAVIA

Yugoslavia emerged from the Peace Conference a great nation by the unification of thirteen southern Slavic states comprising about 12,800,000 people; included was the state of Serbia with 4,500,000 people. Serbia was the only part of the new nation which had been ravished by war. The other states had been parts of the old Austrian Empire and were thus not attacked or subjected to such invasion and plundering as came to Serbia.

The dreadful situation in Serbia at the Peace is indicated by a few extracts from our staff reports:

Belgrade . . . show[s] the results of heavy bombardment. . . .

The war's toll of life was enormous. In the Shabac district, of the prewar population of 270,000 there remain but 170,000. A child census . . . [shows] almost 6,000 full orphans.

. . . Warm winter clothing is very scarce. The coal situation is desperate, and wood is not plentiful, owing to lack of transportation . . . the extensive denuding of houses of their windows and doors has not been [remedied]. . . .

A July 10, 1919, report of the Minister of Health showed:

The number of [fathers killed in the war] 94,935
The number of fatherless children 125,495
The number of full orphans 24,967
The number of half or full orphans under 10 years of age 74,507
The abandoned children and orphans 37,292

Other extracts from our staff reports were:

The war has left Serbia with 500,000 fatherless children, and of these 150,000 are quite destitute while all are in urgent need of care and education. The need in fact is far greater than even these figures suggest owing to the general conditions of life in the country.

. . . The low standard of living and sanitation throughout the land are a serious danger to child life.

The outlook for the orphans is anything but hopeful. An insignificantly small percentage will be taken care of through established orphanages. The rest will be "farmed out," the family taking care of them receiving a bit of State aid. . . . Tuberculosis is very prevalent. . . .

All of the Yugoslav states had a fair grain crop from the 1919 harvest. In one area—the Banat—there was a considerable surplus not available to Serbia because of the lack of rail or water connections. The Yugoslavs were not inclined to give aid to their former oppressors and enemies, Austria and Hungary. It was necessary to secure pressure from the Supreme Council to induce the Yugoslavs to furnish the Banat surplus to these countries. However, they later did so, particularly to Hungary, which country paid in the gold it had seized from the old Austrian National Bank.

In Serbia proper there had been continuous requisitions by the occupying Germans and Austrians during the war and an almost total looting of the food animals by these armies in their retreat at the Armistice. However, with supplies from the other parts of the new kingdom and abundant grain crops, the adult population required no great relief.

OUR RELIEF STAFF

The chief of our Yugoslav mission at the Peace was Major David Klein. He was succeeded by Mowatt Mitchell, and Mr. Mitchell was, in turn, succeeded by Mr. A. P. Shaw.

CHILDREN'S RELIEF

The American Relief Administration's problem thus resolved into one of provisioning for children, mostly in Serbia. We had set up our canteen system during the Armistice, and we expanded it after the Peace. By September, 1919, about 200,000 children were being served by the canteens and through the children's asylums. We had supplied, through our canteens and other services, a total of about 300,000 individuals with 56,500,000 meals.

As for clothing, our staff reported:

The whole of the Yugo-Slav population, with the exception of the wealthier classes, are without any clothes and shoes. Almost seven million people need urgently a complete suit of clothes.

We provided the following materials—amounting to 180 tons with a value of $458,779; the cloth was made up into children's outfits by the Serbian women.

        158,288 yards of 54-inch woolen cloth
          4,030 ready-made children's coats
         69,932 pairs of children's boots
         70,362 pairs of woolen stockings
         66,000 needles
        390,528 buttons
     13,776,000 yards of thread, and
             30 sewing machines

The number of people on relief decreased to about 50,000 by May, 1920, and since the 1920 harvest proved even better than that of 1919, we were able to close our mission in August, 1920.

The American Relief Administration, from its special imports for children from overseas and a gift of grain from the Serbian Government to the canteens, distributed a total of 2,952 tons of supplies of a value of $1,024,382 to Yugoslavia after the Peace. The high cost per ton of our supplies was due to its content of fats, condensed milk, cocoa, and other expensive foods.

AIDS TO YUGOSLAVIA BY OTHER AMERICAN CHARITABLE ORGANIZATIONS

We have performed exhaustive research in an endeavor to record the work of the other American charitable organizations. We found accurate information in the records of only a few organizations. In many cases, only scraps of information were culled from the press or reports of other organizations of the time.

THE AMERICAN RED CROSS

During the Armistice period, the Red Cross performed a yeoman's job in furnishing medical aids and fighting epidemics, particularly typhus. It enlarged its service to Yugoslavia after the Peace. In addition, it provided for the many destitute Russian refugees. There is no better way to indicate the extent of the Red Cross services after the Peace than to show the expenditures carried in its accounts:

Bosnia and Herzegovina	$ 11,922
Montenegro	1,153,519
Yugoslavia	145,807
Serbia	1,201,173
	$2,512,421

Red Cross accounts do not separate expenditures on refugees in Yugoslavia alone. A total of $6,339,701 is given for refugees in Yugoslavia, Greece, Turkey, and Hungary. For statistical purposes, our estimate of expenditures to Yugoslavia after the Peace is about $3,700,000.

TWO CHARITABLE ORGANIZATIONS DEVOTED TO SERBIA

Our research revealed partial information on the following: Serbian Child Welfare Association of America—President, William J. Schieffelin; Treasurer, Murray H. Coggeshall. This organization carried on an extensive program of relief, child welfare, and public health, but we could find no details. Its funds expended in 1921 and 1922 are given as $1,355,072.

Serbian Aid Fund—President, Madame Slavko Grouitch; Treasurer, Otto T. Bannard. This fund engaged in the care of Serbian orphans and other special relief activities. Expenditures for these activities to April 30, 1921, were given as $112,417.

AMERICAN FRIENDS SERVICE COMMITTEE

After the Peace, the American Friends Service Committee undertook construction of homes in Serbia; it established a hospital in Petch; it re-established a former government agricultural school for training orphans. Its total expenditures in Serbia were $105,764.

THE CARNEGIE ENDOWMENT FOR INTERNATIONAL PEACE

On February 28, 1920, the Carnegie Endowment for International Peace voted an allotment of $100,000 to rebuild and equip the library of the University of Belgrade.

THE AMERICAN WOMEN'S HOSPITAL

The American Women's Hospital, which served in many countries, was of great help in Serbia. After the Peace, it sent a fully equipped hospital unit with 50 beds, 16 motor ambulances, drivers, and the requisite number of doctors and nurses. Just how much money the organization expended is not shown in its surviving records. The total expenditures in all countries exceeded $300,000. American Relief Administration records show that after the Peace, the American Women's Hospital purchased from them clothing and material weighing twenty-four tons at a cost of $35,211. Our estimate of total expenditures in Yugoslavia after the Peace is about $130,000.

JEWISH JOINT DISTRIBUTION COMMITTEE

This committee extended its services to Yugoslavia after the Peace, especially in training for trades, but its expenditures or detailed work are not recorded in its surviving records.

METHODIST EPISCOPAL CHURCH

In 1921, the Methodist Episcopal Church established a fund for Serbia. Gifts to this fund were placed directly in the hands of Bishop Nicholai of Serbia in appreciation for his services to his country. Some of the money went for helping orphans of Serbian clergy killed during the war. No details of the relief or expenditures survive.

SERBIAN EDUCATIONAL INSTITUTE

Dr. Rosalie S. Morton was Chairman of the Institute, Paul F. Cooley, Treasurer, and K. S. Ward, Executive Secretary. Funds expended from March 16, 1920, to December 31, 1921, were $31,408.

AMERICAN JUGO-SLAV RELIEF COMMITTEE

This organization raised $315,300 and was headed by Mrs. E. H. Harriman. Further information is not available.

NATIONAL LUTHERAN COUNCIL

From the Peace until 1923, the National Lutheran Council expended, for relief and reconstruction of churches in Yugoslavia, a total of $14,250.

SERBIAN NATIONAL DEFENSE LEAGUE

The only information available with regard to this organization shows a total of $21,867 expended up to March 31, 1920.

OTHER CHARITABLE AGENCIES

Other American organizations which also served in Serbia about which we have no information except their names were:

American Commission to Serbia for Restoration of Serbian Youth
Serbian Hospital Fund
Society of Serbian Mothers
Serbian Relief Committee

TOTAL SUPPLIES TO YUGOSLAVIA
FROM THE PEACE TO 1923 *

	Food	Clothing & Misc.	Total	$ Value
American Relief Administration				
Children's relief	138	180	318	$ 490,705
Yugoslav Government				
donation	2,634		2,634	533,677
American Red Cross	(quantities unknown)			3,700,000
Serbian Child Welfare Associa-				
tion of America	(quantities unknown)			1,355,072
Serbian Aid Fund	(quantities unknown)			112,417
American Friends Service				
Committee	(quantities unknown)			105,764
Carnegie Endowment for Inter-				
national Peace	(quantities unknown)			100,000
American Women's Hospital	(quantities unknown)			130,000
Serbian Educational Institute	(quantities unknown)			31,408
American Jugo-Slav Relief				
Committee	(quantities unknown)			315,300
National Lutheran Council	(quantities unknown)			14,250
Serbian National Defense League .	(quantities unknown)			21,867
				$6,910,460

* In tons.

RUMANIA, GREECE, ARMENIA, CHINA, AND IRELAND

RUMANIA

Rumania emerged from the Peace with an increase in population —from about 7,500,000 to about 16,000,000—and an increase in territory that doubled her prewar area. These gains were due partly to compliance with the promises the Allies had made to secure her entry into the war and partly by her own military conquests after the Armistice.

After Rumania joined in the war at the end of August, 1916, she was quickly invaded by German, Hungarian, and Austrian armies. During their occupation and upon their retreat at the Armistice, these armies engaged in the most complete looting of a country ever known in history. I have given some account of this atrocity earlier in this volume.[1] Rumania's food and work animals were reduced to about 30 per cent of the prewar total. All of her workable agricultural implements, machinery, railway rolling stock, and household goods which the enemy could find were carted off.

During the Armistice, the peasants, by herculean efforts, planted a fair crop. The Rumanians were given Transylvania by the Peace Conference. Having been part of the Austrian Empire, it had not been plundered, and the peasants then brought in a normal crop in the 1919 harvest. The Rumanian peasants, despite their handicaps from the looting of their machinery—and even seed—were able to bring in a considerable crop.

[1] See Chap. 16.

389

During this period, the Rumanians' oil-well equipment, nearly all of which had been destroyed or damaged, was largely repaired, and soon after the Peace Rumania was able to make large oil exports, the profits of which enabled her to buy many needs.

As I related in Chapter 44, the Rumanians invaded Hungary and did an efficient job of looting that country. Since they had suffered from the Hungarian Army (and other armies) prior to the Armistice, they claimed some justification for their actions. They took all they needed—or, rather, all that could be found—of railway rolling stock, agricultural and other machinery, and huge amounts of food, and they even looted the hospitals of surgical supplies and food.

Our appraisals showed that after the Peace the Rumanians had inadequate supplies of special food for restoration of their debilitated children, the ill, and the aged. We had already established our canteen system during the Armistice; we expanded this service and carried it on until November, 1919, when the Rumanian Government took over. During this period our canteens furnished 24,515,000 meals. They also distributed a Rumanian Government contribution of 2,327 tons of grain valued at $1,024,322.

Our staff in Rumania at this time consisted of

COLONEL WILLIAM N. HASKELL, Chief of Mission to Rumania (he remained until August, 1919, when he was transferred to Armenia);
LIEUTENANT COLONEL LYTTON G. AMENT, Chief of Children's Relief;
LIEUTENANT A. N. FREGEAU, Assistant to Chief of Children's Relief;
MAJOR ALAN G. GOLDSMITH, Distribution, Liaison and Executive Officer;
CAPTAIN J. ROLAND FOLLMER, Chief Clerk.

OTHER AMERICAN CHARITABLE ORGANIZATIONS

The American Red Cross had carried on extensive medical aid during the war in a small segment of Rumania not occupied by the German and Hungarian armies. It extended its service during the Armistice and continued it after the Peace. In this latter period, it was mainly engaged in fighting typhus and other infectious epidemics but was also rehabilitating hospitals and clinics. Its total expenditures after the Peace were $2,858,558.

The Jewish Joint Distribution Committee continued its work in Rumania after the Peace. Its work was being carried on through its committee on medical affairs and its committee on orphan and child care. The Jewish Joint Distribution Committee accounts show that it spent $2,203,512 for relief work in Rumania from the Peace until 1923.

After the Peace, four American representatives of the Y.M.C.A. were sent to Rumania to work with the Rumanian Army. They opened their usual huts. Forty-five Americans were recruited to manage the huts and conduct an athletic program. By 1921, the American representatives were released, and the welfare program was taken over by the Rumanian Army. We are not able to determine the Y.M.C.A.'s separate expenditures for Rumania.

In January, 1920, Queen Marie of Rumania requested the aid of the Y.W.C.A. in training social workers. Classes were opened and summer camps created in which the Y.W.C.A. workers taught their ways to the Rumanian women. Later, the American women established clubs for the Rumanian women factory workers. Eventually, the Y.W.C.A. was able to turn these programs over to Rumanian women. Surviving Y.W.C.A. accounts do not afford a statement regarding its expenditures.

The National Lutheran Council expended $78,666 in Rumania. The Southern Baptist Convention, the Presbyterian Church in the U.S.A., the Presbyterian Church, U.S. (South), and the Student Friendship Fund also expended funds in Rumania after the Peace, but we have no record of the work undertaken or the expenditures made.

Our research did, however, disclose two other organizations—the Society of Friends of Rumania, Inc., William Nelson Campbell, President, with expenditures of $7,935 and the Rumanian Relief Committee, T. Tileston Wells, Executive Officer, about which no financial information is available.

Our estimate is that after the Peace, the total expenditures of all American organizations, aside from the American Red Cross and the Jewish Joint Distribution Committee, were possibly $250,000.

TOTAL SUPPLIES TO RUMANIA FROM THE PEACE TO 1923 *

	Food	Clothing & Misc.	$ Value
American Relief Administration:			
Rumanian Government grain contribution	2,327		$1,024,322
American Red Cross	(quantities unknown)		2,858,558
Jewish Joint Distribution Committee	(quantities unknown)		2,203,512
Other American organizations	(quantities unknown)		250,000
			$6,336,392

* In tons.

CHAPTER 47

GREECE

A note on the political background of Greece during the war and its aftermath is necessary for the reader to understand her relief problems. Greece remained neutral until June 27, 1917, when she entered the war on the Allied side. During the war she was mostly self-supporting in essential supplies, and her deficiencies were largely provided by the British from the East Indies and Australia.

Turkey surrendered to the Allies eight months before the Peace. Six months later, Greece, with the approval of the Allies and the United States, landed troops and occupied Smyrna, in Turkish territory, where the population was largely Greek. In June, 1920, a year after the Peace, the Greeks extended the area of their military occupation—again with the approval of the European Allies.

On August 20, 1920, the Treaty of Sèvres was signed by the European Allies with the Sultan of Turkey, Mohammed VI. By its terms, Smyrna and the Ionian hinterland were to be administered by Greece for five years, with a plebiscite at the end of this period. However, the real government of Turkey had passed into the hands of the Nationalist Party, under the leadership of Mustapha Kemal Pasha. The Turkish Nationalists refused to recognize the treaty of August 20, 1920, and began building up the Turkish Army. In the spring of 1922, they attacked the Greeks at Smyrna. In September, the Greek Army collapsed, and a large part of the Greek section of the city was burned.

393

From the panic and continued pressures by Turkish troops came one of the most terrible migrations in history. Nearly one million demoralized Greek troops, Greek civilians, and other non-Moslem minorities escaped by ship, but only because they had the protection of the United States Navy. Mustapha Kemal Pasha and his Nationalist forces completed their victory by proclaiming the abolition of the Sultan on November 1, 1922.

The care of the mass of refugees arriving in Greece after the fall of Smyrna fell upon the great American charitable organizations, whose activities in Greece I will now discuss.

THE AMERICAN RED CROSS

On October 13, 1922, to meet the stupendous problem of relief, the American Red Cross dispatched to Greece a special mission comprised of physicians, surgeons, nurses, and sanitary engineers. During the nine months until June, 1923, when its service was completed and the work turned over to the Greek Government, the Red Cross established 59 hospitals with 1,751 beds. It treated 9,781 injured persons, 233,543 ambulatory cases, 6,091 typhus cases, 2,471 smallpox cases, 218 typhoid cases, 74,777 malaria cases, and 4,849 other cases of contagious diseases. It gave 114,934 vaccinations, 91,061 typhoid treatments, and 84,916 cholera injections. It established 66 typhus delousing stations and deloused 399,483 persons.

The total Red Cross expenditures in Greece from 1914 to December 31, 1923, were $4,805,401, most of which went for the care of the Smyrna refugees. Our estimate was about $4,500,000 expended on the refugees.

THE NEAR EAST RELIEF COMMITTEE

This committee had undertaken a minor role in Greece prior to the Smyrna debacle, its appropriations having been $9,682. But the Committee undertook a major role in mass feeding and provision of shelter for the refugees. Among its distinguished services was the supervision of the exchange of populations between Turkey and Greece. Some 200,000 Greeks and 360,000 Turks were repatriated between the two nations by 1923.

The Near East Relief appropriated, from the beginning of its work in Greece to the end of 1923, a total of $922,540.

THE JEWISH JOINT DISTRIBUTION COMMITTEE

The Jewish Joint Distribution Committee had conducted relief work for its co-religionists as early as 1914. Its expenditures in Greece cannot be separated from those in neighboring states. Under the title "Greece, Turkey, Serbia and Syria," the J.D.C. records a total expenditure of $1,399,181 from 1914 to December, 1923. Our estimate of its expenditures in Greece after the Peace is $400,000.

THE AMERICAN RELIEF ADMINISTRATION

This organization, under my direction, undertook the purchase and transportation of foodstuffs for the Red Cross in its work for the Greek refugees. The A.R.A. delivered 20,374 tons of food at a cost of $1,211,950, which amount was reimbursed to us by the Red Cross. Our contribution was that we made no charge for our overhead expenses, which amounted to about $60,000.

OTHER AMERICAN CHARITABLE ORGANIZATIONS OPERATING IN GREECE

Prior to the Smyrna incident, the Young Men's Christian Association established huts for Greek soldiers in Athens, Corfu, Salonika, and later in Smyrna. By November, 1920, it had 34 huts in operation, with a daily average attendance of between four and five thousand men.

The Young Women's Christian Association joined with the Near

East Relief Committee in providing homes for women released from harems and in promoting and aiding their education. We are not able to make an estimate of its expenditures.

TOTAL SUPPLIES TO GREECE FROM THE PEACE TO 1923 *

	Total	$ Value
American Relief Administration:		
Overhead expenses		$ 60,000
American Red Cross	20,374	1,211,950
Near East Relief Committee	(quantities unknown)	922,540
Jewish Joint Distribution Committee	(quantities unknown)	400,000
American Red Cross (funds in addition to those purchased and transported by the A.R.A.)	(quantities unknown)	3,593,451
		$6,187,941

* In tons.

CHAPTER 48

ARMENIA

The Peace certainly did not bring an end to suffering in Armenia. A day before the Peace Treaty was signed, I wrote to President Wilson proposing a way to continue aid to the Armenians:

PARIS, 27 June 1919

DEAR MR. PRESIDENT:

In accordance with your discussion with Mr. Morgenthau and the several discussions with myself in connection with Armenia, we make the following joint recommendations to be brought to the attention of the Chiefs of State before your departure.

1) We suggest that a single temporary resident Commissioner should be appointed to Armenia, who will have the full authority of the United States, Great Britain, France and Italy in all their relations to the de facto Armenian Government, as the joint representative of these Governments in Armenia. His duties shall be so far as he may consider necessary to supervise and advise upon various governmental matters in the whole of Russian and Turkish Armenia, and to control relief and repatriation questions pending the determination of the political destiny of this area.

2) In case the various Governments should agree to this plan, immediate notification should be made to the de facto Governments of Turkey and of Armenia of his appointment and authority. Furthermore, he will be appointed to represent the American Relief Administration and the . . . Committee for Relief in the Near East, and take entire charge of all their activities in Russian and Turkish Armenia.

The ideal man for this positon would be General Harbord, as I assume under all the circumstances it would probably be desirable to appoint an American. Should General Harbord be unable to undertake the matter, I am wondering whether you would leave it to us to select the man in conjunction with General Pershing.

I assume that the personnel of this Mission would be necessarily comprised of army and navy officers who would retain their rank and emoluments and I understand from the . . . Near East [Relief Committee] that they would be prepared to supply such funds as were required for incidental expenses until such other arrangements could be made.

HERBERT HOOVER

The President secured the approval of the Supreme Council, and it agreed to notify the surrounding governments that they would have to respect the new organization. The Council also agreed that the High Commissioner should be an American.

Major Joseph C. Green and his staff, representing the official American Government relief agencies, had been in continuous service in Eastern Europe and Armenia under nerve-racking conditions for more than six months. At the Peace, they urgently requested that they be allowed to return home. Since General James G. Harbord proved to be unavailable, my colleagues and I decided that Colonel William N. Haskell was the man for this position. He was then administering our relief in Rumania.

On July 3, I wrote to Secretary of State Lansing proposing the appointment of Colonel Haskell and also asking that something more effective be done about the interference in our work by the Georgian Government:

PARIS, 3 July 1919

DEAR MR. SECRETARY:

In respect to the authorization and of the acceptance in principle by the Heads of State that an American should be selected to represent the various Powers . . . at the de facto Government of Russian Armenia, and to take entire charge of the relief measures in that quarter, I beg to . . . suggest . . . Colonel William N. Haskell. Colonel Haskell has had charge of the relief measures in Roumania. . . .

On July 5, the Supreme Council agreed to the appointment of Colonel Haskell. The next day, I notified Major Green of Colonel

Haskell's appointment, requesting that he and his staff remain until the Colonel's arrival and that as many of his staff who felt they could do so remain to aid the Colonel.

We had constantly consulted the Near East Relief Committee with regard to our proposed steps, and it was in full agreement with our action. It continued its magnificent services in providing orphanages, hospitals, and medical aid. I assured the Committee that we would seek financial aid for it if it became necessary.

To replace Major Green and his staff, Colonel Haskell, at my suggestion, enlisted a staff of regular American Army officers—a task in which he was aided by General Pershing.

On July 13, Premier Clemenceau issued the following statement:

Colonel W. N. Haskell, of the United States Army, has been designated by the Supreme Council of the Allied and Associated Powers, under date of July 5, 1919, to fulfill in Armenia the functions of High Commissioner, in the name of the Governments of the United States of America, the British Empire, France and Italy. It is understood that Colonel Haskell will be at the same time charged with all measures tending to aid Armenia, with the assistance of the various aid societies operating in the region. All the American, British, French and Italian representatives in Armenia, Georgia, Azerbaijan and at Constantinople will immediately receive instructions to lend aid and assistance to Colonel Haskell.

CLEMENCEAU
The President of the Peace Conference

On July 16, I sent a note to the Supreme Council through our American delegation concerning the continued holding up of our supplies by the Georgian Government. After a short description of what was going on, I stated:

I quite realize that the situation is one beyond the strength of the Allied Military forces at present in occupation in the Caucasus, but I am well aware of the aspirations of the Georgian authorities for consideration before the Supreme Council. I believe it might do some good if the Council could despatch a very strongly worded telegram to the Georgian authorities . . . and . . . if the Georgian representatives in Paris . . . were given information to the same import. My suggestion is that the telegram should be phrased in somewhat the following manner:—

"The Council has been made aware of the interference of the Georgian authorities with food supplies being sent into Armenia in an endeavor on the part of the Allied Governments to stem the tide of starvation and death amongst these unfortunate people. The Council cannot state in too strong terms that it will not tolerate such interference and that the action taken hitherto by the Georgian authorities and the continuation of such action must entirely prejudice the case of the Georgian authorities, not only before this Council but before the court of public opinion of the world. The Council therefore expects that the authorities in Georgia shall not only give the privilege of transportation over the railway routes which they at present control, but will devote themselves to assisting in the transmission of these supplies without more than the normal charge and remuneration for such service. The Council awaits the reply of the authorities in Georgia as to whether or not they are prepared to acquiesce in this arrangement."

This note was delivered at once to the President of Georgia by the French Mission in Tiflis.

On July 19, I sent a letter of introduction for Colonel Haskell to each of the British, French, and Italian officials representing their affairs in the Caucasus. I also sent the following letter to the President of the Georgian Republic:

PARIS, July 19, 1919

THE PRESIDENT OF THE GOVERNMENT OF GEORGIA
EXCELLENCY:

I have the honor to introduce to you Colonel W. N. Haskell, United States Army, who has been designated by the Council of Heads of Delegations of the Peace Conference, as High Commissioner in Armenia, and in this capacity representing the interests of the United States of America, the British Empire, France and Italy.

In addition to his political office, the High Commissioner in Armenia will have entire direction of the . . . allied relief organizations in Armenia.

This High Commissioner's mission is necessarily of interest to the Georgian people, and . . . I take great pleasure in transmitting this letter to you, with the request that you lend this High Commissioner every possible aid and comfort in his operations.

HERBERT HOOVER

However, our troubles were not solely with Georgia. A united military movement against Armenia by the Azerbaijanese and Turks now began. On July 28, I received from Armenia a much delayed telegram from Major Green. It was dated July 23:

HOOVER, *Paris*

Long conference with Armenian President today. . . . Situation growing worse. Turkish Army well prepared and Tartars [Azerbaijanese] advancing from three sides. If military protection is not . . . [sent to] Armenia immediately disaster will be more terrible than massacres of 1915, and the Armenian nation will be crushed, to everlasting shame of Allied Powers. Predict that relief work will become impossible in present situation unless order is restored. Cannot something be done to have British forces in Caucasus intervene to save Armenia. . . . Green.

On July 24, I received a second telegram from Major Green:

HOOVER, *Paris*

Turks and Tartars advancing [on Armenia]. In districts of Karabagh and Zangezus they now occupy approximately reopened territory of Russian Armenia. Khalil Bey, Turkish Colonel now in command Azerbaijan Tartars. Relief depots and relief trains surrounded and probably seized. British state orders from above prevent their interfering. Armenian Government and people almost in despair. General mobilization ordered yesterday taking away men just as harvest begins. We shall not be able to carry on relief work much longer unless British receive orders to clear all Russian Armenia including Karabagh and Zangezus of Turk and Tartar forces.

GREEN

On August 5, I received a third telegram from him:

HOOVER, *Paris*

Turkish and Tartar military aggressions and massacres in Armenia continue. French Mission considers situation desperate as Armenians running out of cartridges. Long talk with British Commander in Chief this morning. He states [that he] cannot protect relief work and has so . . . [advised] British High Command Constantinople. States orders from above prevent his . . . [interference] Armenia and could do nothing effective with troops under his command even if authorized to do so.

Our magazine Nakhichevan surrounded. . . . Impossible to obtain seed wheat for fall planting until railroad from Persia reopened. Large proportion of present harvest has fallen into hands of Turks and Tartars. Immediate military measures imperative if relief work is to be continued and remnants of Armenian nation saved.

Georgian government given twenty-four hours to reply to note from Clemenceau re[garding] relief traffic. Has let three days pass without reply[ing]. Do not believe [that] Georgian Government much impressed by notes unless backed up by armed forces. . . .

On July 30, 1919, Captain A. M. Barton of the Near East Relief Committee reported on the situation:

Frequent engagements between the local Tartar [Azerbaijanese] and Armenian villagers together with clashes between the local organized forces of the contending factions have occurred, resulting in the burning of villages, murdering of the inhabitants and of the laying waste of crops of both sides, with no prospect of any satisfactory solution being reached or a cessation of hostilities on either side. . . . On June 4th at 10 o'clock in the morning, actual fighting in the town of Shusha between the Armenians and Azerbaidjan forces began. About 50 Armenians who happened [to be] in the Tartar quarter were murdered in the street and a number of Armenian travellers on the road between Shusha and Agdam were also murdered. Firing continued within the town and many casualties resulted. The British Mission made repeated but unsuccessful attempts to stop the fighting. British officers were fired upon by both sides while carrying white flags. . . . In the afternoon of the same date Tartars and Kurds came down from the neighboring hills and started to burn and plunder the villages of Kaibalikend, Djamillon, Palioul and Karaidajan and massacre the population. . . .

On August 5, I received another telegram from Major Green dated July 29:

Hoover, *Paris*

Georgian reply to Clemenceau's note received. Considered . . . generally unsatisfactory by British Commander in Chief, Chief French Mission and self. Do not however anticipate large scale interference on part of Georgia for the present. . . .

Green

On August 9, the following telegram was received by the American Embassy in Paris from American Consul Doolittle in Tiflis:

Situation reported as criticised in recent telegrams from this Consulate has now become tragic if not altogether hopeless. July 20th massacre of 400 Armenians with destruction of six villages is reported from Nakhitchevan. Four American relief workers disappeared in Tiflis district and their fate unknown. One English officer reported killed and another missing. Armed bands of Kurds have passed Turkish frontier and are advancing on Igdir. Fighting is going on in district of Alexandropole. Only 400,000 at best remain in all Armenia. This commences last chapter of Armenian History and unless adequate forces are immediately sent Armenian question will be automatically settled by their practical extinction nation. Unofficial advices indicate that Col. Ingle is arriving to consolidate relief organizations. Under present conditions relief without military support practically amounts to fattening the victim for the slaughtering. . . .

DOOLITTLE

Major Green and Consul Doolittle, no doubt, were too distraught to evaluate the potency of the Clemenceau note. The Georgians corrected their behavior for a while. The Azerbaijanese and the Turks at once withdrew their forces from Armenia.

Again the British wished to remove their forces from the Caucasus, but it was essential that their troops remain until Colonel Haskell could get into action. Since the President was now back in Washington, I sent a telegram to our New York office on August 7 for delivery to Cleveland Dodge of the Near East Relief Committee. I asked him to use his influence in Washington to retain the British forces in the trouble zone. As a result of Mr. Dodge's action, the British again put off the withdrawal for some months.

Colonel Haskell took charge in Armenia on August 15, 1919, with his entirely new personnel from the regular American Army. At once, the Colonel and the prestige of his position began to take effect. He obtained arms from the British for the ragged Armenian Army, and the Near East Relief Committee secured some clothing for them. Soon order was established and the dangers from the surrounding states were under control (with exceptions).

The official American Government relief supplies, which we had piled up in Armenia just before the end of our official life at the Peace, and the supplies secured from our "voyage of the *Kickapoo*," plus those from the American Relief Administration, enabled us to feed the population and provide seed for the 1920 harvest. The Near East Relief Committee carried on its work with devotion in orphanages, hospitals, and schools.

The "voyage of the *Kickapoo*" referred to above was a cargo of trade goods which our organization had obtained, on Mr. Heinz's advice, from American Army surplus before the Peace. These trade goods were exchanged for food from north of the Black Sea in Russia. The trading yielded the Armenians more than 8,000 tons of wheat, which, if shipped from the United States, would have cost about $1,000,000. And there were some trade goods left over, which Colonel Haskell used profitably. But the lives of Colonel Haskell and his staff were filled with constant tribulation.

The whole Transcaucasus was thrown into a ferment at the Peace. The Georgians, the Azerbaijanese, and the Armenians were rightly determined to maintain themselves as independent nations, but, except for the uncertain stay of the British Army, they were dependent upon General Denikin's "White" army to the north of them for protection from Communist invasion. A few quotations from reports involving hundreds of thousands of words will indicate some of the Colonel's problems and also contribute to the history of the Caucasus during that period. He reported on November 6, 1919, as follows:

. . . Georgia attempts to blackmail Armenia on transportation questions, and without our constant intervention would not permit merchandise or foodstuffs to pass freely. We force the matter, however, and Georgia acquiesces.

. . . Georgia's main trouble in life is the fear that Denikin will come south and annex them, and they are consequently always ready to resist him if he attempts to move south of the Caucasus mountains. All other questions are small compared with this great one, but they have their other boundary troubles to the south, east and west.

The Georgians do not know what their future will be, but they care little what it may be so long as they do not go back to the Russians. . . .

In this same report, the Colonel continued:

The Government of Azerbaijan is run by a Clique of Tartars, who are somewhat under the influence of Turkey . . . The Tartars are really savages under their skin.

. . . Armenia's relations with Turkey need no explanation, and while the Turkish army is obeying the armistice, and remaining south of the Russo-Turkish frontier, they do not hesitate to permit roving bands of Kurds to cross into the southern part of Armenia to rob and pillage, and to terrify the population and consequently to pile them up on the already overcrowded villages more to the north. It is even stated, and I believe it, that Turkish officers and enlisted men, some times in uniform, take part in these raids.

Armenia's relations with AZERBAIJAN are as bad as possible short of actual warfare. As a matter of fact, a state of irregular warfare exists continually, to the east of Russian Armenia, with the Tartars, particularly as a result of boundary disputes, and alleged mistreatment of Tartars by Armenians, and of Armenians by Tartars.

In order to pacify this frontier, I have created a neutral zone, under an American Governor [the American Minister at Tiflis], which comprises two districts just north of the Persian frontier and between Russian Armenia and Azerbaijan. By creating this neutral zone, we have re-opened the railroad from Armenia to Persia, and the Indo-European telegraph line, which had been interrupted by hostilities for three months.

Armenia's relation[s] with GEORGIA, are not so bad as with Azerbaijan. The Georgians claim that they desire an Armenia to their south for protection against Turkey, but there are several boundary disputes. . . .

On December 17, 1919, I received a cable from Colonel Haskell on his return to Armenia after a short visit to our Paris and London offices. Some of his paragraphs were:

. . . the condition of affairs, politically, in the Caucasus on my return there rapidly growing worse. . . . the Government of Azerbaijan has not held to the agreement which was concluded before I left, in respect to the neutral zone fixed between Armenia and Azerbaijan. . . . The Governments of Azerbaijan and Georgia are in a state of apprehension, fearing an attack by Denikin from the north. . . . I am making every endeavor to cause hostilities in Zangezour to cease, and also to put a stop to an outbreak which may probably take place near Erivan, but I feel uncertain how long it will be possible for me to keep control of the situation inasmuch as I have no [foreign] troops. In addition there is existing in the Caucasus an undercurrent of Bolshevik sentiment, and this may come to the surface. . . . There is a greater necessity than ever to have troops here. . . . For the purpose of bringing about complete order, we should have here quickly at least 5,000 troops. . . . What Governments shall furnish the troops is a matter of unimportance to me, but in my opinion this is the only method to make peace sure.

Five months later, on May 27, 1920, Colonel Haskell reported on the rising Communist conspiracies:

. . . I went on to Erivan . . . I motored from Erivan into Delijan, the so-called Bolshevik town . . . and found that the [Turkish] government troops from Karaklis had arrived and that after an attempt on the Bolshevik-Armenians to induce the . . . arrivals to become Bolsheviks . . . and upon their refusal to acquiesce, they had all decided to become good Armenians and were all starting out, hand in hand, to fight the Soviet troops from Russia, in the direction of Azerbaidjan.

On this same day an armistice which had been concluded between Georgia and Azerbaidjan for seven days duration, was broken in less than twenty-four hours and hostilities resumed, a new alliance having been made between Georgia and Armenia.

As far as Tiflis is concerned, it might go Bolshevik in twelve hours or twelve months. We hope, however, that it won't go Bolshevik before the middle of July, by which time sufficient flour will have been transported into Armenia to carry them to the harvest.

Incidentally, I motored over most of Armenia this week and found that they have already planted more than 50% larger acreage than ever before in the history of Armenia. The entire planting may reach as high as 75% to 100% over and above any previous year in their history. This is particularly gratifying to me for the reason that my mission undertook to provide seed and other means to make possible this increased planting, and organized the collection and distribution of all seeds, as well as impressed the peasant with the necessity for planting.

For a time here, it looked as though the whole game was over, inasmuch as four or five [Armenian] garrisons in Armenia had gone Bolshevik . . . ultimatums had passed between Georgia and the British Military Government. . . . Traffic, therefore, was absolutely at a standstill at three points. . . .

Twelve days later, I received a letter from the Colonel. It was dated June 8, 1920:

MY DEAR MR. HOOVER:

. . . We have been through everything that I can think of during the past year. We have created neutral zones, appointed governors, changed Ministers, operated railroads, built up and rationed the Armenian army, obtained ammunition for them, made all of their business deals with their neighbors, kept their officials from stealing our supplies, held the Kurds and Turks off of their back, and overcome every known diabolical obstruction . . . the Georgians . . . the Azerbaidjans, [the] Russians and others, have been able to think up and place in our way, to extort either money or supplies from us on one pretense or another. It has many times looked as though the whole thing were over. . . .

. . . A few months ago, after Deniken's collapse, the British government notified the republics of Transcaucasia that arms and ammunition would be furnished them and that instructors would come to assist their armies. They were being encouraged to form a barrier between Bolshevism and the Turk. Nothing was furnished, however. . . . The Bolsheviks came closer and closer and the Transcaucasian republics became more nervous and more nervous. Delegations left the various republics to make some arrangements with the Bolsheviks. Suddenly Baku fell, in the latter part of April. This shook all of Transcaucasia and scared Armenia nearly to death.

. . . They need some assurance as to the future—some encouragement, some recognition, some financing, or at least, some communication which will say to these republics that the Allies are really backing them up and will do something for them. . . .

A further letter from Colonel Haskell on the progress of Communization, dated June 24, states:

MY DEAR MR. HOOVER:

. . . several . . . Americans, reached here from Baku and gave us the story of what has transpired in Azerbaidjan since the Bolsheviks took over the country.

When the old government of Baku [in Azerbaijan] was turned over, late in April, the Turks seemed to be in charge of everything and the people of Azerbaidjan thought that it was a mere change in form of government. By degrees, however, Russian Bolshevik troops increased in number and the reins of government were gradually transferred to Russian hands. As this has taken place, the Turks have been disappearing. Upon the arrival of the Bolsheviks, they sealed all warehouses and requisitioned practically all valuable personal property and began to ship oil rapidly to Russia. The prices of all commodities immediately jumped in value from 500% to 800% and the Tartar [Azerbaijan] population began to become more distressed and more hostile to their new over-lords, day by day. Finally, an organized insurrection was started at Elizabethpol and the Tartars [Azerbaijanese] were in a fair way to drive the Bolsheviks out of Azerbaidjan. . . . At this juncture the Armenians in Azerbaidjan rose up and aligned themselves with the Bolsheviks, with the result that the Tartar insurrection was struck in the back and was completely killed. It is reported by the Americans that nearly 10,000 Tartars [Azerbaijanese] were killed in Elizabethpol as a result of this operation. Immediately thereafter, the entire Tartar section of this city was gutted of everything, to the last box of matches.

The hatred of the Tartars against the Bolsheviks has continually increased, and it is the opinion of these Americans that another effort will be made to drive the Russians out of Azerbaidjan as soon as the harvest has been gathered. . . .

A report by Colonel Haskell on the rehabilitation of the children, the progress of agriculture and industry, and the economic self-sufficiency of the Armenian people was the one ray of sunlight through the threatening clouds of Communism. The Colonel stated that, having assured an abundant harvest for the Armenians and considering that their army was as good as it could be made, he felt his mission was over.

On July 26, 1920, I reviewed the situation in Armenia in a report to Secretary of State Robert Lansing:

Dear Mr. Secretary:

. . . in order to meet the desperate need of the Armenian population . . . at my suggestion . . . Colonel William N. Haskell was appointed High Commissioner to Armenia, representing the United States, Great Britain, France and Italy. His commission was signed by M. Clemenceau as President of the Peace Conference.

The authority centered in the High Commissioner as Joint Representative of the several Allied Powers gave him the powerful support which he required to overcome those racial and political antagonisms . . . which

were threatening the total annihilation of the Armenian people. The work
of this mission was . . . to . . . provide requirements up to the point
when the succeeding crops would render general contributions of food
stuffs from overseas unnecessary . . . [to] extend the charitable work of
the Near East Relief in caring for refugees, orphans and destitutes; to
represent the American Relief Administration; [in provision of supplies
and] . . . to assist in re-establishing stable conditions in the Republic of
Armenia.

Colonel Haskell, supported by an efficient and devoted staff, has carried
out his difficult duties in an admirable manner. . . .

. . . All the American Military Staff are to be withdrawn at once. He
proposes, as of August first . . . to present his resignation to the Council
of Ambassadors in Paris.

With Colonel Haskell's resignation my intervention in the management
of this branch of European Relief will also come to an end.

I respectfully suggest, Mr. Secretary, that the State Department notify
the . . . [Supreme Council] in Paris of the resignation of Colonel Haskell
to be handed to them August 1st, 1920.

HERBERT HOOVER

Although the Colonel and his staff departed, the Near East Relief
Committee continued with its beneficent work—but the end was inevitable. A telegram from Consul-General Charles K. Moser to the
Secretary of State on December 4, 1920, sounded the beginning of
the end of Armenian independence. Moser said:

It is officially announced at Erivan, December 2nd, that Armenia is declared Soviet republic. The new government will consist of five Bolshevik
commissaries and two members of the Dashnak Party, General Dro and
Terterrian, former appointed military dictator in the field with Silin probably Russian Commissary for Military Affairs. Soviet Russian Ambassador
has announced Russia's recognition of the new Soviet republic.

Overthrow of the Armenian Cabinet, formed a week ago, followed
occupation by Russian troops from Baku of the Armenian frontier
towns. . . .

Finding it will be impossible to proceed with the work or to receive
assurance of safety under the Bolshevik regime, Director . . . Yarrow has
secured Turkish military protection and is removing entire Near East personnel and stores to trains going to Kars. Thus he is forced to abandon

orphans and American relief work of five years. Relief work in Armenia proper no longer possible. . . .[1]

MOSER

However, the Near East Relief Committee staff, with an unquenchable faith, carried on for a while under the Communists but finally had to retreat.

TOTAL SUPPLIES TO ARMENIA FROM THE PEACE TO 1923 *

	Food	Clothing & Misc.	Total	$ Value
American Relief Administration:				
Congressional Appropriation (March, 1920)	40,633		40,633	$4,813,744
American Red Cross (freight) . .				500,000
Near East Relief Committee (freight)				532,790
The Commonwealth Fund (child feeding)	3,762		3,762	746,107
Near East Relief Committee	6,858	546	7,404	1,411,330
	51,253	546	51,799	8,003,971

* In tons.

The British transported our supplies [bought with money from the Congressional appropriation] at a cost of $560,000. They probably gave other aid, of which we have no record.

EPILOGUE

Although the free nation and homeland of Armenians was snuffed out, it did not mean the end of the Armenian nationality. Because of the efforts of the Near East Relief Committee, there survived in the Middle East large groups of Armenians who in later years lived amiably with their Turkish and Arabian neighbors. The Armenians who have migrated to the United States are a contribution to our country. With their vitality and an extraordinary intellectual quality, they have contributed to learning, to art, to benevolence, and to enterprise over the whole free world.

[1] *U.S. Foreign Relations, 1930*, Vol. III, pp. 806–807.

CHAPTER 49

CHINA AND IRELAND

There were two countries not engaged in hostilities which required American charitable action: China and Ireland.

FAMINE IN CHINA

A devastating drought in North China greatly reduced the crops of 1920. In response to an appeal for help from the Chinese Government, the American China Famine Fund was organized, with Thomas W. Lamont as Chairman and Norman H. Davis as Treasurer. The Fund secured an investigation by American officials and the various American missionary agencies in China concerning the extent of the famine. The reports showed that the drought had extended over the provinces of Chihli, Shantung, and large sections of Honan, Shansi, and Shensi, and that at least twenty million persons were already affected by acute famine.

On December 10, 1920, President Wilson issued a proclamation supporting the Fund, and on March 21, 1921, President Harding further urged its support. The appeal was aided not only by state organizations but also by religious bodies and groups throughout the country. The total funds raised amounted to $7,750,420, and when the new crop restored supplies, there remained on hand $1,-250,000, which was devoted to creating a foundation that could serve in similar emergencies.

411

THE RELIEF OF IRELAND

The American Committee for Relief to Ireland was organized in 1921, with Morgan J. O'Brien, Chairman; John F. Lucey, National Director; the Honorable Richard Campbell, Secretary; and John J. Pulleyn, Treasurer.

The Committee served to relieve acute distress in parts of Ireland, providing food, shelter, restoration of buildings, and furnishing raw materials. Its funds were distributed through the Irish White Cross. Little information about this Committee survives after more than forty years; however, our research shows that at one time it had raised a total of $4,778,353.

Another fund for Ireland should be mentioned in this narrative, the Shamrock Fund. Only its name survives.

EXPRESSIONS OF APPRECIATION FROM THE EUROPEAN NATIONS

CHAPTER 50

EXPRESSIONS OF GRATITUDE
FROM
CENTRAL AND SOUTHERN EUROPE

Before entering the complicated problems of Russian relief, it is desirable to register the expressions of gratitude of the countries of Central and Eastern Europe. The files of the American Relief Administration contain literally tens of thousands of such expressions. They came in toilsomely prepared books, often of wallpaper and often signed by a thousand children. They came in elaborate leatherbound books signed by local authorities. They came from the highest officials in each country. A few paragraphs from some of these, conveying deep sentiments of thankfulness to the American people, are here reproduced.

LATVIA

RIGA, September 28, 1922

DEAR MR. BROWN:

. . . This important event [recognition] which filled every Latvian patriot's heart with deep enthusiasm reminded our people anew of the great assistance which the unlimited generosity of the American Nation has extended to them during the hardest period of Latvia's struggle for her independence. The Latvian Government and people will always gratefully remember the great work done in Latvia by the American Relief Administration during the past three and a half years. They will never forget the quick help given to our hungering population in the summer of 1919 after the expulsion of the Bolsheviks, and they are aware of the splendid results of the children's relief work most efficiently operated in our country by your Administration on the largest scale. This work which has alleviated so many sufferings has gained our people's wholehearted sympathy for the

American Nation, and it was a deep satisfaction to them to see Latvia recognized by your noble country which has always been upholding the ideals of liberty and humanity.

On behalf of the Government of Latvia, I have the honor to express to the American Relief Administration our heartfelt gratitude for the invaluable assistance extended to the Latvian people during the past three and a half years. . . .

Yours faithfully,
ULMANIS
Prime Minister of Latvia

ESTONIA

REVAL, May 19, 1920

To the American Relief Administration:

. . . The grand help of the American people to the Esthonian children came just during the critical days of our war for independence, when the Esthonian people had not only to defend themselves desperately against a manifold stronger enemy, but also to go through a critical and difficult economic crisis, for the long years of war, the time of the German occupation and the dreadful days of the Bolshevist invasion have completely destroyed the former welfare of Esthonia. The country was deprived of all its most necessary provisions in stock as well as of other goods.

If the [generous] American support would have failed, a great number of Esthonian children might have fallen victims of the heavy shortage of food. Thousands of children would have been deprived of the possibility to attend school owing to the lack of warm clothes and footwear.

The American magnanimous support during the days of hardship has filled the hearts of the Esthonian people with feelings of deep gratitude towards the powerful American nation and with a profound admiration for the perfect arrangement of the Relief work.

The Government of the Esthonian Republic expresses herewith to the American Relief Administration and to its indefatigable collaborators in the name of the thankful Esthonian people and of thousands of joyful Esthonian children their deepest gratitude for all the rich help and support granted to the Esthonian children in their days of privation.

In the name of the Esthonian Republic
Prime Minister, J. TONNISON
For Minister of Labor and Public Works
A. CULP
For Minister of State Affairs
K. TERRAS

POLAND

Christmas 1920

To Mr. Hoover:

From the depths of our hearts we are sending thanks to our friends in America. The gifts of the American people to our children are the more valuable because they represent voluntary offers of countless American households. Today our children rejoice that they eat their Christmas dinner not as mere strangers but as the absent guests of a million of American homes.

Marshal Pilsudski

March 30th, 1920

My dear Mr. Hoover,

I am so happy to have an opportunity to send you once more, a few words of most sincere thanks. You can realize neither the immense amount of good you have done to my people, nor the joy you have given me, to see so many children with rosy cheeks and bright eyes. . . .

Thousands and thousands of blessings from their mothers went to you and I am sure that their prayers were not only for you, but also for your dear ones.

. . . My husband asks me to be an interpreter of his most sincere and affectionate regards. . . .

Most sincerely and gratefully yours,
Helene Paderewska

Warsaw, May 7, 1922 Press Release

The American Relief Administration Mission to Poland, which has brought constant relief to our children during the past three years, will cease its activities on June 1st, 1922. At the time immediately following the world war and during the economic crisis of our country the relief action initiated by Mr. Hoover and conducted by the A.R.A. Mission under his direction rendered immense services to Poland. This work has meant health and life to over one and a half million children, thus preserving a generation for Poland which in large part would otherwise have perished during the hard days through which our country struggled after the war.

The entire population of Poland worships the name of Hoover and surrounds with gratitude and esteem all his countrymen who have cooperated with the relief action in Poland. . . .

As the economic and agricultural conditions of the country have gradually become normal we are in a position, and we consider it our duty, to take over the work carried on up to date by the generous American people. . . .

ANTONI PONIKOWSKI
President of the Ministers

GERMANY

BERLIN, GERMANY, April 9, 1921

THE HON. HERBERT HOOVER:

With regret I have learned that the American Relief Administration has decided to discontinue . . . [at the] end of July of this year. . . . [Thus an end comes to] one of the greatest work of human kindness, a work you have called into being in Europe's . . . [darkest] times.

I desire to express to you on this occasion the appreciation of the German people for the help which has relieved so many suffering families, mothers and children [in Germany]. You have . . . [through your] organization understood . . . [how to find] the way . . . which the natural charitable tendencies of the American [people] could . . . [be called to life]. The German people will not forget the great work with which your name has become known [over] the . . . [whole world]. The bond of humanity . . . [strengthened during the] times of . . . [greatest] suffering . . . [by your work will contribute to] the mutual understanding of the people . . . [of the world]. . . .

. . . You have rendered a service to humanity that will outlive the work of your organization.

It gives me pleasure to take this opportunity to assure you of my . . . [sincerest appreciation.]

EBERT
[President of the German Republic]

CZECHOSLOVAKIA

December 16, 1919

. . . I desire particularly to give thanks for the generous support you and your American friends have given to relieve the distress of our undernourished country. Under the leadership of Mr. Herbert Hoover, the American Relief Administration European Children's fund has been created for the all-important purpose of restoring our children to their rightful status of normal health, and to bring back to them the advantages denied during the war. . . .

T. G. MASARYK,
President of the Czecho-Slovak Republic

HUNGARY

January 1922

To HERBERT HOOVER:

. . . I thank you with full heart in name of Hungary for the saving of Health and Life of many of its children and for goodwill and sympathy . . .

Prime Minister TELEKI of Hungary

January 11, 1923

The Honorable HERBERT HOOVER
Chairman, American Relief Administration
SIR:

I take great pleasure in informing you that, in recognition of its merits in relieving the misery following the World War and the Revolution, as well as in charity work in Hungary generally, His Serene Highness the Regent of Hungary, by his decision of September 25, 1922, in Godello, has awarded the Star of Merit of the Hungarian Red Cross to the American Relief Administration.

. . . Accept, Sir, the renewed assurance of my highest consideration.

L. SZECHENYI,
Royal Hungarian Minister [to the United States]

November, 1922

The people of Hungary are deeply grateful to the people of America for the great and effective relief work done here by The American Relief Administration in its administering of the European Children's Fund. This work has saved from death and disease many of our children. It has noticeably contributed to the improvement of the health of the people of Hungary. It has aided in maintaining satisfactory social conditions and social relationships among our people. The American Relief Administration has been a great help in bringing our people to a more normal state of living and thus curbing any idea of violence or political upheaval. This American Relief work has also aided in the economic recovery of Hungary by permitting the minds of the people to be directed to constructive work rather than to vain consideration of misery and hardship. The economic recovery, which we expect and toward which we are working, has been aided in no small degree, I feel sure, by the valuable and systematic work of the American Relief Administration. It is not only for the lives and health of our children that Hungary is thankful to America, but for the resultant effort in political and economic stability and social improvement.

F. BERNOLAK

Royal Hungarian Minister of Public Affairs

AUSTRIA

VIENNA, 14 December 1921

. . . Our debt to Mr. Hoover, to his band of workers, known and loved here as the American Relief Administration . . . and to the American people who, with open hands, have supported them, can never be repaid. The happier faces and stronger . . . [bodies] of our children tell, better than any words of mine, what we owe. And we are indebted for more than human kindness. The science, research and efficiency which have marked the system of American relief in Austria have been the means of emphasizing not only the permanent necessity of child-care by the State but the best way to attain it. One of the youngest among the Republics is happy thus to acknowledge its debt to the eldest of all the Republics. . . .

I have the honor to be,

Yours sincerely,

HAINISCH

President of Austria

THE VATICAN

MY DEAR MR. HOOVER:

Through our beloved son the Cardinal Archbishop of Baltimore, we have been again informed of the truly wonderful and providential work that you are still carrying on to meet the grave and manifold needs from which Europe is suffering from lack of food. The splendid services you have already rendered in this regard, which assure you without doubt an abiding place in the history of Christian charity and give you an unique title to the gratitude of peoples, fill Us alike with heartful satisfaction and consolation at the prospect of the great good that will thus accrue to the needy multitudes of Europe.

We have learned that you are now devoting your timely and earnest endeavors in a special way in behalf of the suffering little ones. What you did to succor the helpless children of Belgium at a time when the utter lack of proper food threatened their frail lives,—all this is fresh and living in Our memory. . . . We fervently pray God that He may be pleased to bestow upon you His very choicest rewards.

From the Vatican, Rome, January the 9th, 1920.

BENEDICT PP. XV

Austrian children waiting for a physical examination.

Feeding children at a school in Vienna.

A C.R.B. ship with markings for protection against German submarines.

Unloading food from the Bali in Copenhagen.

THE GREEK ORTHODOX CHURCH

[Received April 19, 1921]

The Patriarch of the Greek Orthodox Church
To Herbert Hoover
EXCELLENCY:

The great protection and contribution of Your highly esteemed Excellency to the gigantic relief task carried on from afar here under the American Relief Commission for the Near East, to the everlasting praise of the eminent philanthropy and sympathy of the noble American people for the sufferers, induce us to transmit also to Your Excellency particular deep thanks for the benefits and favors bestowed upon the suffering Greek population by the said Commission. We therefore pray His Excellency to be kind enough to accept also the expression of gratitude and deep thanks of our Orthodox Church of Constantinople and of the Greek Orthodox people for this beneficial and comforting assistance and subscription of the part of the honorable American Commission for the numerous fellow-countrymen of ours, whose sufferings unfortunately, in spite of the close of the war, still continue.

Invoking the holy grace and blessing for the whole noble American people and particularly for His highly esteemed Excellency and His family, We remain with great Honor,

KAPELLAS NICOLAOS
Governor of the Ecumenical Throne

THE CHURCH OF ARMENIA

Blessed may you be, also, who, having taken over the care of Food Control, have spared no effort to supply the needs of nations, and amongst them those of Our people. We have partaken of the bread of affliction, for there was no more for Our people in all Our Land, once an abundant granary and the nursery for nations around us. But they all consumed My people, as food for bread and all other things are exhausted. Through want of victuals our bodies are stunted and our backs bent. Therefore, there rests a great and sacred obligation on you all, whom God had made the possessor of good things, to send the daily sustenance, so that My people who, with wet eyes, have seen the dawn of deliverance and freedom, may not wither altogether.

Our infants and our children seek bread. Crumble bread into their hands. Give your bread to the necessitous and it will count towards your day of reckoning. For in the charity of your people, the Lord will see a great work, and will bless your land and all that are on it.

We pray to God to strengthen you, Sir, and your Colleagues, who are ever distributing the means of the sustenance of life to the ends of the earth.

We beseech the Lord to keep you safe and growing in strength in Our Lord Jesus Christ, Amen.

GEORGE V
Catholicus and Supreme
Patriarch of all Armenians

31, December, 1919
at the Mother See of Ararat,
Holy Etchmiadzin, Vagharshapap.

THE RELIEF OF COMMUNIST RUSSIA
FROM 1921 TO 1923

INTRODUCTION

A brief statement of backgrounds preceding the great Russian famine of 1921–23 is necessary for an understanding of the actions taken at that time.

Before the First World War, I had practiced my profession as an engineer in many parts of Russia. I had witnessed the terrible evils of the Czarist despotism. The workmen were exploited by employers and the peasants by a landlord class. Under the late Czars there were increasing reforms—but these were developed too slowly to check the increasing discontent. In this period there were constant outbreaks of revolution, all of which were put down with an iron hand.

The shaky hold of the regime had much to do with the Russian declaration of war in August, 1914. The Czar apparently adopted the gospel of Machiavelli that to cure domestic difficulties the public mind should be diverted by a foreign war.

Prior to the war, the people, by Asiatic standards, were well fed and reasonably clothed and housed. The public health, medical service, hospitals, and sanitation could only be stated as above Asiatic standards.

The day war was declared, unending miseries came to the Russian people. Constant, disastrous defeats by Germany and Austria finally brought revolt in the Russian armies. The Czar was expelled and a provisional government established in March, 1917, and Alexander Kerensky was chosen Prime Minister in July, 1917. The new government proved unable to cope with accumulated disorder and the increasing miseries of the people.

The Communists, already organized, were given leadership by the surreptitious transport, by the German Army, of Lenin and Trotsky from Switzerland to Russia. Under their leadership, the Communists seized the government on November 7, 1917. Unable to meet the continued German attacks, Russia made peace with the Germans at Brest-Litovsk on March 3, 1918.

Under the Communists, the productivity of industry and agriculture steadily decreased. The services of public health, sanitation, and hospitals, already weakened by the war, deteriorated even further. Physicians and surgeons were driven to common labor in order to live.

Such was the plight of the Russian people when the terrifying famine, caused by drought, swept over South Russia. And their destitution was increased by the depletion of production and thus the exhaustion of food reserves in other parts of the country.

The first stories of the spreading famine appeared in the foreign press in June, 1921. These reports were confirmed by the representative of our American Relief Administration then working along the Russian border in Eastern Europe and later by our official American representatives in bordering countries. Finally, *Pravda,* the official Communist journal, admitted that terrible famine was raging among 25,000,000 people.

At this time I was Secretary of Commerce in Washington and Chairman of the American Relief Administration, which had substantial resources beyond those necessary to complete its tasks in Central Europe.

I was not without experience with the Communists. As Director of Relief and Rehabilitation under the Allied governments during the Armistice from January to September, 1919, I had occasion to deal with a number of Communist attempts to seize many cities in the former enemy countries and one whole state—Hungary.

I have documented and cited statistics extensively in this narrative, and I have given a detailed description of events because this huge American undertaking in compassion has been minimized, and finally, even its existence has been denied in publications of the Soviet government and by Soviet officials throughout the years.

CHAPTER 51

THE CALL FOR HELP

On July 13, 1921, Maxim Gorky, a well-known writer and an ally of the Communist hierarchy in the Kremlin, issued an appeal to the world in general for "bread and medicine" for the children and the sick. He gave no specific information regarding the extent of the famine and, being an "intellectual," emphasized in his appeal the need to save a nationality which had produced many great contributions to science and literature.

Despite my experience with Communist morals and brutalities during the Armistice, I concluded that we should do something about the famine. Western Europe was still struggling with war impoverishment and could give little effective aid. The American Relief Administration, in addition to some spare funds, had a most able and experienced staff from which we could draw personnel. We could at least do something for the sick and the children for whom Gorky had appealed.

Secretary of State Charles Evans Hughes, my colleague, agreed with me that the only possible source of relief should respond to this call of human suffering, that there was a remote possibility that a generous action by a free people might have some moderating influence upon the bloody regime in the Kremlin, with its daily conspiracies against the free world, and that we should distinguish between 140,000,000 terrorized Russian people and the one or two million Communists who oppressed them.

There was some opposition in the Cabinet, where it was contended that with an American staff in Russia, we might get our Government into trouble with the Communist regime. However, I was supported not only by Secretary Hughes but also by Secretary of the Navy Edwin Denby and Secretary of War John W. Weeks. President Harding also approved.

On July 23, 1921, I cabled Gorky that the American Relief Administration would undertake relief for one million Russian children and provide some medical supplies for their hospitals—but subject to certain conditions. On July 31, Leo Kamenev, a high Commissar in the Kremlin, replied to me, accepting the conditions I had laid down to Gorky. He was at that time also Commissar of Famine Relief. He suggested a meeting between Assistant Commissar of Foreign Affairs, Maxim Litvinov, and a representative of the Relief Administration at Riga. I sent Walter Lyman Brown, our director in Europe, to meet with him. Brown was accompanied by Cyril J. C. Quinn, Philip H. Carroll, and John C. Miller, the experienced chiefs of our relief missions to Poland, Germany, and the Baltic States.

On August 2, ten days after my undertaking with Gorky and two days after Kamenev's proposal of a meeting, Georgi V. Chicherin, the Commissar of Foreign Affairs, sent a note to the foreign offices of Europe and to the U.S. Department of State asking for help.[1] That same day, Lenin made an appeal to the "proletariat" of the world for help. The "proletariat" was, however, hardly a source of either food or money.

After tedious negotiations, Mr. Brown signed the following agreement (hereafter referred to as the Riga Agreement) with Litvinov on August 20, 1921. I give the text in full because its terms came into

[1] Aside from the United States, the only response to the appeals from Russia that I know of came from a joint committee of the International Red Cross Societies and the League of Red Cross Societies at Geneva. Their chairman, Gustave Ador, cabled me, proposing joint action and joint management. Knowing full well that because of the financial difficulties of Europe they could produce no substantial funds, I replied that we could not do so under the requirements of our State Department and the Riga Agreement but that we would co-operate at the Moscow level with their representatives. They appointed Dr. Fridtjof Nansen of Norway to administer their relief undertaking. Their appeal for funds produced about $4,000,000, which was quickly expended. Nansen resigned. Their organization finally dissolved at a meeting in Brussels in October, 1921, while the famine was at its worst.

dispute repeatedly during our work, and it has considerable historical interest:

WHEREAS, a famine condition exists in parts of Russia, and

WHEREAS, Mr. Maxim Gorky, with the knowledge of the Russian Socialist Federative Soviet Republic, has appealed through Mr. Hoover to the American people for assistance to the starving and sick people, more particularly the children, of the famine stricken part of Russia, and

WHEREAS, Mr. Hoover and the American people have read with great sympathy this appeal on the part of the Russian people in their distress and are desirous, solely for humanitarian reasons, of coming to their assistance, and

WHEREAS, Mr. Hoover, in his reply to Mr. Gorky, has suggested that supplementary relief might be brought by the American Relief Administration to up to a million children in Russia;

Therefore, it is agreed between the American Relief Administration, an unofficial volunteer American charitable organization under the chairmanship of Mr. Herbert Hoover, hereinafter called the A.R.A., and the Russian Socialist Federative Soviet Republic, hereinafter called the Soviet Authorities,

That the A.R.A. will extend such assistance to the Russian people as is within its power, subject to the acceptance and fulfillment of the following conditions on the part of the Soviet Authorities who hereby declare that there is need of this assistance on the part of the A.R.A.

The Soviet Authorities agree:

First: That the A.R.A. may bring into Russia such personnel as the A.R.A. finds necessary in the carrying out of its work and the Soviet Authorities guarantee them full liberty and protection while in Russia. Non-Americans and Americans who have been detained in Soviet Russia since 1917 will be admitted on approval by the Soviet Authorities.

Second: That they will, on demand of the A.R.A., immediately extend all facilities for the entry into and exit from Russia of the personnel mentioned in (1) and while such personnel are in Russia the Soviet Authorities shall accord them full liberty to come and go and move about Russia on official business and shall provide them with all necessary papers such as safe-conducts, laissez passer, et cetera, to facilitate their travel.

Third: That in securing Russian and other personnel the A.R.A. shall have complete freedom as to selection and the Soviet Authorities will, on request, assist the A.R.A. in securing same.

Fourth: That on delivery by the A.R.A. of its relief supplies at the Russian ports of Petrograd, Murmansk, Archangel, Novorossisk, or other Russian ports as mutually agreed upon, or the nearest practicable available ports in adjacent countries, decision to lie with the A.R.A., the Soviet Authorities will bear all further costs such as discharge, handling, loading, and transportation to interior base points in the areas where the A.R.A. may operate. Should demurrage or storage occur at above ports mutually agreed upon as satisfactory such demurrage and storage is for the account of the Soviet Authorities. For purposes of this agreement the ports of Riga, Reval, Libau, Hango, and Helsingfors are also considered satisfactory ports. Notice of at least five days will be given to Soviet representatives at respective ports in case the Soviet Authorities are expected to take c.i.f. delivery.

Fifth: That they will at their own expense supply the necessary storage at interior base points mentioned in paragraph (4) and handling and transportation from same to all such other interior points as the A.R.A. may designate.

Sixth: That in all above storage and movement of relief supplies they will give the A.R.A. the same priority over all other traffic as the Soviet Authorities give their own relief supplies, and on demand of the A.R.A. will furnish adequate guards and convoys.

Seventh: That they will give free import and re-export and guarantee freedom from requisition to all A.R.A. supplies of whatever nature. The A.R.A. will repay the Soviet Authorities for expenses incurred by them on re-exported supplies.

Eighth: That the relief supplies are intended only for children and the sick, as designated by the A.R.A. in accordance with paragraph (24), and remain the property of the A.R.A. until actually consumed by these children and the sick, and are to be distributed in the name of the A.R.A.

Ninth: That no individual receiving A.R.A. rations shall be deprived of such local supplies as are given to the rest of the population.

Tenth: That they will guarantee and take every step to insure that relief supplies belonging to the A.R.A. will not go to the general adult population nor to the Army, Navy, or Government employees but only to such persons as designated in paragraphs (8) and (24).

Eleventh: That the Soviet Authorities undertake to reimburse the A.R.A. in dollars at c.i.f. cost or replace in kind any misused relief supplies.

Twelfth: That the A.R.A. shall be allowed to set up the necessary organizations for carrying out its relief work free from governmental or other interference. The Central and Local Soviet Authorities have the right of representation thereon.

Thirteenth: That the Soviet Authorities will provide:

A. The necessary premises for kitchens, dispensaries and, in as far as possible, hospitals.

B. The necessary fuel and, when available, cooking, distributing, and feeding equipment for the same.

C. The total cost of local relief administration, food preparation, distribution, et cetera, themselves are in conjunction with local authorities. Mode of payment to be arranged at later date.

D. On demand of the A.R.A. such local medical personnel and assistance, satisfactory to the A.R.A., as are needed to efficiently administer its relief.

E. Without cost railway, motor, water or other transportation for movement of relief supplies and of such personnel as may be necessary to efficiently control relief operations. The Soviet Authorities will for the duration of the A.R.A. operations assign to the A.R.A. for the sole use of its personnel, and transport free of cost, such railway carriages as the A.R.A. may reasonably request.

Fourteenth: In localities where the A.R.A. may be operating and where epidemics are raging, the A.R.A. shall be empowered by the Soviet Authorities to take such steps as may be necessary towards the improvement of sanitary conditions, protection of water supply, et cetera.

Fifteenth: That they will supply free of charge the necessary offices, garages, store-rooms, et cetera, for the transaction of the A.R.A. business and when available heat, light, and water for same. Further that they will place at the disposal of the A.R.A. adequate residential quarters for the A.R.A. personnel in all localities where the A.R.A. may be operating. All such above premises to be free from seizure and requisition. Examination of above premises will not be made except with knowledge and in presence of the chief of the A.R.A. operations in Russia or his representative and except in case of *flagrant delit*, when examiner will be held responsible in case examination unwarranted.

Sixteenth: That they will give to the A.R.A. complete freedom and priority without cost in the use of existing radio, telegraph, telephone, cable, post, and couriers in Russia and will provide the A.R.A., when available and subject to the consent of competent authorities, with private tele-graph and telephone wires and maintenance free of cost.

Seventeenth: To accord the A.R.A. and its American representatives and its couriers the customary diplomatic privileges as to passing the frontiers.

Eighteenth: To supply the A.R.A. free of cost with the necessary gaso-line and oil to operate its motor transportation and to transport such motor transportation by rail or otherwise as may be necessary.

Nineteenth: To furnish at the request of the competent A.R.A. Authori-ties all A.R.A. personnel, together with their impediments and supplies, free transportation in Russia.

Twentieth: To permit the A.R.A. to import and re-export free of duty and requisition such commissary, transport, and office supplies as are necessary for its personnel and administration.

Twenty-first: That they will acquaint the Russian people with the aims and methods of the relief work of the A.R.A. in order to facilitate the rapid development of its efficiency and will assist and facilitate in supply-ing the American people with reliable and non-political information of the existing conditions and the progress of the relief work as an aid in de-veloping financial support in America.

Twenty-second: That they will bear all expenses of the relief operation other than:

A. Cost of relief supplies at port (see paragraph 4).

B. Direct expenses of American control and supervision of relief work in Russia with exceptions as above. In general they will give the A.R.A. all assistance in their power toward the carrying out of its humanitarian relief operations.

The A.R.A. agrees:

Twenty-third: Within the limits of its resources and facilities, to supply, as rapidly as suitable organization can be effected, food, clothing, and medical relief to the sick and particularly to the children within the age limits as decided upon by the A.R.A.

Twenty-fourth: That its relief distribution will be to the children and sick without regard to race, religion, or social or political status.

Twenty-fifth: That its personnel in Russia will confine themselves strictly to the ministration of relief and will engage in no political or commercial activity whatever. In view of paragraph (1) and the freedom of American personnel in Russia from personal search, arrest, and detention, any personnel contravening this will be withdrawn or discharged on the request of the Central Soviet Authorities. The Central Soviet Authorities will submit to the chief officer of the A.R.A. the reasons for this request and the evidence in their possession.

Twenty-sixth: That it will carry on its operations where it finds its relief can be administered most efficiently and to secure best results. Its principal object is to bring relief to the famine stricken areas of the Volga.

Twenty-seventh: That it will import no alcohol in its relief supplies and will permit customs inspection of its imported relief supplies at points to be mutually agreed upon.

The Soviet Authorities having previously agreed as the absolute *sine qua non* of any assistance on the part of the American people to release all Americans detained in Russia and to facilitate the departure from Russia of all Americans so desiring, the A.R.A. reserves to itself the right to suspend temporarily or terminate all of its relief work in Russia in case of failure on the part of the Soviet Authorities to fully comply with this primary condition or with any condition set forth in the above agreement. The Soviet Authorities equally reserve the right of cancelling this agreement in case of non-fulfillment of any of the above clauses on the part of the A.R.A.

Made in Riga, August Twentieth, Nineteen hundred and twenty-one.

On behalf of Council of Peoples Commissaries of the Russian Socialist Federative Soviet Republic.

(*Signed*) Maxim Litvinov
Assistant Peoples Commissary for Foreign Affairs

On behalf of the American Relief Administration.
(*Signed*) Walter Lyman Brown
Director for Europe

The provision for release of American prisoners was suggested by Secretary Hughes, who informed me that the Department knew that there were about twenty of them. More than a hundred American prisoners in Russian dungeons were released on September 1. The number was a surprise, and I may say parenthetically that most of them were Russian-naturalized Americans who had gone to Russia to escape from crimes committed in the United States.

PRELIMINARY ORGANIZATION

With President Harding's approval, we arranged with the Grain Corporation to make the purchases, provide the transportation, and keep our accounts as it was doing for the American Relief Administration in Central Europe.[2]

Upon our instructions, Brown at once dispatched a preliminary staff of seven of the most experienced of our relief hands to Russia. They were: Philip H. Carroll, Chief, with Assistants Harry J. Fink, John P. Gregg, John A. Lehrs, Columba P. Murray, Will Shafroth, and Van Arsdale Turner. They arrived in Moscow on August 27. On the twenty-ninth, they went into session with Kamenev and Litvinov, and on the thirtieth, they secured adequate residential quarters and warehouse space where needed.

Prior to this mission, we had, on August 21, secured the services of Colonel William N. Haskell, who was to direct our organization in Russia. Haskell, then on the General Staff of the American Army, had, as I have mentioned in previous chapters, served as the head of our relief operations in Rumania and Armenia. He therefore had a background of experience in tough relief problems and an insight into the Eastern European mind, as well as into the uncertainties and stupidities of their brand of politicians. Colonel Haskell had a direct, honest mind and a blunt way of expressing himself which commanded respect among such varieties of mankind. He had secured some additional former relief hands, and Brown recruited men among our European staff. As a result, on his arrival in Moscow on September 21, 1921, Colonel Haskell had a hard core of experienced men.[3]

[2] The Grain Corporation was wholly owned by the United States Government and had carried on the purchase, transport, and accounting of American food supplies, under my direction, during the war and after.

[3] Three very adequate and conscientious books have been written on this Russian famine: H. H. Fisher, *The Famine in Soviet Russia: 1919–1923* (New York, The Macmillan Company, 1927); Frank A. Golder and Lincoln Hutchinson, *On the Trail of the Russian Famine* (Stanford University Press, 1927); and Frank M. Surface and Raymond L. Bland, *American Food in the World War and Reconstruction Period* (Stanford, California: Stanford University Press, 1931).

Surface and Bland are largely statistical. Golder and Hutchinson are vividly descriptive of the scene. But Dr. Fisher's book is an extraordinarily interesting and accurate account by an eyewitness. As a member of our headquarters staff, he gained an insight into the workings of the Communist Government, and his book is a notable contribution to the history of the period. Because the full financial and statistical records were not available at the time these books were prepared, the authors necessarily underestimated the resources, expenditures, and volume of commodities distributed by the Relief Administration, and particularly by the affiliates.

Rather than cumber this text with a multitude of footnotes of sources and verifications, I refer students of the relief of Communist Russia to the following:

(1) The extensive American Relief Administration records in the Hoover Institution on War, Revolution, and Peace at Stanford University; and

(2) The Reports, during the famine period, of the organizations listed below.

The American Red Cross

The Jewish Joint Distribution Committee

The United States Department of Commerce

The New York Times

The extensive but unpublished reports of the Federal Bureau of Investigation

Annual Reports of the Federal Council of the Churches of Christ in America

Annual Reports of the Y.M.C.A.

Annual Reports of the Y.W.C.A.

As Between Brothers: The Story of Lutheran Response to World Need, by Richard W. Solberg (Minneapolis, Augsburg Publishing House, 1957)

CHAPTER 52

WE FACE ONE OF THE MOST TERRIBLE FAMINES IN HISTORY

Even before Colonel Haskell's arrival in Russia, our preliminary staff began reporting that the situation was immensely graver than could be served by our commitment to the relief of 1,000,000 children and a modest amount of hospital supplies. We were, in fact, confronted with famine in about 750,000 square miles of the Volga Valley and 85,000 square miles in the Ukraine. About 25,000,000 people in these regions were in the midst of absolute famine, with death for the whole population of these areas only a few months away. Typhus, cholera, typhoid, smallpox, and relapsing fever were sweeping over the area because of a lack of physical resistance and medical and sanitary services. Millions of panic-stricken people were attempting to flee the famine on foot and by rail and every other sort of conveyance. They were moving into other parts of Russia which were already short of food, and they were carrying infections with them.

In order that there can be no doubts regarding the terrifying famine with which we were confronted and from which the Russian people were suffering, I give here a few extracts from our reports, and later I will give reports of the sweep of epidemic disease which faced our medical division. The reader must remember that these reports came from an experienced American staff whose devotion, character, and veracity cannot be challenged. They were written on the spot and under conditions of strain, where perfection in punctu-

436

ation, grammar, and diction cannot be expected. A report on the refugee movement states:

Very large numbers of people are leaving the famine area, coming in from the towns with what supplies they can carry and being shipped by train to sections where food conditions are supposed to be better. All cities are crowded with these refugees awaiting transportation: the floors of stations are covered with persons and their goods, the overflow camps on station platforms or on streets beneath eaves of buildings, under standing freight cars or where not, for days and nights awaiting trains. When these arrive, they all rush up and attempt to board; some are successful, the remainder return and wait. All cars are crowded including coaches, box cars and flat cars, on which families camp for days and nights without protection; refugees even crowd the ledges between cars and stand upon the couplings. The refugee movement seems unsystematized; as many appear to travel from east to west as from west to east; some have Russian cities as their destination, others are travelling to Siberia, Poland, Latvia, etcetera. We met, on the border of Latvia, a train of 58 box cars containing approximately 1,200 refugees. These were travelling from Southeast Russia to Revel, enroute to other points. They had been travelling for twenty one days when we met them and had still far to go.

A report on the so-called "Children's Homes" says:

. . . Collecting Homes are institutions which receive and care for children lost or deserted by their parents until they can be distributed to permanent homes locally or sent to other cities where greater facilities are at hand to provide for them. Our report of October, based on inspections made at the time [stated]. . . .

. . . large numbers of children . . . are brought to collecting homes where they are bathed, clipped and as far as possible reclothed. They are then either shipped to cities outside the famine area or distributed among the local children's homes; the latter being of two varieties: those for children under three years, and those for children from three to sixteen years. The collecting homes vary as to equipment and efficiency of administration. Many are sorry makeshifts without beds, bedding or adequate facilities for feeding, the children lying huddled together on the floors without any covering for days before they can be properly cared for. . . . shortage of clothing blankets and equipment is the rule. . . .

The number of waifs is tremendous. Seven thousand were collected in

Kazan City during the last month, while in the Province of Ufa twenty two thousand are being cared for in these homes, and in Samara there are eight receiving and 58 permanent homes.

At certain hospitals buildings are set aside for . . . bedridden due to starvation. Their condition is pitiable: in the "First Soviet Hospital" at Kazan 180 are housed in a small building containing 100 beds, and as many as four patients occupied a single bed. . . . Many began to cry out for bread as we entered the ward and continued to plead until we left. Inspection of these hospitals is extremely depressing.

Another report states:

After having inspected the kitchens and children's institutions in Mamadysh the committee asked that I go to visit the children's home in one of the suburban villages. We arrived there late and after dark and upon entering care had to be taken that we did not step upon the bodies of the sleeping children which were scattered everywhere about the floor.

Here like many other homes which I visited there were not only no beds but not even blankets or covering and the rags which the children had to clothe themselves with or to protect their naked bodies were scarcely sufficient to keep them warm during the daytime. In their rags, some crouching, some sitting and some reclining upon the floor they resembled in their dirty garments and in their staring lustreless eyes, the figures of animals rather than human beings.

A report from Orenburg said:

Conditions in Orenburg City itself are almost beyond description and relief of the situation will be difficult and might seem hopeless were it not for the fact that the great improvement brought about in other districts, where we have been operating for a longer time, demonstrates that what seems impossible can be accomplished.

Poverty, malnutrition and starvation are evident everywhere and dead are seen lying upon the streets of the city and upon roads leading into towns where they soon become a prey to dogs and birds. Sick and starving are collected into homes without facilities to care for them. "Dom Ivanoff," a collector for adults and children, is one of the worst of these institutions. Its capacity is 3,000, but capacity in these institutions means only the number of persons that can be packed together upon all floors of the building, leaving here and there a narrow aisle to allow ingress and egress and to carry out the dead. Starving, sick and dying are crowded together upon the floors, fifty to one hundred in a room, covered only with thin dirty clothing and accumulations from dead removed. There are no toilet facilities and no bathing accommodations except a cold spigot in the court. The Government ration consists of a quarter pound of bread and hot water daily. The dead—we saw as many as three in a single room lying among the living—are carried out and piled naked together to be transported later to the cemetery where great pits, approximately ten feet deep and accommodating several hundreds of bodies, are dug, and these receive all city dead, a maximum of eight hundred a day being reported.

Another report says:

The Orenburg district office was opened on November 9th, when the death rate from starvation was 400 per day and on the increase. The entire country was under a mantle of six feet of snow. Railroad Station jammed with lousy, filthy refugees of all ages in a starved condition with no hopes of obtaining food. As at all other stations they were waiting for trains to take them anywhere and when they got to anywhere they boarded another train and returned to somewhere. Dead were lying in the streets for days at a time without the bodies being removed. In pest holes termed "Children's Homes" as many as 1,000 children would be housed in space for 400 with no wood, no food, and from forty to fifty dying in one day. Horses, camels dropping in the streets and unable to get up. General conditions in the preemnicks; no mattresses, beds, blankets or clothing. Lying on bare floors huddled together in an effort to keep warm. Inmates alive with vermin; wearing such clothes as they had when they came in. Such a demoralizing, depressing and sickening sight has never before been seen by Americans.

. . . 13th January; cannibalism reported and authenticated in Iseave Dedoval. Bodies which were too numerous to bury and which had died of typhus and other diseases were piled in heaps in buildings, were stolen, and the flesh boiled for food. The punishment meted to offenders was to imprison and then forget them until they died of starvation, with the exception of minors, accessory to the case, who were released after the older persons concerned with them were dead. . . .

A strong guard had to be maintained over the A.R.A. warehouse during the entire winter, and the building was attacked several times by persons who attempted to get past the guards; the latter were forced to fire and several were killed about the entrances attempting to steal in.

Lawlessness, robberies and murders are extremely common and it is not safe to venture out upon the streets at night in Orenburg City. Persons who must be out keep to the center of the streets and avoid passing near vacant buildings as the Khargises, adept with the lasso, are reported to use that means of securing victims, drawing them from the streets to upper floors for purposes of robbery and murder.

A report from Kazan stated:

. . . Typhus, recurrent and typhoid fevers are epidemic: dysentery is prevalent with high mortality, (up to fifty per cent in children). With shortage of personnel and material, these epidemics are difficult to combat. Conditions as regards starvation are bad, and especially so in Spassk and Chistopol where it is estimated seventy-five per cent of the population are starving, and cattle and horses being rapidly consumed. Food substitutes are being extensively used when these can be obtained. Bread is being made from leaves and bark of the birch and elm, sawdust, shells of nuts, rhubarb, rushes, pea husks, straw, potato peels, cabbage, beet leaves, and even horse manure. Blood is also used in making bread. Dead animals are luxuries.

A report from Ufa stated:

. . . the situation here desperate, in the summer of 1921 when it was still possible to get vegetables and substitutes for bread, et cetera, the population fed on them, but with the coming of winter this source of sustaining life was lost and it was necessary to slaughter the last remaining cattle. After these were all eaten, the fight for life was continued by means of feeding on and eating dogs, cats, rats, roots, skins, bones and all manner of refuse. Men lost their reason and became cannibals; cannibalism appearing first in isolated instances, little by little began to increase and by the early part of 1922 had taken on alarming proportions. Many, many cases of cannibalism were discovered, some of them of a nightmare character, such as mothers killing and eating their own children, the stealing of unattended children from the streets, to be slaughtered and eaten and in cases sold on the markets for meat. Horrible though it is to speak of these things, the fact that they are true and did take place will bring home more forcefully the terrible conditions that drove human beings, normally peaceful, stolid and God-fearing, to such extremes. It is very delicate to speak of such occurrences but they are true and the fact that they did occur is beyond doubt. Some authenticated cases are attached but the less said about them the better.

All this provoked all manners of illnesses and disease, which aggravated the dreadful suffering of the famished; seeking food, the exhausted, sick and naked, starved people dragged themselves hither and thither, seeking the larger towns and villages in the hope of finding food there. Cold and exposure finished the work of hunger and thousands of unfortunate souls were frozen to death on the way. In the villages and on the roads one met at every step living skeletons, scarcely able to move, or already completely exhausted and freezing to death where they lay. Hunger and want forced the population to crimes, murders and thefts reached a colossal number, and in order to steal a cow robbers murdered whole families, not sparing infants in arms. Words cannot describe the terrible desolation, the horrible crimes, the awful illnesses and diseases, and the deaths of terrible suffering which famine brought to this formerly flourishing and rich country.

And here is a report from Samara:

Food shortage is extremely acute, affecting two thirds of the population —2,800,000. There are available food products in the cities but prices, rather above those pertaining in Moscow, render these unavailable to the great majority of the urban population. In the country districts, the peasants are subsisting almost exclusively upon food substitutes and 80% are reported to be facing starvation. These conditions become worse in proportion to the distance that one departs from centers, and especially in towns out of touch with railroad communications. We visited, by sledge, the town of Novo Semanko, population of 1,500, located 25 versts from Samara. The peasants here are subsisting upon bread made of ground horse bones mixed with acorn, birch and reed flour and, in many cases, have nothing else to augment this ration.

A report from the Bashkir Republic:

An idea as to crop shortage can be obtained from the following statistics secured at the town of Vichla, Bashkir Republic:

Population 4,000
Normal crop: 150   poods per desyrtina
Crop 1920:   60   "   "   "
Crop, Fall, 1921: 1-½ "   "   "

One hundred families have emigrated and many others have sold their flocks and bought food stuffs. . . . Village population formerly owned 1,500 cattle, 1,500 horses; on hand at present: 200 cattle, 400 horses.

Bread is made of a seed resembling poppy which has a cathartic action and induces dysentery.

A report from Cheliabinsk:

The Cheliabinsk Gubernia has a population of 1,320,461 including 559,-102 children. . . .

Based on official figures, 245,228 adults and 178,000 children in this gubernia are suffering from the famine.

The mortality in this gubernia from all causes, though chiefly from hunger, from July 1st to December 31st, was 71,000.

A further report from Orenburg said:

Conditions in Orenburg are much worse than in any district previously visited. . . . Many of the peasants are nomads and without homes in summer and living in mud huts during the winter. . . . They use camel dung almost exclusively for heating and cooking. These nomads subsist mainly upon mutton and beef but, having gradually lost most of their cattle and sheep . . . during the last few years, raids by bandits and failure of crops making for starvation of surviving herds, a large proportion of them are starving. Mr. Fitzgerald, who is working at Aktyacinsk . . . among the Khargises tells me that 12% are dying monthly from starvation, exposure and disease, and that whole families are at times wiped out in a single night. . . .

A report from Crimea stated:

Mr. Venear reports that seventy thousand persons died of starvation during the last six months according to official figures, and it is estimated that an equal number died from the same cause unregistered.

A report from Petrograd stated:

Petrograd had formerly a population of 2,000,000 . . . the population has been gradually reduced to 700,000.

Sanitary conditions in the city are becoming worse . . . due to the spreading of the typhus . . . overcrowding . . . the lack of fuel . . . adequate food, clothing and soap.

A report from the Ukraine said:

We will shortly be in a position to extend our activities beyond our present sphere of operations; reports of dire conditions, epidemics of typhus, recurrent fever, typhoid fever, lack of hospital facilities and supplies, dearth of disinfectants and what not, are being received, not only from cities bordering the famine area, but from many areas remote from the same and requests for assistance reach us daily, especially from the Ukraine.

Extracts from other reports stated:

. . . the Russian hospitals everywhere are without supplies. Hundreds of thousands of children whose parents could not save them were being gathered into "homes," where as many as could cover the floor slept in utter filth. Cannibalism had started.

In the South Ukraine alone, reliable Russian officials reported twenty-six cases of murder for cannibalism, and in Orenburg a law was passed that meat must be sold in bulk in the markets so that its origin could be identified.

An added horror of the famine is the piling of unburied dead in open heaps in the cemeteries. In one hospital morgue alone . . . there are 500 unburied bodies.

To document the dread nature of the famine, many cases of cannibalism were photographed by our staff and sent to our New York office. However, we did not publish them.

In the chapter on medical aid,[1] I give other reports regarding that situation.

These are but samples of our reports during the years 1921 and 1922. To verify the situation, I immediately sent Dr. Vernon Kellogg to Russia. He had been our relief organization's great expert on famine since 1914. Because we might need verification from some eminent public men, a few days later I dispatched James P. Goodrich, former Governor of Indiana, to the scene. Dr. Kellogg arrived in Russia on September 19, 1921, and Governor Goodrich on October 3. They visited the famine area and soon telegraphed confirmation of the terrible extent of the famine. Both men returned to Washington on November 24, bringing even worse information—with pictures.

At the time we responded to Gorky's appeal for food and medicine for 1,000,000 children, we estimated that the American Relief Administration had about $10,000,000 in assets but had not yet

[1] See Chap. 57.

wholly completed its work in Central and Eastern Europe. But now my colleagues were faced with one of the most trying tasks we had ever undertaken. We could not abandon our commitment to provide for 1,000,000 children. We could not select this number from possibly 8,000,000 who were now involved, and even if we undertook to provide aid for all the children, they could not be saved without also saving the adults. But we had set our hand to the plow.

Huge sums were required immediately. We estimated sixty million dollars at least, together with free services from many quarters for even a minimum program of relief—and it greatly exceeded the estimates.

CHAPTER 53

FINANCING THE RELIEF

My colleagues and I explored the possibility of a great national appeal for funds. However, we were compelled to decide that the American Relief Administration itself could not make a successful appeal. Several months before, we had completed the drive for funds for Central and Eastern European children. In this we had had the support of Americans descended from twelve separate European countries. There were comparatively few Americans of Russian descent and thus no such vast background for an appeal. Moreover, Americans as a whole took a dark view of Communist Russia and blamed the Communists for contributing to the difficulties in which the Russian people had been placed.

Beyond all this, the United States had been plunged into an economic depression from which there were 5,000,000 unemployed who required public support. I had been appointed by President Harding to organize relief for these unemployed. In addition to that task, I was engaged not only in my normal duties as Secretary of Commerce but was also in the midst of a number of reconstruction activities to remedy our own dislocations and losses from the war. But the consciences of myself and my loyal colleagues in the Relief Administration told us that we had to do the best we could where 20,000,000 people were about to die.

There was an effective alternative to a direct appeal by the American Relief Administration—that was the religious organizations in the United States who might effectively call upon their members. At once we took steps to organize them for this purpose. Some of them had already inquired of the State Department whether passports would be issued and whether protection could be given to them.

Our official relations with Russia were under great strain at this time, and Secretary Hughes determined that the State Department could not look after a number of different relief agencies and scores of Americans without making someone responsible for the whole task—and upon whose recommendation passports would be issued. The Secretary secured a letter from the President directed to me as follows:

18 August 1921

MY DEAR SECRETARY HOOVER:

As you are aware, I have given my fullest approval of the action on the part of the American Relief Administration in initiating an effort to mitigate the famine in Russia, particularly to save the lives of children. I know that the entrance of America into the problem of Russia through the full heart of charity is one that will appeal to the whole American people.

My particular purpose in addressing this letter to you is to emphasize my wish that the distribution in Russia of all charity arising in the United States should be carried on through the one American organization. It is only through single American representation and administration that we can assure to both American and Russian people the best service in the use of their funds.

I am asking the Department of State to cooperate in directing that passports be given for travel to Russia on relief work only to persons who may be in the service of the American Relief Administration.

It is also of importance that the American people should be protected so far as we can do so, from those persons who may wish to thrive on great disasters by creating unnecessary organizations to collect charity.

I trust, therefore, that all those in America who are charitably inclined, will give their support either to the American Relief Administration or to such organizations as may undertake to co-operate with that administration.

WARREN G. HARDING

MOBILIZING OTHER AMERICAN CHARITABLE AGENCIES

Eight months previously we had organized unity of action by American charitable agencies for relief in Central Europe. I therefore, on August 24, 1921, four days after signing the Riga Agreement, asked these former colleagues in relief to meet with us for consideration of the Russian problem. Those present were representatives of the American Red Cross, the Jewish Joint Distribution Committee, the National Catholic Welfare Council, the Knights of Columbus, the Federal Council of the Churches of Christ in America, the American Friends Service Committee (Quakers), and the Young Men's and Young Women's Christian associations. All these organizations approved the stipulations in President Harding's letter of August 18.

I proposed that these organizations should select any Russian area or group involved in the famine and that they could add a representative to our central staff in Moscow. I stated that the American Relief Administration would purchase and transport any food, clothing, or other supplies and deliver them to the spots in Russia they wished, for which they could pay our New York office.

A little later we were joined by the National Lutheran Council, the Southern Baptist Convention and the American Mennonite Relief. The Mennonites were a religious sect which had originally come to America from Russia. There were also some Americans descended from the Germans in the Volga Basin, where they had originally been settled by Catherine the Great. They wished to help and at my suggestion formed the Volga Relief Society.

I stated that the American Relief Administration would try to provide relief in those areas which were not covered by these organizations. This proposal was accepted by all the affiliates, and there was never friction among these organizations or between them and the American Relief Administration. The American Friends Service Committee participated with us under a modified arrangement, reasons for which will appear later.

I proposed to our affiliates that each should make its own appeal for funds and that while the American Relief Administration would make no public appeal, we would support the appeal of each of them and we hoped to secure some donations from the great charitable foundations. Aside from the resources of our affiliates, we took the following steps to strengthen the American Relief Administration, of which I give the final realizations.

THE AMERICAN RELIEF ADMINISTRATION'S OWN FUNDS

Because of the long delays in settling accounts for the Armistice period, we were not immediately able to determine what resources the American Relief Administration would have available beyond our obligations in Central and Eastern Europe. As time went on, we drew from our own funds a total of $10,252,795.

THE GRAIN CORPORATION PROFITS

I was aware that the Grain Corporation, which I had created during the war, had in its treasury a residue of about $20,000,000 in profits earned during the war from trading with Neutrals. I appealed to the Congressional committees, requesting that they secure an authorization from Congress for us to use these funds for Russian relief. I was supported by Julius Barnes, President of the Grain Corporation, and we secured the approval of President Harding. In presenting our cause to the Congressional committees, we had the invaluable support of Dr. Kellogg and Governor Goodrich. They presented a mass of convincing statistical material and firsthand observations to the committees.

On December 22, 1921, an act was passed authorizing us to use these profits for relief. The actual amount was $18,662,180.

WAR DEPARTMENT MEDICAL SUPPLIES

Secretary of War John W. Weeks informed me that there remained in his department a great surplus of medical supplies. He joined with me in proposing to the Congress that it authorize the donation of these supplies to the American Relief Administration. President Harding recommended it, and the act was passed on January 20, 1922; it authorized a donation of $4,000,000 worth of medical supplies. The Department, however, was very liberal, and the Red Cross estimated for us that these supplies amounted to a value of over $5,000,000. The Laura Spelman Rockefeller Memorial contributed $267,392 for the transport of these supplies.

FOOD AND CLOTHING DRAFTS

One of our first steps was to extend our food and clothing "draft" system to Russia.[1] We sold drafts to our affiliated organizations. The total value of bulk food drafts purchased by these organizations was $4,374,893. Individual food drafts amounted to $9,305,300 and clothing drafts to $737,317, or a sum total of $14,417,510.

THE AMERICAN RED CROSS

Under the leadership of Chairman Livingston Farrand, the American Red Cross gave us magnificent support. It gave us huge medical supplies; it prepared and packed for shipment all these and the War Department's supplies. It recruited our staff of physicians, surgeons, sanitary engineers, and hospital managers. Where necessary, it gave allowances to this staff from its own funds. Its outlays on our behalf were $4,914,863.

THE RELIEF OF INTELLECTUALS

We extended to Russia our system of support to intellectuals which we had carried on in Central and Eastern Europe. For that purpose we raised and expended $1,206,037 from sources outside our own funds, the details of which are given later.[2]

[1] See Chap. 54.
[2] See Chap. 56.

THE CONTRIBUTION BY WAY OF THE VOLUNTARY STAFF

The majority of the staff of the American Relief Administration and the Grain Corporation which served it, and the officials of our affiliate organizations, were volunteers. Others received only their out-of-pocket expenses. If those Americans—more than three hundred of them—who served in Russia at one time or another for two years or longer had received normal commercial salaries, the excess cost above the actual outlays would have been over $5,000,000. Their services were as much a gift to relief of the famine as the food they purchased, transported, and distributed.

THE CONTRIBUTIONS BY WAY OF FREE SERVICES FROM AMERICAN AND EUROPEAN SOURCES

We sought and received from American business and European governments a large amount of aid that cannot be recorded in exact dollars from each contributor. All the way from the Chicago grain market through New York and Europe, we received free services from private firms and governments. A computation by our American Relief Administration accountants estimated the sum of $1,250,000 as the minimum for these free services.

THE SOVIET GOVERNMENT'S GOLD CONTRIBUTIONS

We decided to demand a contribution in gold by the Soviet Government from the gold reserve they had seized from the Kerensky regime. Kamenev and Litvinov were not averse to making such a contribution. However, they haggled over the amount, but finally Colonel Haskell signed an agreement with the Soviet Government on December 22, 1921, by which they agreed to donate $10,000,000 in gold, part of which was to be used for purchase of seed. The

Ukrainian Soviet Government, which at times maintained a foggy sort of independence from Moscow, also wanted some seed, and Walter Brown signed an agreement in London with Commissar Krassin for $2,000,000 on December 30, 1921. However, when we realized on all the gold, the total actually amounted to $11,357,325. The Soviet Government also made a donation to the relief in commodities valued at $30,026.

OUR TOTAL RESOURCES

I may summarize at this point the resources which we developed to meet the famine:

Our affiliates and others *	$15,275,930
American Relief Administration	10,252,795
Congressional appropriation of Grain Corporation profits	18,662,180
War Department (medical supplies)	5,000,000
Individual food drafts	9,305,300
Bulk food drafts	4,374,893
Clothing and textiles	737,317
American Red Cross	4,914,863
Fund for intellectuals	1,206,037
Voluntary staff services	5,000,000
Free services from businesses and governments	1,250,000
Soviet Gold	11,357,325
Soviet Government contribution of food	30,026
Laura Spelman Rockefeller Memorial (for shipment of medical supplies) †	267,392
	$87,634,058

* For details, see Chap. 61.

† This organization also gave extensive aid for the relief of intellectuals. Its contribution is included in that total above. For details, see Chap. 56.

There are certain duplications in the above items. Some of the affiliates made donations to other affiliates, which amounts appear in both accounts. Many of them purchased bulk food drafts from the

American Relief Administration which appear in the total bulk food-draft sales above. An estimate of the duplication, as close as we can make it, was less than $6,800,000—or a net provision of about $80,834,000 for the relief.

Waiting for an issue of clothing from the C.R.B.

A C.R.B. feeding station.

Camels used to distribute food in the snowy wastes of Russia.

Russian children at a large A.R.A. feeding station in Ufa.

CHAPTER 54

ORGANIZATION IN RUSSIA

The expansion of our task, beyond our original commitment of care for 1,000,000 famine children and provision of some medical supplies, demanded a great and rapid building up of organization.

The first necessity was to secure from the Soviet Government additional rights under the Riga Agreement to cover our increased activities and those of our affiliated organizations. Soon after Colonel Haskell's arrival in Russia, he informed the Soviet authorities that we could not undertake the great relief measures needed unless this were done. They quickly agreed.

STAFF ARRANGEMENTS

Aside from our old and tried hands, whom Brown had sent into Russia, we had to find quickly men who would volunteer for the relief, who would serve with only an allowance for out-of-pocket expenses, and who would be willing to face the hardships and dangers which the job implied. We needed as many Americans who spoke Russian as possible. A few of our staff veterans knew the language, and we found some others, including a number of volunteers from my prewar American engineering associates. For our other staff, we had to recruit Russian interpreters. The total number of Americans who worked in Russia under the Riga Agreement was 327—with a

453

maximum of about 300 at any one time. Of these, 69 were attached to affiliated organizations.

We divided our task into eighteen major districts, generally following the Russian political divisions, each with a director, supervisor, and assistants in charge of subdistricts. One of Colonel Haskell's recurring problems was to shift his men about so that they did not get too unstrung by their surroundings. And a problem of our medical staff was to protect the health of our staff. But two of them made that supreme sacrifice which idealism imposes on its followers.

At one time a cross-section showed the following assignments of the American Relief Administration's own staff:

The director and heads of divisions in the Moscow office ...	12
District supervisors	18
Chiefs of district subdivisions	22
Assistants to the above	80
Accountants and secretaries	81
Representatives of affiliated organizations	15
Total	228

A list of the personnel and their jobs in the Moscow office at one moment indicates the dimensions of the work:

COLONEL WILLIAM N. HASKELL, *Director*
CYRIL J. C. QUINN, *Assistant Director*
COLONEL HENRY BEEUWKES, *Director, Medical Division*
DR. WALTER P. DAVENPORT, *Assistant Director, Medical Division*
LINCOLN HUTCHINSON, *Special Investigator*
DR. FRANK A. GOLDER,[1] JOHN A. LEHRS, and A. C. COOLIDGE, *Chiefs of Liaison Division with Soviet officials*

[1] One of Dr. Golder's missions was to collect historical material (with the aid of our entire staff) for the Hoover Institution on War, Revolution, and Peace at Stanford University. Dr. Golder obtained approval and aid for his collection from the Soviet authorities, among whom Commissars Radek, Rykov, Kamenev and Chicherin were especially helpful. They, of course, believed that the Communist Revolution was one of the great historic events of all history and that certain of its records should be made available to all scholars. They welcomed the opportunity of placing them in the Institution. The collection contained many public addresses of leaders, the minutes of Soviet meetings, decrees, regulations, and complete files of the leading journals. In addition to the records of the Communist regime up to 1923, they gave Dr. Golder

PHILIP H. CARROLL, *Chief, Food Supply Division*
PHILIP MATHEWS, *Chief, Transportation Division*
JOHN P. GREGG, *Chief, Inspection Division*
ARTHUR H. RUHL, *Chief Inspector*
M. FARMER MURPHY, *Chief, Communications Division*
WILLIAM R. KEARNEY, JR., *Chief, Motor Transport Division*
ELMER G. BURLAND, *Chief, Food Drafts Division*
JOHN R. ELLINGSTON, *Chief, Historical Division*
CHARLES TELFORD, *Chief, Accounting Division*

Executive Assistants and special-duty men:

THOMAS C. LONERGAN
JOHN J. MANGAN
LUPTON A. WILKINSON
HAROLD H. FISHER

Of our staff, we had only two minor disappointments. For the rest, they were magnificent men.[2]

FOOD AND CLOTHING DRAFTS

For a full understanding of our operations, I must amplify the previous brief account of our system of food and clothing drafts. They accomplished two things: a method of securing donations and a method of effecting distribution. We varied our system in Russia from that in Europe to the extent that the food or clothing called for by individual drafts was assembled at our principal warehouse in Moscow and packed in containers which were sent to the recipients through our district divisions—instead of having the recipients calling at warehouses to collect the stipulated food or clothing. Elmer G. Burland of our Moscow staff had charge of this division and did an extraordinary job.

---

important records of the Czarist regime. His collection, added to those already in the Institution, constituted the most complete record in any institution of the Communist Revolution and the subsequent events. Under the Riga Agreement, we were able to send all of our internal records to the Institution.

[2] A complete list of American Relief Administration personnel is given in Appendix III.

The Russian assistants in our district offices also did an amazing job of locating the individual recipients. Out of a total of 947,795 individual drafts issued, only 9,762 had to be canceled through failure to find the addressee—mainly because of death or the constant movement of refugees. The undelivered packages went to the children's relief kitchens.

The individual drafts were larger than the units we sold for use in Eastern Europe and averaged about one hundred pounds each. The usual contents of each package were:

Flour	49 pounds
Rice	25 pounds
Tea	3 pounds
Fats	10 pounds
Sugar	10 pounds
Milk	20 tins

The food value of these packages totaled about 200,000 calories. On the basis of a drastic minimum of 1,500 calories per day per person, each package could theoretically sustain life for one person for about nineteen weeks, or, for a family of two adults and three children, about five weeks. The food delivered on individual drafts totaled 54,316 tons.

In order to secure as many individual food drafts as possible, Burland had one million cards printed in Russian and distributed; these explained the method of obtaining a food draft and bore a printed request to some named person abroad to send a draft. Thousands of these cards were sent through our Moscow office to outside relatives and friends around the world.

To keep the railways and docks operating in the famine region, we regularly furnished Burland's packages to their crews at the expense of the Relief Administration.

BULK FOOD DRAFTS

The total bulk food draft purchases by our affiliated organizations were as follows (some clothing draft purchases are also included here):

Jewish Joint Distribution Committee	$1,314,000
American Friends Service Committee	415,000
National Catholic Welfare Council	750,000
Federal Council of the Churches of Christ in America	90,000
Laura Spelman Rockefeller Memorial Fund	830,000
Mennonite Central Committee	400,000
National Lutheran Council	300,000
Volga Relief Society	220,000
Y.M.C.A. and Y.W.C.A. (student relief)	200,000
Seventh-Day Adventists and others	75,000
Total	$4,594,000

The total quantity of food delivered to these organizations amounted to 34,570 tons.

CLOTHING

Russia had been able to provide little clothing for her civilians in the seven years from the outbreak of war in 1914 up to the time we undertook relief in 1921. Moreover, during the war the textile mills and imports were largely devoted to the military forces, and after the Communist Revolution, the mills degenerated from the liquidation of the "bourgeoisie" and lack of imported parts. The members of the Communist Party had priority on such clothing as there was. When we appeared on the scene, except for the Communists, Russia was a nation in rags and patches, with such shortages that children in many places could not go to school for lack of clothes.

We undertook the clothing operation from four directions—purchases of new clothing materials, solicitation of secondhand clothing, and the sale of both "individual" and "bulk" clothing drafts. The following items were purchased:

Woolen cloth (yards)	946,253
Linings (yards)	317,098
Flannel (yards)	639,396
Muslin (yards)	1,293,761
Buttons (1,000 cases)	3,808
Thread (1,000 yards)	69,689

Thread (cases)	17
Needles (number)	20,736
Needles (cases)	2
Miscellaneous (pieces)	12,990
Shoes for children (pairs)	586,991
Stockings for children (pairs)	771,827

The total cost was $2,437,795, of which $971,671 was for children's relief, $301,759 was for general relief, $427,365 was for institutions, and $737,000 to meet the clothing "drafts" and bulk sales shipped from our Moscow central warehouses.

In addition, we purchased and shipped for hospital and medical supplies the following textiles:

Blankets	470,000
Sheets	570,000
Pajamas and nightshirts	675,000
Towels	890,000
Pillow cases and mattress covers	155,000
Slippers	100,000
Suits of Underwear	200,000
Layettes	86,000
Total medical textile items	3,146,000

CHAPTER 55

FOOD FOR CHILDREN AND ADULTS —AND SEED

We began feeding subnormal children on September 7, 1921, with a cargo of food borrowed from our Central European relief. But we quickly discovered that the problem was far different from that of our experience in Central and Eastern Europe. Before the famine in Russia there had been large numbers of orphanages and homes for children, many dating from Czarist days. In the famine region our organization was confronted with huge numbers of orphans and abandoned or neglected children, many of them in emergency and inadequate children's homes. These homes were overcrowded, the number of occupants being limited only to those who—all at the same time—could lie on the floors. Few of these so-called "homes" had any sewer connections. The filth and disease were unspeakable. The children were slowly starving; the daily death rate was appalling.

We soon learned that this was no canteen job of serving one plentiful meal a day, as we had done in Europe. These Russian youngsters had to have adequate housing, with sanitation and medical attention, and had to be completely fed. We established a multitude of kitchens to which the children could come and eat—anywhere they could stand up or sit down. Most of these kitchens represented their sole source of food, and they ate accordingly.

Russian mothers were no different from the mothers of any other nation where children were concerned. They conducted the kitchens devotedly, and their only reward was food for themselves.

459

THE SPECIAL COMMODITIES
IMPORTED FOR CHILDREN

	Tons
Flour	85,987.6
Rice	7,291.5
Beans and peas	3,221.2
Corn grits	928.4
Pork products	7,687.7
Milk	9,459.9
Cocoa	3,325.4
Sugar	12,890.3
Miscellaneous food	578.9
Soap	569.6
Total	131,940.5

I give below such statistics as we have for the number of children directly cared for by the American Relief Administration:

Month	1921	1922	1923
January	...	992,151	919,217
February	...	1,313,027	1,036,428
March	...	1,548,938	1,442,155
April	...	1,739,968	2,033,492
May	...	1,997,501	2,484,025
June	...	2,821,331	2,767,598
July	...	3,613,174	3,000,000
August	...	4,173,339	3,000,000
September	...	3,295,896	...
October	68,598	1,086,905	...
November	183,961	743,453	...
December	565,555	832,380	...

This table is only illustrative. Some children were in the full time, some were taken out when the better crop of 1922 came, and some died. Also, these statistics do not include children supported by our affiliated organizations or those fed in children's homes and hospitals by our medical division, nor do they include children whose parents received food packages.

Taking the listed number cared for during the month of August, 1922, which was 4,173,000 children, and making a rough estimate of those cared for by our affiliated organizations, our medical relief, and those provided for through food drafts, we can list the number who were fed in that month as more than 6,500,000.

RELIEF OF ADULTS

Undertaking to feed the mass of starving adults—in addition to the children—with our slender resources required that we reduce the adult dietary regimen to the lowest common denominator that would preserve life and give the most food value a dollar could buy.

Fortunately, we had a large corn crop in the United States in 1921. This crop and the shrinkage in demand for American food exports brought a great slump in prices of corn and, consequently, pork products. We therefore decided to rely on these two commodities for adults and to spread them as thin as we could to preserve lives. We were able to deliver corn to Russian ports for about seventy cents per bushel and fats for thirty cents a pound. The Russians had never been great corn eaters—but hungry people found methods of using it. Since fifteen hundred calories per day for adults would keep them alive, a ration of about fifty pounds of corn and a pound of fats per month would suffice.

The first full cargo of corn from the Congressional authority sailed on January 4, 1922, and twenty-eight cargoes were en route before the end of that month. At all times before the harvest of 1922, we were delivering this food to the ports as fast or faster than the Russian railways could move it inland, especially since we were delivering clothing, medical supplies, seed, and children's food at the same time.

It is impossible to estimate accurately the number of adults who were fed. Direct rations to 6,317,958 adults were issued by the American Relief Administration in August, 1922, but this figure did not include those supported by our affiliates, by the relief of intellectuals, those receiving individual food drafts, those who died prior to or after that date, or those who received rations at one time and who left our rolls, finding food elsewhere as conditions improved. Neither did it include the several hundred thousand Russians employed by the American Relief Administration food and medical divisions, who were paid in food, or the adults cared for in hospitals.

Our best estimate was that relief was given to about 14,000,000 adults. Adding the children, the total number of individuals who at one time or another were furnished the necessary margins to preserve life was estimated by our staff at more than 20,000,000.

FEEDING OUR RUSSIAN EMPLOYEES

In order for them to live, it was necessary that our Russian staff be furnished a ration of food. For this purpose we used 3,687 tons of food valued at $375,312.

TOTAL SUPPLIES

The total supplies delivered through the American Relief Administration during the famine were:

Item	Tons
Wheat and flour	134,781
Corn grits	96,202
Corn, barley and rye	386,556
Rice	18,915
Beans and peas	7,896
Pork products	12,425
Condensed milk	43,363
Cocoa	3,945
Sugar	21,556
Miscellaneous food	1,351
Feed	2,501
Soap	600
Medical supplies	8,282
Clothing and miscellaneous	3,200
Total	741,573

WE SUPPLY SEED GRAIN

It was obvious that if the famine were to be ended, a large supply of seed would have to be provided for the famine areas—and quickly. The people had eaten their usual savings of seed. Our authority from the Congress and the gold provided us by the Soviet Government were not available until January, 1922. Thus the time required for purchase and transportation of seed from overseas before the spring planting was a tight race, but, as usual, our staff triumphed. Most of the seed was purchased in the United States, since we had varieties corresponding with those of the Russians; in fact, some of our varieties of wheat were originally imported from Russia.

The seed was distributed in time. The deliveries of seed totaled 166,973.5 tons, valued at $9,983,359.54. The following table indicates the varieties of seed in tons:

	American Relief Administration	Soviet Gold
Seed wheat	35,713.3	101,321.0
Seed corn	18,294.3	4.1
Seed rye	. . .	3,810.2
Beans and peas	. . .	4,229.6
Grass seed	. . .	142.0
Oats	. . .	2,359.0
Miscellaneous	1,100.0	. . .
Grand Total ..	55,107.6	111,865.9
Total Value ..	$2,948,485.24	$7,034,874.3

CHAPTER 56

THE RELIEF OF INTELLECTUALS

The problem of the preservation of intellectuals arose in Russia as it had in Central and Eastern Europe. But it was worse in Russia because of the violent attitude of the Communist regime toward all "bourgeoisie."

These destitute groups included teachers, professors, scientists, doctors, engineers, lawyers, and the professional class generally. Some of them received food drafts from friends or relatives abroad, but the majority were not so lucky.

I may well introduce here a statement from a member of our staff:

. . . The first to succumb were the very old, the very young, the weak and infirm. . . . Suspect of the new rulers, with nothing to offer for bread but the ebbing strength of hands unused to labor, these, the intelligentsia . . . were driven from their accustomed work, to fight for food and for sticks to make a fire. Many broke under the heavy burden.[1]

A letter from one of the survivors reports:

Death was now more in evidence than life. Before my eyes there died Feodor Batiushkov, the famous professor of philology, poisoned from eating uneatably filthy cabbage. Another one to die from hunger was S. Bengerov, professor of history and literature, he who gave the Russian people entire editions of Shakespeare, of Schiller, and of Pushkin. I saw him quivering and limping about the bazaar, coveting an apple which

[1] H. H. Fisher, *The Famine in Soviet Russia, 1919–1923* (New York, The Macmillan Company, 1927), p. 385.

his means could not provide him. I saw that talented critic, A. A. Ismailov, die of hunger. At the same period the philosopher, V. V. Rosanov, succumbed to starvation in Moscow. Before his death the latter roamed the streets in search of cigarette ends with which to appease his hunger. . . .

Another letter tells the same story in other words:

Some days ago Professor Khvostoff hanged himself. Yesterday Professor Inostrantseff took potassium cyanide. So dies a great philosopher and the first geologist of Russia. . . . Professor Rosenblatt has just put an end to his life. . . . Professors Rozin, Diakonoff, two Valkoffs, Vilieff, Kapustin, Pokrovsky, Batiushkoff, Kulishev, Ostrogorsky, Karpinsky, Arsenieff, one after another have died and others are dying. Dying from typhus, influenza, pneumonia, and cholera, from starvation and from all the seventy-seven plagues of Egypt. . . . Our faculty meetings are now little more than mournful memorials to our colleagues.[2]

To provide funds for the relief of intellectuals, we made appeals to charitable persons and organizations. The largest contribution for intelligentsia relief was $830,000 from the Laura Spelman Rockefeller Memorial. We also received $95,000 from William Bingham II (for doctors); $25,000 from the Jewish Joint Distribution Committee; and $5,000 each from the Rochester Community Fund and from Dr. Henry Eversole, in addition to many miscellaneous contributions.

These funds were distributed in several different categories, with the approximate amounts as follows:

University professors and other teachers	$ 527,659
Physicians, nurses, and attendants	123,587
Artists and musicians	13,791
Ballet schools	2,900
Writers	4,100
Religious bodies	10,000
Through Committees of Russian Intellectuals	330,000
Individual relief, not specified	194,000
Total	$1,206,037

[2] Pitirim Sorokin, *Leaves from a Russian Diary*, pp. 230–31, as quoted in Fisher, *op. cit.*, p. 386.

To these might be added the individual food drafts of $9,305,300, since these were sent mainly to people in the intellectual groups by friends and relatives abroad. In addition, we distributed rations to these groups from our American Relief Administration funds, and considerable supplies were distributed to the intellectuals by our affiliated organizations.

The whole story of the Russian intelligentsia under the Communist heel was one of the most dreadful tragedies of all history.

Dr. Vernon Kellogg—himself an eminent scientist—who at our request had visited Russia,[3] was at that time the Director of the National Research Council in Washington—a branch of the National Academy. He organized a committee of scientists to solicit books and other publications in any language in an effort to bring to Russian medical men and other scientists data and discoveries made since the Communist eclipse. His drive was most successful. The National Research Council paid the outlays of Dr. Kellogg's committee, and the American Relief Administration contributed the transportation and organized the distribution of the material.

[3] See Chap. 52.

CHAPTER 57

MEDICAL AND SANITARY RELIEF

The American Red Cross was among the organizations attending our meeting of August 24, 1921, represented by its able and devoted Chairman, Dr. Livingston Farrand. At once he directed every resource of the Red Cross to us. In one of my early meetings with Dr. Farrand, Colonel Henry Beeuwkes of the U.S. Army Medical Corps took part. I was greatly impressed with the Colonel's abilities and promptly secured his designation by the Army to direct our medical staff. Colonel Beeuwkes selected a group of skilled and devoted men for his assistants, mostly from the Army Medical Corps, and the Army generously assigned them to our service and continued their Army pay.

Colonel Beeuwkes and his assistants arrived in Moscow on September 21, 1921. They soon began to send back word of a scourge of infectious diseases on a scale unknown in modern history. Their reports showed that not only the famine area but the whole of Russia was being infected, by refugees from the famine-stricken provinces, with typhus, relapsing fever, smallpox, cholera, typhoid, malaria, bubonic plague, tuberculosis, trichinosis, and pellagra. These infections were running unchecked, except by the variation of the seasons.

If anyone wishes to read a story of unspeakable horrors and at the same time a record of American men of highest courage, ability, and devotion, I recommend Colonel Beeuwkes' reports. And at this point

I may mention that the quotations and information in this chapter come from these truly great American medical men.

When Colonel Beeuwkes and his staff arrived, there was little information available beyond the fact that epidemics were on the march. The Soviet authorities had scant data as to the number of cases, and even their statements concerning the number of patients in hospitals and clinics proved inaccurate. In the background were the meager food supplies of the cities and towns during the war, the revolution and the counter-revolution. They left little resistance to these epidemics—except among members of the Communist Party.

Colonel Beeuwkes and his staff reported that the medical, hospital, and sanitary services had deteriorated unbelievably. Added to this, even apart from the famine area caused by the general agricultural degeneration, the shortage of food supplies throughout all of Russia was weakening resistance to disease everywhere. Their reports showed that even before the war Russia was far behind the world in vital medical and sanitary services. There were then only about 26,000 doctors, who, if distributed equally, would each have had to minister to 5,400 people. Many physicians and surgeons had perished in the war. Under the Communists, private practice had not been entirely abolished, but an impoverished population could not pay the doctors sufficiently for them to live. Many had sold their furniture, their libraries, and their instruments and were doing manual or clerical work in order to survive.

Our medical-staff reports show that the Communist Government had no sanitary service to speak of and that of the remaining 24,490 hospitals, only 9,682 had running water, only 6,500 were connected with sewers, and only 3,452 were equipped with central heating, and even those were often without fuel. The reports also show that Russian hospital buildings were dilapidated, the water supply and sewage systems were largely out of action, the mattresses were worn out, sheets were generally lacking, and the terribly worn blankets averaged one per bed. Many patients, on entering the hospitals, were required to bring their own eating utensils and sanitary equipment. The patients were often assigned two, and sometimes three to a bed, and at times the dead lay among the living.

Working in filthy and demoralized surroundings, most of the hospital doctors and nurses, themselves hungry, were lacking in energy and initiative. There were excessive numbers of untrained attendants in the hospitals who had joined the staffs hoping for food. Dr. Beeuwkes' men found that the supply of essential medicines was exhausted, and in most cases the few medicines remaining, in even the large hospitals, could be stored on one or two shelves of a small cabinet. Moreover, the great wave of hungry, vermin-infested refugees from the famine area was moving unrestrained across Russia and was partly responsible for the high incidence of infection which persisted through the winter of 1921 and the spring and summer of 1922.

Lest anyone think the above summary of the situation is an overstatement, I quote the text of some of the early reports of the Medical Division on their problems. Later, I will give their final summaries.

There is a great shortage of medical personnel throughout the famine area. The Russian physicians are, as a rule, well educated, efficient and interested in their work, but their morale is rather low and they are discouraged. However, our promise to help them has given them new life. . . . the medical assistance which will be rendered . . . will not only save many lives but will as well help to rejuvenate the medical profession of Russia and engender in their hearts a very warm and lasting affection for America.

. . . physicians and nurses are leaving the famine area because of the shortage of food. . . .

The feeding of patients in hospitals . . . [is] a very serious problem as the Government ration is uncertain and the appropriate diets impossible. . . .

. . . I know of no class in Russia more deserving of our admiration and assistance than the medical profession, doctors, nurses, feldshers and assistants. A large percentage have died during the last three years from epidemic diseases to which they have been constantly exposed. (Dr. Davenport states that fully 50% of the doctors of the Gubernia of Samara have died). Undernourished and overworked . . . weakened physical condition makes them a ready prey to infections and . . . their mortality rates are out of proportion to those pertaining generally. The mortality rate among physicians from typhus is reported 50% as against 15% for general population.

The larger cities are well supplied with hospitals but the villages are, as a rule, without facilities for treating disease and many towns have no physician and no felcher. The hospitals . . . in Kazan, Samara and Ufa [have] . . . during recent years, received only scant supplies and equipment, broken or worn out, has not been replaced. We find them . . . with much personnel unable to function. Drug and supply rooms exhibit many empty containers; essential drugs being absent. . . . sheets are entirely absent in most institutions, and blankets vary from a maximum of two per bed to a minimum of one for two beds and many are worn out. . . . vessels for administering medicines are rarely seen . . . bed pans are scarce and urinals are entirely wanting. . . . in one hospital of 200 beds there were approximately 30 wooden bowls for feeding the entire personnel.

. . . scalpels, forceps, and the other smaller instruments are badly needed by all, and the stock of dressings is in many institutions practically nil, while bandages are never seen. . . .

Medical famine exists in varying degree throughout Russia. . . . This explains the fact that large well equipped institutions are entirely devoid of expendible articles such as drugs, soap, dressings, surgical instruments, et cetera. . . . patients in practically unlimited numbers are at hand. . . .

Typhus fever has been epidemic in Russia during the last three winters: Approximately 500,000 cases were reported last year, which figure probably represents one half the actual number of cases which occurred. The disease . . . is . . . prevalent and severe . . . no very effective steps are being taken on the part of the Government. . . . Disinfectants are scarce . . . and disinfecting apparatus wholly insufficient, while poverty, crowding and filth are everywhere.

Some sample reports regarding the situation in various localities follow:

SYZRAN

In the City of Syzran . . . due to the influx of refugees from the Volga region to the east, thirty-three hundred cases of typhus and more than twelve hundred cases of recurrent fever were reported. About eight hundred of those afflicted have died.

In the Syzran Ouezd there is but one physician to 45,000 inhabitants. . . . which will explain in part the great number of deaths. . . .

The prevailing illnesses in order of frequency . . . are at present as follows: starvation (hunger edema), typhus, relapsing fever, scarlet fever, typhoid fever, measles, dysentery, influenza and tuberculosis.

THE CRIMEA

Conditions in the Crimea are probably worse than in any other part of Russia at the present time: poverty is general, the incidence of the various infectious diseases is high and cholera is epidemic. . . .

Prior to the civil war, the Crimea was the most important and prosperous health resort in Russia. At the present time Mr. Venear reports that 10–25% of buildings have been destroyed or are not habitable . . . the water supply is inadequate and sewerage systems ruined. The streets are torn up and dirty while trees in the parks have been cut down and used for fuel.

Living under . . . adverse conditions the inhabitants have lost morale and have been unable to maintain decent standards of cleanliness. . . . Crimea has degenerated from a health resort into a hot bed of disease. Early last fall typhus and recurrent fever developed and were spread . . . by refugees. . . . The mortality of typhus reached as high as 35% and many also died of recurrent fever. . . . in addition, cholera appeared in May and is now epidemic in most cities and towns: diphtheria, scarlet fever, scurvy and influenza are also very prevalent and with high mortality rates due to undernourishment of those contracting it.

ODESSA

Over three thousand typhus and recurrent fever cases . . . great shortage of blankets, bedding and medicines particularly salvarsan most essential for treatment recurrent fevers but practically unobtainable. . . . Many hospitals absolutely unheated and condition shivering patients many with only one tattered blanket pathetic beyond words. About 200 typhus patients from surrounding districts arrive Odessa daily.

While conditions Odessa are serious, am advised conditions in rural districts are much worse.

SARATOV

The population of the Saratov District including Saratov is 3,225,000. . . . The homes and hospitals of this district are very unsanitary. In many of the homes and hospitals there is a room set aside in which all the accumulation of human excreta of the institution is dumped. In one institution at Pokrovsk, which we inspected, we found in one room human excreta some eighteen inches to two feet deep on the floor. In many of the institutions you find this excreta deposited in the entrance corridor. We were told that the reason for this is that they have no sanitary system and it is too cold for their patients to go outside the buildings. . . . The majority of these institutions have absolutely no heat whatsoever. The inmates sleep as congested as possible in order to keep warm.

TZARITZIN

The population of the Tzaritzin District is 1,500,000 including the City of Tzaritzin. In general, the sanitary conditions of the district are bad and continue to grow steadily worse.

Typhus, typhoid and recurrent fever are present in epidemic form, their increase being due largely to four factors: (1) inadequacy of housing facilities (2) undernourishment (3) lack of control to prevent congestion in railroad travel (4) lack of bathing and delousing facilities.

SAMARA

. . . In Samara, hospitals have no water supply during the day and only a limited amount is pumped for two or three hours at night. These shortages make efficient functioning of institutions impossible and, during the winter months, many of even the most important hospitals are closed. . . .

THE TARTAR REPUBLIC

The Tartar Republic had last spring, exclusive of the city of Kazan, a population of 3,366,719; on December 1st it was approximately 2,892,200 and, at the present time, is even less. This loss is due . . . to the refugee movement . . . to deaths from hunger and disease. . . .

As a criterion of the food available in the Tartar Republic, a census of the live stock . . . shows a loss of 75% horses, 90% sheep and 80% cows. . . .

PETROGRAD

Petrograd, though far from the actual famine area . . . food supply is not adequate . . . undernourishment approaching starvation claims many victims, either directly or indirectly, by concurrent diseases. . . . Added to this, Petrograd is bearing a burden of 28,000 refugees from the Volga or famine area. The number of waifs in orphanages is 1,500.

. . . on account of the shortage of food, fuel and equipment, the authorities are closing all except five hospitals. . . .

. . . The [food] ration is theoretically . . . 1,400 calories, but actually

1,000 calories, while flour represents three-fourths to four-fifths of the caloric food value. The personnel is allowed theoretically 800 to 900 calories, but on visiting hospitals it is found that personnel are allowed no food whatever except what they can pick up from remains of patients.

I may state at this point that less than 1,500 calories will not preserve life for long.

I have already mentioned the measures we took to secure funds for our Medical Division. The total of these funds and supplies were:

The appropriation from the American Red Cross and the donation of medical and hospital supplies and winter clothing from their Paris stocks $3,804,863

The Red Cross reports show that they expended for salaries and allowances for personnel and for preparation of freight shipments 1,110,000

The Congressional donation of Government surplus medical supplies 5,000,000

The expenses incurred in inspecting, handling, and shipping these supplies were defrayed by the Laura Spelman Rockefeller Memorial Foundation 267,392

I have recounted the three donations for aid of intellectuals which were designated for doctors and which may be recalled here:

Mr. William Bingham II, of Boston, Massachusetts 95,000

Rochester Community Chest 5,000

Dr. Henry O. Eversole 5,000

OUR MEDICAL ORGANIZATION

Colonel Beeuwkes rapidly increased his medical staff to an organization of 40 American physicians and specialists, 21 other American staff workers, and a supervisory staff of some 800 competent Russians. He established central warehouses in Moscow into which our immense medical imports were received and thence dispatched to the areas in need. He established stations in each of the famine districts and also at points where the refugees could be treated. He put two medically equipped trains on the road to deal with refugees from the famine districts. He inaugurated in each famine district sanitary measures in which he employed thousands of Russians, who were paid with a food ration. His major method of attacking the scourge was to equip existing institutions with food, medicines, and medical instruments in order to bring life and tools to Russia's own doctors and technicians.

The Medical Division engaged in a number of other special campaigns. It organized an inspection service at many principal railway centers to spot refugees carrying infectious diseases. In one single center during one month, 2,427 cases of infection were removed to clinics, 2,339 were taken to hospitals, and 12,000 were given immediate aid, including inoculations. The Medical Division also organized a general campaign of vaccination and inoculation; 1,590,136 people were vaccinated, and 6,873,214 were given inoculations.

One of the joint problems of the Medical and Food divisions was providing food regularly to the inmates of the various institutions to which the Medical Division was giving aid. Our Food Division furnished such food as the Medical Division directed.

The children's homes presented a particularly trying problem. As I have indicated previously, the authorities had created homes for deserted children or those whose parents could not support them in the famine. The local governments had made an earnest effort to gather up waifs and orphans and place them in some sort of shelter. Seven thousand waifs were collected from the streets of Kazan alone in the month of November, 1921.

As one of its first objectives, the Medical Division, in conjunction with our food staff, organized Russian teams for clean-up campaigns. The important work of these teams was the removal of refuse from the streets and general cleaning of insanitary conditions. Many hospitals and children's homes—even whole towns—were entirely rehabilitated. The teams were paid with rations.

A bathing campaign was carried out among the children, many of whom were filthy and infested with lice. In Moscow, free baths were provided. In a three-week period in Odessa alone, 37,000 children and students were cleaned up, and in a 100-day period in Samara, like treatment was given to 181,000 children and adults. The clothing of thousands was completely sterilized.

Colonel Beeuwkes' final report read:

The various sanitary measures initiated by the A.R.A. together with the equipping of medical institutions throughout, were important factors in reducing disease and the magnitude of epidemics. . . . food relief extended by the A.R.A. to both adults and children enabled individuals to build up their powers of resistance to disease, undoubtedly playing a very important role in the decreased incidence of . . . [the infections].

Illustrative of the influence of the various measures initiated and carried out by the medical division . . . [was] the incidence of the disease in the city of Samara, the center of the Volga famine and epidemic area. . . . Cases of typhus per thousand of population are shown by months, for the years 1922 and 1923:

1922		1922 and 1923	
January	19.00	August	.03
February	11.70	September	.07
March	10.16	October	.18
April	6.20	November	.37
May	3.50	December	.28
June	1.88	January, 1923	.30
July	.31	February	.22

The official Soviet agencies reported the new typhus cases for the whole of Russia in the famine period:

	1921	1922	1923
January	89,033	151,138	36,938
February	95,455	190,792	24,303
March	87,788	277,710	6,684
April	75,743	295,525	. . . . .
May	59,450	231,747	. . . . .
June	62,179	126,294	. . . . .
July	28,825	64,811	. . . . .
August	13,948	30,192	. . . . .
September	13,494	20,670	. . . . .
October	19,925	18,429	. . . . .
November	44,326	22,091	. . . . .
December	86,005	14,888	. . . . .
	676,171	1,444,287	67,925

The enormity of the task of the Medical Division can be appreciated by medical men from the Division's final statistics:

SURGICAL INSTRUMENTS PROVIDED

648 cases of general operating instruments
435 smaller cases of instruments
336 cases of genito-urinary instruments
156 cases of ear, nose, and throat instruments
136 cases of eye instruments
367 cases of hemostatic forceps
572 medical and surgical chests
200 microscopes
 75 radio tubes and 1,000 plates
120 operating tables
    Thousands of cooking utensils, stoves, and lamps
    One laboratory completely equipped

I have already enumerated, in Chapter 54, some 3,146,000 textile items imported by our medical staff for hospital use.

MEDICAL SUPPLIES

8,000,000 bandages
2,400,000 pounds of soap
800,000 pounds of sulphur
200,000 pounds of creosol
200,000 pounds of formaldehyde
1,000,000 pounds of chloride of lime
60,000 pounds of quinine
700,000 pounds of cod liver oil
12,000,000 doses of vaccines
60,000 bottles of carbolic acid

86,000 bottles of collodion
55,000 bottles of corrosive sublimate
40 tons of ether and chloroform
31 tons of boric acid
57 tons of castor oil
15 tons of aspirin
70 tons of magnesia sulphate
100 tons of petrolatum
700,000 tubes of neosalvarsan

NUMBER OF INSTITUTIONS AIDED

	Number	Capacity for Patients
Hospitals and Sanitariums	5,764	353,332
Ambulatories	4,123	247,087
Children's homes	4,760	336,821

	Number	Capacity for Patients
Day nurseries	372	25,259
Schools	165	17,999
Homes for the aged	248	59,237
Other locations	987	
Total	16,419	1,039,735

This, the greatest foreign peacetime medical crusade ever undertaken, stands as a monument to the whole American medical profession—and to Colonel Beeuwkes.

CHAPTER 58

TROUBLES WITH THE KREMLIN

The major contacts and dealings of our relief staff were with the Kremlin's great Commissars—Kamenev, Dzerzhinsky, Chicherin, Litvinov, Sokolnikov, Rykov, Radek, Lander, and Volodin. Lenin, aside from his original appeal for help, had no direct relations with the American Relief Administration staff. During the period of our work, he was out of action for five months with a stroke—from May to October, 1922. He had a second stroke two months later and died from a third stroke on January 21, 1924, six months after our completion of the relief. During his illness, his place in the Kremlin was for all practical purposes taken, *de jure*, by A. I. Rykov.

Trotsky, who at that time ranked next to Lenin in the Soviet hierarchy, was at all times suspicious of our purposes. His sister violently and openly denounced the relief. In a two-hour speech on March 12, 1922, Trotsky referred to the relief. One of our staff describes this speech as follows:

Trotsky describes the important help of foreign workers and Bourgeious [*sic*] in the Volga disaster, and particularly dwells on the relief of the American Relief Administration. . . . Trotsky says that the United States, giving relief on one side, delivers in the meantime a subsidy to General Wrangel on the other. Thus helping the Russian peasants, they attempt to tighten the slip-knot on the neck of the Russian people. The American people through the intervention of the A.R.A. has rendered us important services. But we are . . . eager to look forward to the day when in Washington and New York it will . . . acknowledge that such experiments as Wrangel and Koltchak are sufficient, that they are not looking for a substitute for them, that they do not support openly or secretly, neither with subsidy nor morally. . . .

Trotsky's knowledge of history was highly deficient. The United States gave no aid to Wrangel or his "White" army. But more pertinent is the fact that Wrangel, supported by the French, was defeated in November, 1920, and evacuated his army from Russia to Constantinople on November 14, 1920. All of this was nine months before our response to the Gorky and Lenin appeal for help in the famine. As for Kolchak, President Wilson did direct some support to him, but his army was dissolved in December, 1919.

Trotsky apparently had a hand in our relations with the Kremlin. One of his henchmen, a minor Commissar named Eiduk, was appointed to keep track of the American Relief Administration activities and to be of aid in our day-to-day operations with the Soviet Government. He established agents wherever we had offices. His setup resembled Trotsky's installation of Commissars in the Red Army and was about as helpful to us as these agents were in battle. As a general rule, local authorities outside Moscow tried at all times to co-operate, but under Eiduk the influence of their good will was diluted by the time it reached the top Commissars.

Stalin was not an important figure during the period of the American Relief Administration work. Our records show no direct contact of our staff with him, but it may be assumed that as a member of the Politburo and Secretary of the Council of Commissars, he was familiar with what Kamenev and the other Commissars were doing. He did not come to high power until later.[1]

Difficulties with the Soviet authorities began two months after Colonel Haskell arrived in Moscow. The Colonel summed up the lack of co-operation and broken promises in a letter to Eiduk on November 11, 1921, two months after his arrival in Moscow:

I regret exceedingly to be compelled to bring to your notice the serious situation in which the American Relief Administration finds itself at the

---

[1] Of the Commissars with whom the relief dealt and who were helpful in its work, Kamenev, Radek, and Sokolnikov were subsequently "liquidated" by Stalin.

present moment in its endeavor to carry out the important work on which it has embarked, and to call particular attention to the lack of coöperation which the American Relief Administration is receiving from the Russian Government and the failure of the Russian Government to carry out their part of the agreement signed at Riga, August 20th. It would be impossible to enumerate all the broken promises and the obstacles placed in the way of progress in our work by officials of the Soviet Government. In most cases the officials who have obstructed our work have been, I believe, subordinates in the various bureaus, but that fact is immaterial, as when obstruction is made, the work stops.

After enumerating cases in point, Haskell referred to our decision to increase the relief, plans for which were already under way in America, and added:

However, I am inclined to feel many misgivings as to the propriety of lending my influence and recommendation to any further assistance for Russia so long as the Russian Government through its representatives is unable to handle and provide the necessary means for handling the operations already under way within this country. If it requires so much pleading, letter writing, and delay to accomplish our present program, I view with great doubt the ability of the Russian Government to carry through any relief program which will double, triple, or quadruple the coöperation necessitated at the present time and which might require perhaps five or ten times the means now required from the Russian Government.

The Colonel did not get very far with that mild protest, and soon greater obstructions appeared in the shape of specific incidents.

ARRESTS OF OUR RUSSIAN EMPLOYEES

Attempts by Eiduk to dominate the Russians working for us and even to prevent them from doing so began within two months after we started (November, 1921) and continued sporadically despite Haskell's many protests. Finally, on February 25, 1922, the Colonel addressed Eiduk in writing on one of his activities—the arrest of one of our Russian employees. The Colonel said:

The operation of the American Relief Administration cannot be subjected to these petty annoyances and personal persecutions on the part of local politicians, and neither can the American Relief Administration be placed in the position where intelligent men [Russians] are afraid to accept employment under it for fear of being persecuted for such employment.

After mature consideration, I consider that it is quite essential to our freedom of action as guaranteed by the Riga Agreement that this employee [a Russian] who, so far as [is] known, has engaged in no action against the Government, should be released from arrest and reinstated in his work at Tzaritzin until such time as the Government can show to the entire satisfaction of Mr. Bowden, District Supervisor at Tzaritzin, that this individual has actually, in fact, been guilty of some criminal activity against the Russian Government, since he has been in the employ of the American Relief Administration.

In view of all the above, I have authorized Mr. Bowden, District Supervisor at Tzaritzin, to use his judgment as to what particular section of the Tzaritzin Government shall receive relief supplies. I am not inclined to insist that he shall feed the city of Tzaritzin if, in his judgment on the ground, he has reason to believe that the local authorities are injecting political matters into the relief work there. There are so many people to be fed in Russia that I can find many places to use that part of our relief supplies which were originally intended to be distributed in the city of Tzaritzin.

Furthermore, I think it most unfortunate that you have injected your personality into this controversy as indicated by the telegram you dispatched recently to Tzaritzin, directing that this man be sent to Moscow and that you would appear against him. I believe that both your action in matters of this kind, as well as my own, should be free from any personal animosity, and that decisions should be taken in matters of this kind simply depending on the merits of the case itself as presented by the facts.

Haskell, under the Riga Agreement of free movement of our staff, established a system of American messengers to Riga to keep our offices in London and New York, Moscow, and Riga informed of ship movements and advised of the work. Their messages were transmitted to New York by code or through the American Legation. Although our messages were scrupulously free from any matters except relief, our Moscow staff seldom used the Soviet mail or telegraph system for communications sent outside Russia.

Colonel Haskell had repeatedly asked for a conference with Kamenev to present his difficulties with Eiduk but was constantly put off. Finally, the various obstructions and the violations of the Riga Agreement reached such dimensions that the Colonel determined upon a showdown.

On April 10, 1922, in order that the Commissars might read something of vital import to them, the Colonel sent me the following *en clair* telegram direct from Moscow:

For last two weeks attitude of Soviets has grown steadily more indifferent and disagreeable towards A.R.A. Less respect for terms of Riga Agreement. Now seizure American relief supplies, especially corn in transit, has begun. Forty cars from Reval under our seals diverted to Petrograd for railway workers. Fifty cars corn under our seals diverted at Balashov for railway workers. This diversion on telegraphic orders from railway authorities at Moscow. I have copy their telegrams. Eleven cars of corn taken at Penza same purpose. . . . Thirty-four cars taken Russaevka same purpose.

Eiduk disavows all these actions and promises reloading with payment or replacement for any shortage. However, abuses continue and promises are only made to be broken.

Meanwhile, for ten days I have tried without success to see Kamenev, his stated reason being too busy. . . . I have coöperated with Soviets fully to insure their seed arrivals, but they have been unappreciative and have sidetracked A.R.A. corn and failed to live up to the reduced demands agreed to by Krassin and myself, which are our minimum requirements children and necessary corn rations. Furthermore, priority of shipments guaranteed by Riga Agreement is ignored. Furthermore, railway authorities at Koslov have begun to unload 400 of our cars without authority and over protest our local representative.

These acts of arbitrary interference and disrespect for our seals, plus the fact that although corn leaves ports rapidly it congests at junction points and does not arrive at Volga in sufficient quantities, leads me to seriously doubt the ability of Russian railways to deliver our program.

I can positively recommend that not another pound of relief supplies should be added to our existing program. I recommend that all pending shipments from America be stopped beyond actual present commitments until such time as I can advise how present difficulties are met here and whether a sincere effort to coöperate with us manifests itself.

No supplies should be collected in America above our program because they could not be transported to the famine areas before harvest.

This message produced an instantaneous result. Kamenev at once came to see Haskell at the latter's office. Commissar Eiduk was present and had to bear a frontal attack from Kamenev on his failure to co-operate. A member of our staff who spoke Russian was present and made a record of the interview. Haskell bluntly went over his entire bill of complaints. Kamenev berated Eiduk, but since Haskell was still not given satisfying assurances, he sent me another open telegram the next day, April 11—no doubt as a reminder to Eiduk.

I have reached the point where plans and promises have little effect and distinctly advised Mr. Kamenev that from to-day the definite record of services rendered by Russian railways and accomplishments in fact were the only evidences acceptable to me from the Soviet Government. This entire situation is in an acute stage and I must have our demands met in fact and not in theory, before I change my recommendations regarding reduction of the Russian feeding program. You may be assured that our demands will be reasonable and all within the power of the Soviet Government to carry out.

Kamenev and Litvinov now took a firm hand. Eiduk was removed on June 27, 1922, and Commissar Karl Lander was given his job. Lander turned out to be much more helpful.

On April 27, we in New York and Washington were greatly relieved by the following telegram from Haskell:

Soviet railways now making every effort [to] coöperate [in the] delivery of program and are fulfilling their guarantees. Transport situation now satisfactory and with increases promised will carry our program as originally planned. Therefore recommend resumption purchases and shipments according to schedules. I am glad to report that general coöperation Soviet authorities has materially improved during the last two weeks in meeting our requirements of control, inspection, et cetera. I hope and believe that a better understanding now exists, that an attitude friendly to our work will be maintained and necessary assistance given.

FAILURE TO PROVIDE TRANSPORTATION

In addition to other difficulties, our staff continued to be bedeviled with the failure of the Soviet railway authorities to transport our supplies from the ports to the starving people inland, sometimes only one hundred miles away. To make clear these failures, it is necessary for me to recite their history from the beginning of our work.

When we had decided in 1921 that we would undertake the huge supply program for adults and enlarge our children's relief, the Communist Railway Commissar in Moscow assured Colonel Haskell that he could handle 200,000 tons of supplies a month out of the ports. He particularized it as 80 cars a day out of Baltic ports and about 240 cars a day out of the Black Sea ports. When our cargoes began to pile up in the ports, there was no such supply of cars. Less than 15 cars a day were made available in Baltic Sea ports. Day after day, our Moscow office reported scores of incidents such as the following:

The first train to leave Odessa with food supplies took one month to reach its destination 1,500 miles away. Instead of the empty cars being sent back from the Volga region to the ports, they were directed on to Siberia. Of the cars loaded at all ports in the Baltic and Black seas in September, 1921, eleven per cent had not yet reached their destinations. In November the non-arrivals from the October loadings were fifteen per cent, and in December the arrivals from the November port landings were twenty-five per cent.

In order to get better railway service, Kamenev directed Commissar Krassin, an engineer then on foreign duty, to return from abroad to take charge of the railways. Krassin made a good fight, but six years of degeneration in the transport system proved too much for him, and he confessed to Colonel Haskell that the previous promises could not be met, that the best he could do would be to furnish about 160 cars daily instead of the 320. The fact was that the competent pre-Revolution railway managers, being bourgeois and anti-Communist, had either escaped, been liquidated, or sent to Siberian work camps.

This small supply of railway cars meant death to millions. In desperation, Colonel Haskell, with Krassin's approval, posted Americans from our staff at critical points where food trains were being jammed up and placed Americans aboard the trains to see them through. He got better results.

At the Black Sea ports, when the dock and railway workers witnessed the piling up of supplies, they promptly struck for higher wages in true capitalist fashion. Trains stood in the yards while people died a few hundred miles away. The Commissars recruited a mob of strikebreakers from the interior—but these men, knowing nothing about stevedoring, made little improvement in the situation.

Then the railway employees demanded more pay and food. They began to seize the food by carload lots. Our staff members secured copies of Eiduk's orders authorizing them to make these seizures. At one time it looked as if the delivery of our food-draft parcels would wholly break down through a failure of rail transportation, but a notice to Kamenev on January 23, 1922, that we would stop selling the drafts at once brought fifty-seven cars, which delivered 17,000 of Burland's packages in four days.

The Colonel was entirely sympathetic with the half-starved, underpaid railway and dock workers. He solved the problem of confiscation of our food and at the same time stimulated the whole railway system to action by issuing monthly food packages, direct from us, to all workers assigned to stevedore and transport our supplies. The packages, designed to support a whole family for a month, contained the following amounts of food:

Corn grits	30 pounds
Cocoa	3 pounds
Evaporated milk	10 cans
Bulk lard	10 pounds
Flour	45 pounds
Sugar	10 pounds

Under this arrangement and with our men at critical points, the supplies moved into the districts where tens of thousands of people were dying.

Another alarming crisis arose in November, 1922, when Lander, obviously under pressure and plainly embarrassed, demanded of Colonel Haskell a complete revision of the Riga Agreement. The Colonel flatly refused and added that we would quit instantly in such a case. He heard no more about it.

CHAPTER 59

TROUBLES WITH
AMERICAN COMMUNISTS

Troubles with the Communists in Russia were not enough for a group of men trying to save their people—we also had to contend with their agents in the United States. Most of our troubles revolved around two persons. The facts regarding their activities came to us from extensive reports of the Federal Bureau of Investigation. The principal person involved was David Dubrowsky, probably an American citizen. He was a Communist agent employed on salary from the Soviet New York office. The secondary light was Walter Liggett, a professional public-relations man. Dubrowsky contracted with Liggett to create a committee called "The American Committee for Russian Famine Relief." Their contract, dated December 5, 1921, provided a cash advance to Liggett of $3,500 and a percentage of the funds he raised. Dubrowsky signed the contract as the representative of the Russian Red Cross. Liggett established his offices in Chicago and secured the sponsorship of thirteen state Governors and ten United States Senators and other influential persons, all of whose names appeared on the letterhead of his committee. He issued extensive publicity appealing for aid for the suffering people in Russia. He raised considerable funds. At once our religious affiliates flooded us with complaints because, although Liggett had secured some religious prelates to support his appeals, he was diverting donations from them.

Liggett requested me to endorse his organization, but on advice from the F.B.I. that there was no assurance these funds would ever reach the Russian people, I refused. He threatened me with dire consequences from his sponsors and at once issued statements to the press. Some of his Governor-sponsors became suspicious of this and other activities and applied to the F.B.I. for information. The F.B.I. replied by telegram as follows:

Following relief committees are officered and managed by well known communists or sympathizers. First Friends of Soviet Russia. Second Russian Red Cross. Third Medical Relief to Soviet Russia. Fourth American Federated Russian Famine Relief Committee. The officers among others comprise Dr. Dubrowsky and Dr. Jacob Hartman formerly connected with Ludwig Martens. Such portion of their funds or supplies as are transmitted by them to Russia are shipped to the Soviet officials for distribution by them. These organizations are apparently opposed to the American Relief Administration which handles the Congressional appropriations and distributes its supplies under American direction as is shown by the letterhead of the Friends of Soviet Russia which bears this statement:

"Our principle. We make the working class appeal. Give not only to feed the starving but to save the Russian workers revolution. Give without imposing imperialistic and reactionary conditions as do Hoover and others."

From the above you will see that these organizations furnished their foodstuffs exclusively to Soviet authorities and the distribution of the food was not under American direction. With this information the decorative sponsors of Liggett's committee quickly abandoned it, but Dubrowsky and Liggett continued their efforts to hold their various organizations together. Liggett engaged in much press vilification of the American Relief Administration and myself. Dubrowsky appealed to his Soviet superior in Moscow, who took up the matter with Colonel Haskell. Having been informed by us, the Colonel gave him the answer.

I was informed by the F.B.I. agents that these committees had collected upwards of $1,500,000. The Customs returns showed that they had shipped about $250,000 worth of supplies from the United States to Russia. Since this sum was the result of American charity, we include this amount in our statements of American supplies furnished.

Later on, the Dies Un-American Activities Committee unearthed the fact that much of the funds raised by Dubrowsky and Liggett was spent on Communist propaganda in the United States. This fact was also exposed by repentant Communists, such as Benjamin Gitlow and others.

Liggett raised funds from somewhere to publish an elaborate book about me. He was later murdered by some of his associates.

CHAPTER 60

WE ENCOUNTER
HARD-BOILED COMMUNISM

We had been hopeful that with our abundant supply of seed and with prospects of favorable weather we might terminate the relief at the harvest of 1922. In June, Dr. Hutchinson, our crop expert, requested our staff to report on the crop prospects resulting from our seed distribution to the famine districts. The conclusion was that there would be sufficient food to carry the adults through the next harvest year, with some grain surplus for other parts of Russia. The Soviet authorities in Moscow confirmed Hutchinson's estimates.

At my suggestion, Edgar Rickard and Walter Brown of our New York and London offices, together with my secretary, Christian Herter, and Governor Goodrich, met with Colonel Haskell and his staff in Moscow on June 17, 1922, to consider whether we should continue after the harvest. Their conclusion was that except for limited regions, mass relief for adults would no longer be necessary —if the Communists handled the situation properly. They recommended that in regard to adults, we should wait for more positive development of the harvest. They concluded, however, that in any event we should continue the children's and medical relief.

Six weeks later, on July 30, 1922, Colonel Haskell came to New York for a conference with our colleagues and myself. A survey of our resources showed that in addition to continuation of the food drafts and the activities of some of our affiliated organizations, we could continue the relief to some one to three million children, along with our medical services, until July, 1923. Upon his return to Russia, Colonel Haskell advised us that there might be a million adults in need of help after January 1.

In the previous year the Kremlin had ordered the confiscation of all the churches' treasures, stating they would be sold abroad for imports of food and other supplies.

We were soon in trouble again. The Soviet Government officials exultantly announced the end of the famine and issued several statistical statements indicating a surplus of food. In late September, 1922, they announced that the surplus warranted exports of grain—which our representatives in the ports reported the Russians were doing. I cabled Colonel Haskell on September 26, 1922, as follows:

Before we undertake the burden of Russian relief beyond our planned child program, we must know more of Soviet intentions. Foodstuffs must be put into motion at once for the one million adults who begin starving on January first, therefore we must know: First, what provision Soviet is making for domestic food supply to these people. Second, as the famine church collections and crown jewels have been widely advertised, what provision is being made to realize on these collections and to apply them to prevent starvation? It will scarcely be possible . . . to make a successful appeal for public charity abroad until evidence is given of complete exhaustion of the above resources. Therefore the whole problem must be threshed out with Soviet authorities:

(a) Do they need imported supplies
(b) Are their resources exhausted
(c) If they still have these [religious] treasures what are they going to do with them in provision for their people.

We of course wish to coöperate in every way practicable.

In line with this cable, Haskell wrote Kamenev on October 9, 1922, reiterating his wish to co-operate with the Government in meeting the problem of a return of famine conditions in some sections and summarizing his latest estimate of the situation. His letter continued:

. . . If I am correct in my conclusions, I feel that I should recommend to Mr. Hoover to seek the finance and set in motion such food supplies as may be necessary beyond those obtainable by the Soviet Government to meet this oncoming famine situation.

However, it will be apparent to you that, before making any recommendations, I must know more of the Soviet Government's food resources and intentions, for the reason that it will be very difficult to obtain funds except to cover so much of the need as is clearly beyond the resources of the Soviet Government.

No successful appeal on behalf of Russia could possibly be made [abroad] for public charity . . . unless evidence is given by the Soviet Government:

(1) That the Soviet Government is making every provision, within its power, for the domestic food supplies for the starving and that, in addition, it is made clear that a real need will exist for imported supplies beyond the domestic availabilities.

(2) That the Soviet Government announces how much of the necessary imported foodstuffs they will be able to purchase with their own resources now available.

(3) That the Soviet Government will state the net difference between the requirements for import and what they will be able to purchase abroad.

You are well aware, Mr. Kameneff, of the wide publicity given abroad concerning the sufficiency of the 1922 harvest to meet all of Russia's food requirements. You are also cognizant of the fact that the . . . [seizure of the] church collections and crown jewels have been widely advertised [for the purposes of relief] and that no official and comprehensive statement has been published as to what provision is being made, if any, to realize on these collections and to apply them to prevent starvation.

I think you will agree with me that, if it is the desire of the Russian Government to obtain American assistance beyond our present program . . . it would clear the atmosphere and make it easier for the friends of Russia to obtain the necessary finances if your Government would publish a frank statement concerning the disposition that has been, or will be made of the assets referred to above, and show that a need exists for imported foodstuffs beyond the remaining available resources of the Soviet Government.

The official reply from the Soviet Government came a few days later, on October 20, 1922, when Haskell conferred with Kamenev and officials representing the Central Statistical Commissariat, the Commissariats of Agriculture, Food Supply, and Health, and the State Planning Commissariat. Haskell reported to us that the Government estimated that by November 1, there would be 4,300,000 people who, though not starving, would need assistance and that by January 1, over eight million would require help. These figures were said to be the absolute minimum. The increased resources available to Russia would enable the Government to care for 4,000,000. Other foreign organizations were thought to be able to support 1,000,000, leaving 3,000,000 whom they thought should be supported by the American Relief Administration.

Medical needs were based on 430,000 beds, for which the Government could provide 50 per cent of requirements. The Soviet authorities requested the American Relief Administration to provide the remainder. At once we reviewed the possibilities of the American Relief Administration's meeting such a program. To do so required asking the American public for funds in the face of the Soviet announcements of a surplus for export.

On October 25, 1922, I sent Colonel Haskell the following stiff cable, to be transmitted to Kamenev:

. . . Interviews by Soviet officials in press indicate intention to export food from Black Sea ports the statement being that this food will be sold in Mediterranean, and other food bought in Northern Europe for import through Baltic the whole because of inability transport by rail from South to North Russia.

1. Since famine areas lie [in] Southern Ukraine and Volga we are unable to reconcile export of food from Black Sea ports as foodstuffs to supply these areas would have to be imported through Black Sea ports and these proposals amount to importing food parallel with exporting from same ports. The export sale of food from Russia from any quarter while threatened by famine and starvation would at once destroy all outside sentiment for relief.

2. Possessions of crown jewels and church treasures and other liquid assets have been widely advertised by Soviet authorities throughout the world and to solicit public charity without full use of these assets to feed starving people would create a hopeless reaction.

3. The A.R.A. is solely a charitable organization dependent upon public good will and generosity. It is prepared to carry out its original children's program in any event but before it could hope for successful strengthening of its resources it would be necessary to have pledges that

A. No foodstuffs would be exported from Russia under any circumstances until next harvest.

B. Liquid assets such as mentioned above would be pledged to some European bank or agency for as much loan as could be obtained, the proceeds of which should be devoted to the import of foodstuffs for the famine sufferers. Otherwise the sincerity of Soviet authorities in relief of their suffering fellow countrymen will be open to constant challenge from all charitably disposed persons who will naturally insist that the first obligation of a government is to prevent starvation of its people and only when every resource of the government has been exhausted can there be rightful or successful call for their charity.

4. If these things were agreed to the A.R.A. would make an effort to increase its program but naturally as much increased resources are dependent upon public charity it is utterly impossible to undertake any guarantee as to positive amounts.

A condensation of Kamenev's written reply November 8, 1922, is as follows:

1. The Government expected to realize from ten to fifteen million dollars and perhaps more on grain exports from South Russia.

2. They proposed to use the money for import of agricultural implements, cattle, etc.

3. They would put up the seized Church jewels as security for a loan, but since the Soviet Government had not been recognized by any country except Germany, and Germany had no money, a loan was not feasible. If however, such a loan could be made, they would use it to buy domestic or import food for relief.

On November 18, 1922, we replied bluntly to Kamenev:

One. The original proposition was the statement from the Soviet Government confirmed by the A.R.A., that some 8,000,000 Russian people including 3,000,000 children were in immediate jeopardy of starvation, together with definite request from the Soviet for our charitable help.

Two. It is obvious that the volume of intended exports of grain now disclosed by their statement would maintain the whole adult population in the famine areas leaving the problem solely one of children.

Three. The A.R.A. cannot enter into argument as to the stated reason of the legal inability of the Soviet Government to sell or borrow upon its liquid assets in order to revolve its foodstuffs internally or to import, further than to mention that Soviet Government has continuously sold confiscated property in England and continental countries for the last two years.

Four. Of major importance however is the fact that the A.R.A. being a charitable organization devoted to saving human life from starvation must protest against the inhumanity of a Government policy of exporting food from starving people in order that through such exports it may secure machinery and raw materials for the economic improvement of the survivors. Any such action imposes the direct responsibility for the death of millions of people upon the Government authorities.

Five. We do not believe that the American people will respond to an appeal for charity to prevent starvation when available food is being hauled by rail across the very areas where millions of people will die and is exported through the very ports into which food must be imported for their salvation.

Colonel Haskell now advised us that the harvest situation was better than the Soviet authorities had estimated and that they were slackening their exports. Our final conclusion was that the American Relief Administration would support 3,000,000 children until the harvest of 1923, that we would continue medical services and food for hospitals, and that with regard to adults, we would wait and see what developed after February or March. As time went on, no acute situation developed among adults, except in a few local spots—which we took care of.

As the 1923 harvest approached, I requested Dr. Hutchinson, who had been abroad recuperating from one of the Russian infections, to return and give us an estimate of the situation over the winter of 1924. On May 14, 1923, he again forecast a surplus. The Soviet Government confirmed his estimates. At my suggestion, Colonel Haskell requested the views of our staff in Moscow and in the field as to whether we should continue during the next harvest year—from August, 1923, to August, 1924. They were unanimous that we should wind up.

We never learned what became of the mass of gold, jeweled icons, and other precious items which were stripped from the churches.

CHAPTER 61

OUR AFFILIATES

I have referred to our affiliate organizations many times, but the record requires a more ample statement of their work. I have postponed such a description of their services until the background picture of the Russian problem was complete. I have already described the early development of our association with the following organizations:

The Jewish Joint Distribution Committee
The National Lutheran Council
The National Catholic Welfare Council
The American Friends Service Committee
The Y.M.C.A. and Y.W.C.A.
The American Mennonite Relief
The Volga Relief Society
The Federal Council of Churches of Christ in America and other religious
 organizations
The aid of the great foundations
The Dubrowsky organizations (not "affiliates")

In preparing this narrative, my research staff has worked in the files, as far as they have been preserved, of all these organizations. The data of some of these organizations are necessarily incomplete.

There were no hard and fast rules in the American Relief Administration's relations with its affiliates, other than those imposed by the Riga Agreement and President Harding's directive of single-

headed control. We were anxious for any responsible body to undertake relief anywhere it liked, and the American Relief Administration, to the extent of the funds we could secure, would fill in the
great gaps in its services. We had no friction with any of our affiliates, and there was no friction among the affiliates themselves. One
reason for smooth working was the appointment of a representative
from each of them to our Moscow office under Colonel Haskell.
These were all able and devoted men who worked not alone in the
direction of their own service but in the general interest of all.

THE JEWISH JOINT DISTRIBUTION COMMITTEE

With the Communist Revolution, the Jewish Joint Distribution
Committee had been forced almost wholly to withdraw aid from its
co-religionists in Russia. But with the coming of the famine and the
Riga Agreement, opportunity came again.

The Committee's representatives working with us in the United
States were Felix Warburg, James Rosenberg, and my former secretary, Lewis L. Strauss. They appointed two able administrators to
our staff in Moscow—Dr. Boris D. Bogen and Dr. Joseph A. Rosen.

The Committee participated in the relief in many directions. It
contributed directly to the funds of the American Relief Administration, to the American Friends Service Committee, and to the
Y.M.C.A.–Y.W.C.A. Student Fund, and undertook a huge program
of rehabilitation of its co-religionists. Its major service, however,
was the creation of its own centers, where, with supplies from our
bulk drafts, it conducted food kitchens and gave rations and medical
care. Its work was mostly in the Ukraine and South Russia, where
the Jewish population was concentrated. The number of people
served by the Committee at one time rose to more than one million.
It undertook the creation of agricultural activities which provided
the means of self-support for the thousands of Jews who were moved
from the cities. It established trade schools, orphanages, hospitals,
and every other form of aid to suffering people. And in every locality
where the Committee operated, it also served those of other faiths

in the neighborhood. Its effort is not to be weighed in dollars, but for lack of any other indicator of dimensions, I give here its account of expenditures in the Russian famine from August, 1921, to January 1, 1923:

I. *Non-Sectarian Relief Work in Cooperation With Other Organizations* $3,827,386.75
    A. American Relief Administration
        1. The distribution of food in the Volga region .... $ 675,000.00
        2. Child feeding program to harvest 1922 in the Ukraine   1,367,386.75
        3. Child feeding and Medical programs to harvest 1922 in the Ukraine and White Russia 1,100,000.00
        4. Adult feeding program in the Ukraine 375,000.00
        5. Student feeding in cooperation with the Y.M.C.A. (Student Friendship Fund) ... 50,000.00
        6. Placed as a discretionary fund with A.R.A. directors for the distribution of food and clothing 10,000.00
    B. American Friends' Service Committee
        1. Cash and food supplies 250,000.00

II. *Relief through Representatives of the American Jewish Joint Distribution Committee* $4,221,324.48
    A. Comprising:
        1. Adult feeding program in the Ukraine .... $ 375,000.00
        2. Direct clothing shipments .. 128,434.96
        3. Relief in cash, food and fuel 450,000.00
        4. Rehabilitation of children's institutions 200,000.00

5. Cash and food relief to Children's internates	250,000.00
6. Direct relief distributed by the J.D.C. representatives . .	657,424.99
7. Other appropriations	31,407.92
8. Advance guarantee to A.R.A. for clothing draft operations	250,000.00
9. Extensive reconstruction work inaugurated by the reconstruction department . .	1,290,000.00
10. To assist in repatriation work in the Ukraine, the Crimea, and on the Russian side of the River Dniester, etc. . . .	76,566.61
11. Assistance to teachers, scholars, etc.	12,490.00
12. Continuance relief activities 1923 appropriation	500,000.00
TOTAL	$8,048,711.23

The J.D.C. operations during the Russian famine, however, did not end on January 1, 1923. Our research into its accounts for the year 1923 indicates a further expenditure during that year of over $1,346,500, or a grand total of more than $9,395,211. From this total must be deducted the item of "Advance guarantee to A.R.A. for clothing draft operations" in the amount of $250,000, leaving a net expenditure of $9,145,211.

THE NATIONAL LUTHERAN COUNCIL

The National Lutheran Council, under the presidency of Dr. Lauritz Larsen, appointed Dr. J. A. Morehead as its representative on our staff at Moscow. He was later succeeded by the Reverend W. L. Scheding. Both were men of unusual courage and character and most valuable additions to our staff.

There was a considerable membership of the Lutheran faith in Russia, mostly in the German settlements in the Volga Valley, but there were also many local pastorates in the Ukraine and South Russia. Altogether, there were 125 Lutheran parishes which embraced 650 villages. The Lutherans distributed their relief through their pastors, who obtained supplies from our food drafts. The Lutheran Council's natural purpose was to aid co-religionists, but in its early work, resources did not permit aid to whole communities. This somewhat complicated the work of the American Relief Administration in administering relief to adults and children in the same villages, but Father Walsh of the National Catholic Welfare Council resolved this problem by a donation of food drafts to enable the Lutherans to aid their Catholic and other neighbors.

The Lutheran Council conducted a nation-wide campaign for clothing, and we furnished free transportation for 393,000 pounds, which the Council valued at $500,000.

As the Council's resources became stronger through larger home support, it gave a monthly donation of $32,000 to the American Relief Administration, which covered our support of the children in the Lutheran parishes.

One of the incidents in the Council's work was the arrest by the Communists of a district supervisor, Pastor C. O. Mees, for espionage. He was sentenced to three years in Siberia. The charge against Mees arose from an innocent report on the economic situation in his district. Colonel Haskell made every effort to secure Mees's release, but to no avail.

Altogether, the Council's expenditures in the famine during the association with the American Relief Administration exceeded $990,000. It carried on its work for a short time after the American Relief Administration withdrew from Russia but was compelled to withdraw soon after.

These men and women, both American and Russian Lutherans, carried on bravely despite the dangers and horrors which surrounded them. There has seldom been a greater effort to alleviate suffering than that of the Lutheran leaders at home and abroad.

After over three years of intensive relief efforts, Dr. Morehead died from overwork and exposure. He was one of the martyrs to the relief of the Russian famine.

THE NATIONAL CATHOLIC WELFARE COUNCIL

This organization sent Father Edmund A. Walsh as its representative on our staff in Moscow, where he arrived on March 22, 1922. The background of his mission was somewhat complicated. Prior to Father Walsh's arrival, His Holiness Pope Benedict XV had made an appeal for aid to European, as well as American, Catholics for relief of the Russian famine, and from European sources he had forwarded about forty carloads of supplies to Russia. Father Walsh arranged that all further funds, both European and American, should funnel through the American Catholic Welfare Council—and thus under his direction. He and the American members of his staff came under the protection of the Riga Agreement. Their supplies were purchased by and transported to their designated spots by the American Relief Administration in the form of bulk food and clothing drafts.

The Council chose Crimea, Orenburg, Rostov-on-Don, Krasnodar, and a part of Moscow as the areas for its relief. In Crimea, Father Walsh took over the whole operation of the American Relief Administration, which he continued until the end of the relief.

The Council established kitchens for distribution of food; it also provided orphanages and gave medical aid. At the maximum point, Father Walsh's kitchens were serving daily about 150,000 men, women, and children.

We had some complications with Father Walsh's organization arising from the appointment of Italians, Spaniards, Germans, Yugoslavians, and Czechoslovakians to represent the Catholic areas of European contributions. However, these complexities were solved by the wholly co-operative character of both Colonel Haskell and Father Walsh. Colonel Haskell finally arranged with the Soviet authorities that although the Riga Agreement applied only to Americans, the European members of Father Walsh's staff were also brought under that protection.

From American Relief Administration records, it appears that

Father Walsh's organization expended about $1,300,000, of which more than $750,000 was for the purchase of bulk food and clothing drafts. It is impossible to determine from the surviving records how much of these funds were American and how much European origin, but apparently more than one-half came from the United States.

In the work of the Council, no discrimination was made regarding race or religion in the areas it served. It was a great manifestation of humane spirit and of the ability and devotion of Father Walsh and his staff.

THE AMERICAN FRIENDS SERVICE COMMITTEE

This committee participated in our meeting of affiliates on August 24, 1921, but its situation was complicated because the organization was jointly operated with the British Friends. Despite President Harding's directive, the two groups made their own agreement for protection with the Soviet Government. Secretary Hughes had a troubled mind in regard to their passports but finally agreed with me to issue them.

The initial resources of the two organizations were indeed meager, but their devotion and administrative ability so impressed the other affiliates that the Jewish Joint Distribution Committee gave them $150,000, the American Red Cross donated $100,000, and we of the A.R.A. donated $100,000. They also received financial support from an organization called the Russian Famine Fund of New York, probably exceeding $50,000. The American Relief Administration furnished them its facilities of purchase and transportation through their purchase of $415,000 of food drafts.

Their reports state that the total expenditures of the two Friends committees in Russia from 1917 to 1924 were $1,523,007. As near as we can estimate, about $300,000 was furnished by British Friends. The probable expenditure of American origin during the famine was about $1,223,000. The Friends also collected and distributed a large amount of clothing, which the A.R.A. transported for them free of charge.

The Friends were easy to co-operate with, since their method was to take over a definite area and provide every sort of relief within its limits. In these areas they not only furnished food, clothing, and medical supplies, but they also undertook agricultural aid and their own medical services, hospitals, and orphanages.

THE YOUNG MEN'S CHRISTIAN ASSOCIATION
AND
THE YOUNG WOMEN'S CHRISTIAN ASSOCIATION

These organizations, under the title "The Student Friendship Fund" and under the chairmanship of Dr. John R. Mott and Treasurer George W. Perkins, Jr., had been contributing relief and other aids to students in Central and Eastern Europe. With the signing of the Riga Agreement, expansion of their work into Communist Russia became possible. E. T. Colton was appointed their representative on our Moscow staff, and Samuel M. Keeny was their administrator in the field. It was estimated that about 100,000 students were attending Russian universities at the beginning of the relief.

A statement issued by this organization related, among other facts, that ten or more students in the Samara area alone died of starvation daily and that all were short of food and underclad. A report by Mr. Colton contains these items:

Clothing insufficient to protect against climate.
Investigation of 3,600 students showed:
   17% had but one set of underclothing
    6% without overcoats
   52% needed shoes
   25% need a complete outfit
Housing inadequate:
   35 to a room
   Board beds
   Overcoats for bed covering
   No heat in rooms
Impossibility of paying for necessary medical care.
Investigation of 3,000 students showed:

15% in good health
33% easily cured if not neglected
33% need special treatment
18% incurable and in many cases should be segregated.
Lack of books and equipment for study
Students often stand in line at the libraries from 6 A.M. until the opening hour in order to use certain reference and text books. . . .
. . . A possible 10% belong to the Communist Party. In the freshman class which should contain the largest percentage, statistics show only 1 party member in 12.

To carry out the work in each university, the American Relief Administration opened, on behalf of the students, food-supply kitchens and issued clothing, and our medical staff gave special services. The student attendance steadily increased and soon our organization was providing for 110,000 students and our affiliates were supplying another 31,000.

The Student Friendship Fund had difficulties raising money in the United States, and we were soon carrying the major burden of their work. Their net financial support to our organization was about $150,000.

Certainly this effort at least contributed to the maintenance for the future of skilled scientists, engineers, doctors, and teachers.

THE AMERICAN MENNONITE CENTRAL COMMITTEE

The Mennonites dated their origins from Zürich, Switzerland, in 1525. The first group of Mennonites settled in America at Germantown, Pennsylvania, in 1683. Of their faith there were possibly 100,000 members in the United States in 1921 and 40,000 in Canada. The principal officers of their relief committee were P. C. Hiebert, Chairman, and Levi Mumaw, Secretary. P. P. Epp represented the Canadians on the Central Committee.

They started their work among Russian refugees in Constantinople. They made their own agreement with the Soviet Government on October 1, 1921, along the lines of the Riga Agreement of a month before. Their representative in Russia, Alvin J. Miller, asked that they become one of the A.R.A. affiliates, and an agreement to that end was signed with them on December 5, 1921, whereby the Mennonite Committee obtained the protections of the Riga Agreement and our purchase and transport facilities. They secured their food supplies through our bulk food drafts, and at one time they were providing for 35,000 persons.

The Mennonites decided to extend their operations of aid in agriculture through the extensive import of tractors and other farm machinery, an agreement which was arranged with the Soviet Government by Colonel Haskell's office. Under this agreement, the Mennonites imported fifty tractors with two plows each, along with some other farm machinery.

An interim report of the Central Committee, dated April 2, 1923, showed total expenditures of $997,712, which with a further expenditure of $100,000 up to the date of the American Relief Administration's withdrawal, brought the total to $1,097,712. Of this, $400,000 was for American Relief Administration food drafts.

The Mennonites continued in their agricultural work for a time after the American Relief Administration completed its work but finally retired. They had saved a multitude of lives.

THE VOLGA RELIEF SOCIETY

This society was composed of descendants of emigrants to the United States, mostly from German settlements in the Volga Valley. The Volga settlements originated from an invitation, issued in the year 1762 by Catherine the Great, to Germans to settle in the Volga River region, where they were assigned fertile farms. By the time of the famine in 1921, this colony probably numbered about 350,000. Although influenced by some Russian customs, the Germans maintained their language and mixed little blood with the Russians. They had built good homes, schools, and many industries, and they were particular victims of Communist persecution.

The emigrants from this colony had spread widely over the United

States. This group, both Protestants and Catholics, comprised about 200,000 American citizens.

In August, 1921, a group in Portland, Oregon, set up the Volga Relief Society. John W. Miller was President and George W. Repp Secretary. Miller and Repp visited me in Washington in September, 1921, and asked to join our organization as one of our affiliates. They made an appeal for funds and established branches of their organization for this purpose in California, Washington, Idaho, Montana, Colorado, North Dakota, South Dakota, Nebraska, Iowa, and Kansas. They appointed Mr. Repp to our Moscow staff, and he quickly organized their work on the usual A.R.A. lines of local committees who issued rations to families or provided public kitchens for others. Our organization filled in in the areas they could not cover.

The Volga Germans, however, were a burden far greater than the resources of the Volga Relief Society. Our other affiliates—the Catholic Welfare Council and the National Lutheran Council—also took part, but the American Relief Administration had to carry the major burden.

The total sum expended by the Volga Society was about $220,000.

THE FEDERAL COUNCIL OF THE CHURCHES OF CHRIST IN AMERICA

The effort of the Federal Council of the Churches of Christ in America was largely directed to urging support to the Protestant denominations affiliated with the American Relief Administration. The Council received some contributions directly, of which it contributed $90,000 to the American Relief Administration and $10,000 to the American Friends Service Committee.

In 1923, the Federal Council organized a drive for clothing on behalf of the American Friends Service Committee. Our organization transported these gifts free of charge.

OTHER AMERICAN RELIGIOUS SUPPORTS

Several American religious denominations gave aid in the relief of the Russian famine. They undertook no distribution of supplies but directed their efforts to the support of the active organizations in Russia.

THE PROTESTANT EPISCOPAL CHURCH

The Protestant Episcopal Church had provided relief to Russia and to Siberia prior to the famine. Its part in the famine was undertaken through an appeal by the Church publication *The Living Church* of November, 1921. The appeal was supported by Bishop Gailor, Bishop Manning, and others to "save the Russian Church" and included an appeal for the purchase of food drafts from the American Relief Administration. These were to be sent to a selected list of persons in Russia.

THE NORTHERN BAPTIST CONVENTION

In 1921–1922 a substantial portion of the Northern Baptist Convention's $166,000 yearly relief fund was expended on Russian famine relief. In the winter of 1922–1923, the Baptists collected and gave to the American Relief Administration 1,200 bales of garments. I have estimated their contribution to Russia to be $50,000.

THE SOUTHERN BAPTIST CONVENTION

Our American Relief Administration records mention the aid of the Southern Baptists, but the surviving records of the Southern Baptist Convention give no information of what it was. I have estimated their contribution to Russia as $50,000.

THE SEVENTH-DAY ADVENTISTS

The Seventh-Day Adventists appear in American Relief Administration records as a contributor of $50,000 to our funds.

AID OF THE GREAT FOUNDATIONS TO THE
RUSSIAN FAMINE RELIEF

The great American charitable foundations cannot be classed as affiliates of the American Relief Administration. None of them engaged in direct distribution in Russia, but they were vitally important contributors to the funds of the American Relief Administration and of our affiliated organizations.

THE DUBROWSKY ORGANIZATIONS

I have already described the various Communist-controlled organizations created by Communist agents. They were certainly not affiliates of the American Relief Administration, and I mention them here only for statistical purposes. They shipped from the United States about $250,000 worth of supplies which were paid for through American charity and should be included in the totals.

OTHER CHARITABLE ORGANIZATIONS

In our research, we have come across names of many other organizations which raised funds for the aid of the Russian people. As I have said in the Introduction to this volume, the information we have received is from old press releases or sometimes incomplete records of those times. For the record, I give what we have:

Organization	Funds raised
Russian Famine Fund, Allen Wardwell, Chairman (raised funds for relief in Russia through the American Friends Service Committee)	$ 50,000
American Relief for Russian Women and Children, Jane Addams, Chairman (raised funds by co-operating with the American Friends Service Committee)	30,594

	Funds
Organization	raised
American Medical Aid to Russia, Mrs. Henry Villard, Chairman (raised funds for medical work in Russia for the American Friends Service Committee)	8,500
American Committee for Relief of Russian Children, Jane Addams, President (co-operated with American Friends Service Committee in sending supplies to Russia)	3,000
American Central Committee for Russian Relief, Princess Cantacuzene, Chairman, Dr. Charles Eliot, President (sent relief in money and supplies to non-Bolshevik Russia. This committee received a $50,000 grant for Russian refugees from the Carnegie Endowment for International Peace.) ..	268,205
Catherine Breshkovsky Russian Relief Fund, Lawrence F. Abbott, Executive Chairman (sent to Russia funds and supplies for relief and education)	46,000
Committee for the Rescue and Education of Russian Children, Mrs. Ralph Adams Cram, Chairman (aid and education to Russian refugee children in Europe and the Near East) ..	3,000
Fund for Relief of Men of Letters and Scientists in Russia, C. M. Oberoutcheff, President (aided Russian professional men and women in need)	16,674

I have estimated, for statistical purposes, that these contributions totaled at least $350,000 in all. This estimate allows for duplication of funds claimed by different organizations.

THE AFFILIATES AND OTHERS

Jewish Joint Distribution Committee	$ 9,145,211
National Catholic Welfare Council (includes $550,000 European)	1,300,000
American Friends Service Committee (includes $300,000 European)	1,523,007
National Lutheran Council	990,000
Y.M.C.A. and Y.W.C.A. (Student Friendship Fund)	150,000
American Mennonite Central Committee	1,097,712
Volga Relief Society	220,000
Federal Council of the Churches of Christ	100,000
Northern Baptist Convention (old clothing)	50,000

Southern Baptist Convention	50,000
Seventh-day Adventists	50,000
Other charitable organizations	350,000
Total	$15,025,930
Dubrowsky Communist Organizations	250,000
Grand Total	$15,275,930

CHAPTER 62

THE SOVIET UNION
WILL NEVER FORGET

Since an abundant harvest in South Russia was now assured, on June 4, 1923, Colonel Haskell formally notified Kamenev of the discontinuation of the American Relief Administration's operations, saying:

   . . . [The Soviet Government's official estimates] for the forthcoming harvest indicate that there will be a substantial surplus of food over all the internal needs of Russia. . . . The surplus, promising as it does a substantial export balance, places the government in a strong position to secure foreign supplies of other materials.

   The American Relief Administration . . . feels that . . . the period of famine relief to the Russian people will have passed with the coming of this year's harvest. . . .

   The Administration will have completed two years in active service of the Russian people and in so doing has given expression of the deep sympathy of the American people for the suffering of Russia.

On June 8, Kamenev replied, expressing the gratitude of his government:

   . . . I completely join you in the viewpoint expressed by you that this year's harvest promises to be quite satisfactory, and that upon its realization the Government hopes to provide for the basic needs of the former famine regions, and to utilize the surplus for the economic reconstruction of the country.

On June 13, the last food shipment from America arrived in Russia. On June 15, all food-draft delivery stations were closed. On the same day, Colonel Haskell signed a liquidation agreement with Kamenev in which all American Relief Administration accounting for Soviet gold furnished us for relief purposes was accepted by the Soviet Government. During June, the supplies on hand were distributed to the children's relief stations in an amount sufficient to take care of 3,000,000 children until after September 1. Within a week after June 27, our district offices were closed.

SOVIET THANKS

There were many farewell ceremonies in the districts, and our American district officials received many gifts which were examples of beautiful local craftsmanship. But the Soviet officials in Moscow ignored a request from us that the high export duties ought not to be placed upon these gifts. Most of them had to be abandoned because our men could not afford the export exaction.

On June 16, Colonel Haskell gave a dinner for the Commissars who had co-operated with the American Relief Administration, including Kamenev, Dzerzhinsky, Chicherin, Litvinov, Sokolnikov, Radek, Lander, and Volodin. Chicherin expressed the point of view reiterated in one form or another in all the speeches made by the Russians when he said, in part:

. . . The work of the A.R.A. is the work of broad masses of the American people who at a most difficult moment have come to the assistance of the Russian people and have thus laid a firm foundation for the future unalterable relations of friendship and mutual understanding between them.
. . . The hour, we hope, is not far distant when the American nation . . . may enter into close economic co-operation with the peoples of Russia. . . .
. . . We shall like to believe that the representatives of the A.R.A. will carry away with them the conviction that so far as the Soviet Government is concerned, it will ever be ready to do its utmost to remove all obstacles to a close and durable co-operation between America and Russia. . . .

On July 18, 1923, the *Sovnarkom* (The Soviet People's Commissars) gave a dinner for our American staff. There were present the Communist dignitaries—Commissars Kamenev, Chicherin, Krassin, and Semashko. In *Izvestia* of July 20, 1923, Kamenev's speech is given as follows:

> . . . Comrade Kamenev expressed profound gratitude to the American people, to the head of the A.R.A.—Hoover, to Colonel Haskell and his co-workers, for the relief, unexampled in history, given by America to Russia in the period of its greatest trial. . . .

Upon learning of the coming departure of the representatives of the ARA, the Sovnarkom passed a resolution, thanking the American people . . . for responding, in the trying year of a great elemental calamity . . . coming self-sacrificingly to its aid, organizing on a tremendous scale the importation and distribution of products and other articles of prime necessity. Thanks to the tremendous, utterly unselfish efforts of the ARA, millions of people of all ages were saved from death, and whole villages and even cities were saved from the terrible catastrophe that was threatening them. At the present time, when with the termination of the famine, the grandiose work of the ARA has come to an end, the Soviet of People's Commissars, in the name of the saved millions and of the whole toiling people of Soviet Russia and its United Republics, considers it its duty to express before the whole world, to this organization, its head Herbert Hoover, Col. Haskell, its representative in Russia, and all his co-workers, its profoundest gratitude, *and to declare that the people populating the Union of Soviet Socialistic Republics will never forget the help given by the American people through the ARA. . . .*[1]

Commissar Chicherin said in part:

> . . . The grandiose, disinterested aid rendered by the American people through the ARA, the self-sacrificing activity of the personnel of the ARA, and the splendid organization of its entire work have left an indelible impression upon our people. . . .

Speeches were made also by Commissars Semashko and Krassin, likewise giving assurances that the Soviet would never forget. They presented to our staff an elaborate scroll which, translated, reads:

> In the trying hour of a great and overwhelming disaster, the people of the United States, represented by the A.R.A., responded to the needs of the population, already exhausted by intervention and blockade, in the famine stricken parts of Russia and Federated Republics.

[1] The italics are mine.

Unselfishly, the A.R.A. came to the aid of the people and organized on a broad scale the supply and distribution of food products and other articles of prime necessity.

Due to the enormous and entirely disinterested efforts of the A.R.A., millions of people of all ages were saved from death, and entire districts and even cities were saved from the horrible catastrophe which threatened them.

Now when the famine is over and the colossal work of the A.R.A. comes to a close, the Soviet of Peoples Commissars, in the name of the millions of people saved and in the name of all the working people of Soviet Russia and the Federated Republics counts it a duty to express before the whole world its deepest thanks to this organization, to its leader, Herbert Hoover, to its representative in Russia, Colonel Haskell, and to all its workers, and to declare that the people inhabiting the Union of Soviet Socialist Republics will never forget the help given them by the American people, through the A.R.A., seeing in it a pledge of the future friendship of the two nations.

L. KAMENEV,
Acting President of the Council of Peoples Commissars.
N. GORBUNOV,
Chief of the Administrative Dept. of the Council of Peoples Commissars.
L. FOTIEVA,
Secretary of the Council of Peoples Commissars.

Moscow, Kremlin,
July 10, 1923.

I may add a letter written prior to this time by Commissar of Foreign Affairs George Chicherin to George Barr Baker, a member of our staff who was returning to the United States:

Moscow, January 23, 1922

DEAR SIR:

Having learned that you are leaving today for America I beg to convey to the American Relief Administration at home and to all American citizens who, by their donations or otherwise, contribute to the work of the . . . [A.R.A.] in Russia, the deep-felt tribute of our gratitude and admiration for its magnificent humanitarian action in saving from suffering and death an ever growing number of children, and later of adults also, in the famine-stricken areas of Russia. Terrible are the sufferings of the hard-working population in an enormous area which has this year been converted into a barren waste by the unprecedented drought. The magnitude of the calamity has rendered it impossible to be dealt with without the most extensive aid from outside. . . .

The calamity is so immense and terrible that only the most grandiose relief is adequate. . . . those innumerable sufferers who, when wandering through the valley of the shadow of death, witnessed a helpful hand held out to them by the American people, *will not forget the succor administered to them in their hour of need.* . . .[2]

GEORGE CHICHERIN

An elaborate illuminated scroll of thanks enclosed in a handsome box was given to me by the Soviet Government. Dated July 10, 1923, it reads, in translation:

MR. HERBERT HOOVER,
CHAIRMAN AMERICAN RELIEF ADMINISTRATION
WASHINGTON, D.C.
SIR:

WHEREAS, in the period of a disastrous national catastrophy, the people of the UNITED STATES, represented by the AMERICAN RELIEF ADMINISTRATION, readily responded to the needs of the population, already emaciated by foreign intervention and blockade, in famine stricken parts of Russia and Confederated Republics;

WHEREAS the AMERICAN RELIEF ADMINISTRATION did organize, on a most extensive scale, the supply and distribution of food products and other articles of prime necessity;

WHEREAS, due to the boundless, and entirely unselfish efforts of the AMERICAN RELIEF ADMINISTRATION, millions of people of all ages were saved from death, and entire localities, including many towns, escaped a threatening fearful calamity;

WHEREAS, at this time, with the cessation of the famine, the magnificent relief work of the AMERICAN RELIEF ADMINISTRATION is being concluded;

BE IT RESOLVED BY THE COUNCIL OF THE PEOPLE'S COMMISSARS in the name of the millions of people who have been saved, as well as in the name of the whole working people of Soviet Russia and of the Confederated Republics and before the whole world, to this organization, to its leader MR. HERBERT HOOVER, to its representative in Russia, Colonel HASKELL, and to all the workers of the organization

[2] The italics are mine.

to express the most deeply felt sentiments of gratitude, and to state, that all the people inhabiting the UNION OF SOCIALIST SOVIET REPUBLICS never will forget the aid rendered to them by the AMERICAN PEOPLE, through the agency of the AMERICAN RELIEF ADMINISTRATION, holding it to be a pledge of the future friendship of the two nations.

KAMENEF

Acting President of the Council of The People's Commissars

N. GRBUROV

Chief of the Administrative Department of the Council of The People's Commissars

L. FOTIEF

Secretary of the Council of The People's Commissars

On July 13, 1923, Colonel Haskell received this tribute from the Tartar Socialist Soviet Republic:

The Central Relief Commission of . . . the Autonomous Tartar Socialist Soviet Republic . . . considers it its duty to express to the American people through you its deep gratitude for the very substantial relief that has been extended in the present exceptionally difficult year of privation to the starving and destitute population of the Tartar Republic through the energetic agency of the American Relief Administration. . . .

. . . the American people have saved tens of thousands of human lives including . . . [a] generation of children. . . .

The timely . . . distribution of food by the American Relief Administration is a proof of your sincere interest in human suffering and the Central Relief Commission begs you to accept its cordial gratitude for the work of the American Relief Administration. . . .

KASAKOFF, Chairman

LAVRINTYEFF, Secretray

I had previously received the following letter from Gorky:

. . . permit me to express my feelings of gratitude . . . and complete satisfaction with the humanitarian work of the American Relief Administration of which you are chairman. In the past year you have saved from death three and one-half million children, five and one-half million adults, fifteen thousand students, and have now added two hundred or more Russians of the learned professions. . . . In all the history of human suffering I know of . . . no accomplishment which in terms of magnitude and generosity can be compared to the relief that you have actually accomplished. . . . It is not only the physical help which is valuable but the spiritual succor to the minds of mankind which are tormented by the events of the past years and sick due to cruelty and hate. . . . Your help will be inscribed in history as a unique gigantic accomplishment worthy of the greatest glory and will long remain in the memory of millions of Russians . . . whom you saved from death. . . .

Far more convincing than speeches and scrolls from commissars were the letters from the people. From thousands of these, I give a few written by children in response to a distribution of clothing. They are, of course, translated from the Russian.

From the children of the School of Sokolnisky:

We children thank the American Mission for taking care of us. Winter has come with its frosts. Many of us have not got warm clothes and must omit school days, and sometimes we are even obliged to leave school. The American Mission came to our aid and helped us to learn, and we would like to express our feelings of most sincere and deep gratitude.

From various schools:

I thank heartily the American children for having sent us children warm clothes. I received a sweater and am very glad. Do you wear yourself such sweaters or don't you?

LJOUDA C.—14 years

We Russians thank the dear American children for having sent us warm clothes.

SEMENOFF MIHAIL

Dear American Children: Thank you for giving us warm clothing. I got a warm suit and heartily thank you for it.

SEMENOFF ALEKSEJ

Thanksgiving to the Americans: I thank you for your present and that you came to help us. I am very glad to have got warm stockings. I thank you very much.

ANNIE KOUSMINE—13 years

We Russian children thank the American children for having sent us warm clothes. I got a warm dress for which I thank you.

KATHERINE KOUSMINE—13 years

We Russian children thank the American children for having made us a present of warm things. I have got warm woolen stockings and gloves and thank you heartily for them.

SCHAPOSHNIKOFF IVAN

I thank the American children for having sent me a warm sweater and a dress to my sister.

OLGA SOKOLOFF—age 7 years

CHAPTER 63

EPILOGUE TO "THE SOVIET UNION WILL NEVER FORGET"

The Communists soon began to realize that an expression of gratitude to a free nation was a violation of the primary tenet of Communism. It would be an acknowledgment to the Russian people of some merit in capitalism.

In 1926, information supplied to some European journals explained that my activities were due to my expectation that I could secure the return of my "Russian mines." I have doubt whether any refutation of Communist lies is worth while, but in case there is a doubting Thomas, I may say that for some years I had been an engineer to several mining enterprises. And I had given up this connection five years before the relief of Russia in order to conduct relief in Europe. If these mines had been returned to their rightful owners, I would not have benefited one dime.

The following quotation from Benjamin Gitlow, a recantant high official in the American Communist Party, is of some interest. He says:

The Bolsheviks never got over the fact that they had to depend on the enormous amount of relief supplies shipped to Russia by the United States, the distribution of which was supervised by Hoover, to extricate the communist fatherland from a famine. To be saved by American capitalism at a time when Russia's communist rulers were plotting the destruction of the capitalist world was too bitter a pill to swallow. Even though they accepted his services, they charged that Hoover was guided by ulterior motives. The Bolsheviks in the Comintern charged that Hoover distributed the supplies for political purposes, seeking to tie in with his relief activities a movement for the overthrow of the Soviet government. . . . The Russian Communists boasted that the Cheka, whose agents honeycombed the Hoover relief set-up in Russia, would prevent him from achieving his counter-revolutionary goal. Ever since that time the communist leaders of Russia, whose regime was saved by the splendid relief job Hoover did, have conducted a vicious campaign against Hoover which has not relaxed in its fury for the past twenty-seven years. . . .[1]

In the Presidential campaigns of 1928 and 1932, the Communists employed and paid speakers to travel and elaborate diligently various defamations.[2] Mr. William Benton published in the *Yale Review* [3] a most interesting study of the anatomy and perfection of this big lie. He gives the following translation from the official *Soviet Great Encyclopedia,* the 1926 edition:

The work of the A.R.A. was limited to supplying children foodstuffs. In 1922 five million children were receiving A.R.A. rations. In that year A.R.A. undertook also to supply adults and a total of ten million people were receiving the rations. . . . In all, 1,814,900,000 daily rations, 602,292 pairs of shoes, 1,929,805 meters of clothing, etc. . . . The total cost of this relief was estimated at $1,455,861.[4]

The 1950 edition said:

The capitalist world tried to use the difficulties of the USSR. Saboteurs and spies were setting fire to Soviet plants or attempting to blow them up. The A.R.A. helped this enemy activity.[5]

The 1956 edition of the *Soviet Great Encyclopedia* presents this further contribution to the liquidation of Herbert Hoover. Mr. Benton says:

. . . This article converts Hoover into the murderer of millions of Rus-

[1] Benjamin Gitlow, *The Whole of Their Lives* (New York, Charles Scribner's Sons, 1948).
[2] Full confessions of this by recanting Communists appear in Gitlow, *op. cit.* See also John T. Pace's statement in the *Congressional Record* of August 31, 1949.
[3] *Yale Review* (June, 1958), pp. 562–63.
[4] This was only about 70 per cent of the truth.
[5] *Yale Review* (June, 1958), p. 563.

sians instead of the savior of millions from starvation as reported a generation earlier.[6]

Further perfection of the big lie came from Soviet First Deputy Premier Kozlov during a tour of the United States. The *New York World-Telegram and Sun* of Thursday, July 2, 1959, stated in part:

Kozlov, making a tour of this country, told President Eisenhower yesterday the U.S. contributions to stem the famine were a loan that this country forced Russia to repay in gold. . . .

I gave a short interview to the press as follows:

The Russians were very thankful at the time for the food we gave them in the 1921–23 famine, but they've been trying to forget our help ever since.

It was not a loan, and not a dime was ever asked for or paid. At the direct request of the Soviet Government we raised about $62,000,000 and provided the Russians with more than 700,000 tons of food, clothing and medical supplies as an absolute gift.

Kozlov repeated his big lie at a reception given him by Vice-President Nixon at which Secretary of State Christian Herter was present. Secretary Herter was a leading member of the American Relief Administration and had been on the staff in the Russian famine. He appropriately placed the lie in Kozlov's teeth again.

Soviet anxiety that I might rise from my liquidation grave had also appeared in 1958. At President Eisenhower's request, on July 4 of that year I made an address at the Brussels Exposition. It was a speech without a word of criticism of the Communists, but in commenting on the ideals of the American people, as exemplified by their great sacrifices in relief of hundreds of millions of people in the great famines after both world wars, I included this innocent sentence: "And this compassion has also been extended to Communist Russia." Six days later, on July 10, an editorial appeared in *Izvestia* under the heading: "Hoover Hypocrisy in Exposition Speech Fails." The article was about four columns long; a few paragraphs will indicate its tenor:

[6] *Ibid.*, p. 563.

For some days now visitors to the worlds fair in Brussels have been having the doubtful pleasure of the seeing a certain 84-year-old American. . . .

The elderly former President, having hardly left his plane, threw himself immediately into the vortex of nasty propaganda and the anti-[Soviet] . . . attitude. . . .

In view of the fact that this venerable orator refrained from giving any more details, we will have to fill in the gap. . . .

In his speech in Brussels explaining U.S. ideals, Hoover laid special emphasis on the spirit of sympathy with the sufferings of mankind, which extended even to communist Russia.

. . . he who, deprived by the October Revolution of his share of capital in our country, took an active part in the anti-Soviet intervention. It was he who headed the notorious American relief committee, which so shamelessly covered its aid to all and sundry enemies of Soviet rule with its alleged concern for the hungry. . . .

The greatest ill that I have suffered from the Communists' perfection in the art of the big lie is that I have been compelled to elaborate this narrative of the relief of Russia so that this lie can rise again only in Communist minds.

WINDING UP THE RELIEF ACTIVITIES

CHAPTER 64

STATISTICS

The American people furnished the margins of food, clothing, and medical aid which saved the lives of millions of human beings in the First World War. The dimensions of this gigantic effort could be partially expressed in tons of food, clothing, and medical supplies or by the dollar value of these supplies if complete statistics were available. However, after more than forty years, they can be only partially assembled from surviving records, and, in many cases, no statistical records were kept.

Statistics are not a major preoccupation in war, and in any event, tons and dollars do not express relief of suffering and saving of life. However, we have assembled such data as we have been able to find, most of which is accurate and some of which is estimated. The following is the record, so far as it is available, pertaining to food and clothing tonnage furnished by the United States or distributed by American organizations during the nine years of the war and its aftermath.

Country	Total Tons
Great Britain *	11,300,000
France *	10,408,840
Italy *	8,471,400
Belgium and Northern France	5,174,431
Neutral Nations (Norway, Sweden, Denmark, Switzerland, Spain, and Holland)	1,898,829

Country	Total Tons
Finland	189,401
Estonia	54,771
Latvia	25,978
Lithuania	12,873
Poland	750,919
Danzig Free State	573
Germany	1,371,513
Austria	821,289
Czechoslovakia	545,439
Hungary	21,394
Bulgaria	22,862
Rumania	229,202
Yugoslavia	127,646
Russia	767,538
Greece, Armenia, and Turkey	171,168
Total	42,366,066 †

* Estimated.

† This total includes about 2,230,000 tons contributed by foreign governments but distributed by our organizations.

The quantities given above are far short of the whole American effort.

For lack of data, the above table does not include the American shipments to the Allies and Neutrals prior to the United States' entry into the war in 1917, nor does it include the purchases made by the Allies and Neutrals after the Peace in June, 1919, from their own funds or from private borrowing in the United States. It does not include the tonnage of unmanufactured and manufactured textiles to the Allies and Neutrals, for such statistics are available only in dollars. These textiles are, however, included in the table representing dollar values. And, in most cases, the tonnage of supplies delivered by the many American charitable organizations is not included, since these organizations kept few quantitative statistics.

If I were to make a rough estimate of the total food and clothing supplies shipped overseas during the nine years of war and its aftermath, the total figure would exceed 56,000,000 tons. If we study the normal export quantities of food and clothing prior to the war, we can well conclude that more than half of this 56,000,000 tons was the result of extra hours of labor on our farms and in our processing plants and the restrictions on waste of food and clothing consumption. Above all, however, the figure illustrates the self-denial in American homes and public places.

The following table gives the supplies of food, clothing, and medical aid in dollars furnished or distributed by American organizations —as far as our records can show them:

Country	$ Value
Great Britain *	$2,548,264,775
France *	1,525,665,002
Italy *	1,046,956,500
Belgium (and Northern France)	363,578,577
Portugal	6,000
Neutrals (Norway, Sweden, Denmark, Switzerland, Spain, and Holland)	357,826,266
Finland	28,663,823
Estonia	19,591,126
Latvia	8,682,492
Lithuania	10,341,725
Poland	224,721,048
Danzig Free State	137,712
Germany	319,827,573
Austria	153,277,326
Czechoslovakia (Bohemia and Slovakia)	116,140,680
Albania	679,724
Hungary	11,785,176
Bulgaria	4,856,647
Rumania	59,886,394
Yugoslavia (Serbia, Croatia, Bosnia, Herzegovina, Banat, Montenegro, Slovenia, and Dalmatia)	53,961,296
Russia ("White" Russia and Communist Russia)	126,997,868
Middle East Countries	108,098,345

Armenia	Egypt
Greece	Saudi Arabia
Turkey	Tunisia

Country		$ Value
Mesopotamia (Iraq)	Algeria	
Palestine (Israel)	Morocco	
Syria	Azerbaijan	
Lebanon	Georgia	
Persia (Iran)	Abyssinia	
China		6,500,420
Ireland		4,778,353
Total		$7,101,224,848

* Estimated.

Again, this total dollar value is incomplete because it does not include the Allies and Neutrals before our entry into the war, nor does it include purchases of some nations after the Peace from their own funds or monies borrowed from American banks and financial institutions. My own estimate of these supplies and services during the nine years of the war and its aftermath would exceed $8,000,000,000.

I estimate that roughly $550,000,000 worth of these supplies and services was from foreign governments and was paid for by them in cash or goods. Roughly $6,000,000,000 was paid for by loans from the United States as shown in the Appendix on foreign debts. These debts were, in reality, never repaid and were thus a gift from the American people. In addition, I estimate that the more than 211 American charitable institutions provided about $1,450,000,000.

CHAPTER 65

AND WHAT OF THE MEN
WHO DID THIS JOB?

In these three volumes of narrative of famine and pestilence during the First World War and its aftermath, I have said little of the spirit of the American men and women who performed these tasks. The great majority of them were volunteers—not for a day, but many of them for years. Many were men in uniform from our armed forces. Their scant remuneration from the United States Government constituted them as sacrificial volunteers. A number paid their own expenses, and others received only their bare out-of-pocket expenses and were no less volunteers. They represented the finest flower of American life.

I would be remiss if I did not pay some tribute to them before I close this account of nearly ten years of fighting famine. Each deserves a personal tribute—but there were over twenty thousand of them. The names of many occur in this narrative. Their children, and their children's children, should know of their devotion, their sacrifices, and their service. And there were hundreds of thousands of nationals in each country where they worked who should have mention in the annals of their governments.

Our American men and women left their professions to perform the dull work of buying millions of tons of food, medical supplies, and clothing; loading and managing great fleets of cargo ships and discharging them; convoying trains and barges from the ports to the place of need; and distributing food to the hungry from tens of thousands of stations and canteens. They operated a telegraph system throughout most of Europe. They managed whole railway systems and great coal districts. They bartered food and coal among nations. They settled little wars. They were called upon to advise new and feeble governments at the highest echelons of statesmanship. And they were called upon by the peacemakers in Paris for many political missions.

I still glow with pride at their reception in the countries where they worked. Many of these Americans serving abroad were officers and doughboys drawn from the American Army and Navy after the Armistice, men who in their civil life had not dealt with these or governmental problems, yet they showed such character and understanding that they won respect and personal affection wherever they went. Never was there such an exhibit of the power of the American way of life as these men presented, and they got a kick out of it—despite the surrounding tragedies. The misfits were so scarce that no one can recall their names.

The quality of these men was proved in later life. One became Secretary of State; one Secretary of Commerce; one a federal judge; four were Senators; four were elected to governorships; three became Congressmen, three were later appointed Ambassadors or Ministers; three rose to Assistant Secretary of State; and one became an Assistant Secretary of Defense. Four rose to high administrative positions in the Government; seven reached important rank in the Army and Navy. Two became presidents of universities; seven were heads of great charitable or research foundations; two became editors of important publications; twelve became heads of large corporations. Hundreds rose to eminent positions in their professions and in service to their communities.[1]

In the Introduction to these volumes, I stated that it was impossible to picture a great famine to our American countrymen. We can

[1] A passing tribute can be made from the records of the small fund which we established upon the liquidation of the residues of our relief activities. The purpose was to give aid by loans to any of our staff who had bad luck. This fund, during thirty-six years, has had so few calls that its capital has increased by more than 100 per cent, out of which increase it has contributed to many good causes.

have little understanding of its realities, for we have never seen real famine in our homeland since the suffering of the Pilgrims. Not even during the Civil War did famine in any town or city reach anywhere near the abyss that it reached in Central and Eastern Europe.

It is impossible to picture the long lines of stumbling refugees trying to carry their children and scant belongings to some destination unknown to them; the pallid faces; the unsmiling eyes; the thin, anemic, and bloated children in the villages and cities; the dead pall over towns where children no longer played in the streets; the empty shops; the dull, listless movements and dumb grief of the women; the sweep of contagious disease and the unending procession of funerals—and the heaps of unburied dead.

In preparation of these memoirs, I had need to refresh my mind from the dusty files of those days—hundreds of thousands of personal letters, telegrams and reports to me which to others would seem only a medley of dead and dry words. But surrounded by these old and dry records, the power of memory began to clothe them with life. I could see again the head offices of these many American organizations in New York, Washington, London, and Paris, with their rooms full of men and women, the clatter of typewriters, adding machines, telegraph instruments, and the voices of direction and instruction. The walls of these offices were covered with maps of countries, their railways, canals, and coal districts; ocean maps upon which every morning little flags showed where hundreds of relief ships were and where they were going; and charts of countries showing what their stocks of food were at the last date and what they would need in the next month.

Somehow, these offices always seemed inhuman and mechanical because there could be no diagrams showing that all this machinery had to do with human suffering, the hopes of freedom, the future of nations, and the prayer for peace. There could be no charts of the warm hearts who were giving their all to save human life and restore hope and faith.

But as I went through these frayed papers from the working front, they again throbbed with human emotion. They portrayed vividly the courage, sympathy, tenderness, indignation, horror, determination, hope and pride of accomplishment, and the native humor in this great group of American men and women.

I fear that such a response can come only to me, for I alone can today draw emotion from the twenty-one Rhodes scholars and four other Americans studying at Oxford who, in a body, joined the Belgian Relief as volunteers, or from a dry telegram from Harrington saying, "This special train of food has encountered blown-up tracks and bridges. Will be delayed some days." That is all that the record shows, but I see that long-delayed train en route to save a quarter of a million lives in Riga. I see the flat car, which their train pushed ahead, jump the rails. I see Harrington, with two American sergeants, rushing for native help to repair the track and urging them along. I see them and their crew shove the pilot car over the embankment. I see them hurrying to gather carts from the villages and farms and then passing through the actual fire of a raging battle to bring life to hundreds of thousands dying from Communist barbarity. And I see Harrington in an empty boxcar, slowly picking out, with one finger and by the light of a fluttering candle, this very original telegram on his typewriter.

From the Belgian Relief files there comes to my mind the faces of President Poincaré, French Foreign Minister Briand, Sir Edward Grey, Lord Robert Cecil, Lord Eustace Percy, and Prime Ministers Asquith and Lloyd George. Not less viewed are the co-operative Foreign Minister of Germany von Jagow, devoted Ambassadors Walter Hines Page and Merry del Val, Ministers Brand Whitlock and the Marquis de Villalobar. And there is Emile Francqui, with his tough face and soft heart, and his host of staunch Belgians devoted to saving their people.

In the telegram files, there again come to me the faces of Edgar Rickard, Captain John F. Lucey, William B. Poland, William L. Honnold, John B. White, and Prentiss N. Gray—stern administrators with tender hearts. The laconic telegram from Poland saying, "Another one sunk," meant number fifteen of our relief ships torpedoed by German submarines. I needed no reminder of his violent indignation.

And from dry reports of many men saying: "I visited," "I called upon," "I suggested"—I know that the way Goodyear, Grove, McCormick, Groome, and Gregory stopped renewed fighting in Eastern Europe was not by politeness. Knowing these men, I understood that when they "suggested," there was no mistake in anyone's mind as to what was meant. I know the language they really used.

And I see Major Green in Rumania, trying to persuade the all-embracing Minister of Commerce, Industry, Labor, Economic Reconstruction, Public Works, and Food that we were not on a commercial mission but one of mercy. And I see the horror of Howard Heinz at the sight of thousands dying—and even cannibalism—in Armenia. I can see Julius Barnes sitting at his telephone in New York directing the purchase of hundreds of thousands of tons of supplies and the loading of thousands of ships. I see Edward Flesh in London directing ships to the nearest ports of the starving. I see Edgar Rickard setting up systems of accounts and statistics which have forever saved thousands of men and women from any charge of corruption. And in the long and detailed reports of Alonzo Taylor, Vernon Kellogg, Colonel William Haskell, and Walter Brown on the needs of nations, I know that behind their dry statistics of sickness and death, calories, and tons there stands out their anxiety that we shall not fail. And I see Colonel Haskell in Moscow, with his stony face challenging the top Commissars in the Kremlin, demanding they cease arresting our Russian employees, demanding they carry out their agreements, and his ultimatum—"or we will quit." And I recall the perfidy of the oft-repeated promises that "Soviet Russia will never forget."

Somehow, when Americans get into uniform, the spark of life is dimmed in their written reports. Yet even then, at times, they break over the stilted style of the services. Captain Miller's longhand postscript says: "Hell has been to this place. It is still here." He went on to say that one out of four of the children in one town had died in the last two months. Captain Gregory summarizes, "Anybody who likes Communists, Germans or war in general ought to come here," and Colonel Groome remarks, "It makes me sick to go on the streets and see these kids." And there is this from Peden: "We can count

food in calories but we have no way to measure human misery."
And Colonel Beeuwkes said: "There has never been in all human
history such sights as these in the Volga." But perhaps all this means
little to anyone else.

And why do civilians in Army clothes get the Army habit of num-
bering paragraphs made of laconic words? Here is Major Ferry
Heath reporting from Finland: ". . . (1) the Prince did not seem to
think the outlook very favorable in Finland [which refers to the abdication by the Kaiser's brother-in-law of his high office as King of
Finland]. (2) . . . (3) Yudenich Army withdraws on Northwest
Front [it was licked]. (4) SS Lake Mary turning round in three days
discharged . . . [its cargo] of condensed milk, according to B.L.
[It meant food of full quality, urgently needed for ten thousand
children]."

And here are the terse reports of an able and staunch American
Army medical officer, Colonel H. L. Gilchrist. We had placed him
in charge of the battle against typhus, which was sweeping west
from the old Russian trenches all the way from the Baltic to the
Black Sea. He had a staff of twenty Regular Army officers and a host
of doughboys, including hundreds of tough sergeants. We had
shipped him, by rail and across Europe, $60,000,000 worth of anti-
typhus equipment. He merely enumerated its arrival.

From this front I am again reminded of the story from Dr. Vernon
Kellogg, whom we had sent to ask Colonel Gilchrist what more we
could do. He had gone behind the sanitary line and in coming out
was deloused by a tough sergeant, despite his indignant protests.
But for years later he proudly exhibited his certificate showing that
he had been deloused.

As I went through these old papers I noticed Goodyear's request
for $10,000 worth of tobacco and our office's laconic reply, "We have
neither $10,000 nor tobacco," and Goodyear's retort, "I have already
sent you $10,000 in American gold certificates, which the banks here
had left over [from before the war], and Mr. Hoover knows a miner
cannot perform without a smoke!"

And what of those great Americans, General Pershing and Admiral
Benson and their men? Through their co-operation in relief, we se-

cured a staff of more than four thousand of the finest American men who were awaiting their return home. On my request to the General asking that I might recruit some of them, he said that I should write him a note telling him what I wanted them for and that he would pick them for me, from doughboys to generals. Admiral Benson said that I could have the entire personnel of the Navy except the men needed to keep the idle ships in order. And he sent me men of all ranks—from sailors to admirals. They were superb and received great joy from their jobs.

I thumbed again the dispatches and the minutes of the Supreme Council relating to the rise and fall of Bela Kun, the Communist dictator of Hungary, and the decline and fall of Archduke Joseph, where Captain Gregory's laconic report read: "Archie on the carpet 7 p.m. Went through the hoop at 7:05 p.m." And of Prime Minister Clemenceau's demand for the original—as the only humor in this war.

I thrill again to the march of the fifty thousand Polish children to express Poland's gratitude, and French General Henrys' leaving the reviewing stand, overcome, saying as he departed: "There has never been a review of honor in all history which I would prefer for myself to that which has been given you today."

As I continued reading these old papers there stood out with vividness that, parallel with providing food and clothing, another major job was being accomplished, that of managing railways, coal mines, canals, ports, restoring currencies, and giving health and reconstruction to demoralized economic life.

And there were the reports of Colonel Causey. He was, in private life, president of a railway but now a magnificent administrator of 10,000 miles of broken railways in southwest Europe—a man of great accomplishment in profanity, which he used for emphasis in his reports. But he moved the supplies which saved the lives of thousands. His colleague, Colonel W. B. Ryan, a railway vice-president in private life, was administering 20,000 miles of railways to the north of Causey. He began almost every communication to me with "Can you not get me more locomotives and cars?"

Parallel with it all ran another operation, not large in quantity of commodities, but high in sympathy and tender feeling—the rehabilitation of undernourished, diseased, and waif children in twenty nations. Allied power politics and the governments of the countries we served had nothing to do with this. That job was American—under the American flag.

And there were the ministrations of the American Red Cross for the wounded, the ill, and those afflicted with pestilence; the Near East Relief Committee striving to preserve the Christians in Turkey and Armenia from extinction; the Jewish Joint Distribution Committee extending generous aid, not only to their co-religionists, but also to their neighbors; and the American Friends Service Committee carrying not only food but gentle words of encouragement and faith into thousands of villages as they administered canteens which restored life to millions of children.

No one can read this mass of documents on children's relief without knowing that these Americans were vicariously caring for their own children at home. The papers still breathe the awakening of millions of kids from lethargy to chatter. Our files contain hundreds of photographs of them. And in all Europe our organizations had restored 15,000,000 children to a healthy future.

Within all this mass of paper, there are the thousands of little items daily giving the evidence that we were succeeding, that starving people had not held out their hands to America in vain. *Those old, yellowing papers live!* And they illuminate the personalities of the men who dominated the world in that war.

As I go over the documents during the Peace Conference in Paris (Why do typewriter ribbons in wartime fade so?), my mind travels to the difficulties of negotiating relief organization with men suspicious of President Wilson—the President, who, in the words of General Smuts, went into "the depths of hell to save the League of Nations." Again I see his stern visage but his unfailing loyalty to me and the relief. One of my vivid memories of him was his mark, "Approved W. W.," on scores of documents I placed before him. The personality of Lloyd George—adroit, yet gentle to suffering; Clemenceau "the old Tiger," adamant for France in negotiations. He was always considerate of me and our work. And I remember my call upon him when I was leaving Europe for home. He expressed the obligation owed to our organization and our work—and added, "There will be another world war in your time and you will be needed back in Europe."

And again I recall the steadfast friendship and support from Colonel House. His face rises in my mind, revealing ineffable serenity, yet he was a great negotiator among tangled problems. And there is Churchill, a hardened militarist, with no patience at idealism in the human race and bitter in his enmity toward Woodrow Wilson.

Vivid as these many events and personalities stand out, I must not stray away from the purpose of this chapter to remind the reader of the quality of men and women who fought the battle of saving human lives on the front lines of human misery itself. Description, statistics of tons and dollars, names and numbers of men and women who served—these can never present the idealism of inspired Americans. It is part of *An American Epic*.

APPENDICES

APPENDIX I

UNITED STATES GOVERNMENT LOANS TO AID VARIOUS COUNTRIES IN THE WAR

At the American entry into the war in April, 1917, the Congress gave authority to the Treasury to make loans in aid of the war. There were two limitations on these loans: they were to be used solely for purchases of supplies in the United States, and they could be extended only to those countries which had joined their military forces with the United States during the war.

At the outset of the war, it was assumed that these loans could be repaid over a term of years through the shipment of goods or in gold. However, as the years waned, it was obvious that payment in goods would create both destitution in the debtor countries and unemployment in the United States and that consequential shipments of gold to the United States would undermine the currency and national bank resources in the debtor countries, thus weakening their financial structures to the point of impeding world economic recovery.

In an effort to solve these dilemmas, on February 3, 1922, the Congress, upon the recommendation of Secretary of the Treasury Andrew W. Mellon, passed an act creating the United States World War Foreign Debt Commission. I was appointed a member. The Commission's purpose was to determine, by agreement with each nation, the amount of its debt and accrued unpaid interest. A further purpose was to enter into an agreement with each nation providing for the funding of the principal of the debts over a term of years and

541

to reach an agreement as to the rates of interest to be paid on unpaid principal. The major policies applied in these negotiations were:

That the debts should be based upon the capacity of the debtor to pay;

That payments on the principal of the debts should be spread over sixty years, beginning with small or no initial payments and continuing with ascending amounts over the years;

That interest on unpaid balances should not be initially required or should be at very low rates, with ascending rates of interest over the years; and

That in every case the rate of interest was to be less than the American taxpayer was paying on long-term United States bonds, by which the funds for these loans were acquired.

The effect of these methods of funding was a great reduction of debt to the debtors, ranging from 30 per cent of the original amount to as much as 70 per cent. In the end, the so-called "loans" were, in fact, gifts. In the Introduction to this volume, I touched upon this subject, but to carry conviction, an account of their history should be more extensive.

Payments on principal and interest were made by some of the debtors from the funding dates until the world-wide depression of 1931. With the financial collapse of Europe (which resulted from their unwise policies of armament, spending, unbalanced budgets, etc.), it was evident that not only could payments on foreign debts to the United States not be met but that the immense amount of debt between other governments, including German reparations, was also a serious depressant on the general world-wide scene.

After securing the approval of the leaders of the Senate and House (not then in session), on June 20, 1931, I, as President, proposed to all nations a moratorium on intergovernmental debt payments, the moratorium to last until December 31, 1932, or about eighteen months. The only consequential objection to the proposal was raised by France, and I was delayed in announcing complete agreement until July 6, 1931.

As the expiration of the moratorium approached on December 31, 1932, I suggested to the nations which were debtors of the United

States that they make that semi-annual payment in order to maintain the integrity of international agreements but that I would urge upon Congress the re-creation of the former United States World War Foreign Debt Commission to revise all the agreements in line with the situation in each country and the world.

I was defeated in the election of 1932, and the President-elect refused to support my recommendations to the Congress. In this situation, practically all debtors to the United States ceased payments of either principal or interest; they were never again to be renewed. The unique exception was Finland, who continued her payments. The payments by other nations were never resumed.

I can therefore sum up the consequences as follows:

(1) The payments of interest during the period when they were paid were less than the American citizens were paying on our national debt.

(2) Our national debt which was issued to make these loans lives with us to this day.

(3) The total cost to the American people in the taxes they have been paying to provide interest on our national debt amounts to two dozen times the payments on principal and interest we received from the debtors.

(4) Therefore, we can rightly conclude that the whole of the World War I loans, with one exception, were gifts. As I have mentioned, that exception is Finland, who in 1961 is still paying installments on the principal and the funded interest rate.

The following table shows the amount of each debt and the percentage paid upon the principal during the years from 1923 to 1932 when payments were being made:

THE FUNDED DEBTS

Country	Principal	Per cent paid on principal
Belgium .... $	417,780,000	4.1%
Czechoslovakia	115,000,000	17.2%
Estonia	13,830,000	
Finland *	9,000,000	28.2%
France	4,025,000,000	4.0%

THE FOUNDED DEBTS *(Continued)*

	Principal	Per cent paid on principal
Great Britain	4,600,000,000	5.0%
Hungary	1,939,000	3.8%
Italy	2,042,000,000	1.8%
Latvia	5,775,000	0.17%
Lithuania	6,030,000	3.8%
Poland	178,560,000	0.72%
Rumania	44,590,000	6.1%
Yugoslavia	62,850,000	1.9%
	$11,522,354,000	

* Finland was still paying in 1958.

There were also some unfunded debts as follows:

Country	Principal	Payments on Principal	Percentage
Greece	$ 15,000,000	$ 981,000	6.5
Armenia *	11,959,917	none	
Austria	24,055,708	862,668	
Russia	138,000,000	none	
Germany †	325,015,940	50,239,595	15.4
	$514,031,565	$52,083,263	

* Payments on principal and interest suspended by Congressional action until 1943, with, apparently, no action since.
† Army occupation costs and mixed claims as finally adjusted.

If it were established to the world that these huge sums were also American gifts, it might give great satisfaction to the American people.

APPENDIX II

DISPOSAL OF
AMERICAN RELIEF ADMINISTRATION
RESIDUAL CHARITABLE FUNDS

I have mentioned in Chapter 31 the long and tedious burden of final settlement of our accounts with the many governments and groups involved in our relief operations. It was not until 1937 that we received the final auditors' certificate that all of our liabilities had been settled. During the entire period from the end of relief operations in September, 1923, to 1937, we were compelled to hold sufficient funds to cover the possible outstanding liabilities.

On December 1, 1923, having completed all of our relief missions in Europe, we incorporated the "American Children's Fund," a non-profit organization into which any balances collected would be credited and any liabilities met. This action would protect creditors, debtors, and staff until we could clearly wind up our accounts. We could then safely distribute to charitable purposes any funds we had left over.

The officers of the American Children's Fund were:

> HERBERT HOOVER, *Chairman*
> EDGAR RICKARD, *President*
> PERRIN GALPIN, *Vice-President*
> RAYMOND SAWTELLE, *Secretary* and *Treasurer*,
> later succeeded by HUGO MEIER

The leading men of our relief staffs comprised the directors and "members." They included such persons as Robert A. Taft and H. Alexander Smith, later United States Senators; Hugh Gibson, later

Ambassador to Poland, Switzerland, Brazil, and Belgium; Harvey A. Bundy, later Assistant Secretary of State; Christian A. Herter, later Governor of Massachusetts and Secretary of State; Lewis L. Strauss, later Chairman of the Atomic Energy Commission; H. L. Spaulding, Governor of New Hampshire; President Ray Lyman Wilbur of Stanford University; Professor Charles M. Bakewell of Yale University; and Judge Edwin F. Shattuck, Hallam Tuck, Sidney Mitchell, John Simpson, Scott Turner, Julius Barnes, and Edward Flesh.

During six years, the Fund received $5,377,990.77 from all the sources. Our investments committee comprised, at various times over the years, Edgar Rickard, Lewis Strauss, Hallam Tuck, Sidney Mitchell, John Simpson, Raymond Sawtelle, and Scott Turner. Thanks to their freely given talents, we earned profits on sale of securities, interest and dividends amounting to $2,378,211.99 making our total resources $7,756,202.76.

The American Children's Fund did not undertake direct service for children but used its resources in grants to promote the health and welfare of children through other organizations as follows:

The American Child Health Association	$2,635,325
White House Conference on Child Health and Protection	725,000
Girl Scouts of America to support child health programs	858,000
Boy Scouts of America to support child health programs	725,902
The President's Conference on Housing, Home Ownership and Slum Improvement	501,371
The American Red Cross to establish certain programs of child health and welfare	500,000
The Boys' Clubs of America to install health programs in the Clubs	311,420
A number of Southern mountain schools and colleges to carry on child health instruction	323,962
The Puerto Rican Relief Committee for the relief of Puerto Rican children	213,773
The American Friends Service Committee to install a canteen system for children in the coal regions	225,000
National Committee on Food for the Small Democracies— for food to children of the small democracies in World War II	52,516

The Allied Jewish Committee for child health programs   50,000
Sundry appropriations for child welfare   133,034

    Total $7,255,303

Having settled every possible liability and having expended the resources of the fund, we placed it in liquidation on April 12, 1950. The sum of $28,000 realized from the liquidation was turned over to the Belgian American Educational Foundation, with which the American Children's Fund shared the expense of office service.

PERSONNEL OF THE AMERICAN RELIEF ADMINISTRATION[1]

FRED K. ABBOTT
WALTER S. ABBOTT
CLARENCE A. ABELE
SGT. CHARLES D. ABRAHAM
PVT. ISADORE ABRAMOVITZ
CAPT. FRANK E. ADAIR
NANCY ADAM
E. D. ADAMS
SGT. RUSH S. ADAMS
JOHN W. H. AICHER
PVT. WM. C. AITKENHEAD
LILLIAN ALEXANDER
LT. CHARLES E. ALLEN
PVT. ELLIOT E. ALLEN
LT. PARKER B. ALLEN
RONALD H. ALLEN
CPL. TRACY W. ALLEN
PVT. HARRY E. ALLTON
MARY ALMAN
MARY ALMAZOV
HENRY G. ALSBERG
SGT. MILTON ALTSCHUL

COL. LYTTON G. AMENT
SGT. ANDREW ANDERKO
CHARLES B. ANDERSON
SGT. CHARLES E. ANDERSON
EDWARD ANDERSON
LT. HAROLD ANDERSON
JOHN G. ANDERSON
OSCAR J. ANDERSON
LT. CLARENCE E. ANDREWS
PVT. THOMAS ANDREWS
MARY ANDRZEJEWSKA
MAJ. MONTGOMERY B. ANGELL
PVT. ALEXANDER M. ANGIUS
CAPT. ROBERT W. ANSTEY
PVT. CHARLES ARION
CAPT. C. ROBERT ARMSTRONG
LT. EDWARD ARMSTRONG
LT. HOWARD C. ARMSTRONG
CAPT. JAMES ARMSTRONG
LAURA M. ARNDT
STANLEY ARNOLD
W. H. ARNOLD

[1] The titles of the military in the Relief are the ones used at the time of entry into the A.R.A. Many of these men later attained promotions in their respective branches of military service; others have dropped their titles in civilian life. However, it is felt desirable to retain the titles shown to indicate those who volunteered from the armed forces after the Armistice.

548

Capt. Hasop H. Aroyan
William A. Arras
Hilda B. Arscot
Cpl. DeVyse W. Atwater
Col. William G. Atwood
Pvt. William L. Auger
Kathryn S. Axtman

Capt. Frank Baacker, Jr.
Nancy Babb
Charles F. Babcock
Guilford C. Babcock
Capt. Ulysses M. Bachman
Sgt. Alfred B. Backer
H. G. Backhouse
Pfc Henry S. Bacon
Anna Bader
Lt. Col. Charles A. Bader
Jewell Bader
Anna Badura
Charles H. Baetjer
Natalie D. Bailey
Ivan H. Baird
Lt. James E. Baird
Simeon P. Baird
Constance Baker
Lt. Comdr. George Barr Baker
J. H. Baker
Sgt. William E. Baker
Elbert Baldwin
Philip S. Baldwin
Maj. Edwin G. Ballinger
Pvt. Harry Baltus
Lt. Arived C. Baltzer
Eugene Banchard
Charles W. Band
Suda L. Bane
Col. Henry M. Bankhead
Capt. Giovanni Barbarino

Col. A. B. Barber
Walter E. Barber
Capt. Victor Barcas
Lt. Arthur Barclay
Vladimir V. Barishnikov
Sgt. Harold L. Barker
Sgt. M. L. Barker
Julius H. Barnes
Pvt. Oral M. Barnes
Paul S. Barrett
Thomas C. Barringer
Isabel M. Barry
Capt. Alexander M. Barton
Maj. Louis A. Barton
Weaver J. Bascombe
Ethel Basely
Sgt. Clay Basset
F. G. Bates
Pvt. Harry Bates
Lt. Charles C. Battershell
Carl Baumgartner
Eugenia L. Baumgartner
Capt. Hugh S. Baumgartner
Bernard J. L. Beard
Donald U. Beck
Otto O. Beck
Cpl. Charles A. Becker
Lt. James H. Becker
Lt. Thomas H. Beckwith
W. Bedwell
Herbert S. Beers
Col. Henry Beeuwkes
Pvt. Charles N. Bell
Pvt. Clifford A. Bell
Maj. Howard H. Bell
Maj. Joseph E. Bell
Lt. Orville C. Bell
Russell W. Bell
Walter L. Bell

Anna Bemish
Pvt. Carrol T. Bengough
Lynn C. Bennett
Sgt. William R. Bennett, Jr.
Cpl. Paul D. Bennis
Edna Benowitz
Sgt. Bernard A. Benson
C. Theodore Benze
Sgt. William H. Bergen
Lt. Harry S. Berman
Alfred M. Bernhards
Lt. Paul Berri
Maj. George W. Berry
Gustav F. Beschorner
Pvt. Dominick Betont
Pvt. Asa W. Bett
Lillian G. Biddles
Pvt. Robert Binkley
Lt. Edward O. Birgfeld
Lt. Morris G. Bishop
Pvt. Troy O. Bishop
Cpl. Earl W. S. Blaauw
Pvt. Ernest H. Black
Sgt. Paul H. Black
Willard C. Blackburn
Kenneth Blackmore
Lt. Clarence W. Blackwell
Cpl. Leonard A. Blackwell
Lily Blair
Maj. Percy Blair
Judson A. Blake
Ivy Blamey
Frank A. Blanche
Lt. Raymond L. Bland
Harold F. Blandy
Benjamin Blattner
Elsie Blau
Frank Blauvelt
Pvt. George M. Bleekman

Elma M. Bliss
Alvin E. Blomquist
Capt. Daniel L. Blount
Lt. Max A. Blumer
Sgt. Fred J. Bodenstein
Cpl. James S. Boders
Capt. Herbert L. Bodman
Cpl. James Bodrero
Emil G. Boerner
Lt. Walter W. Boes
Heinrich Boetticher
Capt. Harry W. Boetzkes
Anna C. Bogart
Boris D. Bogen
Cpl. Emil Bogen
Lucile Boissonade
Sgt. Ernest Boland
Walter G. Bolden
Sgt. John R. Bolin
William H. Bond
Bourdon P. Bondurant
C. E. Bonfield
Alfred C. Boni
Richard W. Bonnevalle
Oscar J. Booman
Pvt. Frank G. Boone
Lovell P. Boone
Sgt. Frank C. Booth
Maj. Shade H. Booth
Carl Borders
Capt. Lemuel E. Boren
Sgt. Joseph E. Borer
Maj. Samuel H. Botsford
Lt. Yves A. Bouget
Marguerite Bouquet
Marguerite C. Bourgeois
Fernande S. Bourgin
Suzanne Bourgin
Lt. Carlton G. Bowden

M. E. Bowes
Pvt. William Bowker
Lt. John H. Boyd
Capt K. J. Boyd
Pvt. Wayland E. Boyd
Blanche Brace
Lt. John C. Brady
Robert G. Bramfit
Maj. William S. Brand
Sfc Walter C. Brandes
Raymond P. Brandt
Sgt. John B. Branstrator
Lt. Clarence R. Braun
Antoine Bravo
James E. Brealey
Elizabeth Bredin
Sgt. Fred J. Brennan
Lt. John A. Bresh
A. J. R. Bridges
Hobart D. Brink
Harry Broadman
Maj. Walter D. Brookings
Sgt. Bert M. Brooks
John B. Brooks
Lt. Sidney Brooks
David Brown
Elizabeth Brown
Capt. Frank A. Brown
George A. Brown
Sgt. Henry R. Brown
Jessie Brown
Lt. John C. Brown
Lt. John F. Brown
Joseph N. Brown
Col. Marshall W. Brown
Omar J. Brown
W. Gordon Brown
Walter Lyman Brown
William J. Brown

Maj. Myron G. Browne
Sgt. Chris D. Browning
Sgt. John J. Brownson
Pvt. Robert Bruce
Harry A. Bruch
Sgt. Sidney W. Brundige
Mitchell C. Bryant
Lt. Norman S. Buck
Pvt. Clarence O. Bucklen
Harold R. Buckley
Florence Bull
Florence Bunger
Friedrich Bunger
Maj. W. A. Burbank
James A. Burden, Jr.
Maj. George E. Burke
Lt. Elmer G. Burland
Frank S. Burland
Francis H. Burnett
J. C. Burnett
Clinton Burns
G. Burton
Lt. John A. Bush
George Bussenot
Sgt. Frank W. Buster
Capt. Adrian M. Butcher
Capt. Allen M. Butler
Sgt. Lee D. Butler
Lt. Matthew B. Butler
Pvt. Roscoe C. Butler
Robert S. Byfield
Maj. Mark C. Byrne

Capt. Paul F. Cadman
Pvt. Arnold F. Caffery
John P. Caffey
Lt. Florian A. Cajori
Constance M. Caleno
Edgar B. Callahan

Pvt. Francis H. Callahan
James E. Callahan
Thomas J. Callahan
Edythe M. Callow
Sgt. Charles A. Campbell
H. J. Campbell
Mabel Campbell
Sgt. E. M. Cannon
Pvt. Henry B. Capehart
Ens. L. W. Capser
Maj. Charles T. Caraker
Godfrey L. Carden
Pvt. Gordon H. Carey
Lt. Col. A. J. Carlson
Sgt. Victor R. Carlson
Edith Carlton
Katherine Carlton
Sgt. E. H. Carmany
Mary Carr
Marion Carroll
Maj. Philip H. Carroll
Lt. Oscar L. Carson
C. B. Carter
Sgt. Leo Carruth
Sgt. Leroy B. Caryl
William J. Casey
Sgt. Oliver H. Cash
Lt. Edmund Caskie
Marion Cassel
Sgt. Albert M. Cauldwell
Lt. Col. William B. Causey
H. Cecil
Maj. Elbridge G. Chadwick
Lt. Walter P. Chambers
Louis Champault
Pvt. Claude Chance
Emma Chandler
Pvt. Elias W. Chapin
Lutie T. Chase

Lt. S. S. Chein
Sgt. Morris Cheriavsky
Jamara Cheshire
Mary Cheshire
Lt. J. Rives Childs
Helen Chmielewska
Frank Chour
Marian Chubb
John A. Chumbley
Helen Cichowicz
Catherine Ciesicka
Capt. Omar V. Claiborne
Capt. Paul S. Clapp
Lorin A. Clark
Roy A. Clark
Capt. Frank J. Clarke
Maj. Harold W. Clarke
Maj. Kilburn D. Clarke
Phyllis Clarke
Capt. Solomon F. Clarke
Clyde W. Cleary
Randolph H. Clement
Sgt. T. Cliff
Capt. Henry Ives Cobb, Jr.
Russell Cobb
F. W. Cobill
A. P. Cochran
Leon J. Cochrane
F. W. Codling
Sgt. Abraham N. Cohen
Jacob S. Cohen
Lt. J. Gerald Cole
Sgt. Thomas J. Coleman
Walter H. A. Coleman
Pvt. Nicholas J. Colleye
Estelle G. Collin
Sgt. Roy T. Collings
P. M. Collins
Ethan T. Colton

PVT. WILLIAM R. COLVIN
LT. MARK H. COLWELL
GEORGE A. CONLON
CAPT. WILLIAM S. CONNERAT
CPL. DAVID W. CONREY
MATTHEW T. CONROY
CHARLES G. COOK
JANET COOK
ARCHIBALD C. COOLIDGE
JESSIE O. COOMBE
LT. COL. JAMES P. COOMBS
ALBERT E. COON
JOHN V. COONLY
G. A. COOPER
CAPT. MARION C. COOPER
LT. CHARLES M. COPE
WILFRED E. COPUS
AUSTIN P. CORCORAN
PVT. HARRY J. CORCORAN
NORAH MEADE CORCORAN
OTTO CORNEL
GEORGE B. CORNICK
CAPT. JAMES F. COSTELLO
MARY COSTELLO
SGT. ROBERT A. COTNER
FORDYCE G. COTTERELL
SGT. THOMAS S. COULTER
CLAUDIA P. COUTURE
I. COWARD
CPL. JOSEPH W. COWARD
JOHN E. COX
WALTER J. COZENS
LAURESTON CRAIG
CAPT. STUART L. CRAIG
CURTIS M. CRAIN
CURTISS M. CRANE
LT. DONALD F. CRANE
CAPT. EDWARD W. CRANE
SGT. HOWARD L. CRANE

LT. GEORGE M. CRAWFORD
HAROLD A. CRAWFORD
CAPT. ROBERT CRESSWELL
ELLISON S. CRIDER
CAPT. R. B. CRISPELL
MARY MARGARET CROKE
PVT. CLEMENT C. CRONIN
HELEN M. CRONIN
MAJ. WALTER C. CROW
PVT. JAMES O. CROWE
NORAH CULHANE
E. CULLEN
WILLIAM W. CUMBERLAND
LT. JOHN P. CUMMING
IRA CUMMINGS
AGNES V. CUNNINGHAM
JAMES J. CUNNINGHAM
SGT. ROY J. CUNNINGHAM
MARGARET CURIO
LT. E. D. CURTIS
JOSEPHA CZARNIK

ELSIE L. DAGLISH
HESTER DAHL
MARIE DAHLERUP
ARTHUR T. DAILEY
PVT. EDWARD E. DAILEY
EDMUND L. DALEY
FRANCISCO J. D'ALMAINE
JOSEPH N. DALTON
LT. FRED D'AMOUR
LT. PAUL DANA
CAPT. JAMES S. DANGERFIELD
CPL. FRANCIS J. D'ARCY
PVT. LAWRENCE D. DARDEN
ALONZO L. DARRAGH
PVT. ROLLIE P. DARST
GEORGE A. DAUM
WALTER P. DAVENPORT

Lt. Carlisle M. Davidson
Ernest Davidson
Cpl. John D. Davies
Eva Davis
Livingston Davis
Lt. Roy C. Davis
Lavern R. Davison
John H. Dawson
Lt. Col. Lee G. Day
Rush O. Day
Denise Dean
William R. Dear
William L. DeBuse
C. B. De Haven
Sgt. Paul Deisler
Frank A. Delgado
Capt. John B. Dempsey
Cpl. Jackson B. Dennison
Olive Dent
Joseph W. Dermody
Reg. Sgt. Maj. Joseph E. Destefano
Catherine M. Devine
Sgt. Paul E. DeVor
R. De Waegenaere
Maj. Louis Dezzi
Pvt. Frank Di Bari
Raymond C. Dickieson
Thomas H. Dickinson
Arthur Dickson
Howard R. Dickson
Maj. Joseph J. Dierkes
Lt. William R. Dillard
Lillian Dilsner
Katherine Dineen
Pvt. Eddie H. Dixon
George H. Dobbin
Sgt. Howard J. Dodd
Earl J. Dodge
Charles P. Doe

Thomas F. Doherty
Eleanor G. Dolan
Sgt. Michael J. Dolan
John J. Donnelly
Pvt. Paul J. Donovan
Sgt. Joseph S. Doran
Corwin M. Doss
Milburn P. Doss
Ralph Z. Doty
Lt. Charles W. Douglas
L. S. Dow
Ernest E. Dowling
Mabel Downey
John J. Doyle
Maj. Luke C. Doyle
Florence Doyne
Myron G. Doyno
Lt. Ralph A. Dracie
Lt. Ralph A. Drain
Marguerite Drennan
Joseph A. Driscoll
Andrew Lewis Drummond
Anna Dubin
Arthur W. DuBois
Lt. R. L. Ducros
Elmore Duero
Bernard Duffy
Ida M. DuFlon
Mary Duggan
Cpl. Donald S. Duncan
Earl T. Dunham
Marcia O. Dunham
Edward Dunn
Lt. Harry L. Dunn
Robert Dunn
Cpl. George F. Duran
E. Dana Durand
Sfc Elmore R. Dutro
Col. Douglas F. Duval

ANNIE DUVERE
HOWARD E. DWINNELLS
DOROTHY DYER

DOLORES EAKINS
GEORGE EAKLAND
CPL. GILBERT C. EARLEY
E. M. EASTER
MAJ. DOYLE L. EASTLAND
CARRIE B. EATON
WEYLAND ECHOLS
LILLIAN ECK
CAPT. ELMER A. ECKMAN
CPL. ERNEST EDWARDS, JR.
PVT. JAMES EDWARDS
LT. GEORGE EDWARDS
PVT. WILLIS G. EDWARDS
MAJ. JOHN A. ELDRIDGE
JOHN R. ELLINGSTON
SGT. CARLISLE B. ELLIOT
LUCY M. ELLIOT
LT. JOHN D. ELLIS
SGT. LUCIEN C. ELLSWORTH
CPL. JOSEPH J. ENGELMAN
MADELEINE T. ENNESER
PATRICK ENRIGHT
ALBERT C. ERNST
SUZANNE JEANNE ETIENNE
SUZANNE MARGARET ETIENNE
ELWYN EVANS
CAPT. HARRY EVANS
W. L. EVELEIGH
LT. FREDERICK EXTON
KINCH W. EXUM

KAREL FAHOUN
CECIL R. FAIRBANK
IDA M. FALKNER
WILLIAM H. FARNHAM

JAMES M. FARR
THOMAS J. FARRAHER
JOSEPH A. FARRELL
PVT. GEORGE K. FAVRET
HOWARD S. FAWCETT
BESSIE E. FAY
MAJ. FRANK H. FAY
RUSSELL B. FEES
CECIL E. FEHRLIN
PVT. JOSEPH F. FEIT
MAJ. GEORGE F. FELKER
SGT. JOHN S. FELL
ESTHER FELSHER
KATHERINE E. FENNESSY
LT. POWELL FENTON
MAJ. HAROLD G. FERGUSON
ROBERT L. FERGUSON
MARGARET FERNIE
PVT. MERLE FERRY
CAPT. RODERICK FIELDS
HARRY J. FINK
PVT. LEON B. FINOUT
PVT. ROBERT J. FIRTH
GRAHAM S. FISHER
HAROLD H. FISHER
SGT. HARRY E. FISHER
M. E. FISHER
SGT. SYLVESTER FISHER
MAJ. ANDREW J. FISK
HERBERT FISKE
PVT. LUDD T. FITZ
JOHN B. FITZGERALD
CAPT. JAMES B. FLAHERTY
FRANCES FLANAGAN
WILLIAM H. FLANNERY
ANNA BELL FLANNIGAN
SGT. WALTER R. FLECK
HAROLD M. FLEMING
EDWARD M. FLESH

Carl E. Floete
Lt. Earl P. Flood
Thomas A. Flynn
William E. Flynn
James V. Foley
Capt. J. Rowland Follmer
Maj. C. Stewart Forbes
Fred L. Ford
Harry Forman
Capt. Evan Howell Forman
Lt. Nathan B. Forrest
Pvt. John J. Fortune
Theodore F. Foster
Frederick H. Foucar
Lt. William K. Fowler
Lt. Charles E. Fox
Pvt. Edward Fox
Sgt. Edward H. Fox
Helen Fox
John A. Foy
Mary A. Foy
Lt. Albert Frank
Capt. George S. Frank
Mrs. George S. Frank
Maj. Jule Frankenheimer
Curtis Franklin
Nina Franstead
Sgt. Louis C. Frantz, Jr.
Fred Fraser
O. J. Frederickson
Pvt. Oscar D. Freedman
Thomas J. Freehily
Lt. Aime N. Fregeau
Lt. David L. Freidman
Capt. Archie W. French
Capt. Norman R. French
Annette Friebe
Emily Friedland
Sgt. Paul C. Friend

Lt. Frank G. Fripp
F. J. Frise
Capt. J. C. Frost
Lt. Kendall P. Frost
Paul S. Fulkerson
Mabel Fullam
Adaline Fuller
Sgt. Charles G. Fuller
George Fuller
Marietta Fuller
W. Palmer Fuller

Maj. Harry R. Gabriel
Maj. Lawrence C. Galbraith
Maj. Benjamin Gallagher
Louis J. Gallagher
Pvt. James A. Galleciez
Sgt. Rupert H. Galloway
Perrin C. Galpin
W. Horsley Gantt
Arthur C. Gardes
Sgt. Charles B. Gardner
Henry Gardner
Nellie E. Gardner
Violet Gardner
Lt. Howard P. Garner
Ruth D. Garner
William C. Garner
Willie Garon
George J. Garrity
Charles S. Gaskill
Helen Gasztowt
Richard Gawith
George I. Gay
Clarence A. Gaynor
Maude Gaynor
Dorothy Geberding
Paul K. Gedman
Raymond H. Geist

Sgt. William D. Geoghegan
Maj. Frank C. Gephart
Sgt. Paul Gepman
August Gerber
Ray Gerber
Albert J. Gerhardus
Lt. Ralph D. Gesner
Irene Gherady
Lt. Edward C. Gibbons
Norah Gibbons
Lt. Carleton B. Gibson
Constance Gibson
Hugh Gibson
Richard Gibson
Harry L. Gilchriese
Lt. Herbert J. Gilkey
Arthur P. Gill
Everett Gill
Irene M. Gillen
Lt. Col. Maurice E. Gilmore
Lucy Gilsinan
Caroline Gilteman
Clarence E. Glass
Mary Goch
Sgt. Allie H. Godfrey
Mark D. Godfrey
Cecila Goldberg
Frank A. Golder
Maj. Alan G. Goldsmith
Lt. Paul Goldstein
A. H. Gooby
Capt. Charles E. Good
Dorothy Margaret Goodhart
John Goodlet
Lawrence J. Goodlet
James P. Goodrich
Lt. W. O. Goodrich
Etta R. Goodwin
Col. Anson C. Goodyear

George H. R. Gosman
Maj. Arthur S. Goss
Cpl. Dan Gostovich
A. Y. Gough
Michael Gough
Michael Gould
Sofia Gould
Maj. Arthur S. Gow
Lila R. Gow
Lish Gow
Martha Graczyk
Ernest S. Graham
Lt. Andrew A. Granstedt
Arthur F. Grant
Malcolm M. Grant
Maud V. Grass
Sgt. John S. Gratkowski
Nora E. Gray
Prentiss N. Gray
Cpl. Robert G. Gray
Cpl. Walter W. Gray
Maj. Joseph C. Green
Lt. Robert M. Green
Pvt. Vinton R. Greene
Curtis K. Greer
Lt. Guy E. Greer
John P. Gregg
Capt. Thomas Gregory
B. Annette Greiner
Lt. Charles H. Griesa
James C. Griffith
Pvt. Luther C. Griffith
Sgt. Pierre J. Grilliere
Matthew J. Grogan
Col. John C. Groome
Sgt. Isador Grosbach
Freda S. Grosser
George W. Grove
Col. William R. Grove

Thomas E. Grubbs
Johann Grumm
Alfreda E. Grundy
Helen Guggenheim
Gustaf A. Gustafson
Herbert L. Gutterson
George Guy
Sgt. Kyle Guy
Lt. William M. Gwynn

J. F. Habegger
Cpl. William Hadley
John C. Hagemann
Lt. Col. Charles S. Haight
Capt. Waldo P. Hair
Capt. Louis E. Halbert
Herbert Dudley Hale
Charles L. Hall
Francis C. Hall
Lt. Fred M. Hall
John C. R. Hall
Elsie Hallback
Cpl. John E. Halstead
C. G. Hambling
Lt. Augustus W. Hamilton
Laurens M. Hamilton
Capt. Minard Hamilton
Capel Hanbury
Harry V. Hand
Lt. Russell R. Hand
Cecil J. Handke
Sgt. Daniel J. Hanley
Sgt. William T. Hanlon
Capt. D. C. Hanrohan
Gustav B. Hansen
Marthe Hansen
Pvt. Fred D. Harding
Harry V. Harding
William J. Harding

Lt. Donald E. Hardy
Harry V. Harlan
James Harrison Harney
Sarah Harper
Lt. George P. Harrington
Lt. Emmett S. Harris
Lt. Harry M. Harris
Pvt. Leonard W. Harris
Veronica Harris
John P. S. Harrison
Stephen P. Harron
Capt. Edward H. Hart
Cpl. Louis J. Hart
Dorothy Hartigan
Capt. John D. Hartigan
L'Engle Hartridge
Henry S. Haskell
Col. William N. Haskell
Walter H. Hastings
Lt. John D. Hatch
Paul L. Hathaway
Capt. John R. Haverty
Maj. David R. Hawkins
Herbert M. Hawley
Cpl. Leigh R. Hawley
Maude Hawley
Julian Hawthorne
Ellen Hay
Maj. David E. Hayes
Lt. Montgomery Haynes
Maj. David E. Hays
Lt. Arthur G. Head
Cpl. Stephen M. Healy
Capt. Thomas Healy
Maj. Ferry K. Heath
Cpl. Arthur H. Hegstrom
Capt. Herbert J. Heiman
Sgt. Anthony J. Heinen
Howard Heinz

Pvt. John G. Heinz
Ruth Heinze
Hanna M. Helberg
Sgt. Fred W. Held
Vera Heller
Edna Henderson
Lt. James O. Henderson
Lt. Thomas W. Henderson
Capt. Victor H. Henderson
Daniel R. Hennessy
Robert W. Herdman
Anna Herkner
Christian A. Herter
Lt. Joseph C. Hertzler
Ralph Herz
Maj. Charles E. Hetrick
Cornell Hewson
Estella Hewson
Maj. Joseph B. Hickerson
Gerhardt C. Hiebert
Peter C. Hiebert
Edward Higgins
Sgt. John T. Higgins
Sgt. Thomas S. Higgins
Sgt. Byron M. Hill
L. H. Hill
Lt. Nathaniel P. Hill
Roland F. Hill
Arthur J. Hillman
Edna M. Hilton
Harold Hines
Lt. Louis Hite
Capt. Harold J. Hockin
H. B. Hodges
James P. Hodgson
D. R. Hoeppner
David M. Hofer
Mrs. David M. Hofer
Piet H. Hofstra

Francis P. Hogan
Frank P. Hogan
Cpl. Arthur H. Hogstrom
Carroll A. Holbrock
John M. Holcombe, Jr.
Capt. Frank H. Holden
Capt. John B. Hollister
Maj. Imla C. Holloway
Lt. William F. Holtzman
William C. Holzhauer
Lt. Reuben Horchow
Daniel Horne
Sgt. John A. Horstman
Lt. Alexander W. Hossack
James T. Houghton
Pvt. Cyril H. Houpert
Sgt. John W. Housel
Lt. Joseph E. Houseworth, Jr.
Capt. Robert LeC. Hovey
Bessie E. Howard
Capt. Conway R. Howard
Lt. George F. Howard
Lt. Robert W. Howard
Lt. Thomas D. Howard
Lt. Austin A. Howe
Capt. James A. Hubbard
Arthur Huber
W. H. Hubert
Capt. William G. Huckel
Sgt. Glenn F. Hudson
Sgt. Charles F. Humme
Capt. Henry Leigh Hunt
Pvt. Joseph P. Hunt
Sgt. George A. Hurd
Beulah A. Hurley
John R. Hurley
N. W. Hurley
William E. Hurley
Pvt. Edward C. Hussey

Lincoln Hutchinson
Maj. William F. Hutson
Lt. George W. Hutton
Lt. Ryland Hutton
John H. Hynes
Kathryn V. Hynes
George K. Hyslop

Sgt. Roy M. Iliff
Lillian E. Ingall
Capt. Rutherford Irones
Pvt. Emerson Isaac
Vida Moss Isles
Eugenia Ivanova
G. M. Ivatt

Charles H. Jacha
Lt. George Jackson
Capt. Robert A. Jackson
Thomas J. Jackson
Willard J. Jackson
Bascombe W. James
Gusta James
Henry James
William James
Joseph Jandacek, Jr.
Pvt. Cornelius M. Janney
Joseph W. Jannicki
Elizabeth L. Jarratt
Capt. Lee Jarrell
Capt. Henry G. Jefferson
Edward Jemmett
Sgt. James G. Jensen
Rene Jensen
Robert Joffe
Lt. Arthur A. Johnson
Lt. Cecil X. Johnson
Charles H. Johnson
Sgt. Frank H. Johnson

Frank O. Johnson
Capt. J. Albin Johnson
Rodney Johnson
Wallace B. Johnson
Lt. William R. Johnson
John Joly
George E. Jones
Gilbert J. Jones
Glenn I. Jones
Harold S. Jones
Lydia T. Jones
Pvt. Max T. Jones
Towner F. Jones
Lt. Col. William A. Jones
Maj. Benjamin Joy
Lt. Walter E. Joyce

Capt. John Kaba
Sgt. John Kaminski
Mabel A. Kamke
Pvt. Aloysius C. Kane
James J. Kann
David Kaplan
Capt. John Karmozin
Joseph Kavanagh
Sgt. Barney Kayser
Sgt. Roy H. Keadle
William R. Kearney, Jr.
Lt. Earl D. Keefer
Spurgeon M. Keeny
Margaret Keevins
Pvt. John Keiser
Cpl. Joseph P. Keller
John K. Kelley
William J. Kelley
Vernon Kellogg
Joseph M. Kelly
George Kelney
Sgt. George W. Kemple

Lt. Col. Owen H. Kenan
Stella Kendzierska
A. J. A. Kennedy
D. W. Kennedy
Pvt. Mark W. Kennedy
Patrick H. Kennedy
Margaret Kent
Murray S. Kenworthy
William F. Kernan
Nancy Kerry
Boris Kesta
Hayward J. Ketcham
A. C. Kidd
Alfred W. Kiddle
Capt. Harry L. Kile
Sgt. John A. Kilroy
Sgt. A. Kimber
Wilfred Kimber
Alice M. King
Capt. Arthur P. King
Jessie A. King
Muriel A. King
Sgt. Edward H. Kinn
David S. Kinne
R. F. Kinnear
J. W. Kinsman
Frank L. Kirby
Rudolph Klassen
Maj. David Klein
Raymond A. Kleindienst
Cpl. Charles H. Klenke
Lt. Allen Klots
Louis R. Knassin
Pvt. Edward W. Knope
Lt. Carroll W. Knowles
Walter Knuth
Lt. Rudolph H. Koch
Pvt. George M. Koenig
P. Tracy Kohl

Lt. David A. Kohler
Lt. H. O. Kohler
Sgt. Fred W. Koller
Anna Kopec
Sgt. Hani J. Korkegi
George Korn, Jr.
Sofia Kosabucka
J. Mayer Kowalsky
Leo E. Kowit
Stephanie Kozlewska
Capt. August A. Krantz
Louis Krapp
Emma Krauss
Christian A. Krehbiel
W. T. Krone
Sgt. Joseph Kropernicki
Lt. Jacob F. Kroske
Maj. Joseph W. Krueger
Felicia Krutewicz
Catherine Krzyzanewska
Preston Kumler
Capt. Robert W. Kunz
Pearl Kyle

Maurice J. Lacey
Maj. Linus B. La Fleur
Cpl. Herman E. Lafsky
Florence A. Lake
Pvt. Fred C. Lake
Roy J. Lamare
Myrle R. Lampson
Cpl. Jack J. Landau
Cpl. Philip J. Landwehr
Louis R. Landy
Capt. Edward C. Lane
Pvt. Charles L. Lang
Sgt. John H. Lang
Walter W. Lang
William C. Lang

John H. Lange
Pvt. Moe Langenthal
Sgt. Edmund C. Langguth
Pvt. Walter Lannigan
Capt. Roger D. Lapham
Marie Larcombe
H. C. Larkin
Lauritz Larsen
Lt. Erwin Larson
Cpl. George N. Larson
James F. La Salle
Pfc. Joseph S. Lassa
Marion H. Lawler
Maj. F. E. Lawrence
Katherine G. Lawrence
Capt. Charles N. Leach
Sgt. Fred Leader
William R. Leary
Lt. Walter J. Leath
Fred Lederer
Pvt. Samuel Ledin
Irving C. Lee
Ernest Leech
Sgt. Stephen J. Leghart
Austin C. Lehmer
John A. Lehrs
J. Leibenguth
Pvt. John C. Leisenberg
Alma Leishman
Mae Leishman
Cpl. Paul P. Lemm
Apolinary L. Lenkowski
Sgt. Fred J. Leonard
Mary A. Leonard
Pvt. Emanuel D. Leshin
Isabelle Levinson
Ray Levinson
Charles S. Levitt

Pvt. Lee Levy
Walter O. Lewis
Edward M. Ley
Howard L'Homme Dieu
Lt. Victor Libretti
I. M. Liddell
Lt. Louis E. Lindemann
Donald A. Lindsay
Katherine Lindsey
Nadejda Lindstrem
Vera Littauer
Robert Littell
Alexander B. Little
S. Grace Little
August Littre
Maj. C. E. Livingston
Lt. John W. Livingston
Sgt. Robert J. Lloyd
Lt. Milton K. Lockwood
Col. James A. Logan
Thomas C. Lonergan
R. F. Lorie
Capt. Pierre L. Loriot
Pvt. John J. Love
Jennie Lovinger
Ernest Lowing
Donald A. Lowrie
Sgt. Syd Lowry
Samuel C. Lucas
George W. Luhrmann
Agnes E. Lulley
Eva Lutyens
Ralph H. Lutz
Capt. Gibbes Lykes
Miriam V. Lyman
Frank Lynam
Thorvald Lynghelm
E. Lyon

Frederick B. Lyon
Cpl. Harris T. Lyon
Stella Lysakowska

Capt. Charles J. Mabbutt
Lt. Col. Daniel W. MacCormack
William A. MacDowell
Malcolm MacFarlane
Sgt. Joseph Mackey
Helen Mackler
Kenneth A. MacPherson
Walter W. Maddux
Lt. Theodore S. Maerker
Lt. Edward N. Mahan
Sgt. James J. Mahaney
Lt. Edward W. Mahon
Martin J. Mahoney
John J. Maitland
Reinhold J. Makowski
Alfred L. Malabre
Capt. A. L. Mallattre
Capt. Paul Malone
Katherine Maloney
Vladimir S. Mameieff
John J. Mangan
William B. Manley
Timothy F. Mannix
Capt. Hector Mansfield
Sgt. Theodore Marceaux
Cpl. Thomas J. Marchand
Mara Marek
Maj. Max E. Mark
Amand L. Marshall
Doris E. Marshall
Arthur F. Martin
Maj. William A. Martin
Mary L. Martin
Stephen Martindale, Jr.

Lt. Frank J. Marvan
Ethel Mason
Violet Masterini
Lt. Col. Lawrence O. Mathews
Philip Mathews
Ernest A. Mathieson
Sgt. Edward C. Matson
Frank Mauran, Jr.
W. L. Mavius
Capt. Allen B. Maxwell
Capt. Arthur D. Mayer
Karl L. Mayer
Raymond C. Mayer
John Mazzaro
Cpl. Charles L. McBride
Sgt. Daniel M. McCaffrey
Maj. Culberson McCall
Dougall McCallum
Pvt. Van McCausland
George H. McClintock
Anthony M. McClusky
Sgt. Carter McConnell
Sgt. Clarence R. McConnell
Maj. Frederick C. McConnell
Capt. Chauncey McCormick
Thomas C. McCormick
John N. McCoy
Walter E. McCreight
Sgt. Cecil V. McCullough
Lt. Charles B. McDaniel
Florence A. McDermott
Katherine McDermott
Alice McDonald
Sgt. Charles R. McDonald
Robert H. McDonald
Jesse L. McElroy
John J. McEnniss
Gates W. McGarrah

Maj. Clare McGinnis
Pvt. William McGinnis
Daniel G. McGuiggan
Vale H. McGuire
William J. McGuire, Jr.
Col. J. W. McIntosh
Maj. Alva E. McKennett
Roscoe A. McKenzie
Capt. Francis H. McKnight
Maj. James S. McKnight
Thomas O. McLaughlin
William C. McMahon
John R. McMillan
Sgt. James McNamara
Maj. Thomas G. McNicholas
Lt. John McM. McPheeters
Daniel McRae
Denis McSweeney
Sgt. Wilbur F. McVey
Sfc Cannon E. McWhorter
Joseph V. Meagher
Cpl. Lucas O. Medicas
A. H. Merriles
Cpl. Joseph H. Merron
Cpl. John M. Mertz
William H. Meserole
Lt. Lucien Messinger
Horace L. Methe
Lt. Jerome Meyer
Pvt. Paul Meyer
Jean Meze
Harry Michael
Anna Michalowska
Helen Mielczarek
Anna V. Mikhailovsky
Sgt. Charlton J. Milam
J. Earl Miles
Alvin J. Miller

Floyd H. Miller
Harlan S. Miller
Sgt. Maj. Henry T. Miller
Howard E. Miller
Capt. John C. Miller
William E. Miller
Margaret Milne
Capt. Eusebius B. Mitchell
Col. Harry D. Mitchell
J. P. Mitchell
Lt. Mowatt M. Mitchell
Cpl. Horace L. Mithe
Lt. J. E. Mock
Sanford Model
Gus H. Moellman
Lt. Charles A. Moes
Ethel L. Moffett
Lt. Arthur L. Moler
Pvt. John Monroe
Robert Montaier
James J. Monteith
Cpl. Augustine Montfort
A. C. Mooney
Justin H. Moore
N. E. Moore
Sgt. Lawrence J. Moran
John A. Morehead
Sgt. Harry H. Morgan, Jr.
Capt. Thomas H. Morgan
Helen R. Moroney
Watson S. Morrell
Capt. Edward K. Morrill
Charles S. Morris
Edna W. Morris
Homer L. Morris
Capt. Joseph C. Morris
Sara E. Morris
James A. Morrow

LT. C. A. MORS
CAPT. LEE C. MORSE
CAPT. RALPH H. MOSHER
CHARLES A. MOSS
LT. JOHN D. MOYER
STELLA MUCHA
PETER U. MUIR
J. BENTLEY MULFORD
PVT. HARRY P. MULLEN
PVT. MAURICE L. MULLEN
WILLIAM C. MULLENDORE
GENEVIEVE MULLIN
CPL. JOHN B. MULVY
EDITH MURDOCK
DENIS P. MURPHY
FRANCIS J. MURPHY
JOSEPH L. MURPHY
LYDIA C. MURPHY
M. FARMER MURPHY
LT. WALTER W. MURPHY
WILLIAM J. MURPHY
COLUMBA P. MURRAY, JR.
JAMES B. MURRAY
WALTER J. MURRAY
WILLIAM MURRAY
AGHA B. MUSA
LOECADIA MUSZYNSKA
WALKER J. MYERS

ROSE NATALIE
LT. CHARLES NEAVE
LT. JAMES S. NEELY
WADE S. NEELY
LT. BERTRAND NEIDECKER
MAJ. WILLIAM R. NELLEGAR
CHARLES EDWARD NELSON
MAJ. JESSE C. NELSON
LT. PAUL D. NELSON

WILLIAM H. NELSON
MARIE A. NESGE
IRVING NETZER
CAPT. MAX M. NEUMANN
A. PARKER NEVIN
ANDREW R. NEVIN
ROBERT F. NEW
LT. COL. FRED H. NEWBERRY
SGT. JOHN M. NEWELL
SGT. ALBERT P. NEWHART
SYDNEY H. NEWMAN
PVT. GEORGE E. NEWTON
CAPT. MAX M. NEYMANN
LT. GEORGE L. NICHOL
EDWARD W. NICHOLLS
SHIRLEY NICHOLSON
W. DONALD NICKELSEN
PAUL R. NICKINSON
ARNOLD G. NIELSON
LT. WILLIAM D. NIXON
LT. CHARLES NODDER
CHARLES NOKES
CATHERINE NOLAN
JOHN B. NOLAN
LT. S. J. NOLAN
WILLIAM F. NOLAN
LT. WILLIS J. NOLAN
EDNA NOONAN
LT. THOMAS W. NOONAN
LT. CHARLES W. NORBY
CAROLINE G. NORMENT
JOHN J. NORRIS
CPL. WILLIAM J. NORRIS
DOROTHY NORTH
LEWIS P. NORTON
LT. LEWIS M. NORTON
LT. JAMES P. NOURSE
CAPT. FRANK NOWAK

Durrell L. Noyes
Albert Noyle
Harold Noziglia

Harry F. O'Brien
Capt. Jolly W. O'Brien
Joseph E. O'Brien
Maj. William L. E. O'Brien
Sgt. Robert E. O'Dea
Sgt. Floyd C. Oden
Charles Edward O'Donnell
Arthur Oehl
Helen Ogden
Lt. Horace O'Higgens
Lt. Edward C. Olds
Sgt. I. Oliff
Pvt. Fay Oliver
Sgt. George R. Oliver
Pvt. Sidney M. Oliver
Grace Olsen
Pvt. Albert W. Olson
Sgt. Edmund F. Oman
Sgt. Daniel W. Orbaugh
Capt. Thomas J. Orbison
Sgt. Earl D. Osborn
Harry Osborn
Rachelle H. Osborne
Lt. John M. Oskison
Maj. Berger Osland
Anne Osterburg
Eugene Oswald
William A. Otis
Maj. Henry S. Otto
Herbert Owen

Thomas A. Pace
William E. Packer
Lewis Padgett
Milton P. Padula

Frank C. Page
Pvt. Earl W. Palmatier
Pvt. Diule Panelli
Cpl. Heger Panier
Capt. Robert B. Park
Edward S. Parker
Ernest B. Parsons
Leonidas M. Parker
Lt. H. T. Partridge
Anna Pastorini
Lt. Maurice Pate
Eunice Patter
Alice N. Patterson
Avis L. Patterson
Elsie B. Patterson
Lt. Col. Frank H. Patterson
Lt. John T. Patterson
Capt. Richard W. Patterson
Robert A. Patterson
Sgt. Alexander Pattison, Jr.
Maj. August W. Paul
Parry H. Paul
Lt. Oliver H. Paxson
Frank J. Pazdera
Frank C. Peabody
Marjorie Peachey
Lt. Ronald H. Pearce
Ralph A. Pearson
Lt. Sedley C. Peck
Allen B. Peden
Edward A. Peden
Inez Pellegrinelli
Harry Penn
Paul H. Penschke
Benjamin Pepper
Pvt. Armand Perrin
Cpl. William E. Perry
Sgt. Benjamin H. Perryman
Lt. Raymond J. Pflaum

PVT. CARL J. PHILLIPS
E. PHILLIPS
WILLIAM B. PHILLIPS
WINIFRED M. PHILLIPS
PVT. RALPH J. PIACHE
LT. GLENN M. PIKE
MAX PINE
HELEN PIOTROWSKA
LT. PHILIP S. PLATT
JUNE PLATTOR
GERALD W. POHLMAN
CAPT. THOMAS W. POINDEXTER
MAGDALEINE POKROVSKAYA
WILLIAM B. POLAND
CPL. THOMAS L. POPP
HOYT E. PORTER
ERNEST M. POST
SGT. FRANK H. POST
PAUL A. POTOUS
MAJ. HYRAM G. POTTER
SGT. HORACE E. POTTER
PHILIP B. K. POTTER
LT. EMERY POTTLE
CPL. FRED POULIN
ETHEL POWELL
CAPT. LISLE S. POWELL
CATHERINE POWERS
LT. JAMES L. POWERS
MAJ. RAY R. POWERS
LESTER S. PRAGER
HERBERT M. PRATT
PVT. EDWARD J. PREBIS
THOMAS PRESSER
I. PRESTON
SGT. WALKER W. PREUSS
FRANK J. PRICE, JR.
HARRY W. F. PRICE
ERNEST L. PRIEST
LT. EDMOND PURCELL

RAYMOND C. PURCELL
LT. CEDRIC E. PYLE
CAPT. DAVID H. N. PYLE

ALICE M. QUAYLE
CAPT. CYRIL J. C. QUINN
LEO F. QUINN
SGT. CHARLES F. QUIRELD

CAPT. SAMUEL L. RACEY
HUGH F. RAMSEY
W. HOWARD RAMSEY
CAPT. ALBERT W. RANDALL
LT. DARLEY RANDALL
CAPT. FRANCIS P. RANDOLPH
MAYER RASKIN
PVT. SVEND O. RASMUSSEN
MAJ. HARRY RATTNER
ARNOLD RATTRAY
JOHN H. RAYMOND
SGT. ERNEST E. RAYNER
LT. WILLIAM J. REA
ALFRED G. READ
MARY REDROFF
LT. HENRY M. REES
PVT. GEORGE F. REID
FANNY REISIG
PVT. LOUIS REITZ
EDWARD J. REMEY
CICELY M. RENAUT
HOWARD H. RENFREW
WILLIAM H. RENFREW
ROSE B. RENGGER
DONALD RENSHAW
EVAN RENSHAW
A. REPINGTON
GEORGE REPP
WILLIAM RESSNICK
SGT. HAYDN W. REX

Kriker M. Satjinn
John M. Saunders
Capt. Shelby M. Saunders
William R. Saunders
Alice Savigny
Walter E. Savill
Raymond H. Sawtelle
August Scapinelli
Capt. Albert A. Schall
Capt. R. S. H. Schaltz
William L. Scheding
Lt. Samuel Scheier
Capt. Alexander V. Schenck
Capt. Ernest R. Schoen
George C. Schrammel
Hugh J. Schuck
William L. Schuckman
Cpl. Alfred W. Schultz
Capt. R. F. H. Schultz
Agnes W. Schultze
John Schuster
Gare Schwartz
Jack Schweitzer
Sgt. Willard H. Scidmore
Capt. James T. Scott
Pvt. Robert P. Scott
Cyrill Scriabine
Eleanore C. Scriabine
Fred O. Seaver
Lt. Reuben L. Sebastian
Frances Sebezynska
Pvt. Anton Sede
Lillian Seffers
James B. Segall
Pvt. William J. Seguin
Sgt. Willard H. Seidmore
Pvt. James R. Seitz
Lt. George H. Selden
John A. Sellards

Arthur B. Selpe
Sgt. Arthur B. Sels
Boris Seltzer
Pvt. Frank J. Sennes
Pvt. Carl S. Serling
John E. Seykora
Lt. Kenneth L. Seymore
Jessica Seymour
Will Shafroth
Ann G. Shankey
M. Cecilia Shankey
Thomas A. Shankey
John D. Shannahan
George P. Shandy
Lt. Alfred P. Shane
Louis L. Shapiro
Edwin P. Shattuck
Dorothea Shaw
Capt. Joseph T. Shaw
Dorothea Shaw
Lt. Frank E. Shearer
James A. Sheehan
Nancy A. Sheehy
Mary V. Sheldon
Edwin Sherman
Roger Sherman
Capt. Fleming B. Sherwood
Philip B. Shield
Lt. William J. Shirley
Sgt. Fenton H. Showl
Frank E. Short
Cpl. James A. Silver
Pvt. Benjamin A. Silvermann
John L. Simpson
Lt. Richard H. Simpson
Maj. William J. Simpson
Sgt. Benjamin R. Sinkinson
Lt. Col. Elijah H. Siter
Capt. Frank E. Slack

John K. Slack
Arthur W. Slagel
Delbert G. Slater
Paul G. Slavic
Caroline Slawinska
Raymond M. Sloan
Sigismund Slonim
Lt. John H. Small
Valentine Smentkowska
Col. Clarence B. Smith
Cedric C. Smith
Pvt. George W. Smith
Pvt. Gerard E. Smith
Lt. Henry B. Smith
Pvt. James V. Smith
Jessica G. Smith
Cpl. J. L. Smith
Maj. Newman Smith
Renoux J. Smith
Lt. Stanley Smith
W. Russell Smith
Albert F. Snook
Alviras E. Snow
Capt. Fletcher J. Snow
Capt. Edward L. Snyder
Cpl. Frank J. Soboata
Andrew J. Sodick
Maj. Everett Somers
Pvt. Marlott G. Somers
James Sommerville, Jr.
Cpl. John H. Son
Benjamin Sonnenberg
Mayme Sonnenstuhl
Luigi Sorieri
Serge M. Sorokin
Capt. Ernest W. Soucey
J. Wendell Southard
Merrill T. B. Spalding
Sylvia Sparks

Sgt. Otis L. Spaulding
John C. Speaks
Cpl. Cecil T. Spear
Lt. William A. Spencer
Lt. William H. Sperry
Andrew Spiers
Dorothy Spratt
James W. Spratt
Lt. Howard E. Spraull
Elise I. Sprott
C. Squibb
Clarice Elizabeth Squire
Lt. Harwood Stacey
N. Stachowsky
John J. Stack
Capt. James A. Stader
Pillar F. Stain
George H. Starr
Walerja Staszka
Theodore Steare
Herbert Steer
Capt. Martinus Stenseth
Capt. F. Dorsey Stephens
Clarence C. Stetson
C. F. Stetzel
Sgt. Raymond J. Stevenson
Norah W. Stewart
Pvt. Robert S. Stewart
Sgt. Robert S. Stickney
Frank Stiff
Lt. Gilchrist B. Stockton
Maj. Edward R. Stoever
Capt. George E. Stookey
Lt. Abram G. Stratton
Lewis L. Strauss
Sgt. Ivan C. Strong
Sgt. Paul B. Stubbs
Philip Sturm
Capt. Marshall C. Sturtevant

JESSIE H. STUTESMAN
LT. HENRY E. SUAVETT
CAPT. EUGENE L. SULLIVAN
CPL. OLAF A. SUMERFIELD
LT. WILBUR B. SUMNER
PVT. WALTER A. SUPPNICK
F. RAYMOND SURBER
FRANK M. SURFACE
CHARLES W. SURLES
MAJ. JOHN J. SUTTON
SFC KNUD SVENDSEN
SGT. JOHN T. SWEENEY
MAGNUS SWENSON
IRENE SZADKOUSAK

ROBERT A. TAFT
PVT. BASIL F. TALBOT
CPL. R. M. TALBOT
CAPT. HAROLD TAPPIN
AMY P. TAPPING
JOSEPHINE TARKOWSKA
SGT. ADOLPH TAUSSIG
MAJ. ALFRED K. TAYLOR
ALONZO E. TAYLOR
LT. DARR K. TAYLOR
JAMES O. TAYLOR
MAY TAYLOR
MARTHA TEGLER
LT. COL. CHARLES G. TELFORD
MAJ. THOMAS M. TEMPLE
GEORGE TEREK
CPL. ARTHUR T. TERRELL
DAISE E. TERRY
CAPT. PRENTISS M. TERRY
RHYS G. THACKWELL
PVT. IKE D. THAMES
LT. CHARLES E. THAYER
CAPT. FRED M. THAYER
CLARENCE J. THOMAS

CLEAVER S. THOMAS
LT. COL. CHARLES F. THOMPSON
ERNEST THOMPSON
FREDERICK L. THOMPSON
HERBERT H. THOMPSON
CPL. ISAAC A. THOMPSON
JAMES F. THOMPSON
J. HUTTON THOMPSON
PVT. KENNETH F. THOMPSON
OSWALD THOMPSON
R. P. THOMPSON
PVT. RALPH V. THOMPSON
LT. THOMAS M. THOMPSON
PVT. WARWICK L. THOMPSON
JESSIE THOMSON
THOMAS G. THOMSON
CHARLES E. THORN
MAJ. DAVID B. THORNTON
SGT. L. B. THORNTON
ROBERT E. THORP
LT. JOHN THORS, JR.
FLORENCE W. THURBER
GEORGE TIFFANY
CPL. ABEL J. TILLES
HARRY G. TIMBERS
REBECCA S. TIMBERS
BEATRICE TINGELY
ANDREW TJARNELL
ALICE TODMAN
JOSEPH L. TOMASELL
VALERIA TOMASIK
JOHN E. TOOLE
JOHN J. TOOLE
PVT. REGINALD N. TOOLEY
ADOLPH TORDY
CAPT. CLARE M. TORREY
THOMAS TOTMAN
RAYMOND R. TOURTILLETT
GEORGE A. TOWNSEND

MAJ. HOWARD L. TRACEY
WILLIAM H. TRACY
RAY P. TRAVIS
FLOYD TRAYNHAM
RALPH TREASURE
PVT. ALBERT W. TREAT
MARY J. TRENCH
PVT. JOSEPH N. TRIERWEILER
CAPT. IRAH H. TRIESTE
VIOLA DOROTHEA TROW
CPL. JACOB G. TRUAS
SGT. LOUIS C. TRUE
SGT. CHARLES L. TUCK
MAJ. W. HALLAM TUCK
JAMES D. TUCKER
CAPT. ABRAHAM TULIN
HERBERT A. TUOHY
SGT. GEORGE F. TURNER
CAPT. HUBERT S. TURNER
VAN ARSDALE TURNER
EUGENIE N. TUROSENSKY
LEON G. TURROU
JOHN M. TUTHER
MARSHALL W. TUTHILL
H. TWINER
LT. SEWELL TYNG
LEO B. TYSON

SGT. JOHN J. ULRIK
WILLIAM F. UPSON
PVT. WILLIAM T. USINGER

LORETTA VACKNER
PVT. WILLIAM VANNEMAN
SIMONE VANNIER
ARTHUR VANPASHTONBECKE
PVT. SIEMON W. VAN VORST
CHARLES E. VARNEY
MARY G. VAUGHAN

CLINTON W. VAUGHT
CHARLES H. VEIL
STEPHEN A. VENEAR
PATRICK S. VERDON
SGT. GUY VERMILLION
PVT. JAMES VESPIA
PVT. ROBERT I. VICKERS
LT. V. R. VISEL
HELEN VIZZARD
SGT. ERNEST C. VOLAND
JACOB VOLZ
JOHN J. VOLZ

SGT. WILBUR R. WADAMS
LT. ALFRED F. WADDEL
JACOB WAGNER
LT. IVAR W. WAHREN
LAURA WAITE
NELLIA WAITE
OLGA WAITE
JOHN WALICKE
C. A. WALKER
DANTON M. WALKER
LT. HERSCHEL C. WALKER
MARY A. WALKER
MATTHEW H. WALKER
MAJ. MICHAEL M. WALKER
LT. MORRIS L. WALKER
SGT. ROBERT S. WALKER
LT. STANTON WALKER
SYDNOR H. WALKER
SGT. HARRY E. WALL
CAPT. M. W. F. WALLACE
JAMES HAROLD WALLIS
EDMUND A. WALSH
HELEN V. WALSH
JAMES B. WALSH
JANE F. WALSH
PVT. FRED WALTERS

Robert Walther
Pvt. Louis L. Warberg
Lt. Angus I. Ward
John P. Ward
Ruth Underhill Ward
Vera Ward
Pvt. Walter E. Ward
Pvt. Edward M. Ware
Lt. Harold J. Warlick
Cpl. James P. Warwick
Eleanor Wasielewska
Henry Waterman, Jr.
Sgt. Mark O. Watkins
M. Watson
Capt. Frank D. Watterson
Lt. Frank C. Webb
Maj. James W. Webb
Frank Wehle
Pvt. Louis L. Weinberg
Charles J. Weindorf
Rudolph Weiss
Ruth Weiss
Pvt. Samuel L. Weiss
Henrietta Weitzman
James H. Welch
Maj. Eugene O. Welcher
Lt. Laurence C. Wellington
Alan W. Wells
Fred S. Wells
Pvt. Cecil Welsh
Joseph Wenderoth
Miriam E. West
Capt. Robert K. West
Samuel Wetherall
Lt. Alexander R. Wheeler
Maj. Carl M. Wheeler
Maj. William A. B. Wheeler
Sgt. John C. Whitaker
Sgt. George A. White

Sgt. Horace B. White
John Beaver White
Theodore F. Whitmarsh
Lt. Alexander D. Whittemore
William E. Whitten
Frederick Whyte
Capt. Francis C. Wickes
Capt. Arthur J. Wicks
Sgt. Charles A. Wikle
Maj. William J. Wilckens
Walter E. Wildman
Donald Wilhelm
Cpl. Herman C. Wilkens
Lupton A. Wilkinson
Lt. Clayton E. Williams
Lt. Frank J. Williams
Capt. George W. Williams
Helen Williams
Marguerite Williams
Ralph Williams
Cpl. Walter J. Williams
Charles M. Willoughby
Ellen Wilson
Sgt. George F. Wilson
Lt. Henry G. Wilson
Randolph C. Wilson
Maj. William J. Wilson
Genevieve Winckiewicz
Harry F. Windholz
Francis Winslow
Edgar C. Winsor
William H. Winters
Marion Wirth
Capt. Richard S. Wise
Lt. Col. Frank C. Wiser
Lt. Robert Withington
Sgt. Adolph Witt
Pvt. Henry Witt
John F. Wolf

MORRIS WOLF
PVT. EVERITT I. WOLFE
HARRY WOLFE
HENRY C. WOLFE
LT. FRANK P. WOOD
LT. GEORGE A. WOOD
LT. FRED H. WOODARD
F. W. WOODFORD
A. WOODLEY
PVT. JAMES V. WOODS
CLARA L. WOODWARD
PVT. GORDON M. WOOLARD
CAPT. THOMAS H. WORK
CPL. WALLACE E. WREDE
MAJ. BOYKIN C. WRIGHT
ROBERT C. WRIGHT
LOUIS C. WULFERS
WILLIS C. WULFERS
LT. ANDREW WYLIE

ROSE WYSZYNSKI
STANISLAV WYSZYNSKI

CORNELIA YOUNG
PVT. E. H. YOUNG
MARJORIE YOUNG
MARIE YOUSHKEYVICH
CPL. JOSEPH M. YOUTZ
OLGA YUREVITCH

PVT. ANTHONY ZANOVICH
CHRISTINE ZDULECZNA
JOHN S. ZELIE
ELEANOR ZIEGLER
FRED H. ZOLIN
ANNA K. ZOLL
BARUSCH ZUCKERMAN
MARIE ZVEGINTZEV

INDEX

INDEX

Albania: conditions in after World War I, 347

Allen, General Henry T., organizer of American Committee for Relief of German Children, 335

Allenby, General Edmund: Near Eastern campaign of, 176; conquest of Palestine by, 179; in Syria, 182

Allied commissions: U.S. membership in, 211

Allied Military Mission to the Baltic: report of conditions in Latvia to, 303

Ament, Lieutenant Colonel Lytton G.: work of with children in Rumania, 146, 390

American Bankers Association: address by Hoover to, 221 and n.

American charitable agencies: share of in relief work, xxii

American Children's Fund: purpose of, 545; directors of, 545-46; aid to other agencies, 546; interest on investment by, 546; total receipts of, 546-47; liquidation of, 547

American China Famine Fund, 411

American Committee for Helping the Blind (Winifred Holt), 12

American Committee for Relief to Ireland, 412

The American Committee for Russian Famine Relief (Communist committee), 486

American Council for the Relief of European Children: funds raised by, 250

American Food in the World War and Reconstruction Period, 241n.

American Friends Service Committee: relief work done by in France, 9; in Russia, 161; in Syria, 182, 184; after the Peace, 243; in Poland, 322; aid to Danzig by, 330; help in Germany, 334-35; in Austria, 354; in Serbia, 383; and Riga Agreement, 447; co-operation with British Friends, 500; funds administered by, 501; total expenditures of, 501; tribute to, 536

American Homes for Children in the Rheinpfalz, 341

American Jugo-Slav Relief Committee, 384

American Mennonite Committee: relief work by, 447, 503

American Overseas Charities and Patriotic League of Britain, 2

American Peace Delegation: expression of appreciation from, 231

American Red Cross, 2, 3, 447; war work of in France, 8, 9; in Italy, 18; for Belgian refugees, 21-22; in Portugal, 23; in Finland, 33; in Baltic States, 58, 298, 304, 307-309, 311; in Poland, 75-76, 320; aid to refugees, 82; to prisoners of war, 82; in Czechoslovakia, 110, 346-47; in Austria, 120, 353; in Hungary, 126, 377-78; in Bulgaria, 130; in Serbia, 136-38; in Rumania, 153, 390-91; in Russia, 160, 163, 258, 283, 449, 467, 473; in Near East, 175; in Palestine,

577